TIES THAT BOUND

TIES THAT BOUND

Founding First Ladies and Slaves

Marie Jenkins Schwartz

The University of Chicago Press CHICAGO AND LONDON

The University of Chicago Press, Chicago 60637
The University of Chicago Press, Ltd., London
© 2017 by Marie Jenkins Schwartz
Published 2017.
Printed in the United States of America

26 25 24 23 22 21 20 19 18 17   1 2 3 4 5

ISBN-13: 978-0-226-14755-0 (cloth)
ISBN-13: 978-0-226-46072-7 (e-book)
DOI: 10.7208/chicago/9780226460727.001.0001

LIBRARY OF CONGRESS CATALOGING-IN-PUBLICATION DATA
Names: Schwartz, Marie Jenkins, 1946– author.
Title: Ties that bound : founding first ladies and slaves / Marie Jenkins Schwartz.
Description: Chicago : The University of Chicago Press, 2017. |
Includes bibliographical references and index.
Identifiers: LCCN 2016054301 | ISBN 9780226147550 (cloth : alk. paper) |
ISBN 9780226460727 (e-book)
Subjects: LCSH: Washington, Martha, 1731–1802. | Randolph, Martha Jefferson, 1772–1836. |
Madison, Dolley, 1768–1849. | Presidents' spouses—United States. | Washington, Martha,
1731–1802—Employees. | Randolph, Martha Jefferson, 1772–1836—Employees. |
Madison, Dolley, 1768–1849—Employees. | Slaves—United States—History—
18th century. | Slaves—United States—History—19th century.
Classification: LCC E176.2 .S39 2017 | DDC 973.4/10922—dc23
LC record available at https://lccn.loc.gov/2016054301

♾ This paper meets the requirements of
ANSI/NISO Z39.48-1992 (Permanence of Paper).

Contents

Author's Note

Many of the figures discussed in this book shared the same last names. To avoid confusion, I generally refer to people in second and subsequent references by first name rather than surname. On occasion, I distinguish characters who share both first and last names by nicknames; for example, Thomas Jefferson's wife and daughter were both named Martha Jefferson, but the latter was commonly known as Patsy. I refer to some enslaved people using only a given name because their surnames are unknown.

I do not use the term White House in this book but rather refer to the official residence as the President's house. The United States capital was first located in New York City and later in Philadelphia. John Adams was the first President to occupy a residence at 1600 Pennsylvania Avenue in Washington, DC. He and First Lady Abigail Adams moved into the home in 1800. The residence burned in 1814 when the British set fire to it during the War of 1812. It was rebuilt, but it was not officially known as the White House until Theodore Roosevelt bestowed the title in 1901.

I have reproduced quoted material as it appears in original sources. In some cases this includes misspellings and grammatical errors.

Seen and Unseen

Much of what has been written about the early First Ladies is more hagiography than biography. Martha Washington and Dolley Madison are acclaimed for their patriotism, social graces, and fashionable attire, and for playing the role of hostess for the nation while their husbands served as President. Martha Washington is especially esteemed for traveling to winter camps to see General Washington and his troops during the American Revolution, as is Dolley Madison for saving a portrait of George Washington from capture and destruction as the British bore down on the nation's capital during the War of 1812. The two remain popular today. A 2014 survey gauging admiration for America's First Ladies ranked Dolley Madison fourth, behind Eleanor Roosevelt, Abigail Adams, and Jacqueline Kennedy. Martha Washington was ranked ninth.[1] Martha Jefferson died before her husband became President and is less well known.

There is more to know about these women. Central to this book is the fact that each was born into a slaveholding family and married a slaveholding man—an elite man who staked his economic, political, and social relationships on slavery.[2] The enslaved people who waited on the women and their families were not incidental to the First Ladies' lives but rather important constituents of their daily experiences and their hopes for the future: their own, their families', and their nation's. Yet most historians and biographers treat the First Ladies' slaves as separate from their mistresses, as if somehow slavery should be relegated to its own sphere (or perhaps a chapter).

When historians and biographers do acknowledge slaveholding by Martha Washington, Martha Jefferson, and Dolley Madison, most portray the women as good mistresses, although what this means is often unclear. Almost all slaveholders claimed that they acted in the best interest of their slaves, but such claims ring hollow today.[3]

The opinions of the inner circle of enslaved servants (mostly girls and women) who waited on the ladies and their families — with the possible exception of the Hemings family who lived at Thomas Jefferson's Monticello — hardly figure into the First Ladies' stories. This book rectifies this oversight by examining the relationships that developed between the First Ladies and their slaves, making visible the domestic spaces where the ladies lived intimately with their help. Knowing about the human relationships that were negotiated between slave mistresses and enslaved servants in these private places gives us a better understanding not only of the First Ladies but of their slaves. For elite women and their families, slaves were more than a workforce that brought profits to planters, although certainly Mount Vernon, Monticello, and Montpelier had agricultural workers who did exactly that. Slavery for ladies was a way of life that reflected and reinforced their elite status.

Slavery, like any human relationship, required ongoing negotiations. Negotiations between mistresses and maids were not between equals, but, within the confines of law and custom, both sets of women made choices. Elite and enslaved women acted and reacted to one another and in the process created a peculiar world of their own — a world that reveals much about class, race, and gender in the early nation.

The growing historical literature on the founding fathers and slavery helped to inspire this book. The new scholarship has enriched the story of the early nation by demonstrating the centrality of slaveholding to the economy, politics, and society.[4] I have not cut the men out of this account completely, but neither do I let them take center stage, as is usually the case. George Washington, Thomas Jefferson, and James Madison were important historical actors. All were present at the nation's founding. They were philosophers of governance who conceived of a nation founded on the principles of freedom and equality, and they gave their ideals legal underpinning in the Declaration of Independence, the U.S. Constitution, and the *Federalist Papers.* As military and political leaders, they translated ideals into practice. They served in state and federal government, and they all rose to the highest office the nation has to offer. But they were also private citizens whose personal relationships gave shape to their daily experiences and informed their thinking. Actions taken within the family circle—in private places upstairs and downstairs—reflected who the Presidents were at least as much as public displays of speech and behavior did. These private spaces fell under the domain of elite women whose enslaved servants were essential to the formation of an elite Virginia household.

The domestic slaves who waited on the Washingtons, Jeffersons, and Madisons were privy to the most intimate aspects of their owners' lives. Other slaves—those who worked in fields and outbuildings—did the work that underwrote the aristocratic lifestyle their owners enjoyed, but it was the house servants who most directly affected the experiences of the presidential families. As Jeffersonian historian Lucia Stanton has observed, "the daily lives of black and white were most inextricably linked" in the slaveholder's home. It was in domestic spaces that blacks and whites shared "intimate secrets" and "had the greatest opportunity to learn from and influence" one another.[5] At Thomas Jefferson's Monticello, the Hemings family filled most of the posts, as dramatically illustrated by Pulitzer Prize–winning historian Annette Gordon-Reed. Domestic slaves worked in similar ways with members of the Washington family at Mount Vernon and with the Madisons at Montpelier.

In recent decades, historians have demonstrated that members of subordinate groups, including women and slaves, help shape history. Yet scholarship on elite women of the early republic continues to emphasize their limited ability to act on their own behalf, while that on enslaved women in the same period emphasizes their ability to find ways to influence everyday affairs. The implication at times seems to be that enslaved women exercised more power over their lives than the women who commanded their labor. In this book, I recognize the agency of both and demonstrate that even in the most patriarchal of societies, elite white women and enslaved black women found ways to shape their own lives and the lives of others. All were constrained by the laws and customs of the time and place in which they lived, but they were not like pieces of furniture that could be moved about as fathers, husbands, and masters would have it. They made choices, and at times managed to thwart the best-laid plans even of Presidents. Responding to one another, slaveholding and enslaved women created a unique, imperfect union of their own that helped to shape the nation.

Many people learn about the First Ladies from the exhibit on them at the Smithsonian Institution's National Museum of American History in Washington, DC. Since opening on 1 February 1914, it has attracted millions of visitors. I first encountered the exhibit years ago when I lived in Virginia. I periodically took my children to the museum in the hope that they would be entertained, and in the process learn about the country's history. On one of these outings we wandered into the space devoted to the First Ladies. It was crowded, quiet, and darker than the rest of the museum (to protect fragile fabrics). Although the children hushed upon entering, I saw immediately that the exhibit's focus on the gowns worn by the women would not hold their attention, and I quickly herded them toward parts of the museum more appealing to youngsters. But I was fascinated. The gowns were displayed on dress forms or manikins, a technique that made the dresses almost come to life. I have never forgotten feeling for a moment as though I were in the presence of the ladies.

I returned to the exhibit in July 2011. By then, I had moved away. I had a PhD in history, and I had decided to write this book. As before, the display on the First Ladies was crowded but quiet. Most of the visitors were women and teenage girls, but there were plenty of men scattered among them. The size of the group dictated that visitors more or less stay in line and snake slowly around the room, viewing the gowns — and related paintings, shoes, and other artifacts — in the order chosen by the curators.

A time line running along the top of the walls identified each First Lady. Paintings or prints represented women from the early era, black-and-white photographs those from the mid-nineteenth century on.

Martha Washington came first, of course, followed by Abigail Adams, wife of John Adams. Martha Jefferson Randolph (often called Patsy) was third in line. Patsy was Thomas Jefferson's oldest child. By the time her father was inaugurated on 4 March 1801, Patsy's mother had been dead for eighteen years. Patsy and her sister Maria Jefferson Eppes (originally named Mary but called Polly in childhood and Maria in adulthood) visited their father in Washington during the winter of 1802–1803. Both daughters were reluctant to leave their Virginia homes, but they came at their father's request and stayed for seven weeks. Patsy might be described as Jefferson's hostess during this time and again in the winter of 1805–1806, when she returned to Washington as the wife of a congressman and lived in the President's house. The exhibit did not explain all of this but simply listed her as First Lady.

I found the designation of Patsy Jefferson Randolph as First Lady somewhat surprising. Not everyone would agree that she deserves the title. The White House website, in fact, identifies Patsy's long-dead mother, Martha Wayles Skelton Jefferson, as First Lady, and some historians credit Dolley Madison with acting as Jefferson's hostess during his two terms.

Thomas Jefferson rarely included women when he entertained as President. He preferred small dinner parties with congressmen or the men in his cabinet. Still, he could not avoid women altogether, and when they were included, he asked Dolley Madison to fill in as hostess. The gregarious and socially skilled Dolley was only too happy to help. She had accompanied her husband, James, to Washington when he became Jefferson's secretary of state. The couple enjoyed entertaining and did so more often than the President.

In writing this book, I have wrestled with the question of who should be designated First Lady during Thomas Jefferson's time in office. He never remarried after his wife's death in 1782. He was close to Patsy, the only one of his children to outlive him. Thomas and Martha Jefferson had the misfortune to see four of their six children die in infancy. Maria lived to adulthood but passed away in 1804, at the age of twenty-five, from complications of childbirth.

Thomas Jefferson's personal relationships are complicated by the existence of his other family. Historians now generally accept that the third President and his slave Sally Hemings had six children together, four of whom lived to adulthood. Neither she nor any of her children accompanied the President to Washington, but he returned to Monticello—a distance of more than a hundred miles—for extended periods during the eight years he held office. Two of their children, Madison and Eston, were born during these years. But if the First Lady is considered to be the President's hostess or wife, Sally Hemings cannot be considered First Lady on either count. She played no public role except in the opposition press, where Jefferson's political enemies did their best to embarrass him by revealing the relationship. On the other hand, Sally Hemings was not a passing fancy, but an important part of Thomas Jefferson's life.

For the purpose of this book, I treat both Martha Wayles Skelton Jefferson and her daughter Patsy Jefferson Randolph as First Lady.[6] I also give prominent space to Thomas Jefferson's consort Sally Hemings.

On that hot July day when I visited the Smithsonian, gowns belonging to Martha Washington and Dolley Madison were both on display. Dolley's silk satin robe—featuring hand-embroidered butterflies (a favorite of hers), flowers, dragonflies, and phoenixes—stood enclosed in an exhibit case, not far from a silk taffeta that belonged to Martha Washington. Like Dolley's gown, Martha's featured flowers and insects, including butterflies, but the species were different and hers were hand-painted. No gown belonging to Martha Jefferson or Patsy Jefferson Randolph was included in the exhibit, although the Smithsonian apparently possesses a shawl worn by Patsy.[7]

In a small room nearby, a large-screen television looped a video clip about Michelle Obama's donation of her first inaugural gown to the Smithsonian. The silk chiffon dress with organza flowers, displayed nearby on a manikin, was creating quite a stir. On the screen, the First Lady remarked on the popularity of the exhibit. Seeing the gowns, she explained, allows Americans to imagine the women who wore them in a way that is not possible from reading a history book or viewing a photograph. The gowns help to make the First Ladies tangible.

She is right. Standing near the case displaying the slim one-shouldered sheath worn by Nancy Reagan one gets a sense of how petite she was. At five feet tall, Martha Washington was four inches shorter, but she was not as thin. Martha lived at a time when ladies laced their corsets tightly. Although she has been described as stout in middle age, her gown accentuates a small waist, conjuring a small woman who stood erect and covered her bosom. Dolley Madison was six inches taller than Martha Washington. Her high-waisted, low-cut gown showed off her stately figure and ample bosom. This much is readily observed, but I wonder about what is unseen. The ladies must have struggled to put on the elegant dresses. By today's standards, the Washington and Madison gowns are voluminous and heavy. The fabrics are beautiful and were expensive. Only someone with proper training could be entrusted to care for them.

Martha Washington and Dolley Madison each had an enslaved lady's maid to oversee their wardrobes. The maids helped them dress, fixed their hair, and completed fancy sewing. Ona (called Oney) Judge, who waited on Martha, was fifteen years old when she journeyed with her mistress to the nation's capital. Dolley's lady's maid, called Sukey, was twelve when she did the same.

As I stood before the gowns, I tried to imagine Oney and Sukey helping their mistresses into them. It is not the most dignified of images. I am certain the exhibit's curators never intended for visitors to think about the First Ladies in their underwear, but I wanted to envision the activities of the First Ladies and their slaves in private spaces. It was difficult to picture the girls because there is no tangible evidence of their height and weight, as there is for Martha and Dolley. Yet the two girls would have known these gowns or ones like them. They would have helped the First Ladies dress for important occasions and for everyday activities.

Enslaved children of that time were small compared to children today. Nevertheless, many began to work as adults around age ten or twelve. By age fifteen most slave youths were working alongside adults, in the house or in fields where tobacco, cotton, or other cash crops were grown. In my research, I have come across an order for slave clothing from an Alabama cotton planter who listed among his enslaved field hands ten- and twelve-year-olds. He had sent his order to the Hazard textile mill in Peace Dale, Rhode Island, only one village away from my current home. The slaveholder had carefully recorded each slave's measurements for use by the manufacturer. I compared his figures to a chart published by the American Academy of Pediatrics on the height and weight of modern boys and girls. To my shock, I saw that the enslaved ten- and twelve-year-olds were about the size of a six- or seven-year-old today. I tried to imagine Oney or Sukey—Sukey the size perhaps of a first or second grader—helping Martha or Dolley don the dresses and fix their hair. I wished the Smithsonian could find a way to make the girls as tangible as the ladies they served.

After my visit in 2011, the Smithsonian took steps to make enslaved people more visible. An exhibit called "Slavery at Jefferson's Monticello" featured artifacts that belonged to the enslaved people who lived and worked on the President's plantation. Included were dominos, doll parts, and clay marbles that were likely enjoyed by enslaved youngsters; pieces of pottery used by slaves for cooking and eating; and pages from a farm book mentioning slaves by name. These items, along with recordings of interviews conducted with descendants of the Jefferson slaves, helped make the enslaved people more tangible, but unfortunately the exhibit closed after fewer than nine months in 2012, despite attracting large crowds.

What can explain the popularity of the Smithsonian's exhibits of artifacts used by slaves and gowns and accessories worn by the First Ladies? The desire to be in the presence of historical objects, especially those belonging to famous people, must be about more than gaining a sense of their physical stature. The objects suggest a type of access that cannot be obtained through text alone.[8] Yet the First Ladies exhibit, as constituted, seems to conceal more than it reveals of the private lives of its slaveholding subjects. I wondered how visitors would react if dresses belonging to Oney and Sukey were displayed alongside those of their mistresses. The exhibit upstairs on the Presidents does little more to enlighten visitors about how the Washingtons, Jeffersons, and Madisons lived as slaveholders. But no one museum exhibit could adequately tell us about life in the private spaces of their homes — and that is one reason I have written this book.

The women who are the focus of *Ties That Bound* grew up in slaveholding families, but their experiences with slaves differed. Martha Dandridge's parents and community accepted slaveholding as the foundation of the economic, political, and social order. Martha married into one of Virginia's grand families, but her first husband died. When she met and married George Washington soon after, she found a like-minded man as ambitious as she to rise in society. Dolley Payne came of age in a family that rejected slaveholding. Her parents, John and Mary, held slaves when Dolley was young, but in 1783 her father freed them and moved the family to Philadelphia, where they became part of a Quaker community strongly opposed to bondage. There was every reason to think that Dolley would remain a devout Quaker, but after her first husband died she married slaveholder James Madison and returned to Virginia. The book begins with Martha Washington and ends with Dolley Madison, not only because Martha was the oldest and Dolley the youngest of the ladies but because their backgrounds represent two extremes: one was raised in a family that embraced slavery, the other in a family that rejected the idea of human property.

Martha Wayles Skelton Jefferson's childhood stands in stark contrast to those of Martha Dandridge and Dolley Payne. Her mother died giving birth to her. Martha's father remarried twice in quick succession, but both stepmothers died young. Her father did not marry a fourth time but instead developed a long-term relationship and had children with his house slave Elizabeth (Betty) Hemings. After Martha married Thomas Jefferson, she inherited Betty and her children (six of them Martha's half siblings). Martha, like her mother, died of complications from childbirth. Her husband never remarried, and their daughters grew up as their mother did: under the watchful eye of Betty Hemings and members of the Hemings family. The absence of an elite white woman to organize and supervise domestic life left Betty and her children (including Sally) to assume responsibilities within the Jefferson household ordinarily assigned to white women. Martha

Jefferson's story allows us to consider the role played by white women in slaveholding households precisely because she and her daughters grew up in households without one.

Virginia was in this period the most populous state in the union, and its elite families exercised extensive political power. Except for the single term of John Adams, Virginians served as President from the nation's founding in 1789 through 1825, when James Monroe left office. Historians usually find it easier to reconstruct the lives of the prominent than those of ordinary citizens. Elite people are more likely to be literate, and their letters, diaries, and other writings are more likely to be saved. Yet these documents pose their own challenges: writers mask the motives behind actions, for example, explaining their behavior in terms that flatter themselves. Dolley Madison in particular embellished and distorted the record. Like other elites, she edited, altered, and excised documents to shape her legacy and that of her husband. Regarding James Madison's papers, she remarked, "If any letter—line—or word struck me as being calculated to injure the feelings of any one or wrong in themselves . . . I would withdraw them or it." At times, she asked correspondents to pass on information to specific people or to destroy letters. One piece of correspondence that has survived did so despite Dolley's command: "Now burn this."[9]

The challenges do not deter historical research. They only complicate it. Instead of relying on one source, a historian must integrate multiple records written from different points of view. Whether the subject is a First Lady or a slave, much can be learned by reading between the lines of correspondence, comparing accounts by disparate observers, scouring financial records for clues about domestic life, and noticing the physical landscape. A floor plan can tell something about how mistresses and slaves interacted. The inscription on a gravestone may suggest what loved ones considered important about the departed. Cookbooks can relay a sense of what it was like to work in the kitchen or consume a meal in the dining room. Details of everyday life emerge from innumerable sources. I have read many firsthand accounts. I have consulted as well the work of other historians and biographers who have painstakingly pieced together parts of the lives of the early first families.

As I left the Smithsonian in the summer of 2011, I thought about how the First Ladies exhibit had changed since I first saw it decades earlier. More First Ladies have come and gone, adding inaugural gowns and accessories to the display. But these recent First Ladies are also represented by text explaining the causes they have championed. No similar panels praise the work of the early First Ladies. Why? Did they champion no causes, or have the causes they championed fallen so far out of favor that they would appear out of place in a laudatory exhibit? None of the First Ladies I consider in this book questioned her dependence on slavery, and each expected her sons and daughters to become the masters and mistresses of slaves. Acknowledging this allows us to understand more fully not only these first First Ladies but also the time in which they lived.

PART 1

Washington

CHAPTER ONE

The Widow Washington

After her husband's death, Martha Washington closed the second-floor bedroom they had shared for decades and moved to one on the floor above. From the window in her garret chamber, she could see parts of Mount Vernon not seen by visitors to the ornate red-roofed mansion. Walls, fences, and shrubbery concealed the areas where slaves labored to provide the mansion's residents with the accoutrements of gentry life, but Martha knew these spaces well. As mistress of Mount Vernon, she supervised the work done there.

The former First Lady presided over a complicated household with a large enslaved staff, from the footman who greeted arriving guests in the impressive elliptical driveway to the scullery maids who washed dishes in a small room above the kitchen. Martha oversaw the gardeners toiling just beyond the kitchen and the cooks they supplied with vegetables. She supervised the work of dairymaids. She kept track of the perishables stored in the larder and the meat that hung in the smokehouse. From an outbuilding on the plantation's North Lane, she distributed fibers to enslaved women who spun them into thread. She oversaw the weaving of thread into cloth and the sewing of cloth into garments and household goods. From her window, she could watch the laundresses boiling wash water and hanging clothes to dry. When she entertained many overnight guests at once, Martha might have her seamstresses embroider owners' initials on items of clothing to ensure they did not get mixed up in the laundry.

Inside the mansion, Martha directed the work of parlor maids and

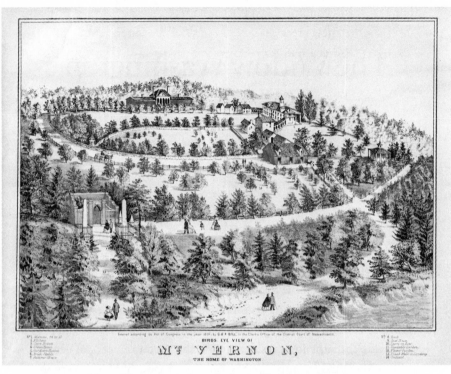

Mount Vernon, artist's rendering, mid-eighteenth century.

dining room waiters. She summoned and supervised the slaves who waited on family and guests, including her lady's maid, who came upstairs to help her dress, do her hair, and sew. When she was not overseeing her domestic help directly, she inspected the results of their labor. She made sure the bedchambers and linens were clean, the staircases polished, the floors swept and washed—passing judgment and giving directions for improvement.

Except for her move to the third floor, Martha's daily routine did not change all that much following her husband's death. While George Washington lived, visitors flocked to Mount Vernon, hoping to engage him in conversation or bask in his presence. After he died, people continued to come, to pay tribute or forge some link to the history he had helped set in motion. Some came specifically to see his widow, who was as well known as her husband. Martha welcomed the vast numbers of strangers, neighbors, friends, and family, though it meant her

domestic duties continued apace. Yet despite the appearance of conti-
nuity, Martha knew great change was in store for Mount Vernon.

A patriarch's death not only represented a personal loss but triggered a financial reckoning. Martha was determined to protect her
family's standing. She and George had worked hard to rise economically, socially, and politically, and she was determined to ensure that
her heirs would maintain elite status. She was most concerned with
her grandchildren, especially the two she and George had raised from
infancy. Family was important to Martha despite — or perhaps because
of — the many losses she had endured. By the time she married George
in 1759, she had already buried one husband, a son, and a daughter.
Two other children from her first marriage, to Daniel Parke Custis, had
died since her move to Mount Vernon. Martha Parke Custis (Patsy)
had passed away at the age of seventeen; John Parke Custis (Jacky)
died at twenty-seven. Jacky left behind four young children, two of
whom Martha and George Washington raised as their own. George
Washington Parke Custis (known as Wash) was age eighteen when his
adoptive grandfather died, and twenty-year-old Eleanor Parke Custis
(called Nelly) had recently given birth to a daughter, giving Martha yet
another generation of loved ones to consider.[1]

Martha understood that slavery supported the economic, social,
and political world in which she and her grandchildren lived, and her
handling of her husband's affairs shows that she accepted this reality.
Her goals and values differed in important ways from those of her
husband. He had been concerned about the fate of Mount Vernon's
slaves and had devised a plan to free some of them after his demise.
She too was concerned about the slaves, but she focused mainly on
how to prevent her husband's plan from adversely affecting her and
her grandchildren.

Martha was present in the second-floor bedroom on the cold day in
December 1799 when George Washington lay dying from what was
probably a bacterial infection. So were a number of slaves. The maids
Caroline, Charlotte, and Molly (sometimes called Moll) were in attendance, as was George's valet, Christopher Sheels, who stood vigil for
hours until George indicated that the young man could sit down. The

other onlookers who remained with the retired President throughout the day and into the night were George's former secretary Tobias Lear, who happened to be visiting, and his longtime physician, James Craik.

The free white housekeeper Eleanor Forbes was in and out of the bedroom throughout the day and evening, and other slaves were in the house or on the grounds. One had been sent, at George's request, to fetch overseer George Rawlins, who knew how to bleed a patient. He came, and over Martha's objections made an incision, extracting half a pint of blood before Martha prevailed upon George to halt the procedure. Physicians at the time believed medical measures should produce a dramatic result, such as fainting, and before the afternoon was over, other doctors would bleed the President three more times. (Two other physicians had been called to consult with Dr. Craik, one at Martha's request and the other at Craik's.) In addition to blood-letting and other measures, the doctors gave their patient calomel, a mercury compound then used as a purgative but today classified as a fungicide and insecticide.[2]

Wash happened to be away, but Nelly and her newborn, Frances Parke Lewis (called Parke), were at Mount Vernon. She and her husband, a nephew of George Washington, had been helping George and Martha host their many visitors. Nelly apparently did not visit her adoptive father's deathbed to say goodbye. It is possible the men who recorded the surviving firsthand accounts simply did not note her presence. More likely, though, she was observing strictly the rules of confinement and stayed away. Like other new mothers from elite families, Nelly limited her activities to the bedchamber and nursery for about a month following her daughter's birth. Family members, servants, and the doctors would have kept her apprised of changes in the President's condition.[3]

George Washington died at the age of sixty-nine surrounded by people he knew well. A crowded death chamber was not unusual at the time. Elite Virginians expected important social relationships to be represented. Close kin, doctors and their helpers, neighbors, clergy, and important household staff were often present. Everyone understood the social importance of the occasion, especially for a man like George Washington. News of his passing would spread quickly, including details of the death scene. The enslaved people were there presumably to fetch whatever household items might be needed, to carry messages, and to make the patient as comfortable as possible by changing sheets and doing the grubby work of nursing. One of them — or perhaps another slave working in the kitchen — would have prepared one of Martha's home remedies for a sore throat: molasses mixed with vinegar and butter.[4]

Enslaved help not only cared for the patient but served the pageantry of the moment. Their presence was a reminder of their owner's mastery and symbolized an important part of his life's work, as did the presence of Lear, his former secretary. Citizens who heard about the President's death would deem it fitting that such assistants were with him at the end.[5]

The slaves had reasons for wanting to be present. A slaveholder's death held danger — the division of an estate among heirs could separate families held in bondage — but also grounds for hope. At times owners manumitted bonded men and women, particularly favored slaves who worked in the intimate setting of the home. Heirs took deathbed declarations seriously. They would be hard-pressed to go against wishes expressed by loved ones ready to meet their maker — whether the wishes concerned emancipating slaves, bequeathing property, or anything else. Deathbed pronouncements were heard by witnesses, some of whom gathered expressly for this purpose. In George Washington's case, rumors of freedom for slaves at his death had circulated for years, and the four people who served him in his final moments may have hoped to be rewarded with release from service.

At some point in the afternoon of December 14, George sent Martha downstairs to his study to retrieve two wills he had written. After looking them over, he indicated that she should throw one in the fire, which she did. By then it was clear to Martha and others in the room that the President was dying. Through the afternoon, he seemed to accept his impending death with stoicism, asking at intervals for the time. Around five or six o'clock he asked that heroic treatments to save his life be stopped. He struggled for breath and said little. In the evening he told his doctor that he could "feel myself going" and asked that he be allowed to "go off quietly." He died between ten and eleven o'clock, shortly after taking his own pulse and asking to be "decently buried" but not before three days had passed.[6] The request apparently reflected his fear of being interred alive. The dread was widespread in the era, and burial services were often postponed accordingly.

It was not the first time George had thought about what would happen to his body. His will specifically rejected the idea that the public be involved in laying him to rest. "It is my express desire that my Corpse may be Interred in a private manner, without — parade, or funeral Oration," he wrote. He wanted his remains laid "with those of my deceased relatives" in a new vault to be built of brick on the mansion grounds. The old one, also located near the mansion house, was too small, "improperly situated," and in need of repair.[7]

If the President's will had been limited to such mundane matters, it might not have garnered much attention, but one provision posed a problem for Martha and electrified the nation. The will he kept from the fire emancipated his slaves upon Martha's (not his) death. No one recorded George's parting words to Martha, if he had any. His secretary and doctor were the only people in the room who wrote about the President's death, and a later memoir by Wash, who was not present but recounted stories passed down in the family, made no mention of any words that passed between them. After George passed, Martha is reported to have said, "All is now over. I shall soon follow him. . . . I have no more trials to pass through."[8] Her words would prove untrue. George's will left Martha with a dilemma: what to do about his slaves?

The writing of a will was one of the rituals that surrounded death, particularly for wealthy white men, and the reading of the will was part of the pageantry and eventually part of the public memory of the man. George crafted his will carefully, attempting to shape the way he would be remembered. Through his will, he did much more than divide his land and stocks. He distributed swords and mourning rings, as well as canes, a Bible, and pistols imbued with historical significance. He publicly affirmed his most important family relationships and friendships through the bequest of personal and prized belongings, as well as through words. Nelly and Wash, for example, received not only land and other property but reassurance that their step-grandfather regarded them "in the same light as I do my own relations."[9]

Through George Washington's will, his slaves received the right to their own persons—eventually, after Martha's passing. He made an exception for one slave, the only one mentioned by name: William Lee, who had been at his master's side through war and peace and who was now disabled. The will granted Lee "immediate freedom" and the right to decide whether to leave or stay at Mount Vernon. Either way, he was to receive an annuity of thirty dollars. Thus, through his bequests, Washington distinguished not only between family, friend, and slave but also among those in each category. Just as some family members and friends were closer than others, so too was one slave.[10]

No one knows the content of the discarded will, although some have speculated that it had been written shortly before Washington took command of the Continental Army in 1775. The surviving one was written in his hand and signed in July 1799. It eventually freed 123 of the 316 slaves who lived and worked on his five farms. The remaining slaves belonged to others. Some had been rented along with a tract of land, but most were part of the estate Martha had inherited from her first husband, the wealthy and well-connected Daniel Parke Custis, who died in 1757. Under Virginia law, Daniel's children or their heirs would eventually take possession of his vast slave and land holdings, as well as other property, but the law also directed that one-third of the estate be allocated for Martha's use over her lifetime. The bulk of Daniel's estate had already been distributed to Jacky's descendants, but Martha's so-called widow's third, or dower property, remained under George's control—as was customary.[11]

The presence of Custis slaves on Washington land complicated the process of emancipating George's slaves. While most of the Custis slaves lived and worked on Custis lands, Martha had brought a dozen or more house servants with her to Mount Vernon in 1759 when she married George, and other Custis slaves had been scattered about on George's four working farms, depending on his need for labor. Custis and Washington slaves formed friendships. They fell in love and married. Children were born, who in turn grew up and had children of their own. By the time of George Washington's death, friendship as well as kinship ties between Washington and Custis slaves were long established.

Shortly before writing his last will, George made lists of the slaves under his management. For each, he recorded name, occupation, place of residence, and name of spouse, if any. He also recorded who owned each slave. Seventy slaves were living at the Mansion House farm. Some were his; others were Martha's. The carpenter Joe was married to Dolshy, a spinner. Joe belonged to George; Dolshy was part of the Custis estate. George's wagoner Godfrey was married to the dower house slave Mima. His carpenter James Carter was married to the knitter Alla, also a dower slave. And so it went.[12] The existence of children only added to the problem. A child's opportunity for freedom depended on whether his or her mother was a Washington or Custis slave. The tangled relationships revealed in the inventories must have weighed heavily on George's mind as he pondered the best way to free his people.

The master of Mount Vernon surely knew that relationships between the Washington and Custis slaves would unravel when his will was implemented. Although George managed the Custis slaves, he had made no plans to free them. He had authority to manumit only those people he had inherited or purchased, along with the children born to enslaved Washington women. He had tried to negotiate with members of the Custis family over some of the others,[13] and the four household servants who attended the dying President—dower slaves all—must have hoped they would be among the Mount Vernon slaves that rumors said would gain freedom at the master's death. But when the content of George's will was made known, it became clear that they would not be freed. Because Custis slaves outnumbered the Washington slaves, most of the enslaved people living at Mount Vernon would remain in bondage.

Martha would have to decide how to carry out the terms of George's will, but first she had to attend to his funeral. As George had requested, burial was delayed until the fourth day after his passing, but little else

George Washington's 1799 census of Mount Vernon slaves, delineating his slaves from Martha's. Courtesy of Mount Vernon Ladies' Association.

was as he had hoped. On 18 December 1799 he was interred in the old family vault near the mansion. Martha had arranged for a new door to be placed on the vault, probably at the same time she ordered his coffin from a cabinetmaker in nearby Alexandria, but no new resting place was erected until 1835.[14]

Most elites at this time buried loved ones at home. Home services were not necessarily simple but could involve elaborate meals, liturgies, and sermons, as well as interment. In George's case, eight slaves, all but one a dower slave, played visible roles. House servants Cyrus and Wilson led the President's horse, saddled but riderless, in a funeral procession. About two hundred family members, friends, and household employees joined the cortège that accompanied the body to the family vault, where the Order of Burial from the Episcopal Prayer Book was read.[15]

Martha chose not to attend the rites, staying in the house with Nelly, and with her other granddaughters, who had traveled to Mount Vernon for the occasion. From the upstairs bedroom windows, the women could hear the funeral procession and see the cortège as it made its way to the vault.

No doubt family members, dignitaries, and other associates offered ideas of what the funeral should entail, including Tobias Lear, who wrote letters informing family and friends of the President's passing and helped with the arrangements. But it is clear that Martha made decisions about how her husband was to be honored, especially with regard to the involvement of slaves. Lear later said that Martha was too grief-stricken to busy herself much with the funeral arrangements, but this may be because he preferred to emphasize his own contributions. He also may have been oblivious to the work women put into funerals or considered it somehow less important than that done by men. Neither Lear nor the eighteen-year-old Wash—both of whom left accounts of the funeral—mentioned the work of women, but neither would have proceeded without consulting the President's widow. George clearly intended that Martha have a say in the events that followed his death because he made her an executrix of his will, along with his nephews and Wash.[16]

Martha would have chosen the eight slaves in the cortège, as well as those who helped behind the scenes to produce a funerary pageant suitable for a Virginia grandee. A slave may have prepared or helped to prepare the body for burial. Slaves certainly prepared food; cleaned and polished; sewed, washed, and pressed clothing; opened and prepared the vault; carried messages; tended horses and carriages; and did the many other tasks necessary to meet the needs of family and guests, some of whom stayed for an extended period. Martha would have decided what food to serve, ordered the supplies, watched the cooks and inspected their results, given directions to the household wait staff, and met with family members, if not with all of the guests.

No one knows exactly what Martha served the guests who attended the burial, but she ordered sixty-one pounds of cheese and forty pounds of pound cake for the mourners. Specially prepared biscuits (often stamped with a cherubim or heart) were customary, and alcohol flowed freely at funerary events; guests attending the funeral of Thomas Jefferson's father in 1757 consumed between thirty-five and a hundred gallons of punch. At least thirty-nine gallons of spirits were brought to Mount Vernon for the President's funeral, twenty-nine from its own nearby distillery and another ten from merchant and friend George Gilpin of Alexandria.[17]

In addition, Martha would have been busy acquiring mourning garb. Not every elite family dressed household slaves in mourning clothing to emphasize their connection to the family, but Martha did, twice. Following Daniel's death, she dressed some of her household slaves in specially ordered clothing. After George died, she purchased black cloth and ribbon to outfit the eight slaves who participated in his funeral rites as well as other house servants. Christopher Sheels got a new pair of shoes.[18] The clothing identified the chosen slaves as part of the mourning pageantry, important members of the Washington household whose role was to honor and serve. George Washington may have done the extraordinary in freeing his slaves, but when it came to his funeral he would be remembered for what he had been in life: an elite slaveholder from Virginia. Martha saw to that.

Perhaps the slaves who helped memorialize George Washington found the experience gratifying. The new clothing may have been welcome, along with the extra food. As was customary, leftovers from the funeral feast were distributed in the slave quarters. The slaves on the Mansion House farm, where the funeral took place, knew their master well and recognized his importance to the nation. But the death of an owner was a troubling affair for slaves. After the guests had left, the Mount Vernon slaves sat down to eat the leftovers, perhaps treasuring all the more family members and friends who shared the feast, knowing some might soon be sold or freed.[19]

Slaves who participated in owners' rituals of mourning were not necessarily allowed time and resources to mourn the loss of their own loved ones. Slaveholders commonly asserted that enslaved people did not feel the pain of parting from family to the same degree as their owners. Incorporating slaves into the owning family's grieving while denying them means to grieve the passing of their own kin was a way of emphasizing to enslaved people that the relationships they formed with one another were secondary to those with their owners.[20] Slaves disagreed and wanted to participate in funerary customs for loved ones. The issue has remained a source of concern not only among descendants of Mount Vernon's slaves but also among scholars and community members who have been working to identify and protect the burial grounds of slaves throughout the country.

At Mount Vernon, as many as seventy-five enslaved people were buried on a hillside overlooking the Potomac, their graves unmarked until 1929 when the Mount Vernon Ladies' Association placed a stone there. An inscription honored the "memory of the many faithful colored servants of the Washington family, buried at Mount Vernon from 1760 to 1860." This marker notwithstanding, the cemetery remained largely inaccessible and ignored until 1983, when—under growing pressure from members of the local community—the group erected a new memorial and added walkways to allow better access. A new inscription describes the dead as "Afro Americans who served as slaves at Mount Vernon," wording that reflects changes in the language of race in the intervening decades and allows for the possibility that the people interred at the site had identities beyond that of slave. Still little is known about those laid to rest in the cemetery.[21]

Freedom under the terms of George's will would be bittersweet for his slaves. With few exceptions, the people who gained freedom would have to leave Washington land, locate places to live, and find work to support them and any of their dependents who were also freed. The situation would be agonizing, for those who left and for those who stayed behind, as wives, mothers, fathers, other relatives, and friends said goodbye. William Lee opted to remain on the Mount Vernon estate, where he worked as a shoemaker, presumably for his own benefit. Even with the annuity promised in his master's will, it would have been difficult for him, at an advanced age and in fragile health, to leave family and friends behind.

In his will, George Washington did not mention by name any slave other than Lee, but he worried about the severing of kinship ties that might accompany a broader emancipation. Careful planning, he hoped, might avert economic chaos and emotional turmoil. To that end, he designated funds for the subsistence of people too old or frail to work and called for the apprenticeship of minor children with no parents to care for them. The children were to be bound out until the age of twenty-five to masters or mistresses who agreed to teach them reading, writing, and other skills needed to engage in useful occupations. George admonished the executors of his estate to follow his plan for emancipation "religiously . . . without evasion, neglect or delay." His forcefulness was prompted by knowledge that not all members of his family shared his vision for a republic shorn of slavery.[22] One family member who harbored doubts about emancipating slaves was Martha. Yet George left the particulars of emancipation to her.

George Washington's directive was no doubt heartfelt, but it also met the requirements of Virginia law. Until 1782, slaveholders who wanted to free a slave had to obtain the approval of the legislature — and the freed slave then had to leave Virginia. Legislators amended the law to stipulate that slaveholders could free enslaved people by will, provided they set aside funding for elderly or infirm adults or minor children who could not be expected to live independently. One purpose of the inventory of slaves George completed shortly before he wrote his will was to calculate how much money would be needed to support the slaves who could not earn a living.

The amended law made private emancipation easier, reflecting changes that were occurring in Virginia and the nation. Virginia, like other states in the upper South, had more enslaved laborers than planters could use efficiently. While Virginians could and did sell "surplus" slaves to planters in places where labor was scarce, some found the practice distasteful, if lucrative. Selling slaves invited criticism, especially in the northern states, where a changing economy, coupled with an emerging political ideology that embraced freedom and equality, was leading toward a general repudiation of slavery. Starting with Vermont in 1777, the northern states one by one agreed to outlaw slavery over time, if not right away. George was perfectly aware of these trends.

Virginia's 1782 law allowed Washington's freed slaves to remain in the state, which meant that families and friends might at least stay nearby if only some of them gained freedom. In 1806 Virginia legislators had second thoughts about having freed slaves in their midst and revoked the provision. The Washington slaves were fortunate in the timing of their master's death.

George Washington expected his slaves to carve out their futures in the time between his death and Martha's. He had no idea how much time that would be, of course, but he thought some period of adjustment would be necessary: "To emancipate them during her life, would tho' earnestly wished by me" result in "insuperable difficulties" stemming from their intermarriage with the Custis slaves, he wrote.[23]

When George on his deathbed told Martha which of his wills should be preserved, he did more than choose between legal documents. He had her burn the second will in the fireplace—in front of witnesses. His action added emotional and moral weight to the remaining document's legal standing. There could be no question of what he wanted done. Martha's later response to the emancipation clause suggests that either she did not know of it in advance or that the two had discussed the matter but come to no resolution.

Word leaked out that the Washington slaves would be freed, forcing Martha to reconsider her relationship to them. She told Abigail Adams during a December 1800 visit that she feared for her life: one of these slaves, knowing that she was an obstacle to freedom, might hasten liberty by hastening her demise. Martha was not so naïve as to believe that enslaved people accepted their fate in bondage. Slaves had fled Mount Vernon during the Revolutionary War, and others had run away during George's presidency. One of the absconders had been Oney Judge, Martha's favorite personal attendant, whose flight appears to have stemmed at least in part from dashed hopes that she might one day be free. By 1799, scores more slaves had disappeared of their own accord.[24]

Talk about a mysterious fire after George's death only added to Martha's anxiety.[25] No one today knows how or even if the flames ignited, but fires were then common and often consumed kitchens and wooden farm structures. Rumors of other dangers circulated as well, including one that the slaves planned to poison Martha. Abigail Adams reported that the President's widow "did not feel as tho her Life was safe in their Hands."[26] Perhaps the fire (or rumor of one) was meant as a warning. Retaliation against slaveholders was not unheard of. Arson, theft, temporary absences, and other like actions on the part of slaves—both real and rumored—encouraged the mitigation of some of slavery's harshest features, because owners feared the wrath of slaves pushed beyond endurance. One or more of the Washington slaves might have set a fire, or talked about the possibility of someone doing so, to frighten Martha into acting. If so, it produced the desired result: Martha freed her husband's slaves sooner than he had intended.

The year after George Washington's death proved a turbulent one in Virginia. News of a thwarted slave rebellion raised fear of slave unrest to new heights. The reported leader and scores more blacks were accused, rounded up, and hanged or transported out of state, but the possibility of more rebels preyed on the minds of white Virginians. Legislators acted to tighten control over slaves and former slaves through measures intended to limit literacy, restrict the ability of enslaved people to "hire out" (work for someone for pay), and prevent freed slaves from staying in the state, but the law did little to alleviate white fright.

Martha likely feared for her life, but her decision to free George's slaves as soon as possible also reflected an economic calculation. Mount Vernon had a surplus of laborers. Abigail Adams repeated Martha's complaint that "at her own expence she had cloalkd [*sic*] them all."[27] While slaves capable of working might have been rented temporarily to area planters, this would have roiled relations on the Washington farmlands and stirred public controversy, especially as word leaked out about the contents of George's will. Martha was a shrewd and experienced businesswoman who had managed her first husband's property between the time of Daniel's death and her marriage to George. Despite her vast wealth, she may well have believed that feeding and clothing the Washington slaves could be done only at the expense of the Custis estate, and she may have wanted to spare her own heirs any financial loss.

George Washington had made his own economic calculations before he wrote his will, and he reached a different conclusion. Mount Vernon was doing well as a result of his decision to diversify his crops—to grow less tobacco and more wheat. Appended to the will was a detailed schedule of his property, which—alongside his inventory of slaves—demonstrated his belief that Mount Vernon could and should support the Washington slaves until the time of Martha's death.

Martha disagreed. In July 1800, seven months after George's death, James Anderson, Washington's plantation manager since 1796, told Martha that the estate was "very unproductive." Expenses, including "Leather for Shoes . . . Linen for the Negroes Shirts Taxes Doctors Bill," could not be covered by the sale of crops. In mid-November Martha wrote, "We have had an uncommon sickly autumn; all my family whites, and Blacks, have been very sick, many of [them] ill— thank god they have all recovered again and I was so fortunate as not to loose any of them."[28] The expense of caring for so many sick slaves must have underscored Anderson's warning of financial crisis. Bills for medicine and doctors' visits could mount, and should slaves die, her assets would diminish further. Survivors who could not work represented a monetary loss of a different type. Anderson had to hire extra hands to help with farming.

Martha knew well the domestic dower slaves, but had little interaction with the Washington slaves, most of whom worked at a distance from the Mount Vernon farm and had been supervised by George or an overseer. Indeed, George had been making the rounds of the farms when he took sick for the last time. Like other Virginia women of the era, Martha placed a high value on the personal relationships she developed with slaves, as well as on economic security.[29] The Washington slaves could be let go without damage to either.

Many slaveholders at the time were reluctant to mix blacks holding aspirations for freedom with their slaves. James Madison, for example, when he returned to his Virginia plantation in 1783, feared his man William Gardner, after some years in Pennsylvania, where slaves were being emancipated, might prove an unfit "companion for fellow slaves." Since slave sales were outlawed in Philadelphia but bound workers could be sold for a set term, Madison sold Gardner for a period of seven years.[30] Martha Washington would have known of Gardner's situation and understood Madison's decision.

Martha knew others with similar fears. Alexander Spotswood, who married George's niece Elizabeth Washington, let an indentured servant of mixed ancestry go free, "not wishing to have female Negroes entitled to freedom among my slaves." During the Revolutionary War, George Washington had expressed reservations over a plan to grant freedom to slaves who joined in fighting the British. Freedom for some and not others would "render slavery more irksome to those who remain in it," he had written.[31] In Philadelphia, George and Martha had mixed free and enslaved servants with disastrous results. Oney Judge had not been the only slave to escape from the city. The cook Hercules had fled in 1797, right before the end of Washington's second term as President.

The idea that promising freedom for some and not others would cause trouble was not groundless, especially given the family and friendship ties that bound members of the Washington-Custis slave community together. Sixteen-year-old Marcus (also known as Billy), who ran away after the President's death, planned to pass himself off as one of the slaves freed by the President's will. Perhaps 7 percent of the slaves at Mount Vernon ran away between 1760 and 1799, a rate similar to that on other Virginia plantations. But the flight of Marcus must have been especially galling to Martha because he was one of the trusted houseboys chosen to participate in the President's funeral. He was the type of slave who tended to be passed along to heirs who would benefit from the careful training he received at Mount Vernon.[32]

The possibility of more slaves escaping was never far away. Even Christopher Sheels had contemplated it. He had married an enslaved woman living on a nearby plantation, and the two had made plans to escape in September 1799. They were found out, but he apparently was never punished.[33]

If Martha Washington worried about how the Custis slaves would react as they watched spouses, children, and other family members leave their homes, she gave no indication. It was the slaveholder's prerogative to decide important matters on behalf of slaves without consulting them. Yet enslaved people found ways of making their wants known. Abigail Adams had no difficulty discerning during her visit that "many of them" were "miserable at the thought" of being parted from loved ones. Slaves often voiced concerns about their fate, especially during times of great change. One can easily imagine Washington and Custis slaves alike beseeching Martha's help in keeping families intact. She told Abigail that she was "distrest for them" and felt a responsibility for the situation, as a parent would for children and as George's wife.[34]

Marriages between slaves were not recognized under law, but enslaved men and women regarded their unions as marriages. The separation of spouses or of young children from mothers was met with anger, dismay, and sorrow. Slaveholders understood this and hesitated to disturb the status quo. They maintained the legal right to sell or separate spouses and other family members, but the process was difficult for all involved, although only the slaves felt the pain of separation from kin and community.

From Martha's perspective, the problem of separating families would only get worse. Freed women who married enslaved men gave birth to free children since children inherited the status of the mother, not the father. Slaveholding Virginians wanted slavery to continue for the foreseeable future, yet the U.S. Constitution included a provision allowing Congress to prohibit traders from importing slaves after 1807.

As a result, the birth of babies in bondage seemed the only practical means to sustain the institution.[35]

Separating slaves from those bound for freedom would increase the chance that those who remained in captivity would find enslaved partners—and the sooner the better, in part because the status of any children born to Washington women in the interim between George's death and the implementation of the emancipation clause in his will would be unclear. Would they be free or enslaved? Martha may have considered it preferable to split couples as soon as possible rather than to wait for this concern to surface.

Given Martha's anxiety about keeping his slaves, it is hard to know what to make of George's decision to condition their freedom on her death. Martha was entitled under law to the use of one-third of his estate. Had he emancipated them before her death, he could have been seen as depriving her of income. Ever one to avoid criticism, George surely would have considered this. Further, a provision in his will suggests that he believed slaveholders, as well as slaves, required time to adjust to the disruptive potential of emancipation. George held legal claim to thirty-three slaves in the possession of Mary Dandridge, the widow of Martha's brother Bartholomew. George's will granted Mary continued use of them (and "their issue") over the course of her lifetime. Upon Mary's death, the slaves age forty and up were to be freed. Those between sixteen and forty would be required to serve Mary's heirs "seven years and no longer." Children and youth under sixteen were to remain in bondage until the age of twenty-five, when they too would become free.[36] Here we see Washington providing for an older woman by leaving slavery, as she had known it, intact during her lifetime. Her heirs and slaves alike would have time to adjust to the changes he had set in motion.

George might have hoped to spare Martha and Mary from the turmoil said to have followed the abolition of slavery in the North. In New England, former slaves were accused of "disorderly conduct," "disturbing the public peace," even "riotous behavior," with some frequency and much alarm. This anxiety helps explain the popularity of schemes to send former slaves out of the United States, most often to Africa. Impractical as the idea of relocating freed slaves might have been, it countered fears of social disorder among those who deemed freed people incapable of exercising self-control.[37] Perhaps George worried that the chaos following emancipation would be worse than the confusion that followed its announcement.

We do not know whether the Washingtons ever discussed slavery or his decision to emancipate his slaves. Following George's death, Martha famously burned all of the letters—probably hundreds of them—she had written him over the course of forty years. She clearly wanted their relationship to remain private. Any dispute—over slavery or other matters—was consigned to the fireplace. Yet Martha's actions show that she disagreed with his plan to free his slaves after her death. He thought his estate could support the Washington slaves until then. She did not. He wanted the Washington and Custis slaves to have time to adjust to the idea that freedom would splinter families. She gave them no more than a year to adapt. George thought that the Washington slaves could be trusted after learning of impending freedom. Martha, again, disagreed. In the end, she did not want the Washington slaves infecting the Custis slaves with ideas of freedom, nor did she want to absorb any expense in maintaining them. Moreover, she could let the Washington slaves go without radically changing her world. Shrewd and calculating, she made her own decision based on what she thought best for herself, her heirs, and her slaves.

The language of George's will and her appointment as executrix left Martha room to maneuver. Few people disapproved of her decision to let the slaves go early. Neither Washington nor Custis relatives complained, and some surely encouraged her efforts. Abigail Adams, however, observed that George's slaves had been set "adrift into the world without horse, Home, or Friend."[38] While George might have been sensitive to such a criticism, Martha apparently was not. Perfectly comfortable with her own slaveholding, she continued to rely on the dower slaves for her livelihood and for personal services. Widely regarded, recognized, and visited, Martha knew her enslaved attendants were highly visible to all she encountered, a fact that seems not to have disturbed her in the least.

The Washington slaves were declared free on New Years' Day 1801. Although George had arranged for the elderly, the infirm, and orphaned children (or children whose parents could not care for them) to receive food, shelter, and clothing—as the 1782 law required—able-bodied adults were expected to find work immediately and to care on their own for freed members of their families. No provision was made for the distribution of land, tools, or other property that would have aided their efforts. Neither Martha nor anyone else left a record of where the Washington slaves went or how Dolshy, Mima, Alla, or other members of Martha's domestic staff fared after their husbands left Mount Vernon.

Only a few stories survive about what happened afterward. Sambo Anderson remained in the neighborhood near his wife and children, who were dower slaves. For support, he hunted wild game and sold his catch to hotels and wealthy households. He earned enough to purchase freedom for two grandchildren and three great-grandchildren. No one knows what became of Christopher Sheels. Caroline ended up (along with her daughter) on the estate of Wash Custis. Frank Lee apparently continued to live on the Mount Vernon estate, but no one knows what happened to his wife, Lucy, who worked in Mount Vernon's kitchen as baker during the Washingtons' retirement years. The Lee's son Philip became Wash's valet.[39]

No record exists that Martha ever spoke against slavery or in favor of her husband's decision to emancipate his slaves, nor did she dissuade her children or grandchildren from claiming the human property in their vast Custis inheritance. Women like Martha understood the importance of slavery to extending the economic well-being of families into future generations. She found no way—or had no desire—to advance the emancipation George had set in motion.

After Martha died in 1802, her dower slaves passed, through the terms of her first husband's will, to her grandchildren. In her own will, dated 22 September 1800, she distributed personal property to family and friends. Her will so closely resembled George's that it is clear she used it as a model.[40] The two wills differ, however, in one crucial matter. Hers freed no slaves. By some unclear means, Martha had come to own one slave in her own name. In a codicil to her will dated 4 March 1802, she declared his fate: "I give to my grandson George Washington Parke Custis my mulatto man Elish—that I bought of mr Butler Washington to him and his hair [*sic*] forever."[41]

Many depictions of elite white women emphasize their inability to act in the face of legal, economic, and social constraints. Yet Martha Washington made decisions in her own interest, as well as the interests of her heirs. If her decisions reflect values that are no longer in favor, they conform to the standards of the time and place in which the Washingtons lived even more than did her husband's. In the patriarchal society of the late eighteenth century, men—as husbands and masters—were by law and custom entitled to make decisions on behalf of wives and slaves; but women of both the slaveholding and enslaved classes found ways to shape their own lives and the lives of others. At times they even thwarted the best-laid plans of the most powerful men.

Sparse records make the task of recreating the world of Martha Washington and her slaves difficult but not impossible. Few documents have survived that were written in Martha's own hand. Letters by her slaves are nonexistent. Yet it is possible to learn something about their thoughts and behaviors by consulting documents written by people who knew them and plantation records composed by George and his overseers. The people who were acquainted with Martha in her youth had little inkling she would end up one of the most famous and admired women in the nation, which makes her early years a good place to begin to know her better.

CHAPTER 2

Martha Dandridge

Martha Dandridge grew up at Chestnut Grove, a tobacco plantation in New Kent County, Virginia. Her parents, John (called Jack) and Frances (called Fanny) Dandridge, were not wealthy, but neither were they poor. Their land and slaveholdings were of the type historians describe as "middling." In eighteenth-century Virginia, the grandees who ruled the colony owned thousands of acres of land and typically held eighty enslaved people who grew agricultural crops for market.[1] Some held more. Most elites lived in large, elaborately furnished homes and were accustomed to having specially trained servants help them dress each day and attend to other personal needs. By custom, Virginia's travelers of the "better sort," who stopped at country estates rather than at hotels or inns, expected to be dined in grand style and waited upon by trained staff. Part of an elite family's reputation rested on its hospitality. The Dandridges were not grandees.

At the time of Martha's birth on 2 June 1731, the Dandridge family resided in a modest two-story wood-frame house with three rooms on each floor. Its size marked Jack Dandridge as an up-and-coming member of the colony's professional class but not part of Virginia's elite. It was large enough to accommodate Jack and Fanny Dandridge's growing family, but there was no wait staff and the family did not dine formally. Some members of the professional class viewed their lack of valets, maids, and footmen as a virtue. David Humphreys, best known today as an aide-de-camp to George Washington during the Revolutionary War, criticized elite men of the mid-eighteenth century for their indolence.[2] But not everyone held this view. Other people of the middling sort aspired to live more like gentry. Jack Dandridge, who in 1715 had come to Virginia from England in the hope of finding a better life, was not prone to criticizing the established order. He accepted the hierarchical structure of Virginia society and sought to rise within it.

Martha's father succeeded to an extent. He found lucrative employment, accumulated funds, purchased land, built a home, and married Frances Orlando Jones, whose family was also of middling rank. He secured an appointment as colonel in the local militia, and he joined St. Peter's Anglican church, where he became a vestryman, that is, an officer of the church who oversaw not only church operations but also civilian matters, including the control of slaves in the community. Fanny Dandridge also became a church member.[3]

The Dandridge house sat on five hundred acres in a region that alternated between flat lands and rolling hills. Homes of the type that Jack built were plentiful. They stood surrounded by gardens and orchards, barns and other outbuildings, as well as slave quarters. Martha's biographer Patricia Brady estimates that Jack and Fanny Dandridge held between fifteen and twenty slaves at Chestnut Grove. At least ten of these were part of the dowry Fanny received from her father. Jack Dandridge's life was typical of men who used their education and connections to acquire and maintain land, slaves, and other property and who managed to live comfortably on income derived from a profession and from planting.[4]

Most adult slaves on plantations like Chestnut Grove worked in tobacco fields. One woman usually cooked. Other enslaved females performed household chores like laundry. Except in the wealthiest of homes, adult slaves who did chores for the owning family did double duty. They helped out about the house or yard—cleaning, sewing, tending animals or vegetable gardens—before or after a day of working in the field. Tobacco cultivation had a cyclical rhythm; work slackened or speeded up depending on the needs of the crop. While fields lay dormant in winter before preparations for spring planting began, slaves could concentrate on domestic chores such as preserving food; constructing and repairing furnishings, housing, and outbuildings; and clothing everyone.

As many as a third of the Dandridge slaves may have been too young for regular field work, although boys and girls as young as ten and twelve worked on farms alongside adults. Younger slaves might be sent to the fields to pick off the hornworms that plague tobacco plants, but hornworms have a short life cycle, which meant the little ones did not spend much of the year in the field. On some farms, children also carried water, food, or messages to the working hands.

On smaller plantations like Chestnut Grove, childcare arrangements for slaves were informal and usually decided between mistresses and mothers, who negotiated such matters as how and when slave babies would be fed, including when they would begin eating supplementary foods intended to stretch out the time between feedings and wean the child. People did not understand germs and the importance of sterilization, but they knew that infants fed bottled milk became sick and died more often than those who were suckled. For this reason, the mother of an infant might be allowed to take the child to the field and stop work periodically to nurse. Women whose breastfeeding children stayed in the slave quarters left the field to nurse the baby at appointed times. How often or how long a woman saw her infant could become a point of contention, but usually enslaved mothers and slaveholders improvised as needed to ensure the survival of the child.

Enslaved children who were past infancy but not old enough to work in the crop did not remain idle during the day. In addition to carrying water, food, and messages, they could gather eggs, dust furniture, beat rugs, tend infants, sew items for household use, hang diapers out to dry, crack nuts, pull weeds from flower and herb gardens, and fetch items wanted by an owner. Very young children sometimes were charged with waving feathered fans in the dining room or by a bedside to keep flies off food or away from a person who was ill.

The children of slaves were expected to do chores not only for owners but also for parents, a situation that, from the owners' perspective, had the advantages of keeping them out of trouble and making it possible for the adults to work longer at their assigned tasks. Parents valued the contributions children made to the family table, which could be substantial. Youngsters gathered nuts and berries, tended small garden patches, trapped rabbits, fished, and gathered wood for the cooking fires. Children also watched younger siblings, helped spin cloth and sew clothing, and swept around the slave cabins.

Like children elsewhere, enslaved youngsters required some supervision to ensure their diligence as well as their safety. While parents were in the field, an older woman working about the house (sometimes the cook) might feed and keep an eye on the children, but anyone could be recruited to check on them. Children could be left to supervise babies barely younger than themselves for long stretches of time, but usually someone in the household checked periodically to ensure the youngsters were doing as they were told. An older daughter like Martha—she was the oldest of Fanny and Jack's eight children— would have been expected to help her mother check to see that rooms were dusted, floors swept, and infants tended.

From this distance, we cannot be sure what methods Martha used to get young slaves to perform their chores. She likely employed the methods of other slaveholders: a combination of rewards and punishments. A special treat given with a smile or a smack on the hand with a stick could remind young slaves to attend to tasks, as could a warning to a child's parent. Slaveholders were not above threatening parents with the sale of children who misbehaved, which encouraged mothers and fathers to use any means necessary to ensure that children obeyed an owner's orders.

Martha learned from her mother to "keep house." It was not simply a matter of knowing how to sweeten jellies and preserves, apply healing potions to cuts and insect bites, make soap, and the like. She also had to learn to manage household slaves. The presence of enslaved children offered girls like Martha the opportunity from a young age to gain experience. As the young mistress and the young slaves matured, they shouldered an increasing number of complex tasks.

Some historians and biographers have sympathized with mistresses of slaves who complained from time to time about the work involved in keeping a plantation's slaves fed, clothed, and healthy.[5] It is true that some slave-owning women spent considerable time cutting fabric for slave clothing, counting out rations for distribution to enslaved families, and growing herbs to be used in home remedies to maintain the health of an enslaved workforce. Such tasks could not be delegated, as owners worried that slaves might prove too generous with cloth or food or opt for their own traditional folk remedies over the ones speci-fied by the mistress. But in truth the bulk of the work mistresses did on behalf of slaves consisted of supervision. Training slaves took time, but it paid off in the long run, as girls and boys gradually learned not simply to clean or cook or sew or garden or gather eggs but to do these things the way the mistress wanted. Fanny Dandridge must have been pleased that Martha could be counted on to help train young slaves to perform domestic chores to satisfaction.

In preparation for her marriage, Martha needed to gain direct ex-perience in managing slaves and performing household chores. The great majority of women from slaveholding families married planters, and their education in the main consisted of learning to do the work necessary for a farm's success. Girls of Martha's background learned to read and write and cipher well enough to keep accounts and cor-respond with family members. Martha's reading skills were sufficient that as an adult she enjoyed a variety of publications, including the Anglican Book of Common Prayer, the Bible, novels, and plays.[6] Her knowledge of arithmetic proved sufficient to allow her, later in life, to keep track of money lent to relatives — and to review George's will and conclude that she and her heirs would be better off financially if she did not follow his instructions to the letter.

Martha's education extended beyond household tasks and aca-demic learning to include personal conduct. This meant learning to walk and talk in a manner befitting the daughter of a property owner. Manners were an important way for Martha and other girls from slaveholding families to help maintain the family's social status. Truly wealthy and well-connected daughters could afford to exhibit eccen-tricities, but not girls like Martha, whose father held limited property for a dowry and whose future would depend on marriage. Martha ac-cordingly learned correct posture, voice modulation, and the proper style of walking (not easy in the wide skirts of the day). She learned to ride a horse in a manner thought appropriate for girls of her class, and she learned to dance the waltzes, country reels, and other steps that were popular and associated with courtship. Martha's studies included the art of setting a table, dressing stylishly, and carrying on conversations. The latter was complicated because the form varied depending on the status of the other conversant. One did not speak to one's betters in the same way one spoke with equals or members of the family, and one did not talk to slaves as one spoke to free servants.[7]

Skills taught girls were both practical and markers of status. Girls first began to sew by making objects of coarse linen for household use. They taught this skill to younger sisters as well as any enslaved children capable of wielding a needle. In time, young mistresses mastered the art of fine sewing, including (if their families could afford fine fabric and multicolored threads) needlepoint and embroidery.[8]

Wealthy women had slaves trained specifically to help with fancy sewing, and they had the financial means to import fine fabrics (including upholstered furniture) from abroad. They also had lady's maids to care for their wardrobes. Martha would have been expected to complete her own fancy sewing under the supervision of her mother and to care for her own clothes. Neither Fanny nor Martha had a lady's maid. Lady's maids were a luxury found only in the homes of Virginia's "best" families. Martha would not acquire one until after she married a man who could afford the expense.

Her upbringing taught Martha Dandridge to accept slavery—even its worst features—as part of life. She grew up in an agricultural community that relied on slave labor to cultivate market crops. At least half of the population in New Kent County was enslaved. She, like other whites, would have understood the danger: slaves might rebel and seek retribution. Individual slaves regularly resisted on local farms, and rumors of slave insurrection abounded in the neighborhood. As a member of the local militia, Martha's father had the duty to guard against slave uprisings, such as the one that had five Virginia counties up in arms the year before Martha was born.[9] Planters in the region guarded zealously against such events by disciplining harshly any slaves caught or suspected of violating plantation rules.

News of slave disobedience, including runaways, traveled swiftly through everyday conversations, letters, and newspapers. During the

1730s, 660 Virginia slaves (1.3 percent of the total) ran away. Most were captured and returned (580 of 660), but those who remained at large left people in the vicinity worrying for their safety. In Martha's day, the Williamsburg newspaper regularly printed advertisements offering rewards for the return of escaped slaves. Suspected fugitives were sometimes captured and jailed until an owner could be identified. Slaves taken up in this manner were often whipped or branded before being returned. Martha would have been well aware of these practices.[10]

Growing up, Martha would have heard dire warnings about slaves out after dark without an owner's written permission. Those caught without a "pass" or congregating in groups without an owner's consent could be punished severely, according to law. Members of the Anglican church, which her family attended, saw no contradiction between holding men, women, and children in captivity and church teachings, including biblical readings. In short, Martha learned in her early years that her community, her governors, even her church, supported a way of life built on slavery.

The privileges that came with slaveholding were on display each Sunday for all to see. Throughout Virginia, grandees drove up to church in elaborate carriages attended by slaves in livery. They waited outside the church until everyone else was seated, and at the last minute made their way to the best seats in the front. When the service was over, congregants of humbler means waited to leave until the ladies and gentlemen had exited. The exalted procession, elaborate dress, coifed hair, and refined deportment of grandees offered visible proof that not all men and women were equal. In this way, the church reinforced the social, economic, and political standing of people within the community.[11]

Slave insurrection and disobedience were discussed openly, but another unsavory feature of slavery was only whispered about: the unsanctioned sexual relationships that occurred between Virginia's patriarchs and slaves. White Virginians maintained that a rigid separation of the races was important, yet white men breached the color line time and again. Politicians and ministers damned interracial liaisons, and wrote laws and preached against them, but with little result. The unspoken rule was that such relationships would be tolerated so long as they were not flaunted. Adults—including the mothers of children born from these unions—knew to be circumspect. Some young children, however, were not told who their fathers were for fear they would tell all they knew, as youngsters are prone to do.[12]

Sex across the color line was not an abstract concept for Martha Dandridge. While married to Fanny, her father had a relationship with a woman of mixed ancestry that resulted in the birth of at least one child. Ann Dandridge was Martha's half sister and lived as a slave in the Dandridge home until Jack died in 1756.[13] No family member acknowledged publicly the relationship between Jack and Ann's mother, but this did not mean that Fanny and her children failed to understand what had occurred.

Ann was raised as a servant in her father's home. She received no monetary compensation for her services. Nor did she reap any of the rights or responsibilities held by the children born to Jack's legally recognized wife, Fanny. She was clothed, fed, and sheltered by her father in exchange for service to the family.

Not all owning families kept biologically related slaves at home. Some sold the children, gave them away to relatives, or in rare cases sent them off to live as free people. Because those raised at home received an education of sorts (careful instruction in the domestic arts), the practice of raising the children to service was viewed in certain circles as charitable, although slavery's critics saw the practice for what it was: an extreme form of labor exploitation and personal subordination.

It is all but impossible given the scarcity of evidence to understand exactly how Ann fit into the Dandridge home, or even much about her. It seems likely that Jack Dandridge's other children accepted Ann's presence without comment or question. Decades later, South Carolina author Mary Boykin Chesnut wrote about the phenomenon of enslaved children born to slaveholding men and raised in the household of the father: "Like the patriarchs of old, our men live all in one house with their wives and their concubines, and the mulattoes one sees in every family exactly resemble the white children—and every lady tells you who is the father of all the mulatto children in everybody's household, but those in her own she seems to think drop from the clouds, or pretends so to think."[14] Chesnut was one of few people who spoke openly of the situation.

Children like Martha did not know instinctively to avoid the subject of half siblings of mixed race. Rather they learned from adults who modeled the behavior. Martha and the other Dandridge children would have followed Fanny's lead. Incorporating slaves like Ann into the family helped perpetuate a class system that kept racially ambiguous people isolated and dependent — and thus in danger. As an adult, Martha Washington took Ann Dandridge to Mount Vernon, where she was apparently raped by a member of Martha's family (see chapter 4). Ann gave birth to a son, who was raised in the Washington family. Evidently, Martha put into practice the lesson she had learned from her mother.

The vast majority of slaveholding men who fathered children with enslaved women never publicly acknowledged their mixed-race sons and daughters, although some came precariously close to doing so by having them baptized. So far as is known, Ann Dandridge was never baptized at St. Peter's Church, but Martha along with her parents and siblings would have witnessed baptismal rites of other slaves. The subject of who fathered them might have been taboo, but the message could be conveyed clearly without spoken words.

Despite Martha's knowledge of slavery's worst features, she aspired — as the next chapter will show — to become the wife of a planter and a mistress of slaves. Her family and community expected her to fulfill a role similar to that of her mother, but Martha's life would differ significantly from Fanny's. When the time came, Martha would marry into one of the largest slaveholding families of Virginia and live as a grandee.

CHAPTER 3

Married Lady

Given the middling status of the Dandridge family, Martha could expect only a modest dowry when she wed, yet she managed to marry into the top tier of elite society. Daniel Parke Custis was the tormented son of John Custis IV, patriarch of Virginia's wealthiest and perhaps most eccentric family. The senior Custis held vast tracks of land (more than seventeen thousand acres) and hundreds of slaves living on multiple plantations, as well as an elaborate home in Williamsburg.[1] His son Daniel lived on the plantation known as White House, just a few miles from the Dandridges' Chestnut Grove.

Somehow Martha and Daniel managed to pledge themselves to one another despite vehement opposition from his father, who judged the Dandridges his inferiors both socially and economically. In the mid-eighteenth century, daughters and sons were exerting more control over their choice of spouses than in an earlier era, but Martha and Daniel nevertheless needed to win the approval of his father, who had threatened to disinherit Daniel should he marry Martha. The matter was complicated further by the existence of a second Custis son, a youth of mixed race. John (called Jack or Black Jack) was born around 1739 to John Custis IV and one of his slaves—a woman known in the record only as Alice. Should Daniel persist in his pursuit of Martha, John Custis VI vowed, he would bestow his fortune on Jack.[2]

So far as can be learned, John cared little for Jack's mother, but he apparently cherished his second son. He was no abolitionist when it came to other slaves, but he planned to emancipate Jack through his last will and testament despite the acrimony it would cause within the family and the potential for public scandal. (His marriage to Daniel's mother, Frances Parke Custis, was, in an age when couples avoided divorce even in the face of extreme irreconcilable differences, legendary for the couple's incessant fighting and mutual hatred.) John not only arranged for Jack's emancipation but bequeathed money for his support and gave Jack land and a legal claim to his mother and four other slaves.[3]

While John appears to have maintained a good relationship with his son born out of wedlock, his bond with Daniel was fraught — one source of the tension being his father's obvious favoring of Jack. Daniel was thirty-eight when he asked to marry eighteen-year-old Martha Dandridge, an age considered rather late for one of Virginia's most eligible bachelors. The delay was the result of his father's incessant faultfinding, not only with Daniel but with any woman Daniel desired.

It may have been Martha who persuaded the elder Custis to accept her as Daniel's bride. She understood the importance John placed on his relationship with Jack, and she evidently convinced him that Daniel would provide a home for his brother until Jack came of age and into his inheritance. In a gesture of goodwill, Martha apparently arranged for a horse, saddle, and bridle to be sent to Jack on Daniel's behalf. John relented and consented to the marriage.[4]

Martha no doubt captivated the senior Custis, but she must also have convinced Daniel to placate his father by accommodating Jack within the family rather than contest the issue and risk losing both property and reputation. This could not have been easy. Daniel was touchy when it came to his family fortune. His grandfather John Parke (on his mother's side) fathered a number of children outside of marriage, and these half siblings disputed Daniel's claim to the Parke fortune. The so-called Dunbar case unfolded over the course of decades on two continents; it posed a real threat to Daniel's fortune but at least unfolded far from home.[5] Jack posed no real threat since he had no standing to sue in court, but a protracted argument over his claims would have brought public condemnation as tongues wagged about Jack's paternity. Better to mend the rift in the family quietly with a modest amount of money.

Yet how did Martha find the courage to confront Daniel's irascible father, who had gone so far as to verbally abuse her and her father in the streets of Williamsburg? It is important to remember that the Dandridges and Custises had known each other for a long time. They lived in the same community and attended the same church. John's treatment of the Dandridges may have dismayed friends and extended family, which in turn may have encouraged Martha to intervene, especially since Daniel was not likely to. Martha may have worried that the elder Custis's defamation of her and her family would have a devastating effect on her future, whether she married Daniel or someone else.

Martha was under no pressure from her parents or from Daniel to act. She could have backed away and left it at that. Perhaps she was driven by love of Daniel. But it seems she also aspired to the life of a grandee. Martha was ambitious enough to be practical about accepting a child of mixed race into the home she would establish with Daniel. She had, after all, already accommodated her father's mixed-race daughter Ann Dandridge at Chestnut Grove.

Martha and Daniel married 15 May 1750, in the familiar, one-story brick Anglican church where both of their fathers had been vestrymen. After the ceremony, the bride and groom took a carriage drawn by four white horses to Daniel's New Kent County mansion, White House, on the Pamunkey River just a few miles from the church. Six enslaved attendants flanked the carriage, riding horseback and dressed in white. Members of the gentry as well as relatives gathered at White House in celebration. Afterward, the servants enjoyed "a holiday . . . made happy with feasting and presents," according to early biographer Benson John Lossing. Perhaps they did, but of course the enslaved domestic staff would have been busy preparing and serving the feast and attending to the needs of the guests. They may have enjoyed extra food and the gaiety of the occasion, but they also would have had reason for concern. The arrival of a new mistress meant the possibility of change, and not necessarily for the better. Of even greater concern, perhaps, was the death of John Custis IV six months before the wedding. With the passing of his father, Daniel came into his inheritance, including five plantations and nearly three hundred slaves. About half of the bondmen and -women resided on the White House estate; the rest were scattered about the other properties.[6]

Twelve of Daniel's slaves worked in the mansion house directly under Martha's supervision. Most young women would have found daunting the transition from a home where household servants were Janes of all trades to one that boasted a bevy of servants with specialized skills. Martha at age eighteen was familiar with managing domestic slaves, but not in an elite household. She had to adapt to the elaborate routines she encountered at White House. For example, during the formal dinners served daily in the homes of grandees, tablecloths were removed after each course. Someone had to wash as well as change them. As mistress of White House, Martha would have been expected to ensure that the tableware was laundered to satisfaction, the silver polished to perfection, and the table laid with precision, all while learning a host of other new duties. At some point, Martha was given a gold watch on which the letters of her new name appeared above the numerals, a gift that would have helped her run the household in a timely manner.[7] She could have consulted the watch throughout the day to ensure that servants were on schedule, but she also would have used it to regulate her own behavior. Daniel would have expected to sit down for dinner at a particular time, and it was Martha's responsibility to ensure that he did. The young mistress faced challenges as she learned to plan menus that pleased her husband and guests and observed the order in which various courses were brought to the table. And meals were not the only thing she had to worry about. Numerous rules governed domestic life at the Custis mansion.

As the wife of a wealthy and well-connected gentleman, Martha Custis was expected to dress herself and her home in the latest fashion. The importance of women as consumers was rising in the eighteenth century, especially with regard to textiles. Certain fabrics were deemed suitable for women's dresses, others for children's clothing, servants' attire, or household furnishings. They were not interchangeable. Women studied trends and ordered what they believed was best suited for each. They also oversaw the construction of clothing and upholstered furnishings, drapes for windows, and bed trimmings.[8]

It was a lot for a young bride to learn, but Martha joined a household in which domestic routines were already in place. The pattern of daily life might have been unfamiliar to her, but this was not true for her domestic slaves. The cook or cooks, for example, would have been familiar with the dishes Daniel wanted served. In the early months, she likely relied on her staff to keep up usual habits. She also received written instructions on running the Custis household. At the time of her marriage, Martha inherited two Custis family cookbooks: *A Booke of Cookery* and *A Booke of Sweetmeats*.[9] Both included recipes for medicinal compounds and household cleansers, as well as food. The pages revealed all manner of things: how to plant asparagus, how to remove stains from linen, how to make a red powder for cleansing open sores and wounds.

The Custis books were not unusual. Elite girls in the era made copies of household cookbooks for their own use upon marriage. The activity allowed them to practice penmanship as they learned to perform household tasks. The practice of copying recipes was a style of learning that was available to literate women only. Women who could not read would have learned to cook and do other household chores by watching and doing. Of course, literate girls who watched servants or slaves or mothers or others perform chores learned this way as well.

Karen Hess, who transcribed the Custis cookbooks for modern publication, explains that the recipes reflect the elite status of the Custis household. Only the rich could afford many of the ingredients, such as oranges, and few housewives would tackle the time-consuming recipes unless they had help. Notably, it would not have been within the means of the Dandridges to make many of the recipes. Martha clearly treasured the cookbooks since she kept them in the family and passed them to her heirs.

Martha must have been grateful at first for servants who were already trained and accustomed to routine, but over time she would have wanted to initiate at least some changes, particularly after she became a mother. Martha gave birth to four children during her marriage to Daniel. For each child, Martha acquired a new enslaved nursemaid, as was customary in elite Virginia families. Daniel Parke Custis Jr. was born in 1751. Three other children followed: Frances in 1753, John (called Jacky) in 1754, and Martha (called Patsy) in 1756. The oldest, Daniel, died in infancy, the year of Jacky's birth.

Change came to White House in other ways. A will written by John Custis IV just eight days before his death required Daniel to look after his younger brother until Jack turned twenty. Apparently, Daniel upheld his obligations to his half brother, but the situation did not last long. Jack died in 1751, probably of meningococcal meningitis. His death proved convenient for Daniel and Martha, not only because it left Daniel as sole heir to the vast Custis estate but because it tamped down any scandal that might have resulted from Jack's presence in the Custis home and neighborhood.[10]

Jack Custis's death did not settle the place of half siblings of mixed ancestry in the Custis household, however. Five years later, Ann Dandridge came to live in the Custis home. We do not know whether Martha felt affection for her half sister, but she apparently viewed her support as an obligation, if not to Ann then to her mother. Although Ann's age is not known for certain, she appears to have been much younger than Martha. By the time she moved to the Custis household, Martha's oldest son had died, but the three other children were still living. Given Martha's age, she and Daniel could expect to have more. Young Ann would fit into the household easily, raised alongside the Custis youngsters—not as an equal but as a nursemaid.

Sadly, death again intervened and altered Martha's future. Her oldest daughter, Frances, died in 1757, and her husband, who had shown no sign of illness, passed away a few months later. Martha and Daniel had been married seven years. Martha, at age twenty-six, was left to raise young Jacky and Patsy without him.

Daniel left no will, but under Virginia law Martha was entitled to the use of one-third of his property, including his slaves. The other two-thirds of his estate went to the children, although until Jacky and Patsy came of age Martha would serve as steward. Daniel's property was vast and far-flung. The estate consisted of more than seventeen thousand acres of land in eastern Virginia, nearly three hundred slaves, livestock, household and farm furnishings, Six Chimney House in Williamsburg, White House in New Kent County, bank stock in England, and thousands of pounds in cash and English treasury notes.[11]

By some accounts, Martha looked immediately for a man to help her run the extensive estate, which at the time of Daniel's death was worth thirty thousand pounds, without factoring in the value of the land.[12] Others posit that Martha managed well on her own. The editor of Martha's papers, Joseph E. Fields, concludes that the management of Daniel's estate "was a crushing burden that [Martha] was ill prepared to meet." The Dunbar suit—a massive collection of claims and counterclaims involving the Parke/Custis fortune that predated Martha's marriage to Daniel—was still pending, which meant she needed to consider legal matters in addition to managing an extensive agricultural estate worked by hundreds of slaves. A husband who could help deal with Daniel's complicated finances, Fields suggests, would have been welcome. Biographer Patricia Brady, on the other hand, maintains that Martha took charge and made decisions that were in her and her children's best interests. There is truth in both claims. Martha remarried eighteen months after Daniel's death but in the meantime made her own decisions with the help of Daniel's plantation manager, as well as other advisors. Each of the Custis plantations had an overseer, and a crowd of lawyers, friends, family members, merchants, and planters offered assistance.[13]

Following Daniel's death, Martha began at once to settle his accounts, sell his tobacco, insure his crop, and renegotiate legal representation in lawsuits involving him and her late father-in-law. She ordered goods, lent money to neighbors and relatives, secured services, and paid taxes. Her purchases ranged from a tombstone for Daniel and black mourning clothes for the male slaves who worked in the house to quantities of osnaburg, a coarse, plain-woven fabric used to make grain bags and clothing for field hands. She bought stockings for herself and carpeting for the mansion. From London she purchased spices, raisins, and nuts. She ordered salad oil by the gallon and candy by the pound. Martha's brother Bartholomew Dandridge and her maternal uncle Lane Jones both borrowed Custis funds.[14]

In the two months following Daniel's death, Dr. James Carter at-

tended Martha, her son, and an enslaved woman, and supplied astrin-
gents, cordials, and powders to cure or ward off various ailments. A
local seamstress, Elizabeth Vaughan, sewed mourning clothing and
altered some of Martha's gowns (presumably to suit her new status as
a widow). Martha paid tailor George Heath to make Jacky's clothing
and for cutting out clothing for the male slaves. (In September and
October 1757 he collected the same amount for making a silk coat,
scarlet waistcoat, and breeches for Jacky as he did for making sixty
"Negro suits.")[15]

Above all, Martha sought to assure Daniel's creditors and business
associates that the estate would remain intact. "As Mr. Custis died
Without Will and left but two Children his Estate will be kept together
for some time," she told Daniel's former tobacco sellers in London.
She hoped his arrangement with them would continue as before.[16]

Slaves as well as business and legal associates could take comfort
in the knowledge that the estate would not be dismantled. Following the death of a master, slave families and friends could find themselves scattered as heirs claimed the human property to which they
were legally due or, worse, sold them to pay off debts or to divide more
easily the property among multiple heirs. It no doubt came as a relief
to the Custis slaves to see the estate functioning as before, although
surely they were not so naïve as to consider themselves beyond danger
of sale or separation. After all, Martha was young and there was a good
chance she would remarry. If so, her new husband would decide their
fate, since law and custom put decisions about land, people, and other
property into the hands of men when they were around.

The widow Custis would have been an attractive marriage prospect
for men throughout Virginia and beyond. Whoever married Daniel
Parke Custis's widow would immediately command a fortune. From
many potential suitors, Martha chose George Washington, a man
whose ambitions—if not his wealth—matched her own.

CHAPTER 4

Mistress of
Mount Vernon

Martha Dandridge Custis married George Washington on 6 January
1759. Family lore maintains that she wore a gold dress overlaying a
petticoat shimmering with silver threads. A pincushion handed down
in the family is said to have been fashioned from cloth cut from the
petticoat,[1] but this has not been authenticated. An "interpretation" of
the wedding dress is on display at Mount Vernon. The yellow silk and
damask garment appears alongside a reproduction of what are said to
be Martha's gold and purple wedding slippers. The gallery also holds
a necklace that once belonged to Martha and earrings that may have
been hers. A portrait of Martha based on an "age-regression" analysis
and reflective of period portraiture looms over the items, giving the
impression that we know more than we do about how Martha looked
as a bride.

No one knows for certain where Martha and George exchanged
their vows. Some say it was in the same church where she married
Daniel Parke Custis nine years earlier. More say the ceremony took
place at White House, the home she had shared with Daniel. Today St.
Peter's Church in New Kent County acknowledges the dispute while
proudly proclaiming its connection to the nation's first First Lady. In
1960 Virginia's state legislature officially designated St. Peter's—now
restored to resemble the building Martha knew growing up—as "The
First Church of the First Lady."[2]

An elaborate reception at the Custis country estate followed the
marriage ceremony. For days, guests feasted on turkey, ham, fruit, and

cake; danced minuets, quadrilles, and country reels; and drank wine, whiskey, and punch. Martha's second wedding party would have resembled her first, except this time it was the groom who was marrying up instead of the bride. George's wealth did not match Martha's. He had inherited land on the Rappahannock River and ten slaves from his father, but George's mother was still living on the land and relying on the labor of the slaves. George owned Mount Vernon plantation on the Potomac River and other slaves, but when he courted the widow Custis his elite status was more aspiration than actuality. George's Mount Vernon simply did not match the splendor of Daniel's White House, but as Martha's marriage to Daniel had catapulted her into high society and turned her into a lady, so her marriage to George Washington elevated his status to that of gentlemen. Over time, George would use his newfound wealth to transform Mount Vernon from a farm to the country "seat" he hoped for, with a mansion worthy of a grandee, but at the time of his marriage to Martha, Mount Vernon was a work in progress.

White House's domestic slaves worked hard to make the celebration of George and Martha's marriage festive, but the women and men who prepared and served the food, looked after guests, and cared for their horses must have been anxious for the future. Marriages in slaveholding families, like deaths, were harbingers of change, as the Custis slaves well knew. In less than ten years, they had gained one mistress (Martha) and lost two masters (Daniel and his father). Now they were to have a third master. Routines were bound to change. Martha's impending move to the home of her new husband was especially worrisome to members of her domestic staff. Families might be separated as the newlyweds decided which slaves would remain on the vast Custis holdings and which would live and work at Mount Vernon.

George must have anticipated some of the nervousness; while he was courting Martha he made a point of tipping her domestic slaves well. It was not unusual for guests to provide enslaved attendants with small sums for services rendered, but George would have had a special reason for convincing them of his generosity. If Martha consented to marriage, she would bring to Mount Vernon her highly trained domestic help. He hoped the move from New Kent to Fairfax County would go smoothly. Disgruntled servants, everyone knew, could create havoc in an otherwise tranquil home.

The Washingtons took their time moving Martha, her children, and her belongings to Mount Vernon. First the couple traveled to Williamsburg, where George served in the House of Burgesses. Next they visited relatives, including George's mother, Mary Ball Washington. Finally in April they arrived at Mount Vernon accompanied by wagonloads of property, some of which was human.

By the mid-eighteenth century, Virginia elites were building elaborate homes with formal dining rooms and halls big enough to accommodate formal dancing. They were collecting specialized tableware for use in entertaining[3] and staffing their mansions with servants who specialized in particular occupations. George had made considerable progress in refashioning his house on the bank of the Potomac, but it remained far more modest than the twenty-room mansion visitors see today. George had done his best to spruce it up before Martha's arrival. He ordered his slaves to polish the staircase, clean everything else, and bring beds, tables, and chairs out of storage. It was a start, but it would be years before the house came to reflect the elite status of one of Virginia's most illustrious citizens.

Which household servants to bring from White House to Mount Vernon was a matter for Martha to decide, but George took an interest in the details. She brought with her the trained help necessary for entertaining in grand fashion, as well as slave attendants who would see to the personal needs of her family. George began ordering livery for the staff, and sometime that year he made a list of the slaves who worked in the house, noting their occupations and ages. Martha's dower slaves inherited from Daniel Custis included Sally, Breechy, Mulatto Jack, Doll, Beck, and Jenny. Other slaves working at the house were part of her children's inheritance: Julius, Rose, and Moll (also called Molly), Mima, and Phillis. There may have been others. Austin was a dower slave who likely worked at the mansion. And at some point Martha brought Caroline Branham from White House to make beds, sew shirts, and help tend to the needs of guests.[4] Ann Dandridge came too.

Although moving slaves was the prerogative of the mistress and master, the Custis slaves would have had some sway over who went to Mount Vernon and who remained behind. Trouble could arise when owners separated slaves from kin and community, and no owner wanted to be constantly whipping or threatening to sell uncooperative slaves who worked in the intimate setting of a personal residence or nearby in the yard. The Washingtons would have favored slaves who seemed willing to relocate and whose past behavior indicated the disposition to work closely with family members in a domestic setting. While none of the Custis slaves left accounts of what happened, there is some evidence of dissatisfaction and a willingness to act secretly to maintain personal relationships over time and distance. A dower slave named Jemmy attempted to escape the year after the Washingtons married, and in February 1788, Martha's nephew John Dandridge shared the good news (to him) that a runaway slave belonging to the Dandridges had been captured in the vicinity of Mount Vernon and returned to his New Kent County estate.[5] The latter event suggests ties between slaves at Mount Vernon and back home decades after some of them had been moved from one location to the other.

Some of the Custis slaves served as personal attendants to Martha and her children. The presence of youngsters was new at Mount Vernon, which meant that a nursery had to be established and staffed. Jacky was five years old and Patsy three when their mother remarried. George as well as Martha understood that they would need to learn the ways of elite slaveholders and be raised in a manner typical of Virginia's gentry, complete with personal servants brought from White House. Ten-year-old Julius served as Jacky's valet, and twelve-year-old Rose served as Patsy's maid. Fifteen-year-old Sally served as Martha's lady's maid, helping her dress and do her hair each day. Adult slaves were available to supervise the younger attendants and perform jobs that were beyond their abilities. Much of this oversight fell to the housemaid Moll, who was nineteen and also served as seamstress. Breechy (age twenty-four) and Mulatto Jack (age forty-one) waited on the family in the dining room, and Betty (age twenty-one) did much of the family's sewing. Old Doll (age thirty-eight) cooked with the help of the scullion Beck (age twenty-three).[6] Jenny (age thirty-nine) washed the clothes and household linens, which were later ironed by Mima (also thirty-nine). Twenty-five-year-old Phillis spun thread that went to make items needed by the family.

In his inventory, George listed more Custis slaves who had been brought to work at Mount Vernon. Two were shirt makers; one (Scomberg, age forty-two) was apparently part of Martha's dower property, and the other (Crispin) was part of the children's inheritance. Eleven were carpenters, three belonging to Martha and eight to the children. A tanner was part of the children's inheritance.[7] As husband of Martha and guardian of Jacky and Patsy, George assumed responsibility for managing these slaves, along with the rest of the Custis fortune. Yet Martha maintained authority over certain slaves, depending on occupation.

For a time, the rest of the Custis slaves remained on Custis lands. There would be no large-scale disruption to kin and community until family circumstances forced the issue. When Martha's children came of age, they would claim their shares of the Custis estate. Martha's death would also prompt a redistribution of Custis property, including slaves. So would, eventually, the deaths of Martha's children or their heirs. But in 1759, Martha was only twenty-seven years old, her children were young, and any further division and redistribution of the estate seemed to the Washingtons far in the future. As we shall see, the time came sooner than expected.

As George and Martha went about establishing their home in a way that advertised their elite status, they turned to Europe for luxury goods. They ordered fine china, silverware, and damask tablecloths, as well as chairs, couches, and bedsteads. Even soaps were imported. Although soap could easily be made on the plantation, perfumed soaps from abroad were considered more genteel. The Washingtons imported wine, cheese, nuts, candies, teas, citrus fruits, sweetmeats, and spices, reflecting their desire to eat well and entertain lavishly.

George's importation of luxury items for Martha and her children began with their arrival at Mount Vernon and increased over time. An order for "Sundry Goods for a Bride" placed in September 1759 included silk hose, gloves, a bonnet, hairpins, Spirit of Lavender (thought to ease menstrual pain), ruffles of Brussels lace for a night-gown, and powdered perfume. At the same time, George requested consumable items such as wine, mustard, and sugar; practical farm implements; "hose fit for Negro servants"; hats, shoes, and knee buckles; fabric for slave clothing; and "2 Postillion Caps," tall beaver hats with narrow brims.[8]

Although Martha often relied on George to secure the things she wanted, she also purchased items on her own, as she had done before their marriage. Elite women of Martha's time were taking more interest in fashion than ever before, and her purchases of the latest styles included jewelry and corset stays "good, easy made, and very thin." Martha was particular and voiced disapproval when orders went wrong or she thought prices too high. She once complained that a fine suit of Brussels lace ordered for Patsy (which cost twenty pounds) was not only incomplete but also of no better quality than could be found in the shops of Virginia. Like other elite women, she had to leave the details of many items in the hands of the agents who filled orders overseas. When ordering clothing for herself and Patsy in 1772, Martha reminded her milliner to make caps "to suit a Person of 16 yrs old" and another to suit a lady "of 40."[9] She kept track of expenses, explaining that items ordered for her daughter were to be charged separately from those for herself—an accounting necessitated by the terms of her and her daughter's inheritances from Daniel Parke Custis.

A reputation for gentility required more than money and the goods it bought, however. It also reflected ease in welcoming guests. Even before George became famous, he and Martha entertained constantly, and at great expense. In 1768 the Washingtons had at least 130 overnight guests. At least 82 more people came to Mount Vernon that year and stayed for dinner. In the 1760s and 1770s as many as four hundred guests a year came to Mount Vernon. So accustomed were the Washingtons to entertaining friends, relatives, and strangers that George took note of a remarkable day when they had no guests.[10] Although the crowds of people could prove wearisome at times, theirs was a style of life both Martha and George desired. In sustaining this style, economic means and material goods had to be joined with charm on the part of the host and hostess. The appearance and conduct of enslaved servants counted too.

A slave who waited on guests represented the family and its place in the social hierarchy. No wonder, then, that enslaved servants who helped elite families entertain received years of training. Waiters, for instance, had to know the correct way to serve a particular dish. Their interactions with guests — including their demeanor — could be judged by direct observation, but the help also had to demonstrate a quality that in retrospect seems rather intangible and hard to judge: trustworthiness. Owners worried about the access slaves who carried out domestic service had to expensive food and other goods, and their diligence in performing their duties. A slave could not be watched every minute of every day. Elite mistresses did, however, spend a great deal of time investigating the results of maids' work. A mistress could readily see whether a bed was made properly, but periodically she also had to count and inspect the bed linens to ensure none had been stolen and that all were being cared for. Martha began each day by carrying a set of keys downstairs. Without access to the larder, the cook and cook's helpers could not begin their day's work. Maids coming into the mansion house from nearby sleeping quarters could not access clean sheets or tablecloths or other needed items until Martha unlocked the storerooms.

Genteel ladies, to be sure, had more leisure time than many other women. Martha was not, for instance, actually churning the butter or making cheese in the dairy George established shortly after their wedding, as many women of the time did. She had time to read and listen to music and attend balls and other types of dances, but she also had responsibilities that involved checking to ensure her orders were being followed, on matters ranging from the cleaning of drapes to the repair of gowns and the preparation of mince pies. Martha could be quite busy on any given day inspecting the contents of the larder, telling the cook what to prepare for dinner, and ensuring that the laundry was being done properly.

Martha had learned as a child to pitch in to help with guests, and had entertained visitors as the lady of White House, but the constant work of entertaining at Mount Vernon taxed both mistress and slaves. Martha was enthusiastic, however, and had access to substantial resources, including domestic servants who were ready at a moment's notice to kill and pluck poultry or to change out a soiled tablecloth. Her cooks baked biscuits, cakes, and pies, and her maids cleaned for guests who might show up unexpectedly and stay for days or even weeks.

The Washingtons were not always the hosts but left Mount Vernon to attend balls and plays and dinner parties in town and at the homes of others. Personal maids and valets accompanied them on their visits to Williamsburg and Annapolis and the homes of relatives and friends. Additional servants cared for and drove their elegant carriage, alongside which men or boys in liveried costumes rode postilion. A carriage and four or six made quite a sight rumbling through the countryside or the streets of a colonial capital. It announced the arrival of an important lady and gentleman.

Considerable time and effort went into ensuring one's children—when they grew old enough to be out in society—made a positive impression at such events. Martha not only bought hers the finest clothing from Europe, but paid to bring a dance instructor to Mount Vernon. Children in elite families all took lessons to learn the elaborate dances that were popular. Such instruction was considered so important that George once fetched Jacky home from boarding school to participate in a dance lesson Martha had arranged.[11]

At the time of George and Martha's marriage, he held about twenty slaves. After his marriage, George inventoried and appraised the vast Custis estate that was now his to manage. Not content with living well on another man's property, George took deliberate steps to increase his slaveholdings. He purchased thirteen slaves in 1759. Two years later, he bought ten more. He continued to purchase slaves with some regularity until 1772. By then he had spent more than two thousand pounds expanding his labor force.[12]

Two of the slaves George bought were brothers of mixed ancestry, William and Arthur Lee. Like other planters of his time, George believed that people of mixed European and African descent were su-

perior in intellect to those of exclusively African ancestry, and he preferred light-skinned blacks as house servants. Accordingly, he paid
three times more for the Lees in 1768 than he paid for other young
men purchased the same day, whose darker skin destined them for
fieldwork. Both Lee brothers went to work in the house, William as
George's valet and Arthur as dining room attendant. Arthur would
eventually assume the position of butler.[13] Although Custis slaves
made up the bulk of the domestic staff at Mount Vernon, George apparently wanted his own men in key posts.

During the first year of George and Martha's marriage, about forty-
two Custis slaves were brought to live and work on Washington land.
The incorporation of the Custis slaves and the slaves George purchased meant change for the bondmen and -women already there,
some of whom found their tasks and place of residence shifting.
George had no compunction about relocating slaves from one farm
to another depending on his estimation of what workers were needed
where. Later, he would express concern about practices that separated
slave families, but on his own plantation he displayed remarkable indifference toward the effect of such moves on family relationships. For
example, Harry, an African purchased by George in 1763, settled in on
one of his master's outlying farms and found a wife. In 1766 George
moved Harry to the Mansion House farm. Harry's wife, Nan, was dispatched to George's Muddy Hole farm. Such transfers heightened tension at Mount Vernon and sometimes resulted in the "problem" (from
George's point of view) of "night walking": slaves sneaking out in the
dark to visit loved ones.[14]

Mount Vernon's slave force grew not only through George's marriage to Martha and through purchases, but through the birth of babies
in bondage. By 1772, however, the master of Mount Vernon was expressing reservations about acquiring more slaves. He still negotiated
from time to time for slaves to serve a particular purpose, but overall his purchases decreased. In November 1786, he agreed somewhat
reluctantly to accept in payment for a debt "Six or more Negroes,"
provided they were all men and "none of them addicted to running
away." John Francis Mercer, who owed his friend George money, was
strapped for cash and offered enslaved boys instead. George and John

haggled over the value assigned the slaves. At one point, George—perhaps having doubts about the transaction—sought reassurance that the boys (barely old enough to be put to a trade) would not suffer by the separation from their families. In the end, the deal did not go through.[15] George's earlier eagerness to acquire slaves had demonstrably cooled.

Mount Vernon's increasing slave force corresponded with its transition from a small-scale tobacco farm to a vast and diversified agricultural operation. Changes of this nature often strained relations between owners and slaves. The year 1761 saw the escape of four men from George's Dogue Run farm. Two had been purchased within the previous two years; the other two men may have been purchased earlier from the same region of Africa as their comrades. Slaves newly arrived from Africa were more apt to run away than those who were more acculturated, but from the time of Martha and George's marriage to his death in 1799, one or two slaves were missing for at least part of each year.[16] Harry, whom George had separated from his wife, was among them. Harry was quickly recaptured, but his disappearance, however brief (and that of other runaways), served as a reminder that slave owners might pay a price when slaves were pushed beyond their endurance.

George did what he could to deter runaways. Like other planters, he sold those who proved recalcitrant. In 1766 Tom was sold to the West Indies; Will Shag was dispatched to St. Domingue in 1771. After Sam's fourth attempt to escape, he was apparently sold to a Maryland planter.[17] Martha and George might have envisioned that a slowing of Mount Vernon's expansion would usher in a comfortable, relatively quiet life marked by only an occasional runaway.

In 1773 Jacky, off at college, assured his mother in a heartfelt letter that he was living in the aristocratic style that she and he expected. The professors were drawing a "distinction" between him and the other students. Rather than dining with the other scholars, Jacky ate with the faculty, except for breakfast, which was brought to him by his enslaved valet Joe. Jacky also participated in the faculty's entertainments. His apartment was spacious and consisted of two rooms, one of which served as his study and sleeping chamber. Joe slept in the other.[18] The letter must have offered some hope to the Washingtons that Jacky was settling down. His behavior had not always been all that they had hoped.

The Washingtons had raised Jacky to assume the prerogatives of his class. Unfortunately, one such supposed prerogative was the sexual exploitation of enslaved women. The forms this took varied widely. At times, slaveholding men raped using physical force. In other cases, coercion was less overt, but since slavery itself was upheld by violence or the threat of violence, any degree of cooperation on the part of the woman is difficult to assess. When enslaved women complied or did not resist, they did so in hopes of improving their lives or the lives of their children in some way.

Circumstantial, but persuasive, evidence suggests that while in his teens, Jacky fathered a child with one of the slaves at Mount Vernon. This in itself was not unusual. But if the charge against Jacky is true, his case is shocking even by the standards of a society that abided egregious cases of rape because Jacky's victim was Ann Dandridge, his mother's half sister and Jacky's aunt.[19] Ann had lived in the Dandridge home until her father died and Martha brought her to live at White House. After Martha married George, Ann moved to Mount Vernon and likely sewed or performed other domestic chores during the day. At night, she retreated to the barracks-style housing the Washingtons provided for their domestic help. (No slaves slept in the mansion house.) Ann's relation to Martha was known within the family, although it is possible that Martha contrived to hide Ann's parentage from her son. Whether she did or not, Jacky's violation of Ann broke the taboo of incest.

Martha handled her son's sexual offense as she had her father's. She pretended it had not occurred and incorporated the resulting child into her domestic circle. Why the child, William (who later assumed the name William Custis Costin), was allowed to grow up as a free person, although his mother was enslaved, is not entirely clear. Martha may have felt she had no choice. The circumstances of Williams's conception surely upset not only his mother but other members of Mount

Vernon's domestic staff. The tension must have been palpable. The promise of freedom for William might have eased Ann's distress as well as the anger and resentment of the rest of the enslaved help. It would have been preferable to pacify her servants with freedom for baby William than to let the matter fester and risk the consequences of their ire.

Ann Dandridge was not part of the Custis estate. She was among the property Martha inherited from her parents, and so Martha probably believed the decision of what to do about William was hers to make. The fact that William would have been considered inheritable property if listed as a slave and passed on to Martha's heirs, possibly Jacky, no doubt factored into her decision. The idea that William might end up the property of his father would only have exacerbated the outrage. As it turned out, William was the only enslaved person Martha ever freed, but even in his case she could not bring herself to execute a formal deed of manumission. His name was simply omitted from any list of Mount Vernon slaves.[20]

Martha may have been encouraged in her decision by notions of race. Certain theorists in the day posited that racial mixing could result in the birth of a child whose race was different from that of his or her mother. For many Virginians, including Thomas Jefferson, a child who had only one great-grandparent who was black was white. This was true in William's case, and he looked white. The situation in which seemingly white people ended up enslaved troubled many Virginians, Jefferson among them.[21] Rather than emancipate William, which would have called attention to his identity and perhaps raised questions about it, the Washingtons simply treated him as if he were free.

Despite such turmoil, things seemed relatively calm at Mount Vernon by the middle of 1773. Martha and George had achieved their ambition of turning his home on the Potomac into one worthy of admiration. They were popular and wealthy, even when measured against Virginia's upper echelon. But the good times did not last long. On June 19, Patsy died of an epileptic seizure after Sunday dinner. She was just seventeen years old, the third of Martha's four children to die young.

There was the personal loss to be coped with, and once again an estate had to be settled. Patsy's share of the Custis fortune was divided between her mother and her brother.

At the same time, friction between Britain and the American colonies was growing. A year later, the Continental Congress, convened to negotiate the troubles between the Americans and the mother country, declared independence and commissioned George Washington to take command of the Continental Army. War had begun. For the next eight years, Martha shuttled between Mount Vernon and the winter camps that General Washington established for his troops.

CHAPTER 5

Revolutionary War

Martha and George Washington were separated for much of the American Revolution. Over the course of eight and a half years, George spent about two months in residence at Mount Vernon.[1] Martha joined him in winter, but she managed at home on her own the rest of the time, though George kept abreast of domestic matters through correspondence. Martha was experienced at running a large plantation, of course, and she had the help of farm managers and family members, but Mount Vernon was her responsibility during the war. She could have abandoned it for the home of a kinsman or friend, and no one would have faulted her. But she stayed.

Martha's decision to remain put her at risk, and Americans have rightly admired her courage in the face of a very real British threat. Many expected British troops to sail up the Potomac, trash the plantation belonging to the head of the Continental Army, and take Martha as a prize of war. When the British did sail up the Potomac, Martha had no way of knowing in advance that she and Mount Vernon would both be spared.

But there were reasons beyond overt military threats that made slaveholders fear leaving mistresses, Martha included, alone on the home front. No one knew what slaves might do while their masters were off fighting the British or serving in government posts. Reports came from all around—not just Virginia—of slave impudence and escape. While Thomas Pinckney was serving as a delegate to the Continental Congress, his wife at home in South Carolina reported that

the slaves became "insolent and quite their own masters." When he returned home in spring 1779, he found the plantation almost deserted;
many slaves had taken the opportunity to escape.[2] His absence and
the absence of other masters offered unprecedented opportunities for
slaves to run away, especially where the British were nearby and offering refuge, as they were in Virginia.

Managing slaves under the best of circumstances was not easy because they had multiple ways of expressing discontent, including running away permanently or hiding out for a time. They could and did
misplace items, break or damage utensils, forget recipes, misunder-
stand directions, feign illness or injury, work slowly, and rush through
jobs so that they were only half or poorly done. In extreme cases they
might refuse to carry out chores or sabotage the work. Slaves also
talked. Even when complaints never left the plantation, a slave might
stir discontent among others. Mistresses, like masters, could never be
quite sure how far protests would go. Nor could they tell for certain
whether a slave was ill, had forgotten how to complete a task, or could
not locate a needed tool. For this reason slaveholders, when giving
orders, took into consideration a slave's personality as well as any objection she or he might raise to carrying out duties. The war heightened such sensitivities.

Over time slaves developed strategies that played upon the slaveholders' fears and consciences. For example, a slave's public display of
grief at sale might be orchestrated to evoke pity for the slave and condemnation of the seller. This is not to imply that the grief was not real;
it was. But especially dramatic displays of emotional agony by parents or spouses being parted from loved ones could make an owner
think twice about completing the transaction. At Mount Vernon,
Bett and her mother were able to thwart Bett's sale by begging long
and loud not to be separated. Although owners had the legal right to
sell whichever slaves they wished, more reform-minded slaveholders
held to the idea that families should remain intact, which encouraged
slaveholders who did not share this view to forgo such sales or at least
keep them secret. George Washington himself had developed scruples
about separating enslaved families through sale. He was willing to do
it but only so long as it was not publicly known. At times he vacillated

on the matter, which frustrated his plantation manager Lund Washington. In April 1778, Lund wrote George, "You say again you wish to be quit of negroes," but you have not told me "in plain terms, whether I should sell your negroes at Public sale or not, & how many of them & indeed who."[3] By then George and Martha were both public figures, which heightened their concern about what people would think. Public pleas by slaves who wanted to remain with loved ones gave them pause.

In November 1775, Virginia's royal governor, John Murray, the fourth Lord Dunmore, had announced that slaves who helped defend the colony against American insurgents would be emancipated. Dunmore was no abolitionist—indeed, he was an aristocrat who had invested in slaveholding enterprises in both Virginia and the Caribbean—but he was determined to command an army sufficient for maintaining control over the colony. If arming slaves (or Indians, for that matter) would help, he would do so.[4]

Word of Dunmore's proclamation spread like a shockwave throughout the black and white populations. Some slaves heeded his call and took up arms on behalf of the British cause to secure their own freedom and the liberty of others. Some emblazoned the words "Liberty to Slaves" on their uniforms. Washington and Custis slaves were among those who joined the British. Dunmore armed the escaped slaves with muskets and used them to help defeat the local militia in Norfolk.[5] Dunmore's decree and the actions of the slaves horrified white Virginians, who feared a wholesale uprising. Blacks at the time made up about 40 percent of Virginia's population. The defection of slaves raised questions that challenged the most cherished beliefs of slaveholders. Many slave owners had convinced themselves that people of African descent benefited from enslavement. Others likely agreed with Benjamin Franklin that "sheep will never make any insurrection."[6] But slaves were not sheep. Rather than acknowledge that their laborers had valid complaints and a natural desire for freedom, slaveholders blamed Lord Dunmore for enticing slaves to run away.

For a time, Lord Dunmore was the most hated man in Virginia. John Tayloe II, writing from his Mount Airy plantation in the northern neck of Virginia, called him a "D——l." Members of the Washington-

Custis family were among those who reviled him. In March 1778, Martha called him "cruel." Jacky, who had mistakenly believed that Dunmore had died, opined, "I wish it may be true."[7]

Rumors circulated that Dunmore would stop at nothing short of freeing all of Virginia's slaves and turning its social hierarchy upside down. White Virginians were appalled at the idea that "dishonored" people would take up arms against their "honorable" masters.[8] Rumors further painted Lord Dunmore as a scoundrel. He was said to have black lovers and to have held a ball where black women and white men danced together. While today, these charges do not seem insulting, in that place and time — despite the common occurrence of sexual relationships across the color line — they were. Those who engaged in such liaisons — among them Jack Dandridge and Jacky Custis — kept them quiet.

Some slaves who heeded Dunmore's call did escape slavery. Harry Washington, for one, fought with the British and traveled north with the troops when Dunmore left Virginia for New York City. But others were less fortunate. When runaways were recaptured, the response of white Virginians was harsh and swift. The Virginia Committee of Safety, one of many shadow governments established during the American Revolution to organize militias and carry out other civic duties, executed two slaves who had indicated a willingness to serve the British cause.[9]

Anxiety ran high during the war years. Worries about the possibility of a general uprising were nothing new. The worst fear now was not that runaway slaves would never be found. Rather, it was that they might return to a plantation as British soldiers, armed and seeking revenge for past wrongs. South Carolina mistress Eliza Wilkinson was one of few white women who recorded on paper her reaction to seeing black soldiers carrying arms. When the British raided her home in 1782, she reacted with anger and indignation, fueled in part by the fact that the British "had several armed Negroes with them, who threatened and abused us greatly."[10]

These facts hit home at Mount Vernon in the spring of 1781 when British captain Thomas Graves anchored the sloop *Savage* in the Potomac nearby. Fourteen men and three women left to join him. At least two of the women were house servants who worked closely with Martha: Lucy, age twenty, and Esther, age eighteen. The disappearance of the housemaids must have been particularly upsetting. Martha would have chosen the women with care. Their defection suggested that even her closest slaves could not be trusted. Lucy and Esther were retaken when the Americans defeated the British in the final battle of the war at Yorktown, as were most of the others, but the third woman—Deborah Squash, age twenty—and two of the men eluded recapture.[11]

It was customary in those days for armies to wait out the winter months and resume fighting after the spring thaw. Throughout the American Revolution, George asked Martha to join him after he had settled his troops, at locations in Massachusetts, New Jersey, New York, and Pennsylvania. The wives of other officers came too. Each had her reasons for being there. Some thought it safer to be with the army than at home. Others took pleasure in camp life. Still others, including Martha, wanted to support a husband or the revolutionary cause.[12]

Martha left Mount Vernon to join her husband in winter camps eight times over the course of eight years. In 1775 she traveled to Cambridge, Massachusetts, the following year to Morristown, New Jersey. It took Martha ten days to travel from Mount Vernon to Valley Forge, Pennsylvania, her third winter camp. Family members and slaves accompanied her on these journeys. Their travels over rutted roads, rivers, and streams in all types of weather could be treacherous, but the trips were broken up by stops in small cities and towns where crowds of people gathered to greet and fete her.[13]

As the wife of the acclaimed General Washington, Martha enjoyed a great deal of celebrity. Observers commented on her comings and goings, as they did his. She traveled in elaborate style, with an entourage that included a military escort for at least part of the way. Throughout slaves attended to her and her children's every need. On the way to and from the winter camps, she often stayed in houses of friends, who put up the slaves along with the rest of her party. Friends of the

Washingtons and the Revolution seemed to have had no compunction about supporting a war in the name of freedom while accommodating the captive humans who traveled with the general's wife.

At military camps, Martha acted as hostess and determined domestic routines as she did at home. George employed a housekeeper at his winter headquarters to oversee the domestic help, but Martha made decisions about menus and social activities and inspected the results of others' labor. The housekeeper at Valley Forge was seventy-four-year-old Elizabeth Thompson, a white woman who served the general throughout the Revolution. She supervised the cooks, the laundresses, and the packing and unpacking of household goods, and she took inventory of and purchased supplies for his headquarters. "Mrs. Thompson," as she was called in the military records, reported to Martha when she was in camp but to George when Martha was not around.[14]

While in camp, Martha and the other wives kept up familiar social activities as much as possible, organizing entertainments as circumstances allowed. The women visited and sang and celebrated patriotic events such as the cementing of an American alliance with France. During the winter at Valley Forge, the ladies and officers saw at least one play, although eventually Congress made clear its disapproval of such activities. Martha and the other ladies and gentlemen at Valley Forge also had their portraits painted by Charles Willson Peale, and they attended worship services. Martha hosted many dinner parties, planning festive foods as supplies allowed. At New Windsor, New York, for example, she apparently oversaw the baking of holiday fruitcakes. While in Morristown, she requested currants and citron, presumably for the same purpose.[15]

The married couple Hannah and Isaac Till did the cooking at the Valley Forge headquarters. Their working arrangements were unusual for slaves. Each received forty shillings a month in pay; an additional sum went to their respective owners to pay off their purchase price. (Hannah's was set at fifty-six pounds; Isaac's likely was a similar amount.) Hannah's owner was a Presbyterian minister from New York: Reverend John Mason. Isaac belonged to another New Yorker: Captain John Johnson. In other words, the arrangements allowed the

Tills to pay for their freedom through their work for General Washington. Neither of the Tills was young. Hannah was fifty-six years old; Isaac must have been of a similar age.[16] Had they been younger, their self-purchase prices would have been higher, probably too high for either of them to accumulate sufficient funds.

The two cooks served up delicacies unavailable to the common soldiers because the officers and their wives at headquarters had access to a greater variety, quantity, and quality of food. An expense report from the period lists deliveries of turkeys and other fowl, butter, eggs, veal, apples, cabbages, potatoes, and parsnips, as well as hams that were specifically wanted by Martha Washington. In addition, locals presented food as gifts to the Washingtons and officers. Hannah and Isaac also cooked food gained as spoils of war, including cheese and pickled oysters. The Tills were responsible for feeding up to thirty people, including residents and guests.[17]

Hannah and Isaac Till were not the only blacks working at the Valley Forge headquarters. A free black woman named Margaret Thomas helped George's enslaved valet, William Lee, care for the general's clothes. She also washed and mended the better household linen, and she helped care for the clothing worn by Martha and the wives of the officers when they were in camp. She and William Lee were married, if not in law then in their own eyes. It remains unclear which slaves Martha brought to camp from Mount Vernon, but she may have brought most of the house servants. There was plenty of work for them to do, and having them in camp was preferable to leaving them at home, where they might abscond with the British.[18]

While Martha and her husband were away, they worried about what was happening at Mount Vernon. He concerned himself mainly with agricultural operations, while Martha focused more on the mansion, its inhabitants, and guests. She expected and received reports about the people at home during her time away. Lund Washington had been left in charge of planting operations, and his wife helped to oversee the house, including the slaves who were spinning cotton. Martha expected one of them to write regularly about the status of domestic work at the Mansion House farm. Among other things, Martha wanted to know how many yards of cloth had been made from the cotton that was spun and whether the cloth had been whitened. She checked not only on output but also on the productivity of individual workers. Had seamstress Betty kept busy all winter spinning? Martha left bundled work at Mount Vernon for her maid Charlotte to complete. Had she finished? Most of Martha's letters have not survived, but it is clear from those that do that she sought to manage Mount Vernon's domestic affairs from afar.[19]

The enslaved people who worked at the army's headquarters or who accompanied Martha and George from Mount Vernon were not the only ones there. About four hundred women and an unknown number of children followed the army from camp to camp, cooking, washing, and sewing for the troops. Some were enslaved; it is impossible to say how many. Some camp followers like Rachel of Maryland may have claimed the status of free women and said they were married to soldiers when in fact they were runaway slaves.[20]

George did not like the female camp followers, and he refused to acknowledge them during the war's first years. At one point, he ordered his officers to rid the camp of women, but this proved impractical. The army required their services. A revised order exempted all women who were "absolutely necessary." Over the course of the war, the number of women traveling with the Continental Army increased. Attempts were made to regulate rather than rid the army of them. Each woman had to submit to an inspection for venereal disease, although husbands could be examined instead of their wives. One rule prohibited women from riding in wagons and relegated them to the end of the line when the troops were on the move. Yet existing documents show that it was hard to keep women out of the wagons or the men from falling back and marching in their company. Some women received rations and pay. Where the women stayed at night is unclear, but they must have slept in tents with the men as the troops moved from place to place.[21] It does not appear that Martha or any of the other ladies concerned themselves with the plight of camp followers.

Some believe that Martha Washington interacted personally with the troops at Valley Forge, sewing for common soldiers, visiting and caring for the sick, and generally being a popular figure in the camps.

As Nancy K. Loane has shown, these are myths created by early biographers (one of them Martha's grandson George Washington Parke Custis who, like the sources he consulted, wished to paint Martha in the best possible light). The truth is that Martha was a class-conscious woman who came to camp at her husband's bidding and who interacted socially with the officers and officer's wives and elites who visited the camps, all the while waited on by slaves.[22]

Martha Washington was nearly forty-seven when she left Mount Vernon for Valley Forge in late January 1778. She and George stayed at the Isaac Potts House, which served not only as their home but also as military headquarters. The house is open to tourists today. A film at the visitor's center orients tourists to the park and helps them understand events leading up to the winter of 1777–1778 when the Continental Army camped there. It focuses on the plight of the enlisted soldiers and explains how troops built the cabins, foraged for food, and suffered from illness, hunger, and lack of clothing. Viewers learn how to load a musket and how sick soldiers were cared for. The ill men were not left in camp but rather taken to hospitals some distance away. It rained a lot that winter. It snowed too. About twenty thousand men lived on the grounds. The film makes no mention of ladies at Valley Forge, and the mention of other women—the camp followers who traveled with the army—is brief. Some of the female followers were paid to care for the sick soldiers in the hospitals, it says.

A driving tour takes visitors past a set of reconstructed huts like the ones that housed the soldiers and gives the visitor a sense of how large the camp was. The tour covers ten miles and takes anywhere from twenty minutes to two hours to complete. Tourists can park at designated lots, walk around, and enter some of the cabins. One can see immediately that the space would have been cramped for the twelve men who lived in each, but the cabins kept the men dry and protected from the wind. Each had a fireplace and twelve beds made of boards. The film notes that blankets were in short supply.

Visitors to Valley Forge can also stop at Washington's headquarters. The gray stone Georgian-style house was big by standards of the day, but it too would have been cramped given that more than twenty people stayed in it. The main floor consisted of two large rooms and a foyer. The two rooms today are furnished as work areas, but George and Martha actually slept in the back room. The rooms are large, but it is nevertheless difficult to imagine how a play might have been performed in one of them. The furniture must have been moved out to make space.

The house includes a second floor, an attic, and a basement, as well as a kitchen attached by a breezeway. A sign near the headquarters says that slaves slept in the house, but no documentation exists to confirm this. George and Martha's enslaved servants apparently did not sleep overnight in the house at Mount Vernon, and it is hard to imagine them being crowded into the Potts House, although they might have put pallets in the foyers or on the stair landings or in the basement or in the kitchen connected to the house. The attic likely housed some of Washington's aides. The other rooms would have quartered officers and their wives. The general's personal guard lived in huts located in back of the headquarters. The hundred soldiers who made up the security force were — per Washington's orders — clean, neat, sober, honest, well behaved, and between five-foot-eight and five-foot-ten-inches tall. They lived in huts much like the rest of the troops.[23] At least some of the Washingtons' domestic slaves might have slept in a hut or huts similar to the ones that have been reconstructed at Valley Forge, which are not dissimilar to the housing many planters furnished slaves.

In Morristown during the winter of 1779–1780, the Washingtons and his officers crowded into the home of widow Theodosia Ford, who remained in residence with her four children and slaves. At one point, the general complained that the Washington and Ford slaves were packed into the same kitchen—eighteen all together. In such cramped conditions disease could spread rapidly, and George reported that nearly all had colds. He eventually had an extra kitchen made of logs built near the mansion.[24] Presumably at least some of the slaves were moved there.

Martha seems to have become fast friends with the other officers' wives at the different winter headquarters. Some of her friendships lasted a lifetime. Seeing the size of the Potts House, one can understand why. The weather was bad that winter, and most of the ladies' activities, including entertaining, would have been conducted in close quarters. So confined, they would of necessity have found ways to get along.

One might wonder whether Martha Washington's travels to the North caused her to question slavery's place within the nation. George's officers and their wives came from different states, including those that were abolishing the institution. George himself changed his attitude toward bonded people and the institution of slavery. Over the course of the war, he began to rethink his own plantation practices, including the separation of enslaved families and harsh whippings. At first he opposed recruitment of black soldiers to the patriot cause, even signing an order forbidding it, but war needs pressed, and he changed his mind. Once he saw black troops on the battlefield, he realized their worth as soldiers and began to question their rightful place in the nation. Martha appears not to have gone through a similar evolution in thinking. Some of the officers or ladies Martha encountered may have been offended by slavery and the presence of Washington slaves within the camps. If so, no record of protest survives. At least one lady, Catharine Greene of Rhode Island (wife of General Nathanael Greene), appears to have envied Martha her enslaved help. In February 1779, she inquired about purchasing a slave to wait on her during her winter stays in camp. After the war, the Greenes moved to Georgia, where they operated a rice plantation with slave labor.[25]

Although George came over time to question the place of slavery in the United States, both he and Martha remained committed to the institution at the end of the war, as evidenced by their desire to reclaim the slaves who had run away from Mount Vernon and joined the British. From a camp at Yorktown in 1781, Jacky—who had secured a civilian appointment as his stepfather's aide-de-camp when it became apparent that the battle there would be decisive—assured his mother that he had "made every possible Enquiry" in an attempt to locate Mount Vernon's missing slaves, but he had not seen any. Jacky had heard that Ned was imprisoned in New York and that Old Joe was lurking in the neighborhood, but that Joe's wife was dead. Others were likely dead or too ill to return home.[26] Jacky hoped his mother would pass on the information to his stepfather.

It appears that Martha was comfortable with the hierarchical society she had known from childhood and saw no need to change. Slaves and people she viewed as "other" seemed threatening unless they were properly subdued. In May 1779 she watched in horror as her husband reviewed troops that included Indians. To Martha, "They appeared like cutthroats all." She had trouble understanding why they were included even after George explained the necessity of maintaining the friendship of native peoples during the war.[27]

This attitude could make Martha appear callous. Upon hearing that a black child belonging to her niece had died, Martha consoled Fanny Bassett Washington by pointing out that "Black children are liable to so many accidents and complaints that one is heardly sure of keeping them." She hoped Fanny would not attempt to console his grieving family too much. "Blacks," she wrote, "are so bad in thair nature that they have not the least gratatude for the kindness that may be shewed to them."[28] In this passage, Martha demonstrates not only an acceptance of the high death rates that plagued enslaved children throughout the South, but a disregard for people outside of her class. Even the death of a child was no excuse for parents to shirk duty.

Martha seems to have considered her slaves only in terms of what was best for her and her family, even when it came to breaking up families. When her brother Bartholomew Dandridge Sr. died in 1785, it fell to his son John Dandridge to settle the estate, which apparently included 103 taxable slaves and scores more children too young to tax. His will prohibited the sale of slaves before the land had been disposed of, but land sales were depressed after the war and debts had to be paid. John worried about the economic security of his mother and grandmother. The slaves had been left for the use of the two women during their lifetime. Presumably they could have been rented out to others, including whoever bought the land, to provide an income for the women, yet to settle the estate and pay pressing debts John wanted to sell them right away. Many of the slaves were women or children who could not be put to good use, he complained. John proposed a scheme whereby George Washington and kinsman David Stuart would

The WASHINGTON FAMILY.   *La* FAMILLE *de* WASHINGTON.

Martha and George Washington, with Nelly, Wash, and enslaved attendant.

accept slaves in exchange for a bond. They could then force the sale of the slaves before the sale of the land, which John presumed would help clear his father's debts. He explained his proposal to Martha and asked her to share it with her husband, but only if she approved. "If you see any impropriety in it," he wrote, "stop it & pardon my weakness."[29]

John Dandridge apparently calculated that Martha would be more sympathetic to his plan than George. She in fact did not object and shared the details of the scheme with George, who agreed to help. John wrote a note of thanks to his aunt in February 1788. He also shared the "good" news that a runaway slave belonging to the Dandridges had been captured and returned to the estate.[30]

The American Revolution effectively ended on 19 October 1781 at Yorktown, Virginia, when the British general Lord Cornwallis surrendered to George Washington. Two more years would pass before the warring nations signed the Treaty of Paris outlining the terms of the peace, but George and Martha looked forward to retiring to Mount Vernon and living a life much like the one they had known before the war. Although there had been death and destruction throughout the British colonies, and many of Virginia's slaves had used the chaos of war to find freedom behind enemy lines, Mount Vernon had been largely spared. Martha and George Washington's wealth had survived the war, and their stature had been enhanced. But George's homecoming was not the happy occasion they had hoped. In the last days of the war, Martha's only surviving child, Jacky, contracted "camp fever" (probably epidemic typhus) and died at twenty-six, leaving behind a wife and four young children: three daughters and a son.

Martha and George assumed parental responsibilities for Jacky's two youngest children: Eleanor Parke Custis (Nelly) and George Washington Parke Custis (Wash). The Washingtons planned to raise them at Mount Vernon, but as it turned out, Nelly and Wash were slated for a different upbringing. The desire of his countrymen to have the distinguished and victorious gentleman from Virginia serve as the nation's first President changed the course of their lives — and the lives of Martha, George, and their slaves — once again.

CHAPTER 6

First Lady

George Washington became the nation's first President when he took the oath of office on 30 April 1789 on the balcony of the Federal Hall building in New York City, the nation's temporary capitol. Martha joined him in New York a month later. Her departure from Mount Vernon that May was tearful. In addition to her two grandchildren, Nelly (age ten) and Wash (age eight), Martha's traveling party included six slaves: Ona (Oney) Judge, Molly, Giles, Austin, Paris, and Christopher Sheels. George Washington's nephew Robert Lewis, who also journeyed to New York with Martha, said that the house slaves and some of the field workers were "greatly affected" by the separation. Lewis did not make clear exactly who was upset and why, but it is easy to imagine that the seamstress Betty was "greatly affected": two of her children were leaving with Martha. Austin was a grown man who left behind a wife, children, and other family members in addition to his mother. Betty's other child, Oney Judge, was only fifteen years old. Like Austin and Oney, the other slaves traveling to New York bid goodbye to family and friends. Christopher's mother was one of the spinners at the Mansion House farm. His grandmother, Old Doll, was a cook who had been brought from New Kent County to Mount Vernon by Martha soon after she married George.[1]

No one could say for sure when the Washingtons and the servants would return. George Washington had signed on for a term of four years, but there was nothing in the U.S. Constitution to prevent the President from being reelected multiple times. He was popular enough that many Americans hoped he would remain in office for life. As it turned out, he declined to serve more than two terms, but even so he, Martha, the Custis children, and the six slaves were away from Mount Vernon for the better part of eight years. After the nation's capital shifted from New York to Philadelphia in December 1790, two more Mount Vernon slaves joined them there, and although Philadelphia lies a hundred miles closer to Mount Vernon than does New York, they were still far from home.

Most historians who have written about Martha Washington as First Lady focus on what she did in the capital; yet when Martha left for the nation's capital, she did not leave behind her identity as mistress of Mount Vernon. For the Washingtons, the slaveholding plantation on the Potomac River was not only a means of livelihood but also tangible evidence of their grandee status. Mount Vernon anchored the Washingtons in elite society as much as did the presidency.

Most of Martha's domestic slaves remained at Mount Vernon, and Martha struggled throughout her years as First Lady to manage them from a distance. She was experienced at this, having left Mount Vernon to be with her husband in winter camps during the Revolutionary War. But now she would be gone for longer stretches of time. She continued to assume responsibility for domestic activities at Mount Vernon and labored to keep her enslaved staff busy with tasks ranging from making tablecloths to preserving food. Her long-distance management produced results, as the Mount Vernon slaves supplied the President's house in Philadelphia with services and needed items (sewing and hams, for example). Moreover, the mansion had to be ready to house the Washingtons whenever they returned home, which meant cleaning and maintenance tasks continued. On these visits, the Washingtons often brought along guests, and visitors sometimes showed up at Mount Vernon even when the Washingtons were not in residence. Throughout Washington's presidency, the work of the household continued apace.

Yet the Washingtons' absence from Mount Vernon made management of the estate—and of slaves—more difficult. The Washingtons were never free of worry about what was going on at home. They appointed plantation managers, some of them relatives, to ensure Mount Vernon's productivity and profitability. George's nephew George Augustine Washington and his wife, Fanny, for example, together managed Mount Vernon for a time, she indoors and he outside. They were ideally suited to the task because they had lived at Mount Vernon since 1785 and were familiar with the slaves and plantation routines.

The Washingtons wrote their proxies letters filled with instructions, and in return they wanted regular reports. Apparently unhappy with the letters she was getting (or perhaps dismayed by a lack of them), Martha at one point told Fanny that she should write each week. For her part, Martha would write Fanny every Monday. Martha's inquiries and instructions focused mainly on domestic matters; she asked, for example, whether linen clothing had been made for the house slaves as she directed, and ordered hams by the dozen, bacon, artichoke seeds, and shad, all of which had to be gathered or processed and delivered to Philadelphia. George focused on agricultural concerns, but these at times crossed into Martha's realm. "Mrs. Washington desires you will order the Ashes to be taken care of, that there may be no want of Soap," he once wrote. He instructed the gardener's wife to oversee the spinning of thread and the gardener to plant a particular type of lima bean. Martha sent word that Old Doll should "distil a good deal of Rose and Mint Water." On another occasion, she hoped Frank Lee had been gathering and storing "indian" walnuts since other types of nuts were so expensive. Charlotte should make ruffles for Wash's shirts, hemming and sending them to Philadelphia six at a time. Apparently Martha or one of her maids would attach them once they arrived.[2]

Martha was determined to keep her domestic slaves busy whether they were in the country or the city. Once, in 1784, the enslaved women at Mount Vernon had finished spinning the wool Martha had on hand, which left them with "little to doe"; to prevent their sitting idle, she procured cotton from her sister-in-law Hannah Bushrod Washington. Martha knew cotton was scarce and that Hannah would feel its loss, but asked her to send some anyway.[3]

Nevertheless, Martha's slaves tended to work at their own pace and sometimes not at all. In June 1794, Martha complained to Fanny that despite her specific order Frank Lee had not yet sent a spinet piano to

Philadelphia for Nelly. Frank, one of the Washingtons' more dependable house slaves, held the important position of butler. Yet "There is not much dependance on him," Martha wrote in a letter asking Fanny to take charge of the matter. In spring 1795, Martha wanted Old Doll to make gooseberry preserves and to dry some "morelly" cherries. (Sour morello cherries were often used to make pies, jams, and preserves.) Perhaps anticipating Old Doll's demurral, she told Fanny that Old Doll could get directions for making the preserves from the plantation manager's white housekeeper.[4] The experienced cook surely knew how to make fruit preserves, but Martha's phrasing suggests that servants had previously used the excuse of having "forgotten" how to carry out a task. In this case, she knew she had an ally on hand to guard against strategic forgetfulness.

After becoming First Lady, Martha Washington relied heavily on her maid and seamstress Charlotte to get things done at home. Martha expected Charlotte to complete various projects for her while also providing maid service for Fanny and George Augustine Washington. Yet Martha did not trust Charlotte to do everything she was told and tried to keep tabs on her. As part of their weekly reports from Mount Vernon, the Washingtons wanted news of Charlotte. "Charlot will lay herself up for as little as any one will," Martha wrote Fanny soon after leaving for New York. By this, she meant that Charlotte feigned illness to keep from working whenever she could. Once when Charlotte was sick for several weeks, Martha decided that the plantation manager should look in on her and determine whether to call a doctor. While her motive may have been to ensure Charlotte's health, slaveholders at times called a doctor to determine whether a slave was malingering.[5] Like other mistresses, Martha thought that domestic slaves should be supervised closely by a white person; otherwise, they would slacken the pace of work, feign illness or injury to avoid work, take goods for their own use, and break or damage tools and other family property.

The taking of goods by slaves was a constant concern. During 1795, Martha worried in particular about Kitty, who had access to meat, milk, and butter and who in Martha's opinion did not give a sufficient accounting of what had been used and what was still on hand. Martha complained in general about the women who performed domestic work at Mount Vernon. "They always idle half their time away," taking care of their own business rather than hers, she said. They laundered clothing so poorly that it was "not fitt to use."[6] It is difficult to know at this juncture whether the enslaved women at Mount Vernon were in fact slacking off, or whether Martha had unrealistic expectations.

Sewing was one of the principal activities of Mount Vernon maids. Martha regularly sent sewing jobs back and forth with people traveling between Mount Vernon and Philadelphia. The system was efficient, and Fanny or another supervisor stepped in only when something went wrong. When Martha wanted sewing done, she made up bundles that included the thread, cloth, and anything else necessary to complete the garments or household items. Bundling supplies supposedly obviated any worry that a seamstress would take thread or cloth for personal use. It also made it easy to keep track of how much sewing each maid finished. Despite such precautions, Martha found the productivity of the Mount Vernon seamstresses disappointing. On at least one occasion, they stopped work altogether because, they said, the mistress had not sent enough thread. To get them working again, Fanny had to give them more.[7]

Whether the seamstresses ran short of thread in this instance is open to question, but in general mistresses struggled to get as much work as possible from the domestic help at the least cost. Enslaved women in turn struggled to find time and energy to meet their own needs and those of their families. Getting enslaved maids to complete tasks was in some ways like a dance, but each partner had her own idea of how quickly the steps should be taken, and neither could control entirely the resulting performance. Maids consistently disappointed mistresses like Martha who tended to think them lazy and capable of doing more.

Martha expected her seamstresses to sew not only for members of her family but also for "the people," by which she meant the other slaves on the Mount Vernon estate. "House people" wore clothing made of linen, rather than of the coarser fabric given field slaves. As

President, George sometimes purchased cloth in bulk to be turned into garments for tradesmen and field hands, but Martha obtained smaller parcels of fabric thought suitable for family members, house slaves, and the enslaved babies born at Mount Vernon. In August 1793, she sent material "to make Babe clothes — for the negro women." The fabric was for shirts and caps and other necessities.[8]

Coarse cloth was not all purchased. Some of it was made at Mount Vernon. George helped Martha keep an eye on the spinners, particularly when they were outfitting the field hands. "I do not perceive by the Spinning report, that any of the Girls are employed in making woolen cloathes for the people," he wrote his plantation manager in 1794. He wanted to know what material the weavers had produced and whether it would be ready to give to the hands by the start of November. George may have been sensitive because the Mount Vernon slaves complained when they did not receive their annual allotment of clothing and blankets at the customary time. In fall 1791, George had delayed purchasing two hundred blankets for the slaves as he researched which seller could provide the best quality at the least cost. In early October, his enslaved hands were "all teazing me" for them, he reported from Mount Vernon. He asked his secretary Tobias Lear to send them by the "first vessel."[9]

The grotesque dance continued on every level, every day. All slaves — whether in the house or in the field — could find ways to resist an owner's orders, but few did so openly. Charlotte appears to have been bolder than most, even intrepid. She once in Martha's absence went to town on an errand, only to be accused of wearing a stolen dress. When its alleged owner tried to examine the garment, Charlotte objected vociferously — enough to attract attention — and physically threatened her accuser. She also gave several different explanations of how she had come to own the dress.[10]

More than one supervisor found Charlotte hard to handle. The gardener's wife, who for a time oversaw the seamstresses, reported having trouble getting Charlotte to do her assigned work. One of George's farm managers, Anthony Whiting (who worked at Mount Vernon from 1790 until his death in 1793), encountered the same problem and whipped Charlotte for it.[11] The beating did not produce the desired result, however. Charlotte refused to return to work, and Whiting beat her again.

Refusal to work was a weapon slaves sometimes wielded against an owner when they found their working or living conditions intolerable. Under their moral and economic calculus, slaveholders expected a certain amount of work in exchange for the food, shelter, and other services they provided slaves. Slaves tended to cooperate until an owner pushed them to perform more work than usual or inflicted particularly egregious treatment. Trying to extract extra work or punishing harshly for a minor infraction, then, might prove counterproductive. This may have been the case with Charlotte, who was doing work for Fanny as well as for her mistress. After she was beaten, she took her time returning to work. She did not explicitly state that she was retaliating for the whipping, but Whiting and the Washingtons probably understood her action as protest. Charlotte was smart enough to know that an outright statement of defiance would result in even harsher treatment. Instead Charlotte said she had hurt her finger.[12]

Whiting was concerned enough about the matter to contact his employer. Although one of George's plantation rules prohibited slaves from running to owners with complaints, Charlotte was threatening to tell Martha about the incident. It was also possible that Austin or another slave transporting goods between Mount Vernon and Philadelphia would carry Charlotte's tale. George gave his full support to Whiting and pronounced the whippings he had given Charlotte "very proper." Any slave acting insolent or refusing to work must be corrected, he said. But afterward, George's support for his manager began to wane, and he was soon making derogatory comments about Whiting.[13] Charlotte, in contrast, did not fall completely out of Martha's (or George's) good graces at this or at other times when she defied orders. She was, after all, one of the dower slaves who attended the President during his final illness.

Charlotte was not the only housemaid to challenge authority. Another, Caroline, is described today at Mount Vernon as "one of Martha Washington's house slaves" who "sometimes annoyed the Washingtons because of her slow work and failure to make production quotas—acts most likely practiced as passive resistance to being enslaved." Periodically, "the Washingtons threatened to move her to the fields but never followed through." Caroline, too, was one of the slaves in the room when George Washington died.[14]

Martha's tolerance of Charlotte's and Caroline's behavior may seem odd given the maids' enslaved status, but the Washingtons prized their highly skilled house staff and worried about angering them. George warned his plantation manager in summer 1794 against provoking the mother of Boatswain by separating the two. Boatswain was working as a waiter while recovering from an accident on a cart. For three months his mother had been insisting that he work inside the house rather than outside. George was not sure what she might do if the manager interfered, but he was certain she would do whatever it took to keep her son from being assigned more physically taxing work.[15]

Boatswain's and Charlotte's and Caroline's situations show that domestic staff could, within the constraints of slavery, bargain to improve their own or their children's working and living conditions. The dance between the enslavers and the enslaved was cruel, complex, ongoing, and full of seeming contradictions. While most of the power lay with the owners, who could employ violence, psychological pressure, or the threat of violence and sale to make slaves do as they were told, slaveholders relied on their slaves to carry out chores and (especially in the case of domestic staff) to demonstrate through their behavior the gentility of the family. Slaves who worked closely with family members in the home could inflict major damage on material possessions or even persons. They could also damage reputations by refusing to go along with the stylized behavior that passed for evidence of a slaveholder's upper-class status. Everyone knew that when an important matter was at stake (such as the full recovery of a son from illness or injury), slaves sometimes stood their ground.

No one knew better than the enslaved children of domestic workers how to get away with breaking the rules set by the Washingtons. For years, George and Martha tried to keep them from playing on the mansion house grounds, but still they frolicked on the well-manicured lawn, ruining shrubs and doing other damage in the process. In fall

1793, the newly appointed farm manager, William Pearce, reported his failure to keep "a great many" of them away. Policing the children was difficult in part because the children of Frank and Lucy Lee (Phil, Patty, and Burwell) were allowed on the grounds. Frank served as butler at the mansion, and Lucy as a cook, and the family lived above the kitchen. Lucy was the daughter of Old Doll, who had accompanied Martha to Mount Vernon when she married George, so the family had a long history with Martha. The children of the other domestic workers were supposed to play in the slave quarters, but they did not. It is unclear whose children were trespassing. Charlotte had at least two boys, Timothy and Elvey. She may have wanted them nearby while she worked. Caroline had three children: Wilson, Rachel, and Jemima. No doubt the children had ideas of their own about where they wanted to be. For his part, George Washington seemed resigned to the situation, but he was not without hope. He would find it "very agreeable" if Pearce could break the children's habit of coming into the yard.[16]

Like other elite men of his time, George Washington prized elaborate gardens. He was so eager to improve his that he once had slaves dig holes for trees and shrubs before the snow was off the ground. It proved to be difficult work and of little value since some of the plants froze.[17] Yet George apparently tolerated enslaved children playing in the yard, to the detriment of the gardens. This suggests that the Washingtons walked a fine line when it came to discipline.

William Pearce would have been keenly aware of the children on the lawn because he was living in the mansion, where he commanded the services of Frank and Lucy Lee as well as "a boy in the house." The arrangement was unusual. A manager usually stayed in another house on the grounds, but the manager's home at Mount Vernon was undergoing renovation. George Augustine Washington had died in February 1793, and his widow, Fanny, had moved. George and Martha may have preferred to have the mansion occupied by a white person, since guests continued to stop by while they were in Philadelphia. "I shall lay in such things as will be necessary," George assured Pearce, who otherwise might have found himself paying the cost of entertaining the Washingtons' guests.[18]

Some of the visitors were strangers, but others arrived at the invitation of the Washingtons. Martha knew in advance that the daughter of Senator Ralph Izard would stop by and wanted "every thing their to be made as agreeable" as possible for the traveling party. Martha asked Fanny, who at the time was living in nearby Alexandria, Virginia, to put things in order for the visit, but she was unavailable. Tobias Lear, George's secretary, was expected at Mount Vernon, but he never arrived. Making the situation worse, Pearce was away on business, which left the butler Frank Lee to greet the guests on his own. Apparently, Izard found Frank Lee's efforts satisfactory; she complimented the slave on his "politeness and kindness." Martha must have breathed a sigh of relief because she did not trust Frank to work well without supervision: less than three weeks later she was accusing him of "drinking as much wine as he gives to the visitors."[19]

Martha seems to have wanted a white housekeeper who could free her from "the drudgery" of supervising the domestic slaves.[20] Yet neither she nor her husband seemed able to free themselves from such tasks. In summer 1794, George took time from matters of state to comment on who should attend Mount Vernon's enslaved women at childbirth. He had been hiring a midwife from off the plantation, but now he raised the possibility of using the services of a Mount Vernon slave named Kate. Kate had asked to assume the role of midwife, and her husband Will had proposed the idea to their master. George directed his plantation manager to look into the matter. Was Kate as well qualified as she said she was? The only reason he had hired someone from outside was because "none [at home] seemed disposed to undertake" the job.[21]

George may or may not have discussed the use of midwives with Martha. Mistresses on small estates were involved intimately with most aspects of slavery on their husband's farms, but ladies like Martha concentrated their efforts on the household. Whereas Martha's mother Fanny probably became involved in decisions about childbirth and childcare among slaves on the Dandridge farm, on larger plantations like Mount Vernon these decisions—at least for field hands—might fall to the master or plantation manager. Which is not to say Martha

was disengaged from the economics of Mount Vernon and the slaves
who made her grand style of life possible. Once when Mount Vernon's
tobacco failed to sell and sat in a warehouse over a long stretch of time,
she reminded her husband of the need to dispose of it.[22] But for the
most part, she left "agricultural matters"—including the pregnancies
of enslaved women and livestock—to George. Thus the fortunes of
parturient enslaved women who worked in Mount Vernon's fields fell
under the purview of the President or his farm managers rather than
Martha, her femininity notwithstanding.

During the eight years of Washington's presidency, Martha and
George returned periodically to Mount Vernon. Most of the trips occurred during summer or early fall, when Congress was not in session. During a yellow fever epidemic that hit Philadelphia hard in July
1793 and peaked in October, the seat of the government shifted to
nearby Germantown, Pennsylvania. Both Martha and George went
home, though George soon returned to duties in Germantown. The
next summer, George, Martha, and the children went to Germantown, partly out of fear that yellow fever would return and partly in
the hope that they could avoid the heat of the summer season, but also
because William Pearce had moved into the mansion at Mount Vernon. His presence made journeys home more difficult, especially after
his family arrived in spring 1794. George made a brief trip that summer without Martha, who stayed away in part because there would
be no "room for the servants that we should be obliged to carry."[23]
Leaving them behind was unthinkable: Martha and her family would
have been without their personal attendants, and slaves left in Philadelphia would have been difficult to police.

   Each trip to Mount Vernon resulted in flurry of activity on the part
of slaves and their supervisors. In summer 1791, Martha told Fanny
to prepare the mansion for their imminent arrival by having Frank
clean it "from the garret to the sellers." All of the beds should be aired
and the bedclothes cleaned and mended. The bedsteads themselves
were to be "well scalded," and some smaller beds should be taken out
of storage and set up so they could be carried from room to room in
the event of company. The china closet was to be cleaned, along with

everything in it, and the contents organized so they could be located easily. "I have not a doubt but we shall have company all the time we are at home," Martha explained. Fanny should hurry the house slaves to finish other work so they would be free to wait on the Washingtons and their guests. The seamstresses, for example, would have to finish weaving the cotton for Martha's tablecloths quickly so they could act as "servants when we come home."[24]

"Make Nathan clean his kitchen and everything in it . . . very well," Martha wrote Fanny on another occasion before she and George arrived at Mount Vernon. Charlotte was to be done with other chores so that she could complete work (presumably sewing) that Martha was bringing with her. Charlotte and other of the Washingtons' domestic slaves should "get your family business done as fast as they can." After Martha and George arrived, they would need to shift their attention to waiting on the President and First Lady.[25]

One year Martha directed the butler Frank to whitewash the kitchen as well as "his room in the seller." In a letter to Fanny in August 1793, Martha said, "Make him clean every part of the House constantly every week sellers and all." Martha was hoping to come home the following month and wanted "things in tolerable order."[26]

In June 1794, Martha asked Fanny to "make Caroline put all the things of every kind out to air and Brush and Clean all the places and rooms that they were in." Although Martha was not coming and George's stay would be brief, George was bringing with him "two white men" who would need to be accommodated in the mansion house. There was also the usual round of cleaning to be done.[27]

In spring 1795, Martha wanted "every part of the House cleaned from the garrets to the sellers" before she returned for a summer stay. The bedclothes must be aired, the beds aired and cleaned. No work of that kind should remain to be done after she came home. One summer Martha told Fanny she should ensure the gardener had a ready supply of vegetables. The tablecloths should be as clean as possible, and the window and bed curtains hung. Martha was sending a new carpet for the parlor, and she advised Fanny to watch for it and make sure it was placed in the room before her arrival.[28]

The Washingtons' travels between Philadelphia and Mount Vernon posed problems with servants on both ends, whether the servants were free or enslaved. During visits home, both Washingtons worried that the white servants left behind in Philadelphia would not listen to the steward and housekeeper. Any insolence on their part would not be tolerated, George warned in a passage of a letter that he probably intended to have read aloud; the managers were employed "to take trouble off the hands of Mrs. Washington and myself." If workers succeeded in driving the managers away, others just as severe would be appointed in their stead, and the remaining servants would be held accountable for bad behavior.[29]

At times, the Washingtons sent slaves alone to Mount Vernon. Although Martha received reports from plantation and household managers, she also heard of conditions at home from the slaves. She apparently grilled Austin about conditions at Mount Vernon upon his return to Philadelphia in August 1793. When he reported that bacon had spoiled, she followed up with a letter to Fanny asking whether it was true.[30] The incident suggests that Martha put store in what slaves said despite her husband's insistence that slaves carry no tales.

Slaves who returned home alone to Mount Vernon arrived with specific instructions to complete chores. Once Martha lamented that neither she nor Fanny had thought to have Austin whitewash some of the rooms while there. Austin and others regularly carried items back and forth, such as "Stays for the young women" and "seeds for the plantation's garden," as well as the sewing bundles Martha made up for Charlotte. The cook Hercules took muslin for Wash's shirt ruffles to Charlotte for hemming in June 1791. Martha had planned to send silk as well, but sickness prevented her from obtaining the material in time.[31] The silk would have been intended for her own garments or perhaps Nelly's. On another occasion, Martha sent muslin for Charlotte to hem a week before Austin visited in the hope that he could bring the finished "borders" to her when he returned. Austin's stay was to be short, because she "could but illy spare him at this time." He was coming to Mount Vernon, Martha wrote, solely to "fulfill my promise to his wife" that he would return to see her and the children.[32] As we will see, she had another motive as well.

CHAPTER 7

Slaves in the President's House

After George Washington assumed the presidency, everything he and Martha did was scrutinized. Each action taken by the President and First Lady—no matter how mundane—seemed to set precedent and hold significance for the success of the United States. Would the first couple model themselves on royalty? Or would their appearance and behavior mark a significant turning point? Americans were divided. Some thought George should be addressed as "His Excellency" and Martha as "Lady." Others—the majority—spurned royal trappings and touted the less aristocratic titles "Mr. President" and "Mrs. Washington." Although disputants on both sides trusted George Washington to set the country on a proper course, the public was riveted by the new day-to-day making of America.

Everything Martha Washington did—what she wore, how she entertained, whom she associated with—evoked a public response. Critics found her bearing and manners too aristocratic. She once had her image engraved for publication with the title "Lady Washington." Her Friday evening levees, which attracted great numbers of people dressed in formal attire, were said to resemble official receptions in long-established European capitals. Martha sat slightly above the others on a platform and nodded as new arrivals were announced. The guests curtsied or bowed in her direction before moving on to the buffet. Martha also presided with the President over formal dinners. Each Thursday at 4:00 p.m. the Washingtons dined formally (some said tediously) with government officials, including ten to twenty congressmen.[1] The First Lady's supporters believed such rituals were necessary for the United States to gain the respect of European nations.

The level of scrutiny given Martha took some getting used to. In October 1789, she wrote from New York that she felt "more like a state prisoner than anything else." Boundaries of all sorts were being set that she dared not venture outside. Because she did not like the public's incessant gaze and subsequent judgment, she remained at home more than she would have preferred. After more than a year, she was still complaining: "I have been so long accustomed to conform to events which are governed by the public voice that I hardly dare indulge any personal wishes which cannot yield to that," she wrote a friend.[2]

Martha believed that her personal appearance and behavior reflected on her husband and the nation. "My Hair is set and dressed every day," she told Fanny Bassett Washington, with whom she was particularly close. Martha had been accustomed to dressing fashionably, but now she worried about public reaction to her outfits. She once asked Fanny to retrieve from her closet at Mount Vernon "my Black lace apron and handkerchief," along with some black netting from her chest of drawers, because she thought they would go over well in the capital city. If Fanny had trouble finding them, Martha's maid Charlotte could help.[3]

Despite the commentary that attended the First Lady's and President's every move, one thing seemed to evoke little discussion. The Washingtons had brought six slaves with them to New York. When people did complain, it was not always the attendants' enslaved status that offended. For some, the idea of a lady's maid or gentleman's valet smacked of European-style aristocracy, which seemed inappropriate for democratic America. Tobias Lear found particularly offensive the degree of the servants' subservience to the children, Nelly and Wash. Raising young Wash with an emphasis on his wealth and standing seemed out of place in America. Lear feared it would put him "on the road to ruin." His concern reflected changing attitudes about a man's status. In the colonial era, family connections and wealth had determined a man's place in society, but a new type of man was emerging. Wealth and breeding were still important, but in the new order of things, Wash would need knowledge and talent to make his mark upon the world. Wash was receiving an excellent education and mastering his lessons, but Martha seemed to overemphasize the "servile respect" she considered Wash's due.[4] Lear had originally been hired in 1784 to tutor the Custis children as well as to act as George's secretary, which explains in part his attention to Wash's education, but in commenting on Wash's upbringing, he was echoing a worry shared by others about imitating European aristocracy in America.

Lear went further than many other Americans, however: he found it troubling that the President and his family owned slaves. In fact, before agreeing to work for the President in an official capacity, Lear elicited a promise that the chief executive would eventually free his. At a time when many reformers spoke of alleviating slavery's worst features, Lear rejected the approach in favor of abolition. He once observed of the Mount Vernon slaves that they were well clothed and fed and not subject to harsh beatings, *"but still they are slaves."*[5] Antislavery sentiment was growing in the nation, particularly in northern states and among Quakers, but the majority of Americans did not share Lear's concern. In George Washington, Americans north and south had knowingly chosen as President a man who counted certain men as his equals but others as his property. By bringing slaves to New York, he and the First Lady established the precedent that slaves had a place in the President's house. Of the eleven men elected to the presidency after George Washington left office and before the Civil War, seven staffed the President's house with slaves.[6]

The Washingtons chose the slaves who accompanied them to New York carefully. All six had a history of delivering impeccable service, and all had proven their loyalty. Those who would be most visible to the public were young, healthy, well groomed, and light-skinned — traits the Washingtons valued. They were determined to have the slaves make a good appearance.

Martha chose as her personal attendant fifteen-year-old Ona Judge (Oney), the daughter of Martha's enslaved seamstress Betty and a white tailor named Andrew Judge.[7] Her mistress prized in particular Oney's fancy sewing skills, but the young girl had other attributes

Martha valued in a lady's maid. She knew how Martha wanted her hair done, how to care for Martha's clothing, and how to attend to her other personal needs. She also knew how to behave with Martha both in private and in front of company. Just as her mistress had learned the art of walking, talking, and dressing as a lady, Oney mastered the behavior expected of a lady's maid. She learned to anticipate her mistress's every demand, to stand aside when her mistress did not need her but always within reach or hearing for the times she did. A lady's maid saw nothing she was not supposed to see, heard nothing she was not supposed to hear, and kept her facial expression pleasant and friendly. Had Oney not mastered her lessons well, she would have been relegated to a less public region of the household where she could use her needle behind the scenes instead of in plain view of her mistress's friends and acquaintances. Oney pleased her mistress on all scores, including physical appearance. She kept her person and clothing clean, and she was light-skinned. People who interviewed Oney in the 1840s described her as "very much freckled" and "nearly white."[8]

It took years to train a lady's maid. The sewing was difficult and beyond the ability of many to master. Most elite mistresses began by teaching a number of young enslaved girls to sew. Only those who demonstrated a knack for needlework and the patience to complete time-consuming projects were considered for the position. Girls who did not work out were redirected toward other, less exacting chores. They could become spinners or weavers or general seamstresses who made household goods and sewed for the plantation workers. A girl who displayed little talent with the needle or who was careless about her appearance or who did not learn the mannerisms expected of a house slave could take on the role of washerwoman or perform any number of other domestic tasks carried out beyond the gaze of ladies and gentlemen. Incompetent or uncooperative girls could be relegated to the field or another worksite or even sold.

A lady's maid was not valued solely for the product of her labor. A well-trained lady's maid signaled the owner's wealth and high social standing. The most important attribute for a lady's maid was loyalty. She lived and worked in such close proximity to her mistress that her character had to be beyond reproach. Because a lady's maid was uniquely trained to serve the needs of an individual mistress, it was difficult if not impossible to purchase one in the market. Lady's maids were not bought and sold so much as brought up to the occupation. On occasion a lady's maid might change hands because a mistress had died, but most were passed down in families rather than sold to strangers. An enormous calamity—perhaps a serious breach of loyalty—could convince a mistress to sell a lady's maid, but many believed sending the woman to work in the field was a better alternative.

By the time Oney arrived in New York, she had already spent countless hours with Martha, and by all accounts the mistress was pleased with her. Besides her husband, Oney was the last person whom Martha saw at night and the first person to greet her in the morning.

In some ways, Oney's training in domestic service was akin to that of millions of girls from impoverished families who today perform domestic labor. Economic need and custom often determine the age at which they begin service, but a recent worldwide study of child domestic workers suggests that most begin work by the age of twelve.[9] This was the age when many enslaved girls like Oney began service as a lady's maid.

The idea of training children like Oney to perform skilled labor fit at least superficially with Enlightenment ideals that considered childhood a time for education. Maids in training certainly learned skills, but enslaved girls never came of age and used their education to their own advantage. Instead of establishing homes of their own, they continued to serve the mistress. Because the skills of a lady's maid were highly prized, she was ostensibly protected from unwanted (in the mistress's eye) attention from male suitors and (in some cases) abusers. Any personal relationships were carefully monitored, forbidden or encouraged according to criteria established by the mistress.

The private nature of domestic work even today makes the girls and boys engaged in it particularly vulnerable to abuse by employers, especially if the child has no relatives or other supportive adults nearby to appeal to for help. By virtue of their limited knowledge and inexperience, children find it more difficult than adults to protest abusive treatment or difficult working conditions. Children tend to accept their fate because they know no other way to live, according to an expert on modern-day child workers.[10] Of course, employers (including slaveholders) might prefer a child for this reason. When it came to providing personal service (as with a lady's maid or gentleman's valet), children might have to be corrected physically or verbally. Because children were assumed to require discipline as well as education and training, a mistress or master might punish a child servant without worrying too much about the reactions of friends or family. Most adults accepted the correction of children as a "normal" part of life, as long as it was not unusually harsh. Although a slave, Oney had a degree of protection in the world, with her mother and other family members nearby at Mount Vernon and her older brother Austin with her in the capital. But it was not others that the Washingtons feared when it came to Oney; it was her own knowledge of her enslaved state. And as they dreaded, she soon came to learn that she was not fated to live as a slave.

Oney was not the only female slave in the President's house. The older woman Moll (also called Molly) came to serve as nursemaid for Nelly and Wash. Martha had brought Moll, a Custis slave, to Mount Vernon as a maid for her daughter Patsy. After Patsy died, Moll continued to work as a domestic and eventually took on the responsibility of caring for Martha's grandchildren. She continued in service many years after that, and she, too, was one of the slaves in the room when the President lay dying. So far as is known, she never had a family of her own but instead spent her life tending the needs of the Washington family.

Oney's half brother Austin was much older than she. He had been born in New Kent County and had come to Mount Vernon with his mother as an infant. He was said to have hair and skin typical of an American descended from European stock. He started out in his teens as a waiter in the Washington dining room and gradually assumed more responsibility. Dressed in a scarlet waistcoat and lace, he was soon accompanying Martha and other family members on their travels, possibly in the role of footman. He often carried messages or other items to friends and neighbors on behalf of his owners. In 1776 he had been inoculated against smallpox, probably because he traveled so much. Austin tended carefully to his appearance, taking the time to clean his leather breeches regularly with clay. His boots and other clothing were generally spotless.[11] Austin was exactly the type of servant the Washingtons wanted in the nation's capital.

Christopher Sheels, like Austin, began his life of service as a waiter and gradually assumed more responsibility. But while Austin was a grown man when he left for New York, Christopher was but a boy. He too was of mixed ancestry. His mother Alice was one of Martha's enslaved spinners, but his father was a free white man, most likely one of those hired to remodel the mansion at Mount Vernon. William Lee had served as George's valet throughout the Revolutionary War, but he had been crippled in a series of falls. Christopher went to New York as Lee's replacement. George Washington once spelled out in writing what he expected of a valet. He had to look good and meet the standard of excellence in his work. He had to know how to shave his master and dress his hair, and to wait on his personal needs throughout the day.[12] A valet also cared for a gentleman's clothing.

Christopher Sheel's appointment as the President's manservant represented an important shift in the Washington household, as the fourteen-year-old Christopher was a dower slave, not one of Washington's own. Sheels served George Washington for the remainder of the President's life. He too was among the slaves who attended the President as he lay dying. Like Moll, he was not among the slaves freed by Washington's will.

The other two slaves brought to the capital—Paris and Giles—worked in the stable. Both were teenagers who could ride postilion or drive the Washingtons' carriage. Although the two went to Philadelphia with the President and First Lady when the capital was relocated, neither stayed through George Washington's first term in office. Paris displeased the President in some way, and Giles suffered an injury. Both apparently died while in their twenties at Mount Vernon.

The presence of slaves in the President's house was noteworthy because New York was in the process of abolishing slavery within its borders. The year before Washington's inauguration, the legislature had voted to end the slave trade (with certain exceptions), and legislators for some years had been debating the passage of a gradual emancipation act. Such a law would not have freed any slaves right away. Instead, children born after a particular date would be free. Ten years would pass before New York passed the proposal, but even in 1789 many observers thought that emancipation was just a matter of time. Gradual emancipation seemed to be a northern phenomenon. Whereas slavery had been legal in all of the colonies before the Revolution, the North and South had begun to develop in different ways. In the North, where slavery had been legal but merely one component of a mixed economy, Americans embraced the idea espoused by many supporters of the Revolution that liberty was the order of the day and slavery had no place in the nation. Southern states, on the other hand, remained committed to slave labor and were equally sure that liberty for some could coexist with the enslavement of others.

If George and Martha had concerns from the start that New Yorkers might object to the presence of their slaves, they left no account of them. On the contrary, the highly visible presence of their enslaved attendants seemed to announce their certainty that they could rely on slave labor in the nation's capital. Yet New York's debate over slavery must have captured their attention and encouraged both to ensure that the behavior, even the appearance, of their enslaved servants was irreproachable. George himself took time from his official duties to decide how the hair of enslaved servants should be cut and groomed.[13]

George Washington was keenly aware that he was President of the South *and* the North. As if to reassure both southern and northern interests, the Washingtons set about establishing a household that incorporated both enslaved and free workers. But the Washingtons found the free laborers difficult to supervise. Accustomed as they were to servants trained from birth to yield to an owner's every demand, they were taken aback when the new servants refused to behave in an obsequious manner or to perform their duties exactly as directed. In December 1790, when the national capital moved to Philadelphia, the Washingtons hardly hesitated in their decision to "carry" slaves there (in the parlance of the day), even though Pennsylvania was moving faster than New York toward emancipating human property.

The Washingtons took eight slaves to Philadelphia, including the dower slaves who had been with them in New York. Hercules and Richmond, two Washington slaves, now joined them. Another Mount Vernon slave named Joe came later. Hercules was the Mount Vernon cook. It was he — not George and Martha — who insisted that his son Richmond come along to work as a scullion in the kitchen.[14] Hercules may have wanted to mentor his son and teach him to cook. The children of domestic servants frequently took jobs similar to those of parents. For parents, the practice conveniently ensured that their child's training would be left to them rather than to someone who might not have the child's best interest at heart. It may seem peculiar that Hercules was able to get his way in this matter, but skilled and trusted attendants exercised a degree of leverage over their living and working conditions. The Washingtons would not have wanted to drag disgruntled slaves to Philadelphia. It was much better to have slaves who were reasonably satisfied with their situations.

Austin and Hercules traveled by stage ahead of the others to put things in order. Richmond and Christopher Sheels soon followed.[15] The other two men, Giles and Paris, rode postilion and cared for the horses that brought Martha, her children, Moll, and Oney Judge to Philadelphia. Hercules, Giles, and Paris sported new hats purchased by the Washingtons before they left Mount Vernon.[16] The Washingtons seemed oddly unaware (or perhaps uncaring) that the people of Philadelphia might object to the presence of enslaved attendants no matter how decked out they were. They would learn soon enough.

Philadelphia was a free city in a free state. Pennsylvania — considered the cradle of liberty — had passed a gradual emancipation law in 1780. Americans watched the state carefully on account of its experiment with emancipation. Philadelphia was in the forefront of the abolition movement, and citizens formed the first abolition society there in 1774. There were still slaves in the city in 1790, but they numbered only a couple hundred out of a population of roughly 28,500.[17]

The architects of Pennsylvania's liberation law recognized that southerners doing business in the state might want to bring slaves along, and the law gave them that right. Commercial ties between Pennsylvania and slaveholding states to the east and south needed to be accommodated. But no one had the right to bring slaves into the state permanently. Slaves brought into the state could stay no longer than six months. Owners whose slaves remained longer would relinquish claim to them. At the end of six months of residence, a slave could petition for freedom, and presumably gain it.

Martha learned firsthand from U.S. attorney general Edmund Randolph that some of the slaves she brought with her to Philadelphia might be eligible for freedom after half a year.[18] Because her husband's four-year term in office did not end until 1793, the slaves working in the President's house would meet the residency requirement. There was an exemption for members of Congress who had brought slaves with them to Philadelphia, but it was not clear that the exemption applied to members of the executive branch of government. The slaves the Washingtons brought with them were among their most skilled and prized, which meant the Washingtons would feel their loss keenly if it came to that.

Neither Martha nor George could be certain what would happen if the slaves stayed. They might not apply for freedom even if eligible. Oney, Christopher, and Richmond seemed too young to lodge an appeal without help, but there was no guarantee, and the others had to be considered. The Washingtons worried because, in George's words, "the idea of freedom might be too great a temptation for them to resist." Together he and Martha hatched a secret plan to avoid complying with the law. They would make sure the slaves did not stay in Philadelphia for six months by sending them periodically to Mount Vernon for temporary stays. They told no one but the trusted Tobias Lear. When Martha made plans to return to Mount Vernon in May 1791, she "would naturally bring her maid and Austin," and Hercules could go along to cook. The scheme could "be known to none but *your self &* *Mrs. Washington*," George told Lear.[19]

The reason for the visits had to be kept from the slaves. Knowing that they might have "a right" to freedom could encourage them to lodge a petition. It might also make them "insolent," especially if they realized that the Washingtons were attempting to skirt the law. If word of the conspiracy leaked out to the general public, opinion would likely go against the Washingtons — especially since the law, originally passed in 1788, had been amended to make it illegal for slaveholders to send their slaves out of state in an effort to subvert the law's intent. Some local citizens were already criticizing the Washingtons for holding slaves or for bringing them to Philadelphia in the first place. "I wish to have it accomplished under pretext that may deceive both them [the slaves] and the Public," George Washington wrote Lear. All but two of the slaves with them in Philadelphia were dower slaves who would be passed eventually as property to the heirs of Daniel Parke Custis. If any of these slaves were to find a path to freedom, I "may have to pay," he wrote.[20]

Martha planned to send Austin home under the pretext that she had promised his wife he could come. She made a point of telling her niece Fanny Bassett Washington that this was why she was sending him in the spring of 1791. Martha may have felt the need to recruit Fanny in the subterfuge in case anyone questioned whether the Washingtons were evading the Pennsylvania law. It is of course possible that Martha had made such a promise to Austin's wife. We know that the Washingtons negotiated with Hercules about bringing his son to Philadelphia, but some time went by before she mentioned the promise to Fanny, and other documentary evidence about why Austin was sent home renders her statement suspect.[21]

Austin was highly trusted by both Martha and George. As we have seen, he ran errands for the Washingtons and traveled about on his own or with other slaves. He saw at least one play in Philadelphia in the company of Hercules and Oney Judge, and he went with Hercules to the circus.[22] Austin also accompanied his mistress when she traveled by carriage, lending his protection to her person. The efforts by both Washingtons to deceive Austin about their motive in sending him to Mount Vernon speaks a truth about slavery that the Washingtons tried not to acknowledge: no matter how well they were treated, bonded men and women wanted to be free.

Unfortunately, the decision to send Austin home to see his wife (who may have been Charlotte) in the spring of 1791 had tragic consequences. Somewhere near Harford, Maryland, the thirty-six-year-old was thrown from his horse and died.[23]

The Washingtons may have gotten the idea to send slaves back and forth to Mount Vernon from the residents of Philadelphia's Carolina Row. A large contingent of elite southerners had homes in that neighborhood and regularly sent slaves back and forth between the city and their home plantations. The Washingtons mixed socially with Carolina Row residents, who represented some of the nation's most prominent and conservative families — elite men and women from both North and South who prized nationalism and feared anti-elite sentiment among ordinary Americans. The Carolina Row elites joined other men and women with aristocratic leanings to found a salon in the city where they could express reactionary ideas that were out of favor in the democratizing nation.[24]

The city of Philadelphia was of two minds when it came to slavery. On the one hand, it was a stronghold for abolitionists — particularly within its Quaker communities. On the other hand, it was known for a reactionary "quasi-monarchial circle" that excluded all but the top echelon from its luxurious entertainments. More democratic elements found the quasi-monarchists scandalous. Wealth was an important factor in the determination of who would be invited to join the circle, but it was not the only one. Family connections, education, social skills, dress, and travel to Europe and elsewhere were all taken into account.[25]

While in Philadelphia, the Washingtons lived in the three-and-a-half-story Robert Morris house on Market Street. Their personal servants, on call morning and night, lived in the brick home too. Oney Judge stayed in a room on the second floor above the kitchen, as did Moll. The attic housed three of the male slaves: Hercules, Richmond, and Christopher Sheels. A smokehouse was converted into living quarters for the other slaves.[26]

Wage laborers outnumbered slaves at the President's house. A servants' hall provided space where a staff of about twenty-five (free and enslaved) took their meals. The two sets of workers may have had trouble getting along. The Washingtons employed a steward and housekeeper to oversee household management. John Hyde and his wife had worked for the Washingtons in New York and relocated to Philadelphia with them. Hercules was the more capable cook, but social convention dictated that Mrs. Hyde take charge of the kitchen. The situation frustrated the President, who knew the meals would be "more tasty" if Hercules exercised "more agency." He had no doubt that Hercules could plan and execute menus better than she, but neither Mrs. Hyde nor her husband would "submit to" placing Hercules in charge.[27] One can well imagine the tension that developed as enslaved and free servants tried to sort out who was in charge of what within the constraints of racial conventions that decreed a free white person superior to an enslaved black one no matter who possessed greater skill. The Hydes would have had their hands full trying to keep order in such a household.

Martha relied on the Hydes to handle everyday matters, but she exercised considerable discretion in running the President's house. She maintained the power of the purse and the right to make executive decisions related to the home's management. Her husband directed Lear, who paid the President's expenses, to give her "what money she may want." George Washington had turned down the offer of a salary when he accepted the office of President, but he did ask that Congress pay his expenses. George told his secretary to inquire from time to time whether his wife needed additional funds because, he said, she did not like to ask for them.[28]

By all accounts, the Washingtons' slaves in Philadelphia lived well in comparison to other bonded people, which made Oney Judge's defection so shocking to them. The Washington family was making preparations to visit Mount Vernon in May 1796 when she ran away. The impending move provided a perfect cover. Because the slaves were packing for the trip, Oney was able to gather her things without arousing suspicion. Someone (who is unclear) removed her bag from the house, and when the Washingtons sat down to dinner, she left.[29] It was easy enough to disappear in the streets of Philadelphia; the city had become known as a haven for runaway slaves. When two slaves disappeared from the Virginia home of George Washington's sister in 1794, Betty Lewis sought her brother's help in retrieving them on the presumption they were headed to Philadelphia.[30] We know now that Oney stayed in the city with friends for a month and then boarded a ship bound for Portsmouth, New Hampshire. She later said that she wanted to live as a free woman, maybe learn to read and write.

Oney's disappearance was a personal loss for Martha, but it was also an embarrassment to the President and First Lady. Oney's escape revealed all too clearly the discontent that slaveholders denied existed among the people they held in bondage. At first the Washingtons put out word that Oney had been led astray: she was a simple woman seduced into acting against her own self-interest. They went so far as to make up a story about a Frenchman who had enticed Oney to run. Because Oney was young and unmarried, the story seemed plausible, but there was no Frenchman, as the Washingtons knew. They were in fact worried that Oney had fled with another man: Martha's nephew Bartholomew (Bat) Dandridge Jr., who had disappeared from Philadelphia around the same time. Bat, who had been serving as George's personal secretary, was nowhere to be found. Nor had he left word of his whereabouts. The disappearance of Oney and Bat became a source of gossip near and far. Vice President John Adams wrote about the matter in his diary. Meanwhile, Martha and George worried that the unfolding public scandal could get worse. Oney might be pregnant.[31]

This was not an unfounded fear. Martha and George both had blood relatives of mixed race. On Martha's side, Ann Dandridge and her son William Custis Costin stood as proof that such liaisons existed. Martha's first husband had competed with his half brother Jack for the affections of their father, and Martha's eldest granddaughter Elizabeth Parke Custis (called Eliza or Betsey) had, two months previous to Oney's disappearance, married a man whose three sons were not "pure Anglo-Saxons." Thomas Law, an Englishman, had fathered his children while serving in India as an official of the East India Company. Like many other gentlemen in his situation, he had taken an Indian woman as mistress. Eliza had not only married Thomas but also agreed to mother the three boys.[32]

On George's side, there was West Ford, a child of mixed ancestry born either in 1785 or 1786. Some of his descendants (and certain scholars) maintain that West was George's son by one of his brother's slaves. West's mother Venus lived at Bushfield, a plantation belonging to John Augustine Washington about ninety-five miles south of Mount Vernon. For years, historians dismissed the idea that West could be George's son, since it was said that George Washington was nowhere near West's mother at the time of West's conception. But recent scholarship has shown that West may have been older than historians have believed. If so, Venus was visiting Mount Vernon around the time of West's conception, making it possible — if not probable — that George was West's father. Even if the President was not West's father, it seems likely that West was a close relative, the child perhaps of his brother or one of his nephews.[33]

Martha would have known about West. She was close to her sister-in-law Hannah Bushrod Washington, and while such matters were not discussed publicly, family, friends, and neighbors whispered aplenty, as did slaves. Mount Vernon was but a short boat ride along the Potomac River from Bushfield, making it easy for people to carry back and forth news along with goods.

The Washingtons eventually heard from Bat in Greenbrier, Virginia (now West Virginia). He assured his aunt and uncle that his disappearance — though sudden and unexplained — could not be attributed to any "unworthy motives." His words did little to alleviate their concern. When word arrived that Oney was in New Hampshire, the Washingtons must have breathed a sigh of relief, but there was still the question of what to do.

Oney's escape had gone as she had planned until Elizabeth Langdon, daughter of New Hampshire senator John Langdon and friend of Martha's daughter Nelly, spotted her on a Portsmouth street. Elizabeth, who had often been a guest in the Washington home, asked Oney why she was in the city. Oney's truthful answer shocked Elizabeth. Elizabeth reported the encounter to her parents, who in turn informed the Washingtons. Martha and George immediately launched a campaign to have Oney returned.[34]

Martha was incensed. It was bad enough to have lost Oney; it was worse to have her found and publicly declaring that she was not content to be Martha's slave. Elizabeth and other of Martha's friends knew that Oney's living conditions were better than those of most slaves.

In Philadelphia, Oney not only had a room of her own but dressed more stylishly and ate more and better food. Oney returned periodically to Virginia, so was not cut off completely from family and friends. She also had liberty to move around the city unaccompanied by her owner. Martha had given Oney and other slaves tickets to the circus and theater because she thought "gay amusements" were important for lifting "the gloom" of difficult times.[35] But of course Oney's material conditions of living had not been what had driven her toward New Hampshire.

By the time of her escape, Oney had lived away from Mount Vernon for nearly seven years, brief periodic visits notwithstanding. She must have known that she was entitled to freedom under Pennsylvania law. The Washingtons, however, seem to have assumed that Oney's fate had been settled under Virginia law and by the terms of Daniel Parke Custis's will, under which Oney was to be passed as property to one of Martha's granddaughters at Martha's death. It seems not to have occurred to Martha that Oney might hold out hope for a different fate. At any rate, she told Oney shortly before she absconded that one day she would become the property of Eliza Parke Custis Law. It is possible that until then Oney believed she would be liberated at the end of her master's presidency or at his death. She had probably heard rumors that the President planned to free his slaves through his will. He had discussed with others, including David Humphreys, his onetime aide-de-camp and authorized biographer, certain schemes for freeing his slaves.[36] It was highly unlikely that these conversations had all taken place out of the earshot of servants. Even if Oney had not overheard talk of manumission herself, she could have learned about it from other servants in the President's house.

Decades after her flight, Oney told abolitionist interviewers that she had decided she would not become the slave of Martha's oldest granddaughter. Eliza and her sister Martha Custis were coming of age, marrying, and inheriting their portions of their father's fortune, including slaves. Martha Custis had married Thomas Peter in 1795, and by the following year he was selling some of the slaves and breaking up families in the process.[37] What would stop Eliza's husband, Thomas Law, from doing the same?

George hesitated to pursue Oney. There were legal procedures for returning runaway slaves, as the President well knew. He had signed the Fugitive Slave Act of 1793 into law. The problem from his perspective was that it required public proceedings, which he wished to avoid. He worried about how it would look for the President of the United States to chase after a runaway slave, but Martha was unwilling to let her maid go. He decided to use underhanded, even illegal, means to bring Oney home in order to keep the matter out of the public eye.

The President enlisted the help of one of his cabinet members as well as the customs official in Portsmouth to seize and return Oney to Philadelphia or better yet to Virginia. The plan failed, in part because New Hampshire customs official Joseph Whipple refused to break the law as the President requested. He had been told that Oney was enticed to escape, but he realized upon meeting her that she had come to New Hampshire of her own accord in search of freedom. Slavery remained legal in New Hampshire, but it was not important economically except to the small number of residents who held slaves. Slavery was dying out there as in the other New England states, and slaves who managed to escape were making their way to the region in search of freedom as they could.

George explained to New Hampshire officials and others that his efforts to bring Oney home were undertaken at Martha's behest, as if to absolve himself of any responsibility. He also said that Oney was a Custis slave, one he would have to account for later when Daniel Parke Custis's estate was finally settled. This may have been less of a worry than he made out. After all, George was a very wealthy man. He had no children of his own to provide for; Martha's heirs would inherit the sizable estate of her first husband. Still, George was contemplating a general emancipation of his slaves, and he knew this would require money. He was also accustomed to being in control. However much he may have sympathized with a slave's desire for freedom, he would have considered it the prerogative of an owner to say when and under what circumstances freedom would come.

At one point, Oney tried to negotiate with her former master. She would return to Mount Vernon but only if the President could guarantee that she would receive freedom through his will. This George could not or would not do. He might have purchased Oney from the Custis estate and added her to the list of slaves he intended to emancipate, but he did not. It may not have occurred to him to do so since decisions about her domestic help had always fallen to Martha, and Martha wanted Oney returned. Instead, George decided to do what he could to recapture Oney, short of taking her by force or creating a public stir.

The First Lady was willing to use force and schemed with a nephew, Burwell Bassett Jr., to return Oney to Mount Vernon using any means necessary. Burwell happened to be on his way to Portsmouth in July 1799 when he stopped by to see his aunt. The conversation at some point must have turned to Oney because two weeks later George wrote Burwell asking his help in retrieving Martha's maid. He emphasized that he did not wish to use improper means, but if Oney could be *persuaded* to come back he and Martha would be pleased.

By the time Burwell arrived in Portsmouth in fall 1799, Oney was married and the mother of an infant. She had wed John Staines, a free sailor of mixed race, in January 1797 and given birth to a daughter named Eliza. When Burwell appeared on her doorstep, her husband was away at sea. Burwell claimed to be delivering a message from the President. If Oney returned to Virginia, she would be free. Oney refused, explaining, "I am free now." Burwell, who was staying at the home of Senator John Langdon, confessed to his host that he had "orders to bring [Oney] and her infant child [to Mount Vernon] by force" if she did not return of her own volition.[38] The statement alarmed Langdon, who somehow let Oney know she was in danger. She fled with her infant to friends in the nearby town of Greenland. Unable to determine their location, Burwell left without them.

Burwell had recently written a will emancipating his own slaves. He hardly seems the type to have acted on his own to retrieve Oney through force or other illegal means, especially since the President had asked him not to. Historian Henry Wiencek says Martha persuaded Burwell to go against the President's wishes and, it would seem, his own inclinations.[39] The fact that Burwell listened to his aunt rather than to the President suggests that she was a formidable figure. He and his family had benefited in important ways from Martha's connections with the Custis family and her marriage to George. Caught in the middle, Burwell preferred not to antagonize her.

Exactly what would have happened to Oney in the short run if she had been returned remains unclear. She had proven herself untrustworthy as a lady's maid, "ungrateful" for the privileges her mistress had bestowed upon her. Martha might have put Oney to work elsewhere on the Mansion House farm or moved her to one of George's other four farms or one of the many Custis holdings. Or Oney might have been sold. George had pledged to sell no more slaves, but Martha had made no such vow.

Oney Judge was not the only servant to escape enslavement in Philadelphia. The cook Hercules, like Oney a well-trained and trusted slave, fled to parts unknown. He had been brought to Philadelphia because the free cooks the Washingtons hired in New York City had not lived up to their exacting standards. To ensure Hercules's cooperation, the Washingtons extended privileges that were customarily given to chefs who worked for other elite families in U.S. and European cities, including Philadelphia. For example, Hercules was allowed to sell leftovers from the kitchen, including used tea leaves and chicken feathers, and pocket the money for himself. Three blocks away on High Street, Thomas Jefferson extended similar privileges to his enslaved cook, James Hemings.[40]

Hercules had discretion in spending his income and the Washingtons' permission to travel about the city. He attended the circus, the theater, and other ticketed events, as was the custom among free servants who could afford the price of admission. Hercules purchased clothing and a gold-headed cane with some of the money. Martha and George wanted Hercules in Philadelphia, so much that against their better judgment they had allowed his son Richmond to join him as a chef's assistant.[41]

The Washingtons worried that Hercules, having enjoyed a degree of freedom in Philadelphia, would refuse to return to Mount Vernon when George retired from the presidency. When they plotted to circumvent Pennsylvania's freedom law, they had been especially con-

Presumed portrait of Hercules, the Washingtons' prized cook.

cerned about Hercules. But when they concocted a reason for him to return with Martha to Mount Vernon before six months elapsed, Hercules saw through the ruse and called the Washingtons on the scheme. Professing loyalty, he complained of the Washingtons' lack of trust. He made such a fuss that the couple relented. He would not be required to return to Mount Vernon before six months elapsed, Martha told him.[42] Hercules stayed in Philadelphia for more than six months before he went to Mount Vernon. He had returned and seemed to settle back into his Philadelphia life when Oney Judge's escape demonstrated that Pennsylvania's liberation law was not the only path to freedom.

Perhaps Martha believed that Hercules's situation in Philadelphia was so near freedom that he would not experience any difference. After all, he made money and spent it as he pleased. He had developed friendships and enjoyed the entertainments that the city had to offer. Like Oney Judge, Hercules had family and friends back at Mount Vernon whom he would want to see again. And she may have known that her husband intended to bequeath freedom to Hercules and the other Washington slaves. If this was Martha's thinking, she was wrong. Hercules bided his time, waiting for the right moment to disappear. The opportunity came on the President's sixty-fifth birthday. After preparing food for the occasion, he used the chaos of the celebration to walk away. He must have calculated that his master would spend little time tracking him down. If George Washington worried—as he had in the case of Oney Judge—that it would be unseemly for the President of the United States to chase after her, how much worse would it have looked were he to track down and return to slavery a highly skilled, well known, and well regarded man who under Pennsylvania law was clearly entitled to his freedom?

One cannot be sure why Hercules did not simply petition for freedom, but it may have had something to do with his son. Richmond had originally been among the slaves taken to Philadelphia by the Washingtons, but he had been returned to Virginia. Hercules may have resented the turn of events. Perhaps he had envisioned that he and his son would both gain freedom under Pennsylvania law. Although he may have believed they would be emancipated under George's will, he had no way of knowing when this would occur since no one knew how long the President would live. By the time Hercules disappeared in 1797, he apparently had concluded that his best path to freedom was not through Pennsylvania law or the largesse of his owner but through his own effort. Martha and George appealed to friends and acquaintances for help in locating the runaway, but none of them knew where Hercules had gone. When a visitor to Mount Vernon asked Hercules's daughter whether she was sorry that she would not see her father again, she said no. She was happy he was free.[43] Whether he had discussed his plans with family is unknown, but her answer suggests that she understood his desire to escape bondage.

The loss of Hercules was a great blow to the Washingtons. They took steps to locate him, but they were low-key, at least compared to the search for Oney. A prized cook was just as valuable and as hard to train as a lady's maid, but Hercules belonged to George. Flamboyant in style, he was well known around town, and he might accuse the Washingtons publicly of trying to break the law. The First Lady probably felt she had no good choice in the matter. She and the President asked people they knew to be on the lookout for Hercules, but there was no newspaper announcement offering a reward for his return, as there had been for Oney Judge.[44]

George had previously vowed not to purchase any more slaves. In truth, he had more than he could use on his farms, and with his step-grandchildren well provided for through their Custis inheritance, he did not have to worry about increasing his slaveholdings. This was already happening anyway, through human reproduction. On his estate, as on many others, the number of babies born in bondage who would live to adulthood exceeded the number who died each year. But he and Martha needed to replace their cook right away. Hercules's disappearance did not obviate the need to entertain, and the Washingtons did not have time to wait while another Custis or Washington slave learned the skills necessary to put food fit for a President on the table. In mid-November, the Washingtons were still without a cook, and George wrote his nephew George Lewis about purchasing a replacement for Hercules. He admitted that buying a slave went against a previous resolution. He explained his reversal this way: "The running off of my Cook, has been a most inconvenient thing to this family." He had already "endeavoured to hire, black or white," but had not been able to secure someone suitable. A previous letter to another nephew, Bushrod Washington, brought information that the only cook for sale in Richmond had a fondness for alcohol, which was why he was being sold in the first place.[45] Apparently, an inebriated cook did not appeal to the Washingtons.

George wrote letters and made inquiries about purchasing a cook, but Martha took the lead. The President maintained an interest in the minute details of running the household, but the kitchen was the domain of the mistress. She and George ended up hiring a white cook for the remainder of their time in Philadelphia. Honoré Julien, a Frenchman, served in the Washingtons' kitchen for the last four months of George's presidency.[46] Finding a permanent replacement for Hercules would await the President's retirement.

CHAPTER 8

Home Again

Martha and George Washington looked forward to retirement at the end of the President's second term, but their retreat to the country-side did not usher in a quiet life. The Washingtons in 1797 were big-ger celebrities than ever. "Almost every day some stranger" showed up expecting food and lodging, Martha wrote a friend, "and we cannot refuse" hospitality. On 31 July of that year George noted, "Unless some one pops in, unexpectedly—Mrs. Washington & myself will do what I believe has not been done within the last twenty Years by us,—that is to set down to dinner by ourselves." The absence of visitors that eve-ning was indeed remarkable. The number of people coming to Mount Vernon increased substantially after the President's retirement. In 1798 alone, at least 656 people sat down to dinner; 677 stayed overnight.[1]

Household help was essential to maintaining Mount Vernon's do-mestic tranquility in the face of so many guests. The former First Lady and President had enslaved maids, footmen, cooks, kitchen assistants, seamstresses, laundresses, and other servants sufficient for hosting a large number of people, but they were still reeling from the loss of Hercules, who had not only overseen the preparation of the elegant dishes that graced the President's table each day in Philadelphia but also ensured that the kitchen and pantries were stocked, well orga-nized, and cleaned. The Washingtons also wanted help with oversee-ing Mount Vernon's large household staff and entertaining its many visitors.

Eleanor (Nelly) Parke Custis, who turned twenty the year George

Washington retired from office, was old enough to be of assistance. Like other girls of her social class, she had been groomed to keep house—which involved managing slaves—and to assume a place as hostess in the family parlor and ballroom. Youthful experience managing a complex household like Mount Vernon was considered good preparation for becoming the wife of a prominent and wealthy man.

Lawrence Lewis arrived at Mount Vernon soon after the Washingtons' return to assist his uncle with correspondence and to help with the constant rounds of entertaining. As the educated son of slaveholders, Lawrence would have fit in well. He had grown up learning to manage slaves, and his formal education had prepared him to serve as the former President's secretary. Lawrence was also a relative, the child of George's sister Betty and her husband Fielding Lewis.

Together Nelly and Lawrence helped relieve the Washingtons of the hosting duties they were finding increasingly onerous, but the kitchen remained a problem. Primary responsibility for meal preparation fell to Lucy Lee and Nathan, who had begun cooking at Mount Vernon while Hercules was managing the kitchen in Philadelphia. After the President's retirement, they continued as before: Lucy did the baking; Nathan tended the pots and pans. It was hard work that kept them busy throughout the day. Nathan not only cooked but chopped wood for the fire and fed the poultry. Together, the couple saw that the kitchen was clean at the end of the day. Even with the help of underlings to carry out much of the drudgery, they began their workday at 4:30 a.m. and did not finish until 8:00 p.m. This was assuming the Washingtons did not request a late supper. If they did, Lucy and Nathan worked another hour. The problem as Martha saw it was that she could not trust them to work alone. She wanted someone to "superintend boath and make others perform the duties allotted them." She had plenty of servants, in other words, but no one she trusted to provide the constant supervision she thought all slaves needed. For Martha, the difficulty was grounded in race and class: many blacks, she explained, "will impose when they can do it."[2]

The former First Lady hoped to find one person who, like Hercules, could act as chef and steward. Finding the right candidate would not be easy, in part because the job—which was really two jobs—was so demanding.[3] It would be difficult enough to find a head chef who knew how to prepare the seafood dishes Martha preferred, along with the meats, poultry, vegetables, pies, puddings, pancakes, and fritters the Washingtons regularly wanted on the table. Dinner could easily involve the making of fifteen dishes, and this did not include the custards, ice creams, fruits, and other sweets typically served after the main meal. Holiday dinners were especially laborious, featuring such time-consuming dishes as Yorkshire Christmas Pie and Martha's Great Cake. The Christmas pie alone took two days to prepare. The poultry that went into it had to be selected, slaughtered, deboned, and flavored with savories before being baked with vegetables into a pastry shell strong enough to hold it together.[4]

Hercules's replacement would also need to oversee an enslaved staff, which complicated the search. The Washingtons found a skilled white cook in Philadelphia who was willing to come. Although he was said to be honest, sober, obliging, and meticulous in performing his duties, he proved unable to prepare food and arrange the table to suit the Washingtons' tastes. Nor did he know how to manage the slaves. "He cannot understand them, nor they him," Martha wrote a friend. "The loss of my cook is very great and rendered still more sevear for want of a steward" who knew how to direct enslaved workers.[5]

Martha held white men who could not manage blacks in disdain. She once criticized Thomas Green, hired to oversee the Mount Vernon carpenters, because he had "but little influence" over the enslaved men who worked under him. He had proven unable "to keep them to their worke." George shared her contempt, especially for Green. Martha's desire to find someone accustomed to managing slaves was so great that she rejected a qualified cook recommended by her friend Elizabeth Willing Powel. He was French, and the wages he requested were high by Martha's standards, but her primary objection was that he was "unacquainted with blacks."[6]

The Washingtons' search for a white steward or head chef did not mean they gave up trying to find Hercules. They continued to seek his return through contacts with friends and acquaintances. It is not clear why they wanted him back. Much as they wished for a chef of his caliber, they would have hesitated to employ him again. Shortly before Lawrence Lewis arrived at Mount Vernon, his valet had run away. George worried about having the enslaved man—if found—at Mount Vernon. He was sympathetic to his nephew's loss but averse to having a known runaway on the plantation. Slaves who have been re-captured "should never be retained . . . as they are sure to contaminate and discontent others," he wrote. Would George have sold Hercules had he been recaptured? The former President thought the problem of runaways would grow more frequent and saw no solution other than emancipation at the state level: "I wish from my Soul that the Legisla-ture of this State could see the policy of a gradual abolition of Slavery" because "it might prevt much future mischief."[7] The escape of Her-cules and Oney Judge had moved the former President forward in his thinking about emancipation. Martha, on the other hand, was rattled. She was unwilling to give up on enslaved servants, but she wanted the help of another white person who could wield the oversight she thought necessary to keep them in line.

Events over the years had given Martha pause when it came to slaveholding. Slaves wanted freedom, she knew. The Washington and Custis slaves who had run away during the Revolution and during her husband's presidency had made this evident. But instead of granting slaves freedom, she tried to exert tighter control. Closer supervision could prevent acts of disloyalty, especially in Virginia, far from Penn-sylvania, where the law seemed to encourage insubordination and as-pirations for a life beyond slavery.

In August 1797, Martha remained without a head cook or steward. She complained to a niece that she was still serving as her own house-keeper, a job that took up most of her time. Two months later, George described Martha as "exceedingly fatiegued & distressed for want of a good housekeeper." Shortly after that, the Washingtons hired Eleanor Forbes, a white woman who had previously worked for one of Vir-ginia's governors and whose experience apparently included supervis-ing enslaved help.[8]

Martha did not give up the search for Hercules until December 1801. By then her husband had died, and she may have felt less need to entertain lavishly. She had also hired a white cook—one she found satisfactory. "I have thought it therefore better to decline taking Hercules back," she explained in a letter to Colonel Richard Varick of New Jersey, one of many people she and George had enlisted to help in their hunt for Hercules.[9] It was, of course, a moot point. Hercules was entitled to freedom not only under Pennsylvania law but also under George's will.

Martha passed away at noon on 22 May 1802. She had been sickly for some time, and in early May her condition had grown dire. James Craik—the same physician who had been with her husband during his final days—attended her, reporting regularly on her condition to the throngs of people who continued to visit Mount Vernon despite Martha's illness. She lingered for weeks, which gave her time to take communion and to say goodbye to family and friends, as well as to choose a dress for her funeral. She was buried on 25 May beside George in the family vault.[10]

Martha's death left the dower slaves once again subject to separation, perhaps sale. Inheritance laws in Virginia required that the slaves (or their worth in other forms of property) be turned over to the heirs of Daniel Parke Custis—Jacky's children.

George Washington may have hoped that other slaveholders— including members of his and Martha's family—would follow his example and put their slaves on a path toward freedom. Perhaps he believed Martha might accomplish what he had not: convince Washington and Custis relatives to abandon any claim to human property. If so, he would have been greatly disappointed.

Bushrod Washington, George's nephew and an associate Supreme Court justice, inherited Mount Vernon after Martha's death and continued to operate it with slave labor. He worried about the precedent set by his uncle and went out of his way to let the slaves he owned know they could not expect freedom at his death. Bushrod inherited some of the slaves from his father. Others he purchased. Still others were born into bondage at Mount Vernon. Over time, Bushrod came to own more workers than he needed, but by then extravagant spending had landed him in debt. Slave sales became a way to resolve both problems. Bushrod sold his "surplus" slaves, an act that upset the many people who had celebrated the liberation of his uncle's people, as well as members of the American Colonization Society, an organization Bushrod had helped to found in 1816, whose stated purpose was to remove free blacks (including freed slaves) from the United States and send them to Africa. After a Leesburg, Virginia, newspaper published an account of Bushrod's slaves passing through town in chains, bound for labor elsewhere in the South, a host of editors at other papers began to follow the story, none of them happy about the turn of events.[11] Despite George's intent to encourage the emancipation of slaves, his individual act was limited in its effect even at Mount Vernon, where Washington family slaves continued to be subject to sale and separation from loved ones.

It was not just Bushrod who clung to slaveholding. Nelly Custis and Lawrence Lewis did as well. Nelly and Lawrence fell in love and on 22 February 1799 — George's sixty-ninth birthday — married at Mount Vernon. Shortly before the wedding, George formally adopted Nelly, which is why historians sometimes refer to her as his adopted daughter instead of as his step-granddaughter. For a wedding gift, George gave the couple land, a gift he reconfirmed in his will. Nelly later inherited some of Martha's dower slaves, who came to work on the Lewis plantation, known as Woodlawn. As on Bushrod's Mount Vernon plantation, Woodlawn produced crops for market with slave labor, and slaves continued to provide domestic services for Washington descendants.

Nelly was as dependent on slaves as her grandmother. At the time of her marriage to Lawrence, Martha gave her the two Custis family cookbooks that had been handed down to her when she married Daniel Parke Custis.[12] Years later, Nelly compiled another housekeeping book for her daughter, Frances Parke Lewis (called Parke), who had married Edward George Washington Butler and eventually moved with him to a slaveholding plantation in Louisiana. Nelly's book, like the Custis volumes, included recipes for food, medicine, cleaning products, and other household necessities. It was also intended to enlighten Parke about managing her enslaved domestic help.[13] Some of the recipes were apparently family favorites, originating with Nelly or her acquaintances, but others went back generations. Nelly recorded "Old

Dolls Method of Washing Color'd Dresses" and "Old Letty's Peach Chips," for example—the latter a time-consuming means of drying peach slices that only someone with a large contingent of household help would consider making. By having her slaves follow the recipes, Parke could recreate a part of home. "Old Doll" was one of the slaves Martha had brought with her to Mount Vernon when she married George. In such ways, elite women like Martha Washington and her granddaughter Nelly Custis Lewis passed along from one generation to another a manner of living dependent on enslaved help.

Nelly eventually divided her portion of the Custis slaves among her children. When she died at the age of seventy-three, Nelly laid claim to one slave only: Sam, an old man who had given her years of service. In a gesture reminiscent of her beloved adoptive father, she set him free and bequeathed him fifty dollars "as a remembrance from his old mistress." Nelly left no deathbed message.[14]

Wash Custis established a plantation on nearby Custis land that he inherited from his father. Between 1802 and 1818, Wash put slaves to work constructing the mansion still known today as Arlington House. Some of the slaves had grown up at Mount Vernon and been inherited upon Martha's death. Caroline—who had been with the President when he died—and one of her daughters ended up on Wash's estate, as did Frank Lee's son Philip.[15] Wash purchased slaves to add to those he inherited and eventually claimed ownership of about two hundred people who lived and worked on three farms: Arlington House, White House (where Martha had lived during her marriage to Daniel), and Romancoke near Richmond. Perhaps this would not have surprised and disappointed George Washington as much as what transpired later. Wash's daughter Mary Anna in 1831 married Robert E. Lee. Although President Abraham Lincoln offered to appoint Lee to a senior command, the career military man declined. He remained loyal to Virginia when it seceded from the United States in 1861 and took charge of the Confederate Army of Northern Virginia in 1862. His and Mary's sons followed in their father's footsteps by enlisting in the Confederate forces.

Following the emancipation of George Washington's slaves, there was no outpouring of sentiment in Virginia or other parts of the South for ending slavery. His will was widely published and applauded in places, particularly in the North, where slavery was already collapsing, but it triggered no wave of antislavery activity even among his family members or the men who followed him in office. Although a small number of Virginians would do as George Washington had done and manumit their slaves, such individual acts did little to bring an end to slavery in the state or in the nation.

It would be easy for modern readers to dismiss George Washington's decision to free his slaves as ineffectual, but certain slaves did gain freedom through his action. Others clung to the hope that they too might be freed at their owner's death if not before, and hope can nurture resolve to survive difficult circumstances. George Washington, his slaves, and others who heard about his action were able to envision the possibility of a nation without slavery, even if they could not bring it about. Although few other slaveholders freed their slaves, each instance of emancipation kept alive the hope that slavery would end and that the nation would live up to its founding principles espoused in the Declaration authored by Thomas Jefferson.

PART 2

Jefferson

CHAPTER 9

Martha Wayles

Route 5 is a scenic byway that runs between Richmond and Williamsburg in Virginia. Charles City County lies halfway between the two. Contrary to its name, Charles City County is a rural landscape bounded on the south by the James River, where many grand homes of the colonial era still stand. Martha Jefferson grew up here. Her home, on a tobacco plantation known as The Forest, no longer exists, but a state historic marker just off the highway pinpoints the location and identifies it as the place where Thomas Jefferson married the widow Martha Wayles Skelton:

V 15

SCENE OF JEFFERSON'S WEDDING

TWO MILES EAST IS THE SITE OF "THE FOREST," HOME OF MARTHA WAYLES SKELTON, WIDOW OF BATHURST SKELTON. THERE SHE WAS MARRIED TO THOMAS JEFFERSON, JANUARY 1, 1772. THE BRIDAL COUPLE DROVE THROUGH IN THE SNOW TO JEFFERSON'S HOME, MONTICELLO.

The sign implies that Martha Wayles Skelton Jefferson's importance lies in her connection to one of the nation's founders. Certainly in that time and place marriage defined much about a woman, but there is more to know about Martha.

Virginia was a British colony when Martha Wayles was born on 19 October 1748. She came of age, married, and married again before Virginia joined with twelve other colonies to declare independence. Martha experienced the Revolutionary War as a young wife and mother. She died after the decisive American victory at Yorktown in 1781 but before the peace treaty was signed in Paris in 1783. She was only thirty-three years old, too young to have had much influence on national politics or society. Eighteen years were to pass before her widowed husband became President. Still, she saw a lot of history in the making. During her lifetime, her husband served in the Continental Congress, where he wrote the Declaration of Independence; in the Virginia legislature, where he attempted to revise its code of laws; and as Virginia's governor, while war raged about him. Despite her husband's prominence, Martha's life was not all that different from that of other elite women of her time and place.

Women like Martha had wealth and standing, but their lives were circumscribed by social conventions (including expectations of fathers and husbands), the biology of human reproduction, and the contours of slavery. A woman's place was in the domicile of first her father and later her husband, and her domestic duties were undertaken on behalf of family. A high mortality rate meant that most women suffered the loss of family members, including children, more often and at younger ages than do modern American women. They risked their lives in childbirth and died from medical conditions that do not today pose the same threat. Martha's early life was marked by these tragic facts. Her mother died soon after she was born. She was raised by a series of stepmothers who also died. After that, her father's enslaved concubine Elizabeth (Betty) Hemings took charge of Martha's care, along with that of her three half sisters born to her father and his second wife. Betty Hemings simultaneously cared for her own ten children, six of whom were also Martha's half siblings. Truth *can* be stranger than fiction.

An examination of Martha Jefferson's too-short life reveals something of what it was like to live with a "shadow family." Sex across the color line was at once forbidden and common, and women (white and black) lived with the complicated relationships it produced. In Martha's household, some family members enjoyed great wealth and other advantages because of their biological ties. Other family members did not because they were owned. Law, cultural beliefs, and custom shaped the way in which Martha viewed each of her relatives. It was a peculiar way of life, in different ways, for both mistresses and slaves.

Martha Jefferson is today less well known than Martha Washington and Dolley Madison, in large part because she died so young but also because few documents survive in her own handwriting. Thomas Jefferson (or perhaps someone else) destroyed the letters she and he wrote to each other. Only one piece of correspondence is known to exist in Martha's hand: an appeal sent to another Virginia woman asking for her help in alleviating the plight of imprisoned Revolutionary War soldiers. A passage she copied from one of her favorite novels, *Tristram Shandy*, and some musical notations still survive.[1] The Library of Congress holds a leather-bound volume of her household accounts for the years 1772–1782. Other sources include a newspaper advertisement she placed asking the women of Virginia to help clothe Revolutionary War soldiers. Some of the people who knew her recorded their recollections. Important milestones that marked transitions in the lives of women — birth, marriage, childbearing, and death — have been recorded in public and private places, including gravestones in cemeteries. Floor plans exist for the places she lived. Information about her family, as well as the historical context, also help in reconstructing her world.

Although Martha's childhood home no longer stands, the Virginia Historical Society in Richmond has a drawing of the layout of The Forest's first floor as it was when Martha married Thomas Jefferson.[2] The document indicates an elevated house facing south with wide windows to the front and back, one that was large and imposing by colonial standards. Martha's father, John Wayles, built the home to his liking. He had risen from lowly origins by amassing a fortune in the slave trade and marrying well. Martha Eppes Wayles, Martha Jefferson's mother, was from a prominent Virginia family.[3] When she married John in May 1746, she had substantial property, comprising a sizable marriage settlement from her father and an inheritance from a deceased husband. In addition to nine slaves, she owned twelve hundred acres of land, silver, furniture, and a horse and saddle. A contract signed a few days before the marriage gave John the use of his wife's property over his lifetime only. Upon his death, it would revert to her control if she survived him or to her heirs if she did not.[4] Such premarital arrangements, not uncommon among elite families, ensured that a bride's property would stay in her family if after she died her husband remarried and had other children. Absent such an agreement, a husband would retain complete control of his wife's property, and it would pass to his heirs.

Martha Eppes and John Wayles lived in a world in which parents passed their station in life to their children. Daughters from wealthy southern families commonly received movable property (usually slaves), which enhanced the value of any real property (usually land) their husbands brought to the marriage. The Virginia ideal of independent families was rooted in land and bound labor. John Wayles had accumulated property and forged his place in society through exertion of effort and a fortuitous marriage, albeit through the exploitation of others. His wife inherited her property and social standing. Their children could expect to inherit wealth and status from both.

As it turned out, John and Martha Eppes Wayles had only one child, who was named after her mother. Martha Eppes Wayles died on 5 November 1748, six days after giving birth.

In that day, childbirth posed considerable dangers for mother and child. Doctors little understood the role of germs in causing infection, and few took the hygienic precautions that would have protected women from infectious disease. Physicians moved from one bedside to another without washing their hands carefully or seeing to the thorough cleaning of obstetrical instruments. When the inevitable infections followed, people did not blame the doctor but rather assumed fate or Providence had decided the outcome. Sometimes other attendants — especially black midwives or nurses — came in for criticism, but apparently not in this case. The death of Martha Eppes Wayles was not unusual and aroused no suspicion.

John Wayles remarried quickly, and when his second wife, Mary Cocke, died, he remarried again. His third wife, Elizabeth Lomas Skelton, died in 1761, just a year after she married John. By then, Martha was thirteen years old. Her family had expanded to include three half sisters (Elizabeth, Tabitha, and Anne). Another half sister had died in infancy.

Martha's father never remarried after the death of his third wife, but he did not forgo physical intimacy. He took as a concubine Betty Hemings, one of the slaves Martha Eppes had brought with her. The relationship between John and Betty developed soon after his third wife's death (if not before), and Betty gave birth to their first child in 1762. Judging by Martha's later behavior toward Betty and Betty's children, she at least accepted—perhaps condoned—her father's new domestic arrangement.

Betty Hemings, of mixed ancestry, was a light-skinned woman, according to one of the slaves who knew her.[5] She was the daughter of an English ship captain and an African woman and had come to The Forest with her mistress at the age of thirteen. After Martha Eppes Wayles died, Betty Hemings continued to work in the Wayles household while raising her own family. Although already the mother of four—Mary (born 1753), Martin (born 1755), Betty Brown (born 1759), and Nancy (born 1761)—she was still young when her intimate relationship with John Wayles began.

How the relationship started and what Betty thought of it is difficult to say. It is possible that John Wayles banished Betty's husband from her bed and forcefully claimed his place, but Betty might have played a less passive role. It was not unheard of for enslaved women to see opportunity in sexual relationships with owners. The fact that hers with John Wayles lasted over his lifetime and that after his death she formed a similar attachment to another white man suggests she might have accepted John Wayles's overtures or even welcomed them as a means of securing a measure of stability for her family.

Betty Hemings and John Wayles eventually had six children to-gether (Robert, born 1762; James, born 1765; Thenia, born 1767; Critta, born 1769; Peter, born 1770; and Sally, born 1773), all of whom were the half brothers and sisters of Martha Wayles. Under her parents' mar-riage contract, Betty and all of her children belonged to the young mistress Martha Wayles.[6] It seems that Betty worked hard to mother young Martha and ensure she formed an attachment of some sort to her children.

Did Martha Wayles know that her slaves were also her biological relatives? No documents prove conclusively that she did, but as we shall see, she kept them close throughout her life and even wanted them with her when she died. It seems highly unlikely that she did not know who they were.

Only rarely do historians find documentary evidence about sex across the color line. Interracial unions were common enough in Vir-ginia but were not discussed publicly, at least not in polite society. If they were written about, it was usually in an attempt to slander some-one for political reasons or because of a legal dispute over an inheri-tance. Occasionally someone held in bondage sued for freedom on the basis of having a free white parent or grandparent, and at times someone charged that an heir was not legitimately entitled to a be-quest because of his or her racial identity. Disgruntled family members could ask the court to prevent an "illegitimate" relative from inheriting property. This was rare, however. Mostly family, friends, and neighbors whispered privately about such matters and refrained from commit-ting their thoughts to paper, even when a relationship was common knowledge in the neighborhood.

Somehow Betty satisfied a need in Martha that her stepmothers had not. Perhaps her presence and the presence of her children gave Martha a sense of control over her relationships, not unimportant for someone who had lost three mothers in thirteen years and who might have resented her stepmothers' authority.

John Wayles's involvement with the slave trade rendered his connec-tion to the gentry suspect, but his four daughters had the financial means to attract suitors, and all found opportunities to marry into elite Virginia families. With no brothers to contend for the family fortune, each could expect an attractive marriage settlement and later inheritance of a portion of the family's land and labor.

Martha married Bathurst Skelton, the youngest brother of her second stepmother's first husband, on 20 November 1766. She was eighteen; he was twenty-two, the son of James and Jane Meriwether Bathurst Skelton. Bathurst owned a thousand acres of land on Elk Island in Goochland County and slaves to work it. Martha's father grew tobacco with slave labor on the same island. Martha and Bathurst began married life there on a plantation known as Elk Hill. The house overlooking the James River was grand enough to allow the young couple to host visiting family and friends in style.[7]

Marriages were viewed by elites as alliances between families, but this did not mean that patriarchs dictated the choice of marriage partners. Parents and others recognized particularly that a woman's life would be constrained by the circumstances of her husband's wealth, social status, business interests, place of residence, slaveholdings, personality, and temperament. Divorce was difficult, nearly impossible; legal separation of a couple required approval of the state legislature. Families expected relationships to last a lifetime. The choice of spouse was crucial to a couple's happiness.

By all accounts, Martha and Bathurst Skelton were happy together. Their son John was born on 7 November 1767. Martha might have lived out her life at Elk Hill, as wife, mother, and mistress, had not Bathurst died unexpectedly on 30 September 1768 while visiting Williamsburg. The widowed Martha returned with baby John to her paternal home, but visited Elk Hill periodically. Bathurst's will divided his slaves—his principle form of property—evenly between his wife and son, but left them all to Martha should his son die before reaching adulthood.[8] As it happened, John Skelton died of a fever in June 1771 at age three, shortly before his mother married Thomas Jefferson.

Martha did not need to remarry for financial security. Like Martha Dandridge Custis, Martha Wayles Skelton was well provided for by her deceased husband. She also had the support of her father and an inheritance from her mother. At The Forest, members of the Hemings family were available to help care for her child, but in that day, only older women tended to remain single following the death of a spouse.

Martha Wayles Skelton married Thomas Jefferson in the drawing room of The Forest on New Year's Day 1772. The Reverend William Coutts performed the Anglican ceremony that united the couple. No portrait survives of Martha, but she has been described as attractive and slender, of medium height, with auburn hair and hazel eyes. She and her tall, thin, red-haired groom must have made a striking couple as they stood together and said their vows. She promised to obey, love, honor, and serve her husband. He pledged to love, honor, and comfort his wife. Three days of music and dancing followed as guests celebrated the marriage and the New Year.[9]

Betty Hemings and her seventeen-year-old son Martin helped serve the guests.[10] This posed a challenge since food had to be brought from the kitchen, which was outside the main house. Servants braved bitter cold, balancing plates and bottles as they made their way up the back steps and through the door into the center hallway.

The newlyweds did not leave for Monticello until mid-January. En route they stopped at Shirley plantation to have their carriage repaired and at Tuckahoe plantation to see family. Thomas Jefferson's manservant Jupiter Evans probably rode with his master. Betty Brown — Betty Hemings's fourteen-year-old daughter, unrelated to Martha — no doubt traveled with her mistress. The last leg of the journey was on horseback through a blinding snowstorm. Accounts suggest that the Jeffersons made this part of the journey alone and arrived at a cold, dark house late at night, the slaves at Monticello having already gone to bed. If the story is true, it may have been the only time Martha traveled without servants. It was unusual for an elite woman to travel without a maid.[11]

The home awaiting Martha on that January night was more symbolic of her husband's aspirations than of achievement. In 1768 Thomas had begun building a great country estate, a European-style house on the top of a mountain in Albemarle County, Virginia, on land inherited from his father. Four years later it was still more construction site than mansion. Like her husband, Martha could dream of the elegant estate that would mark the couple's prominent place in society, but when she first arrived the living space consisted of a one-room cottage that had served as Thomas's bachelor home. He once described the structure (today called the South Pavilion) as hall, parlor, kitchen, bedchamber, and study all in one, but the kitchen was actually located in the cellar.

Visitors to Monticello today can see a reproduction of the Jeffersons' first home. It is not open to the public, but, peering through the glass door, one can get a sense of how it might have been furnished with a large bedstead and an upholstered chair. A crib for an infant sits just inside the doorway. A sign says that Thomas Jefferson had the finest upholsterer in Williamsburg make "bed furniture" (i.e., curtains and counterpanes) for the room in anticipation of his bride's arrival. Martha and Thomas's first child, a daughter called Patsy, was born here and may have slept in the crib on display.

This is all true, but the newlyweds did not stay long at the South Pavilion. Thomas Jefferson was prosperous by any measure. Born at Shadwell plantation in 1743, he had inherited about thirty slaves from his father's estate when he turned twenty-one, along with an estimated five thousand acres of land. Since his father's death, some of his enslaved women had given birth, which increased his slaveholdings. Thomas calculated his and his wife's financial worth as about equal. But Martha was accustomed to a more lavish and genteel way of life than he was prepared to provide. While Thomas had been living as a bachelor in a one-room outbuilding, she had enjoyed all the privileges of a gentrified life, first at her father's plantation and later at Elk Hill. The difference was not simply in the physical structure but also in the home's furnishings and other trappings, including the presence of trained household help. Thomas had slaves, but he did not have a trained domestic staff of the type found in Virginia's grandest homes. Because Martha preferred Elk Hill, she and Thomas lived there for much of their first two years of marriage. And when business or politics took Thomas to Williamsburg, Martha went home to The Forest.[12]

Elk Hill stood in stark contrast to Monticello in other, important ways. Monticello was undergoing constant construction. Building went slowly, in part because materials such as windows were hard to come by. Elk Hill was already an elegantly furnished mansion, and its amenities allowed the Jeffersons to host the kind of parties favored by Virginia's elite. For example, the Jeffersons could hold hunting parties with fox and hounds at Elk Hill—an activity more to Martha's liking than her husband's. (Thomas hunted small game from time to time and kept guns for this purpose. Like other planters, he often took along a young slave to help when he went after squirrels and partridges and such. But these were individual excursions, not the formal parties that entertained Virginia's gentry.) Martha enjoyed playing whist, a card game for four players.[13] Dancing too was popular at gatherings of the gentry. During the Jeffersons' first years of marriage, Monticello suffered by comparison, although eventually Martha and her husband would transform Monticello into a home even grander than Elk Hill.

CHAPTER 10

Mistress of Monticello I

Gradually a mansion emerged from the construction materials Thomas Jefferson had assembled on his mountain. Martha and her husband moved into the home, dubbed Monticello (Italian for "little mountain"), two years after they married. A 1782 visitor described the structure as unique in Albemarle County. One entered "through two porticoes ornamented with columns." A drawing room took up most of the ground floor. Above it was a library. Two wings off the ground floor led to "the kitchen, offices, etc." The home was half as large as the one that sits atop the mountain today. No dome crowned the Monticello Martha knew. She died long before her husband embarked on his ambitious plan to enlarge the house, but even without the dome and extra square footage, Monticello was a home worthy of notice.[1] But the newlyweds understood that it would take more than bricks and mortar to earn a place among Virginia's elite. They needed a household staff. Thomas Jefferson may have believed it was possible to make do and live happily with one or two house servants, as he once wrote,[2] but he and Martha aspired to more. A grand home required a full complement of household help.

At the time of their marriage, Martha and Thomas Jefferson each had personal attendants they had known since childhood: Betty Brown and Jupiter Evans. Betty Brown, the second oldest daughter of Betty Hemings, was young, pretty, light-skinned, and skilled in the dressing room and in the parlor—all valued attributes in a lady's maid. She traveled with her mistress wherever Martha went. Similarly, Jupiter Evans traveled with his owner. Jupiter had been born at Shadwell around the same time as Thomas and trained from childhood to act as his valet. Jupiter's varied duties in adulthood included paying fees for ferry crossings and carriage repairs; purchasing books, wig powder, and other items; and paying the people who baked his master's bread, mended his shoes, and washed his clothing when he was away from home. Jupiter was also responsible for keeping his master's clothes clean and in good repair. He shaved Thomas and dressed his hair.[3]

Soon after their marriage, if not before, Martha and Thomas discussed enlarging the household staff. Within a month of the wedding, Martha was pregnant, making the matter seem urgent. Martha made up her mind to acquire, in her husband's words, "a favorite house woman of the name of Ursula," whom she learned was to be sold at an estate sale fifty miles away in Cumberland County. She sent her husband in the dead of winter to make the purchase. He returned in January 1773 with Ursula Granger and her two sons—fourteen-year-old George Jr. and five-year-old Bagwell—having paid 210 pounds for the three of them. Ursula had a husband in Cumberland County who belonged to a different owner. Thomas arranged to purchase George Granger Sr. for an additional 130 pounds. Not all slaves who were sold managed to stay with family members, but Ursula was an accomplished housekeeper. Women with her set of skills were considered crucial to the functioning of an elite household. George Sr., too, was a proficient worker and said to be reliable. The 340 pounds Thomas Jefferson paid for the family must have seemed a reasonable price for ensuring that his family's domestic needs would be met by capable hands.[4]

Patsy, born 27 September 1772, had been failing to thrive. (She was named Martha after her mother but called Patsy.) She "recovered almost instantaneously" at six months when Ursula began to breastfeed her. The house woman's ability to act as wet nurse may have been one of the reasons Martha was so keen to have her specifically, not just any competent house woman. Martha must have known that Ursula was pregnant or had recently given birth—her son Archy was born in early 1773—and would be able to nurse an infant. Thomas Jefferson attributed Patsy's improved health to "a good breast of milk,"[5] which emphasized Ursula Granger's functional purpose over her personhood.

Together, Martha Jefferson and Ursula Granger worked to realize the Jeffersons' aspiration to live like gentry. Ursula was already trained as a pastry chef when she joined the Jefferson household. In the kitchen, she cooked cakes and tarts and other family favorites. Few documents mention Martha at Monticello, but one of them—a memoir by Ursula's son Isaac (who was born after the Jeffersons purchased the Grangers and later took the surname Jefferson)—describes her reading a recipe to Ursula while holding a "cookery book in hand."[6] Mistresses consulted cookbooks for elaborate dishes, not everyday fare. Martha's reading of recipes indicates that she and Ursula were trying out unfamiliar dishes. The two would have had no need to consult written recipes to make food that appeared regularly on the table, such as turkey or biscuits or sweet peas.

Martha and Ursula probably took stock of the ingredients on hand before Martha decided on a menu that reflected the Jeffersons' tastes and local customs for entertaining. Martha would have stayed at least some of the time to watch Ursula cook. Her presence helped ensure that Ursula did not waste or confiscate food, but it also allowed Martha to learn how the dishes should be prepared. Ursula was no mere scullion, following each step as her mistress dictated. Written recipes did not often include complete directions, and the quantities of ingredients could be vague. Cooks did not have modern stoves or ovens with precisely regulated temperatures. Seasonings would need to be adjusted, depending on whether herbs were fresh or dried, vinegars tart or sweet, and other factors. It was up the cook to figure out how to make the recipe work. Cooking a new dish was always an experiment.

The love that Martha and Thomas are said to have shared was born of many things, including a fondness for music and literature, a desire for family and intimacy, and a vision for a country estate that would announce their place among Virginia's elite. Thomas Jefferson well knew that extravagant food was associated with gentry status. His interest in the culinary arts lasted a lifetime, not only because he took pleasure in eating but also because setting a fine table supported his ambitions. Martha's interest in fancy cooking and her desire to have a cook who could execute elaborate dishes shows that they held this goal in common.

Martha and Ursula's culinary efforts included brewing beer. Every two weeks, they made fifteen gallons. In this, they were like many other Virginians who prepared alcoholic beverages for household consumption. Early Americans considered alcohol a healthy alternative to water. The home brew tended to be darker, sweeter, and more alcoholic than the commercially produced beer of today. A recipe penned by George Washington in 1757 demonstrates the amount of work involved. The brewer boiled bran and hops for three hours, strained the mixture, and then added molasses while the brew was "boiling Hot." After the mixture cooled, she added yeast and waited for the beer to ferment before putting it into bottles.[7]

Ursula's workspace extended beyond the kitchen. She supervised the bottling of cider and beer and its storage in the cellar. In the smokehouse, she supervised the curing of meat. She washed and ironed clothing in the yard, presumably with the help of other servants. The Jeffersons dutifully recorded the results of Ursula's labor, as well as that of George Sr., who proved to be as capable as his wife. George Sr. gradually assumed major responsibilities outside of the home, rising to become the only black overseer Jefferson ever employed.[8]

The world in which Martha Jefferson and Ursula Granger lived and worked was one in which—in the words of one former slave—the owner's children "had dainties and we had crusts." It was also a world in which a slaveholding parent could claim a black breast for a white child. Once fed Ursula's breast milk, Patsy thrived. But Ursula's infant Archy died. It is not clear how long he lived, but he had passed away before the end of his second summer, in 1774.[9] By then, Martha Jefferson had given birth to another daughter, Jane. Ursula helped raise all of her mistress's children, and she may have suckled Jane as she had Patsy.

There is no way of knowing whether Ursula's breastfeeding of Patsy or Jane contributed to Archy's demise. Perhaps he caught one of the contagious diseases that circulated on plantations in Virginia during the summer months. Or maybe he met death by accident, tumbling into a fireplace or a well. Whatever the case, his mother's many duties could not have helped his chances for survival. Enslaved mothers (and fathers) often lacked time to supervise their children and means to provide for their nourishment, even when the mother was not acting as wet nurse to an owner's child. Jane Jefferson did not survive infancy either, dying in October 1775.

The death of Martha's father in May 1773 increased the financial standing of the Jeffersons and set in motion the transfer of the Hemings family—including his mixed-race children—from The Forest to Monticello. John Wayles's youngest child, Sally Hemings, was born the year her father died. His oldest, Martha Jefferson, was a married lady of twenty-three who (with her husband) would inherit Sally and five other half siblings.

John Wayles held considerable property at the time of his death: more than twenty thousand acres of land and some three hundred slaves.[10] A will written while he was married to his third wife specified that no division of property could occur until after her death. Elizabeth Lomax Skelton Wayles was to have the slaves she brought to the marriage, as well as the use over her lifetime of her husband's plantation and twenty-five additional slaves, including Betty Hemings and the cook Jenney.[11] By the terms of the contract between John Wayles and Martha's mother, Betty Hemings and Jenney belonged to Martha Jefferson. This provision in her father's will may have been the impetus behind Martha's dying request that her husband not remarry and submit their children to the rule of a stepmother—a story that will be taken up in a later chapter. If Thomas Jefferson married again and died before his second wife, the Hemingses might become the property of his widow, who might sell them, give them away, or bequeath them to her heirs.

John Wayles had intended to update his will after Elizabeth died in 1761, but the closest he came to doing so was a codicil dated 12 February 1772 in which he added his son-in-law Thomas Jefferson to the list of executors and made a few additional bequests. By then, John Wayles was grandfather to three infants: Patsy Jefferson and two grandsons (Richard Eppes and John Wayles Eppes) born to one of his other daughters. Each of them, according to the codicil, was to have "a female slave between twelve & fifteen," to be purchased on the market "within five years after my death" and not taken from his existing stock.[12]

Why would John Wayles leave each of his grandchildren money to purchase an enslaved girl? There were multiple economic incentives: a girl between the ages of twelve and fifteen would be old enough to begin adult work and be on the verge of sexual maturation. The buyer of a prepubescent girl could expect monetary reward in the form of babies born in bondage, while avoiding the problems that came with a slave who already had children: mothers with children had either to be purchased together or parted from one another. What seems cruel today—separating a young teen from her family—would have been viewed as compassionate by slaveholders, who had no problem separating children on the verge of maturation from their parents. Only the separation of younger children from a mother provoked concern.

Martha's inheritance included 135 people and two large plantations: Elk Hill and Willis Creek. Added to Thomas's plantations, the inheritance catapulted the couple into Virginia's wealthiest class. By his own tally, the master of Monticello held 187 men, women, and children as property,[13] a number that did not vary significantly over the rest of his life. Thomas Jefferson became Albemarle County's second largest slaveholder and assumed membership in the class of men who were expected to rule the colony—within the constraints imposed by the king of England.

John Wayles did not attempt to free any members of the Hemings family. To do so would have required legislative approval (Virginia had not yet liberalized its manumission laws allowing freed slaves to remain in the state), and he may not have wished to flaunt his relationship with Betty in this way. More likely, he did not think the Hemingses were his to liberate. They belonged to his daughter Martha. It was one thing to lend his widow the use of Betty Hemings for a number of years, as specified in his will. It was quite another to deed her away. Had he done so, Martha and her husband could have objected, and it is likely a court would have sided with the Jeffersons.

Although John Wayles made no attempt to free his shadow family, there is evidence that he thought about his children's future, or at least that of his sons. His oldest, Robert (also called Bob) and James, learned to read and write. The youngest, Peter, age three when Wayles died, might have learned as well had his father lived longer. Slaves who learned to read and write with an owner's approval were trusted to put the skill to work on the owner's behalf, but literacy proved useful for freedmen as well. Robert and James enjoyed special privileges. They traveled by themselves, as did their older half brother Martin, and at times they found work and kept the money they earned. As we shall see, Robert and James eventually found paths to freedom. Years later, Eston Hemings, one of Sally's sons, named his first son (born in 1835) after his great-grandfather, strongly suggesting that the family saw John Wayles as an important progenitor.[14]

In January 1774 Betty and at least six of her children arrived at Monticello already trained in the ways of wealthy households and took over most of the domestic positions in the house. Betty Hemings's oldest daughter, Mary, was a seamstress, and Betty Brown probably became a parlor maid. Their half sisters Critta and Sally, daughters of John Wayles, personally attended Martha Jefferson and her daughters while practicing the fine sewing expected of lady's maids.[15]

Betty Heming's oldest son, Martin, assumed the position of butler despite his reputation for being prickly. James and Peter Hemings worked in the house under their half brother's supervision. Robert became Thomas's valet, replacing Jupiter Evans, who took over as hostler and keeper of the stables. Robert assumed his duties at the age of twelve and accompanied his master to Philadelphia when Thomas Jefferson served in the Continental Congress. The two were residing at Seventh and Market Street when Thomas famously wrote, "all men are created equal." Robert was one of more than 180 slaves owned by Thomas Jefferson at the time. He provided many personal services for his master, including the dressing of his hair. In 1784 Jefferson placed him with a barber in Annapolis so that he could learn the latest techniques.[16]

Martin's duties as butler were extensive. He assumed responsibility for keeping the household staff in line, most of them relatives. As keeper of the keys, he had access to storage areas and checked to ensure that wine and other alcoholic beverages, food, and valuables such as china and silver did not disappear. Like other slaveholders, the Jeffersons counted and recounted their possessions to ensure that their slaves were not taking items without authorization. In 1774 Thomas Jefferson tallied his bottles of rum to see whether Martin could be trusted.[17] Every black slave was thought to require a white superintendent.

Some household slaves acquired through the settlement of the Wayles estate were not Hemingses. Suck, a sixteen-year-old who came to Monticello to cook, was married to Jupiter. The two had probably met at The Forest when Thomas was courting Martha. Isabel Hern worked in the house, while her husband David worked at multiple outdoor tasks.[18] The Grangers continued to work hard, she indoors and he outside.

With the addition of the Hemings family and other domestic slaves from The Forest, the home atop Jefferson's mountain began to take on the semblance of an elaborate country estate. Duties became more specialized as the newcomers took on positions found only in the grandest of homes. A sous chef and scullions entered the kitchen, and a butler answered the door. Nursemaids looked after the growing number of Jefferson children. As more help arrived, Martha devoted less time to physical tasks such as dressing her children and making beer. Instead, she supervised staff members who cared for her children, made soap, sewed clothes, butchered and cured meat, cleaned the home, and did a host of other chores, at Monticello and on the other plantations owned by the Jeffersons.

In bringing the Hemings family to work at Monticello, Martha Jefferson, like Martha Washington, demonstrated a willingness to tolerate slavery's most unsavory side so long as the work of the family members advanced her own position and those of her husband and children. For their part, the Hemingses—as will be discussed more fully later—took advantage of their positions close to Martha and Thomas to maintain their family ties, advance their education, improve their working conditions, and better their standard of living. A few even achieved freedom, although it was a long time coming. As more Hemingses were born, they took on yet more positions in the house.

Martha Jefferson's account book shows her keeping track of expenses, inventorying possessions, and making note of butchering and other work done at Monticello, Elk Hill, Bedford, and (after her mother-in-law died in 1776) Shadwell. Her entries in the small leather-bound volume start with her marriage to Thomas in 1772 and end with her death ten years later. There were some gaps. She made no entries during the two years she lived in Williamsburg and Richmond while her husband served as governor, for example. The account book's thirty pages reveal Martha Jefferson to have been a typical, wealthy plantation mistress reigning over her domain. She planned ahead to feed and clothe her family and the Jefferson slaves; made sure the household did not run short of linens, candles, and other necessities; and tried to prevent the unauthorized taking of goods from the pantry, storehouse, and smokehouse. Martha monitored the work of her domestic servants to ensure they met her standard for productivity.

Given the size of her staff, it is unlikely Martha undertook much physical labor herself. She would have given orders about such matters as when to kill a goose for the table and what to do with its feathers, and perhaps told the cook how she wanted the goose prepared and other slaves which pillows needed stuffing, but ladies did not personally slaughter animals or perform other unclean or arduous labor. Later, after Martha died and Thomas Jefferson went to France as minister plenipotentiary, he expressed revulsion at witnessing white women in the countryside engaged in hard physical labor. He thought such work better suited to men or servants. His remark suggests that he never witnessed Martha hard at work. She may have pitched in to help Ursula Granger cook fancy dishes, but she left the more taxing chores to others. Monticello's enslaved women, like its enslaved men, regularly engaged in difficult labor. Strictures about proper work for ladies never applied to bondwomen.[19]

The fact that Martha did not perform arduous labor did not mean that she was aimless or idle. Clothing her family and the Jefferson slaves took considerable time and effort. Martha purchased some fabric and clothes and supervised the manufacture of others. In the process, she made choices that reinforced the custom of distinguishing social class through dress.

Wearing homespun became a patriotic duty during the Revolutionary War. Foreign goods could not be imported legally and were difficult to obtain through extralegal channels. Virginia women had to make or make do — to manufacture textiles at home, have them made locally, or recycle what they had on hand. Most elite women did all three, and Martha was no exception.

The Jeffersons hired a weaver in 1781 to turn cotton, hemp, flax, and wool into various grades of cloth for garments and household items. Coarse cloth was for the workers, better cloth for the house servants and children, and fine cloth for the master and mistress. In the early part of that year, the weaver made "hemp linen, cotton, and 'coarse linen'" for the slaves. "Mixt cloth" clothed the younger children and the house servants. "Fine mixt cloth" was to be turned into a coat for Thomas Jefferson; "Fine linen" was for his shirts and Patsy's shifts. It went like this for much of the year, except for November and December, when the concentration was on linen to clothe the field slaves.[20]

Martha kept a written record not only of woven cloth but of unspun fibers. Flax, hemp, wool, and cotton were grown (and probably processed) at Elk Hill and Shadwell plantations, in addition to Monticello. Someone, presumably Jefferson slaves, carded the fibers and spun them into thread before they were turned over to the weaver. Spinning was almost always an important part of textile production on plantations like Monticello. In 1775 Monticello's Aggy spent six days a week spinning yarn.[21]

Once cloth was made or purchased, it had to be cut and sewn. Bedclothes, tablecloths, and pillows, along with garments, were made, stored, counted, and distributed according to the needs of the household, its guests, and its slaves. In September 1777, Martha counted twenty sheets: two at Elk Hill, two at Bedford, and the rest at Monticello. She inventoried everything from ruffled shirts and gowns to handkerchiefs and nightcaps. Among the Jeffersons' possessions were

"2 new clokes & one bonnet," "13 pr of white silk stockings," "5 red waistcoats," and "15 old rags." Fabric maintained value, even when it was well used.[22]

Martha distributed clothing to the slaves each year at the end of June. In 1774 she gave Ursula Granger two outfits but no apron. Mary Hemings and a woman listed in the records as Siller also got two outfits each, along with aprons. Ursula and Bet (probably Betty Brown) each received a white shift. Bob (probably Robert Hemings) got two pairs of breeches and two white shirts. Martin Hemings got four shirts, three of them white. Jupiter Evans received four shirts, two of which were white. Ned and Jim each got a pair of trousers. Juno and Lund got coats.[23]

The dress of Monticello's domestic servants set them apart from the slaves who toiled in the field. The housemaids wore patterned clothing made of muslin, Irish linen, and calico, while the majority of enslaved women at Monticello dressed in osnaburg. The Hemings women and other house servants wore knitted stockings, in contrast to the ill-fitting woven stockings worn by the majority of enslaved women. The male servants—Martin, Robert, and James—also wore distinctive clothing, some of it custom-made or hand-me-downs from the master.[24]

Making regular entries into an account book allowed Martha to guard against shortages of household supplies, as well as pilfering. In the first five months of 1777, she recorded the making of 220 candles. She already had 134 stored in the cellar.[25] Her records helped her determine when her slaves would need to make more. If stores seemed to diminish too quickly, she could hold the help accountable. Everyone knew that at times slaves took items they needed or wanted. When federal officials interviewed former slaves during the 1930s to record their stories for future generations, they elicited numerous confessions from people who said that they had, in the antebellum era, taken or "borrowed" items from masters and mistresses.[26] A black market flourished throughout the South, making it possible for slaves to trade or sell purloined items. Martha's habit of counting food, clothing, china, pewter, and other household goods was considered best practice in the management of slaveholding households. Yet it is not clear that frequent inventories prevented unauthorized taking or that slaves were always to blame when supplies ran low.

It was difficult to keep accurate records, particularly for food and other consumable goods. Martha tried, however, especially for valuable foods like meat, sugar, and flour (as opposed to, say, peas and beans). She noted in her account book, for example, each time she opened a barrel of flour or broke a loaf of sugar. On her return home from visiting in the summer of 1773, Martha made this note: "a loaf of sugar & barrel of flour opened in my absence."[27] But there was more to monitoring stores of food than jotting down brief records here and there. To know if food was missing, a mistress had to keep track of all that had been consumed legitimately. Shortly after the note about sugar and flour being opened in her absence, Martha wrote, "eat 6 hams 4 shoulders 2 middlings in 3 weeks & 2 days." But each week was not the same. The amount of meat eaten depended on such factors as who was at home and whether guests had come by. The amount of sugar used depended on what foods had been prepared.[28] Because the help made preserves now and then, "normal" sugar consumption could vary a lot week to week.

Martha took special care in overseeing the slaughtering of animals, particularly hogs, cows, and sheep. She was not necessarily physically present when butchering occurred. After all, large numbers of animals were butchered on several Jefferson farms. But she knew the number of hogs that were killed and could estimate the amount of meat, lard, and tallow that should have been produced. She not only needed to plan meals for her family and guests but to make sure meat was available for distribution to the slaves. As she inventoried the ham, bacon, and pork in the smokehouse, she designated certain cuts "for our own eating" and others for the workers.[29] In January through March 1778, ninety-two hogs were butchered at the Monticello, Elk Hill, and Bedford plantations. In addition, twenty-three cows and one sheep were slaughtered. Sixty gallons of beef fat were stored in the cellar at Monticello. Fifty-two pounds of tallow (used to make candles and soap) arrived at Monticello from Elk Hill.[30]

Housekeeping was both time-consuming and tedious, as Martha's account book makes clear. On one page she wrote directions for obtaining rennet, a substance found in the lining of a calf's stomach that is used to curdle milk and in the process of making cheese or junket. It involved butchering a calf and extracting its stomach, and required careful handling of the curds. This part of the process alone took more than three days. When it was finished, there was no cheese, only the rennet to make the cheese:

> Let the calf suck just before you kill it, then wash the bag and curd very clean, salt it and let it lie three days, put the curd in the bag with a little mace, and put the bag into a linen bag, when you use the curd boil the water, and let stand till it is cold, then put the curd in, and let it lay twelve hours, then salt your curd and put it in the bag.

On the next page of the account book, Martha recorded directions for making cream cheese.[31] Soft and hard cheeses were often made at home. Both required a commitment of time and a readiness to adjust the technique based on observation. Women like Martha kept busy, despite having plenty of household help.

A plantation home — even that of a grandee — was very much a workspace. From Martha's records and other sources we can get a sense of how Monticello sounded and smelled on a workday. The crunch of wagon wheels and the shouted greetings of the wagoners who brought goods to the plantation can be easily imagined. The men probably laughed and cursed as they unloaded the carts and told news of friends and family at Elk Hill or Bedford. Their voices would have mingled with the talk of women doing laundry in the yard, the occasional squawk of a chicken about to be slaughtered, the tinkle of cowbells, and the sound of a barking dog. Smells emanating from the kitchen might have included the fragrance of bread baking in the oven, the stench of cheese in the making, or the aroma of hops beginning to boil. Walking down Mulberry Row, where many of the workshops and other outbuildings stood, a blindfolded visitor could easily detect the smokehouse where meat hung to cure, as well as the privy where workers went to relieve themselves.[32] Enslaved children added to the sounds and smells on the plantation street as they went about their chores or played after work was done. Inside the mansion or off in the distance, a baby might cry for its mother.

What type of slave mistress was Martha Jefferson? It is difficult to know. Household accounts tell us only so much, but her efforts to keep track of the consumption of food and other items at Monticello suggest that she was exacting. She appears to have been a difficult task-master when it came to her children. Her husband once reprimanded her for demanding too much of little Patsy. After she grew up and had children of her own, Patsy told her own daughter that Martha Jefferson displayed a "vivacity of temper" and could be severe.[33] Given this, it would be surprising to learn that Martha Jefferson was anything other than a demanding mistress who sometimes lost her temper with the enslaved help.

After work for their owner was done, slaves returned to their quarters where loved ones awaited them, along with additional chores. At Monticello, the plantation street near the mansion (Mulberry Row) included shelter for house slaves and their families, as well as workshops and storehouses. During Martha's time, wooden barracks housed multiple families. Later in the century, the dwellings would undergo a transformation. One-room cabins for individual families replaced the larger barracks and were said to represent an improvement in the slaves' standard of living.[34] Perhaps they did, though both barracks and cabins were cramped and cold in winter and hot in summer.

Ursula and George Granger's three sons (George Jr., Bagwell, and Isaac) grew up on Mulberry Row, as did a new generation of Hemingses. Here, enslaved people assumed identities as family member and friend. Children learned from their elders how to survive in a dangerous world, as well as how to have fun telling stories, singing, and dancing. Evenings and Sundays (typical times when enslaved people were "off duty") allowed time for gardening, fishing, raising poultry, cooking, bathing, worshipping, and a host of other activities that defined enslaved people as more than the mistress's cook, seamstress, or laundress. On Mulberry Row, and wherever slaves lived, they loved, laughed, fought, cried, competed, and engaged in behavior that re-

Pages from Martha Jefferson's household account book.

flected their human condition rather than their enslaved status. As Martha and Thomas Jefferson assembled their household staff on the mountain, they brought together a community of slaves who forged ties of friendship and kinship that enriched their lives. Only a select few — most of them Hemingses — would ever break out of slavery, but the others did more than survive: they resisted the dehumanization that enslavement implied.

Some of the activities undertaken by slaves in their off hours had economic value. Slaves raised chickens and ducks and grew peas and watermelons for their own tables, but some they sold or traded for cash or goods. They often used Martha Jefferson's need for poultry, eggs, and vegetables to their own advantage by selling directly to her. During her first summer at Monticello, Martha acquired almost a hundred chickens from them, along with eggs. Over the years, Martha continued to purchase or trade with slaves for poultry. Old Jenny, Juno,

Jackson, Squire, Jupiter, Phill, and Will were among the slaves who traded chickens for bacon in 1777. Martha recorded these transactions in her ledger in a clear, even hand, although an occasional word is indecipherable, including the name of another slave who traded four chickens for bacon that year.[35]

Martha's account book shows her securing food for Monticello's family and guests by borrowing or purchasing items from neighbors as well as slaves. In January 1774 she borrowed ten pounds of sugar from her mother-in-law. A month later she repaid Jane Jefferson the sugar she owed and sent a loaf to Elk Hill.[36] Martha's purchases included butter, beef, poultry, eggs, coffee, corn, and wheat, but in the summer of 1777 she had poultry very much on her mind (and table). In addition to chickens, she purchased outright nineteen ducks, ten geese, and seven dozen eggs, all apparently raised by slaves. The eggs came from Elk Hill. "Mr Scot" furnished eight more chickens. Duck was more popular table fare than goose. Martha had fourteen ducks killed to eight geese. She also had three shoats, one lamb, and one sheep slaughtered. On the page in her account book where she jotted down these quantities, she also sketched a picture of two ducks,[37] suggesting that she had time during the day for less practical matters than feeding and clothing her family. Martha's account book obscures as much as it reveals, however. The Jeffersons built and staffed the mansion at Monticello in the years preceding the Revolutionary War. Although at first the war seemed far away, eventually it made its way to their mountain.

CHAPTER 11

War in Virginia

American and British forces clashed on the coast of Virginia at the start of the Revolutionary War, but until 1779 the state was largely spared from military action. Both Jeffersons became involved in the war effort nevertheless: he joined the governing body that declared independence and organized the military force that made it real; she restructured everyday routines at Monticello in response to interruptions in overseas trade and out of a sense of patriotism. Rather than guns, the Jeffersons fought the British with paper documents and weaving looms. But in 1779 the war returned to Virginia. The British marshaled large numbers of troops to subdue the state and take the capital. Thomas and Martha Jefferson, having witnessed firsthand no fighting until then, saw their lives and property threatened. The arrival of the British in central Virginia held a different meaning for the slaves, some of whom saw opportunities for freedom.

After two years of serving in the Continental Congress, Thomas Jefferson had been elected to the Virginia House of Delegates. From 1776 to 1779 he lived part of the year in Williamsburg at the two-story brick house belonging to George and Elizabeth Wythe. It was during these years that he proposed (as part of a general revision of the Virginia code of laws) to end slavery. He was likely influenced in his thinking by his former teacher and mentor and now host. Though born into a slaveholding family, George Wythe held a lifelong aversion to slavery.

When government business took Thomas Jefferson away from

Albemarle County, Martha and Patsy did not usually go with him, but mother and daughter made an exception when he moved to the Wythes' elegant home situated along the Palace Green.[1] During these years, the Jeffersons returned to Monticello when the governing body was not in session, and Martha gave birth to two children, a son born in 1777, who lived only seventeen days, and a daughter, Polly (named Mary and later called Maria), the following year.

Thomas Jefferson was elected governor of Virginia in 1779 and re-elected in 1780. He, Martha, Patsy, and Polly moved into the Governor's Palace along with some of their slaves. The palace was a Georgian-style structure of more than three thousand square feet—quite large by colonial standards. It had been the center of Virginia's high society during the colonial period, and its elegant balls had attracted George and Martha Washington along with other men and women of standing from near and far.

Not much is known about Martha Jefferson's time as Virginia's first lady or her support of the patriot cause. When asked by Martha Washington to help clothe the Continental soldiers, she put her slaves to work spinning, weaving, and sewing garments needed by the men. One of the few surviving examples of her handwriting is a letter written in 1780 to another Virginia woman, Eleanor Madison (wife of the Reverend James Madison, not to be confused with the future President), asking her to do the same.[2]

The war was not going well for the Americans in 1779. The British burned Portsmouth and Norfolk in May. The governor and state assembly moved Virginia's capital from Williamsburg to Richmond in the hope that the inland location would make it more difficult for the British to seize the site of government. The Jeffersons with their slaves moved into a rented property on Shockoe Hill.[3] The strategy failed. In late December 1779, the British launched a full-scale assault on Richmond, and the Jeffersons woke up on New Year's Day to news of a pending attack. The governor hesitated to call out the militia and waited for confirmation of the report. The British were just outside the city by the time he acted; he and members of the state assembly barely managed to escape. After ransacking Richmond, the troops moved on in search of the governor and what was left of the legislature, whose members had reconvened in Charlottesville. The Jeffersons stayed ahead of the troops and reconnected at Monticello.

The British targeted Thomas Jefferson not only because he was governor but because he was a member of the Continental Congress. His hand was all over the Declaration of Independence. There was worry that Martha and her daughters might be overtaken on their harrowing journey home. The trusted Jupiter Evans transported them safely, but there was talk that wherever the British troops went, they played "the very Devil with the girls and even old women to satisfy their libidinous appetites. There is scarcely a virgin to be found in the part of the country that they have passed through," according to Virginia politician Thomas Nelson.[4] Although the idea that the British could or would sexually violate every woman they encountered seems far-fetched, the danger of assault was real enough.

The Jeffersons' fears about the fate of women in the British path apparently extended only to white women. Some members of Monticello's household staff who had accompanied the Jeffersons to the state capital were left behind in the city, including the Grangers and sisters Betty Brown and Mary Hemings. Mary had two children with her: seven-year-old Daniel Farley and two-year-old Molly. Suck Evans, the cook, was also in Richmond with her child. Her husband, Jupiter, had been serving as hostler and coachman in the capital, aided by John Hemings, Betty's youngest son. Betty's oldest, Martin, had assumed the duty of butler, the position he held at home. His brothers Robert and James had come to Richmond as personal attendants to the governor. The men all left with the Jeffersons except for George Granger Sr., who stayed with the enslaved women and children. It was he who met the British troops when they arrived at the door of the Shockoe Hill home. The British marched the slaves to Yorktown on foot.[5] It was a long walk—more than sixty miles—for all but the youngest children, who rode in wagons.

The British scoured the countryside between the capital and Monticello in pursuit of Jefferson and other government officials. The Jeffersons had stopped at Monticello only briefly before moving further west. Martha and the girls and two slaves went to a nearby plantation and then to Poplar Forest, Jefferson's Bedford County property.

Thomas himself lingered so long at Monticello that he only narrowly evaded capture, but he soon joined Martha and his children. Martin Hemings remained at Monticello and refused to tell the British where his master had gone despite the threat of being shot. He managed to hide the family silver under Monticello's front porch before the British arrived, trapping a slave under the floorboards in his haste. The story of Martin's bravery has been handed down by generations of Jeffersons, who have emphasized the loyalty of family slaves in the face of British danger.

Yet elsewhere a different story was unfolding. More than twenty Jefferson slaves fled behind British lines in 1781. Four men left Monticello, and nineteen men, women, and children left Elk Hill and Willis Creek. Some of the runaways were members of families who fled together. The enslaved people joined many others who sought freedom in the chaos of war. Altogether, an estimated eighty thousand ran in search of freedom during the Revolutionary War years.[6]

Few of the slaves who escaped captivity on the Jefferson properties found all they hoped for in the British camps. At least fifteen of them died, like Jacky Custis, victims of disease. The Grangers' son Isaac, who was only seven years old at the time, recalled in a memoir the deplorable conditions in the internment camp at Yorktown where the British kept both captured and runaway slaves. The Jefferson slaves who had been taken from Richmond to Yorktown were returned after the fighting ended. Suck Evans and her child who survived the British camp were finally reunited with Jupiter after six months. When the war was over, Thomas Jefferson distinguished between slaves who had run away of their own volition and those who had been carried off. The former were either given away or sold.[7] Apparently the architect of American liberty did not relish the idea of owning enslaved people who shared his ideals.

The American victory at Yorktown marked the end of the fighting, but death still stalked the country, tempering any celebrations. As runaway slaves and soldiers returned from the war, smallpox contracted in the camps exacted a toll on the home front. Nurses, family, and friends were among those who sickened and died.[8] The Washingtons were not the only patriots mourning the loss of loved ones who in the last days of war contracted an enemy impervious to guns.

On 4 June 1781, Jefferson's term as governor ended. Later that year he penned *Notes on the State of Virginia*, which he revised and enlarged over the next couple of years. In it, he discussed ideas about government, including the idea that church and state should be separate and that government should be subject to checks and balances. He also addressed the issue of slavery. Blacks and whites could never live together if slaves were set free, he said. He had expressed this idea as a member of the House of Delegates when he helped to draft a revision in Virginia's code of laws, but *Notes* showed that his thinking on race was evolving. Black people, he said, were improved through interracial sex. He must have had the Hemingses in mind as he wrote these words, particularly their behavior during the days when the British were advancing through Virginia. All of the Hemingses had remained loyal to the Jeffersons throughout the turmoil of the British assault. Even the women and children who had been "carried off" from Richmond seemed steadfast in their loyalty once they returned to Monticello. But if this is what Thomas Jefferson had in mind, he conveniently forgot about the Grangers, whose experiences were similar to those of the Hemingses but who had no white ancestors between them. He also forgot about Jupiter and Suck Evans, as well as the many other slaves at Monticello, Elk Hill, Willis Creek, and the Bedford property who had not run. Jefferson was wrong on race, and he was wrong about the Hemingses. As Annette Gordon-Reed has pointed out, the Hemingses likely calculated that their chances for freedom were better with the Jeffersons than with the British.[9] They had obtained privileged positions within the household, and their mistress treasured their service. As it turned out, they calculated well. Some of them eventually gained freedom, although Martha did not live to see it.

At the end of the war, the home that Thomas and Martha had constructed on top of an Albemarle mountain remained largely intact. The British troops spared Monticello major damage, although at Elk Hill and at Willis Creek crops had been burned, buildings damaged, and fences destroyed. Some of the Jefferson slaves were gone, but most of the human property upon which the family's grandee status rested was still there. It would not be a cataclysmic event that destroyed the Jeffersons' dreams but an ordinary one: the birth of another child.

Martha had become pregnant soon after the British siege on Richmond. On 3 November 1780 she delivered a girl, Lucy Elizabeth Jefferson, who lived only five months. Four months after baby Lucy died, Martha was pregnant again. This daughter, named Lucy Elizabeth after her older sister, was born 8 May 1782. Complications from the birth of the second Lucy would leave Jefferson and his daughters without the woman who had helped create Monticello.

CHAPTER 12

Birth and Death at Monticello

The American Revolution ushered in a great experiment in democracy that continues to reverberate today. But change often comes to individuals and families through ordinary events—a birth, a marriage, a chance encounter—rather than through historical upheaval. Toward the end of his life, Thomas Jefferson identified his three greatest accomplishments as authoring the Declaration of Independence, writing Virginia's Statute of Religious Freedom, and founding the University of Virginia.[1] Each action had changed the course of history. Something more ordinary altered the course of his personal life: the death of his wife at age thirty-three from complications of childbirth. Her passing not only rocked his world but changed the lives of his daughters and slaves. Members of the enslaved Hemings family filled the void in Monticello's domestic arrangements left by Martha's death, and Martha and Thomas Jefferson's daughter Patsy stepped into the role of First Lady when, eighteen years later, her father became the nation's third President.

Childbirth was a dangerous event for women in the late eighteenth century. High morbidity and mortality rates for birthing mothers and a high incidence of miscarriage, stillbirth, and infant death meant that many women greeted the news of pregnancy with trepidation. For married women, there was no effective means of family planning. Some tried to limit family size, but mostly without effect. Methods used to prevent pregnancy were unreliable except for abstinence, which was impractical. The most effective means of postponing pregnancy was extended breastfeeding, since lactation tends to delay ovulation, but while statisticians can detect wider spacing of children among women in societies that practice prolonged breastfeeding, it is not a dependable means of birth control for individual women.

There is no reason to think that Martha tried to limit the size of her family. Newly married women in her day expected to become mothers soon and often, and most women rejoiced in their children. Martha gave birth to John less than a year after marrying her first husband. She lost him to a sudden illness shortly before she married Thomas Jefferson. Patsy was born within nine months of Martha's second marriage. Martha became pregnant five more times in the next nine years. Her second child, Jane, died in infancy; her second son, Peter, lived only seventeen days. Martha gave birth to Mary Jefferson (called Polly in childhood) on 1 August 1778. Perhaps because of her history with childbirth, both a white midwife (Mrs. Gaines) and a physician (Dr. Gilmer) attended subsequent births.[2] Martha gave birth to two more daughters in November 1780 and May 1782, only one of whom outlived her mother. The spacing of Martha's pregnancies suggests that she was using a wet nurse rather than breastfeeding her children.

Pregnant or not, Martha apparently carried out her duties as plantation mistress. She saw to it that beer was brewed as usual the week before Patsy was born. Her seventh and last pregnancy may have forced her to alter her activities, however. A visitor to Monticello in 1782 recalled that Thomas would not accompany him to the Natural Bridge, some eighty miles southwest of Monticello, out of concern for his wife's health. Martha had retired early in the evening during his stay. It was not unusual for plantation mistresses to leave their husbands to entertain visitors — in this case to enjoy a combination of poetry and punch. But the chevalier de Chastellux said specifically that Thomas would not venture far because of Martha's impending confinement. Husbands were concerned generally for the welfare of wives at childbirth, particularly when there had been a history of infant deaths, as in the Jefferson household. But there might have been particular concerns about this pregnancy. Martha lived only a few months beyond the baby's birth.[3]

Pregnancy and childbirth punctuated the lives of enslaved women, as it did Martha's. Some of their experiences were similar. Around the time Martha gave birth to Peter, Suck Evans gave birth to a daughter, Aggy, who died at two months.[4] The death of a child or new mother or both was a tragedy experienced all too often by slaveholders and enslaved people alike.

Yet, not all birthing experiences of slaveholding and enslaved women were similar. For one thing, slave owners claimed ownership of the children of enslaved mothers and assumed the right to decide their fate. About the time Martha gave birth to Polly, the enslaved Nell gave birth to Scilla. When Polly married nineteen years later, her father gave her Scilla as a wedding gift.[5] The practice of "gifting" a slave who was close in age to a daughter or son was common among slaveholders. Usually, the black child grew up knowing she "belonged" to the young mistress or master and served as the white child's playmate. The practice helped, from the owner's standpoint, to emphasize that the black child did not belong to her parents. The young mistress or master customarily gave special treats or favors to the youngster, which was thought to foster loyalty. We cannot know for sure that this happened with Polly and Scilla, but the fact that Scilla was given to Polly as a wedding present suggests that the Jeffersons followed customary practice.

Thomas Jefferson paid a local, white midwife to assist with both Scilla's and Polly's births,[6] but the record shows he paid Mrs. Grimes twenty shillings for attending the slave and twenty pounds for attending Martha, suggesting she visited Martha much more often. He also paid Dr. Gilmer to visit Martha. There is no record of payment to him or another doctor for seeing Nell. Although doctors sometimes attended slaves at childbed, owners called them only when the mother, the child, or both were in imminent danger. Grimes appears to have been called for Martha Jefferson as a precaution.

Slaves did not necessarily want a white midwife or doctor in attendance at childbed. When a slaveholder paid a white practitioner to attend an enslaved woman in labor, one goal was to ensure that the parturient woman followed their notions of proper procedures. Everyone wanted the mother and child to live, but some of a midwife's advice had more to do with cultural predilections than knowledge of what was best for mother and child. Childbirth practices that seemed rooted in biology and nature or even common sense were often grounded more in tradition. This still holds true to an extent, but it was especially so in the early national era, when medical men little understood parturition. Slaveholders often believed they should impose their thinking about proper procedures on the women they held in bondage. The women, in contrast, had serious reservations about departing from the customs they held essential for a successful birth.

Enslaved women preferred lay midwives from the slave quarters as birthing attendants. They knew not only about the physical changes women experienced in birthing a baby but also how to handle rare but critical events like the birth of twins or the birth of a child with a caul (part of the birth membrane) covering its face. At such portentous moments, black midwives, friends, and relatives offered advice about what to do. Their advice differed from that offered up by white doctors, midwives, and owners who little understood the assumptions behind the traditional birthing practices of slaves.[7]

Although no document spells out what childbirth practices were like among slaves at Monticello, there is evidence that at least some of the domestic slaves trusted traditional healers over white physicians. Jupiter Evans is a case in point. After starting out for Philadelphia in 1799 with his master, he became ill and feared that he had been poisoned. Instead of returning to Monticello, where Patsy or another member of the Jefferson household might have intervened with his treatment, Jupiter sought a cure from a black doctor twenty miles away in Buckingham County. Shortly after, Jupiter began to convulse. The doctor had reportedly given him a dose of something that he said would either *"kill or cure."* Jupiter lingered nine days, then died. Patsy relayed these events by letter to her father in Philadelphia. Neither father nor daughter expressed the slightest surprise that Jupiter had sought help from a traditional healer. That same year three members of the Granger family, Ursula, George Sr., and George Jr., died after consulting the doctor who had treated Jupiter. All three experienced "constant puking, shortness of breath and swelling." George Jr. died first, in summer. His father's death followed in the fall, and Ursula passed away a week later. Patsy termed the deaths of the Grangers "murders" and believed the doctor should be held accountable, though there is no evidence that he was. He had fled the area.[8] The stories of Jupiter Evans and the Grangers demonstrate how difficult it was for slaveholders to impose ideas about medicine on slaves, even those who worked most closely with them. None of the four slaves sought help from a white doctor through their owners.

Given that Ursula Granger maintained faith in traditional healers when she was fatally ill, it would be surprising to learn that she did not earlier in life follow traditional childbirth practices. And it seems unlikely that either Suck Evans or her husband Jupiter would have been content with a white midwife.

Jupiter Evans and the Grangers apparently were suspicious of white people's medicine and put faith in folk remedies handed down through generations, some of which may have had their origins in Africa. The embrace of folk healing practices by slaves was in part an instance of resistance to domination by the owning class. Traditional methods of treating illness and handling childbirth helped preserve cultural and bodily integrity within the degrading system that was slavery.[9] But they also helped avoid the poor outcomes associated with white doctors. This was an age, after all, when physicians relied on drastic measures—puking, poking, purging, cutting, bleeding, and dosing with strong medicines—to achieve drastic results. It should come as no surprise that enslaved people preferred less extreme measures, often herbal teas.

At 11:45 a.m. on 6 September 1782, Martha Wayles Skelton Jefferson died from complications of childbirth.[10] The war had been won at Yorktown the previous October, although the peace treaty had not yet been signed. (This would occur on 15 April 1783.) Martha had given birth to the second Lucy Elizabeth Jefferson four months before. Thomas remained by her side in the downstairs bedchamber at Monticello as she lingered. Visitors included her three daughters: Patsy, Polly, and the infant whose birth had prompted the crisis. The doctor came and went, as did the enslaved Ursula Granger, whose fixed presence in the home must have comforted the children.

Other relatives visited Martha as she lay dying. Her legally recognized half sisters and sisters-in-law tried to see that her physical and emotional needs were met and her daughters cared for. Members of the Hemings family were present, including Betty and Betty's youngest daughter, Sally.[11] All were important to Martha's sense of herself as wife, mother, and mistress. Her half sister Sally—who was not legally recognized as kin—would eventually become Thomas Jefferson's paramour, but no one in the room that day foresaw this development. Thomas Jefferson was thirty-nine years old and grieving the impending loss of his wife and the mother of his children. Sally Hemings was only nine years old and there to help her mother care for her dying mistress.

The presence of the actors in the room offered Martha reassurance that her husband and children would be cherished after she was gone. She knew that her legally recognized relatives could be counted on to help her widowed husband raise three motherless daughters, but she also knew it would be the Hemingses who would provide the day-to-day care her husband and girls required. Betty Hemings had nurtured Martha following the death of her mother and through a series of stepmothers. Martha preferred that her children be left in Betty's hands rather than those of someone else, particularly a stepmother.

Later, the Hemingses recalled that Martha Jefferson became distraught. She "wept and could not speak for some time" when she attempted to talk about the children. "She said she could not die happy, if she thought her . . . children were ever to have a stepmother brought over them. Holding her hand, Mr. Jefferson promised her solemnly that he would never marry again."[12] Elite women of the late eighteenth century were not expected to speak their minds freely or forcefully, but the deathbed was an exception. As she lay dying, Martha spoke and extracted a promise, one that was remembered and repeated long after she passed away.

One cannot know exactly what lay behind Martha's plea and Thomas's pledge. Her experiences with one or both of her stepmothers may have been a factor. Perhaps they had been less than nurturing, or maybe Martha resented the idea that her father shared his love, attention, and fortune with others. She may have hoped to spare her children the hurt of losing more than one mother. Whatever the truth, one must ask why Thomas made and kept his promise. Part of the answer may lie in the Enlightenment ideals both he and his wife embraced. Although stepparents were a common feature of family life at the time, prejudice against them was growing. Stepparenting was a practical way to cope with high death rates among women and men in the prime of life, but Enlightenment thought romanticized the idea of the family and defined it as an affectionate unit of companionate biological parents devoted to one another and to their children.[13] The destruction of the family through death was about the loss of a loved one, of course, but it was also about the forfeiture of this ideal. Martha's entreaty and her husband's vow not to take another wife reflected their devotion to one another but also their commitment to the idea of the sentimental family depicted in Enlightenment literature of the day.

As it turned out, Thomas Jefferson kept his promise never to remarry, but he did not give up sexual intimacy. He lived in an age when people believed that abstinence was unhealthy. Scientific thinking prescribed sex for men in moderation. Too much or too little sexual activity was thought to be bad for health, but the right amount promoted it. Eventually Thomas did what many other slave masters without wives did (as well as some with wives): he established a sexual relationship with one of his slaves.

In telling the story of Martha's death and Thomas's promise, the Hemingses not only asserted their own importance but made subsequent events seem fated. It was understood by everyone in the room that Betty would step in to help raise Patsy, Polly, and Lucy in the absence of a mother or stepmother. She and her family had been *chosen* to care for the young Jefferson girls and to keep house for the widowed master.

Whether Martha intended it or not, Thomas's promise not to remarry meant that none of the Hemingses would have to answer to a white mistress for the foreseeable future. For Betty, it meant that there would be no repeat of the time when her former master John Wayles bequeathed her—albeit for a limited term—to his third wife. Later on, it would offer a measure of reassurance that subsequent events involving the widower and his slave Sally had a logical, even a moral, dimension.

The Hemings family told another story about Martha's death, this one involving the gift of a bell. Members of the Hemings family had been Martha's constant companions since she was a child. Now as Martha lay dying, she singled them out for a special gift: the bell she used to summon servants. Sally Hemings likely accepted it.[14] Martha may have meant to acknowledge that she would need it no longer. More likely she wanted her Hemings relatives to have an object that would signify their connection and help them recall her after death. As we have seen with the Washingtons, elites bequeathed objects as remembrances of important relationships. Though significant, Martha's relationship with the Hemingses was unequal, a fact perfectly reflected in the choice of souvenir.

Whatever Martha envisioned for the future, the Hemingses attached their own meaning to the bell. For them, the valuable silver piece was no mere material object but rather an acknowledgment of the deep ties that linked the Wayles, Hemings, and Jefferson families and a symbol of change. While she lived, the mistress had used the bell to summon the Hemings women, who could not refuse. After her death, there would be no mistress to demand service, at least for the foreseeable future. The bell was a highly valued object kept in the Hemings family for years.

The Robert H. and Clarice Smith Gallery at Monticello's visitor's center now displays the bell that the dying Martha Jefferson is said to have handed Sally Hemings. Text behind the small silver object reads, "Servant bell, late eighteenth century. The sisters who inherited this bell always heard that Martha Jefferson on her deathbed gave it to Sally Hemings." The exhibit also includes this statement: "Based on documentary, scientific, statistical studies and oral history, many historians now believe that years after his wife's death Thomas Jefferson was the father of Sally Hemings' children."

Martha lies buried at the family graveyard at Monticello. An inscription from the *Iliad*, in Greek, recalls the words of Achilles as he stood over the dead body of Hector. The translation offered by the official Monticello website reads:

> Nay if even in the house of Hades the dead forget their dead,
> yet will I even there be mindful of my dear comrade.

These words are followed by this inscription:

> To the memory of
> Martha Jefferson,
> Daughter of John Wayles;
> Born October 19th, 1748, O.S.
> Intermarried with
> Thomas Jefferson
> January 1st, 1772;
> Torn from him by death
> September 6th, 1782:
> This monument of his love is inscribed.[15]

Martha died in 1782 believing that her husband and children would be taken care of by the same Hemings family who had nurtured her through many losses and who were already familiar with their needs, but events did not unfold as she hoped. Her grieving husband decided not to remain at Monticello, the scene of so much heartache.[16] Instead, he agreed, at the request of President George Washington, to serve as minister to France.

Thomas Jefferson considered Patsy old enough to accompany him to Paris, but before they could leave, he had to arrange care for his younger daughters. The infant Lucy was too young to wean, and Polly had only recently turned four. He sent them to live with their mother's half sister Elizabeth Wayles Eppes. She and her husband, Francis

Eppes IV (one of Martha's cousins), lived in an imposing two-story Georgian-style colonial, which still stands on the banks of the Appomattox River in Chesterfield County. The two Jefferson girls were welcomed and beloved at Eppington, as the plantation was called.

Sally Hemings and Isabel Hern were also sent to Eppington to wait on the girls. Sally was aunt to Polly and Lucy, half sister to Elizabeth Wayles Eppes, and cousin to Francis Eppes IV. Although her Eppes relatives did not cherish her as they did the Jefferson girls, they welcomed her as Lucy's nursemaid. Isabel Hern, whose husband David remained behind at Monticello, served as nursemaid to Polly.[17] Sally was nine years old when she began her life of service, rather young to be separated from her mother (who remained at Monticello), even by slaveholder standards.

Thomas Jefferson and Patsy (who had turned age ten a few weeks following her mother's death) left Monticello for Philadelphia on 19 December 1782, where they hoped to board a ship bound for France. The continued interference of Britain with shipping following the Battle of Yorktown delayed their departure. At one point, father and daughter traveled to Baltimore and back in an unsuccessful effort to find an outbound ship. So much time passed that Congress rescinded Thomas's appointment but then reinstated it. While he waited, Jefferson served a six-month term in Congress, which met in Annapolis. (Patsy remained in Philadelphia.) Finally, father and daughter traveled to Boston, where they obtained a berth aboard the *Ceres*.[18]

Nineteen-year-old James Hemings sailed with them. Robert Hemings had served as his master's valet in Philadelphia, but Thomas Jefferson wanted the younger brother to come instead so he could learn the art of French cooking. James, who had been raised in the Wayles and Jefferson households, had proven to be a quick learner. He was literate and knew how to please.[19] He was exactly the type of slave Jefferson wanted in France: someone who could take advantage of the opportunities Paris offered people of color to learn a skilled trade.

The Atlantic crossing took nineteen days. After an overland carriage ride, the travelers finally reached their destination in August 1784. The city must have awed the travelers when they finally arrived. Its population, at six hundred thousand, was almost fifteen times that of Philadelphia, the second largest city in the United States.[20] Momentous changes with worldwide implications were under way in France, which surely impressed them as well. A shifting political landscape was threatening to turn the hierarchical world upside down. Within the Jefferson household, relationships were also in flux. By the time Thomas Jefferson returned to his mountain five years later, much had been altered by what happened in Paris.

CHAPTER 13

Patsy Jefferson and Sally Hemings

Martha Jefferson's death altered the lives of everyone at Monticello. The Jefferson and Hemings families dispersed, some traveling as far away as France, but long-term changes had more to do with transformed relationships than with geography. Sally Hemings was not supposed to go to France, but she did. She accompanied Polly Jefferson to Paris, stayed to become Patsy Jefferson's maid, and returned to America as her master's concubine. After Thomas Jefferson and Sally Hemings became intimate, other family connections shifted as well.

What happened in Paris between Thomas Jefferson and Sally Hemings was long shrouded in secrecy. Forbidden relationships do not often make it into the documentary record, or at least they did not in the 1780s. But scholars working diligently with fragmentary and circumstantial evidence have made a compelling case that master and slave had a decades-long relationship that began in France. DNA evidence has corroborated their findings. What is less clear is what type of relationship existed between Thomas Jefferson's daughter and his slave.

The move to France distanced Patsy Jefferson from Virginia's slaveholding society and exposed her to new ideas. She received an education fit for a queen, literally, since the school in which she enrolled—the Abbaye Royale de Panthemont—provided elite French girls, including members of the court, with a classical education. Patsy's convent school ostensibly shielded its charges from the everyday world that was Paris. Yet outside influences crept in. Schoolgirls talked about what happened outside the convent gates, and Patsy visited her father in Paris, where radical social and political ideas were fomenting the French Revolution. People were openly questioning the privileges of king, church, and class. One of the subjects discussed in the Abbaye Royale de Panthemont and nearly everywhere in Paris was whether one human being should own another. Although few slaves lived in France, Frenchmen were heavily invested in the slave trade and in slaveholding enterprises across the Atlantic, which made slavery a contentious topic. Patsy responded sympathetically to the plight of the slave. "It grieves my heart," she wrote her father, to think that slaves are so horribly treated "by many of our country men." "I wish with all my soul that the poor negroes were all freed."[1] There is no record of her father's response, if in fact he acknowledged her sentiment.

It was not solely the status of slaves but also the place of people of mixed race that was up for discussion in France. Artists with part-African ancestry were performing before white audiences, who were responding positively. In May 1789, nine-year-old violin prodigy George Bridgetower—the son of a white Polish mother and a black Barbadian father—played to rave reviews at the Panthemont before an audience that included Patsy and her father.[2] And certain people of mixed ancestry—the children of wealthy men who had returned to France from its slaveholding colonies after making fortunes and fathering children with enslaved women—mingled in polite society.

Given the Parisian environment, one might wonder why Thomas Jefferson had brought James Hemings to the city. The simple answer may be that he was accustomed to traveling with a valet and he wanted a French-trained chef. He knew James would do on both counts. He also would have known that slaves brought into France by masters were not guaranteed freedom. People who called for "liberté, égalité, and fraternité" did not necessarily include people of African ancestry in their prescriptions. In the United States, his fellow countrymen, after all, had sought independence from Britain in the name of freedom while tolerating the enslavement of others. Why should France be any different?

Yet there was cause for concern. The number of colonials traveling to France with servants clearly designated as slaves had been rising during the eighteenth century, particularly after the 1750s, and many of the slaves had successfully challenged their enslaved status in court.[3] It seemed to many people — though not to all government officials — that in France the presumption was in favor of freedom.

Not long after Jefferson arrived in Paris, Baltimorean Paul Bentalou sought advice from the U.S. minister about an enslaved boy he and his wife had brought there. Apprehensive that the youth might take advantage of the Parisian environment to secure freedom, the Bentalous asked how to ensure that the boy remained in bondage. Thomas Jefferson made "enquiries on the subject" and responded in August 1786. French law was clear: it granted the boy "freedom if he claims it," Jefferson wrote, and it would "be difficult, if not impossible, to interrupt the course of the law." Even so, he was optimistic: "I have known an instance where a person bringing in a slave, and saying nothing about it, has not been disturbed in his possession." The person was, of course, himself, and the servant was James Hemings. Jefferson advised Bentalou not to seek an exemption to keep his boy enslaved, since doing so would call attention to the situation and possibly produce the opposite of the desired result. The boy's youth, he suggested, made it "not probable he will think of claiming freedom." But if you are threatened with the loss of the boy, Jefferson added, let me know and I will see what can be done. The next year, Sally Hemings came to France.[4]

In July 1787 Sally came to Paris with Polly Jefferson. Lucy, the Jefferson baby, had died of whooping cough not long after her father and sister left for France, although news did not reach them until May 1785. Polly and her cousin had caught the disease too. Only Polly recovered. Thomas Jefferson decided at once to bring Polly to Paris. He asked her guardians back home to arrange for a suitable companion to accompany her: a lady or gentleman or a mature enslaved woman. Isabel Hern, Polly's maid, would have been a logical choice, but she had become ill following the birth of a child. Polly (now age nine) was sent abroad instead under the supervision of fourteen-year-old Sally Hemings. After Lucy's death, Sally was no longer needed at Eppington, and Polly knew Sally. Polly put up quite a fuss about leaving the only family she knew, but her father insisted. Even so, she had to be tricked into boarding the boat that carried her and Sally to France. Some of the Eppeses boarded the ship and stayed with her until she fell asleep. They left before the boat set sail and Polly awoke.[5]

Sally might have been sent home once Polly was safely in her father's care. Polly, like Patsy, was enrolled at the Abbaye Royale de Panthemont. But the sisters came home from school periodically, and there was no need for Sally at either Eppington or Monticello. The Jeffersons' Parisian home was spacious and required a large staff. All of the current servants were men.[6] A lady's maid could prove useful, especially since Patsy was of an age to come out in society.

Paris offered an unparalleled opportunity for Sally to train as a lady's maid. She could help Patsy and Polly with their toilette, learn about the latest fashions, and practice the sewing and other skills necessary to care for the girls' wardrobes. Besides, Jefferson's daughters would need to readjust to the slave society of Virginia once they returned home. Having experience with an enslaved maid in France could aid in the transition. Sally, for her part, may have had no objections. Her brother James was there to watch out for her and to fill her in on the opportunities Paris offered people of color.

One obstacle to Sally's remaining in Paris was her lack of immunity to smallpox. Thomas Jefferson was a great believer in inoculation. About three months after Sally's arrival, he sent her to the leading physician of the era, Robert Sutton, who, with his brother, had famously improved the process of inoculation. Sally's treatment was expensive, in part because anyone undergoing inoculation had to be quarantined for forty days. The doctor owned and operated a country estate on the outskirts of Paris for this purpose. Jefferson paid Sutton the equivalent of forty dollars to inoculate and care for Sally.[7] Afterward, she moved into the Jeffersons' opulent home, the Hôtel de Langeac, on the Champs-Élysées.

Sally had to adjust to a new social order, as had her brother. James—like other Parisian apprentice cooks—earned a salary and sold leftovers from the kitchen to supplement the wages paid by his master. He traveled freely and spent his money as he wished. He became proficient in French as he moved about the city meeting other cooks and servants. He hired a French tutor to teach him grammar for at least five months during his five-year stay.[8] James also learned about Parisian law, which held out the hope of freedom for slaves who petitioned for it. By the time Sally came, he was able to help her acclimate to the city by negotiating her terms of service, teaching her French, and showing her how to move about the city. He surely also explained the status of slaves in Paris.

No one knows for sure when and how a sexual relationship developed between Thomas Jefferson and Sally Hemings. Sally had been a small child when he left Monticello, but she had matured. Ursula and George Granger's son Isaac remembered Sally as a pretty woman whose long hair and fair skin made her look almost white. Indeed, the enslaved girl was said to have looked like her half sister, Thomas's late wife. Because she spent so much time in the homes of the Jeffersons and Eppeses, Sally's speech probably resembled that of an elite white woman from Virginia. Abigail Adams, who saw fourteen-year-old Sally around this time, said that she appeared to be about sixteen.[9] If so, Sally looked to be old enough to marry by Virginia standards. In that time and place, older men could take an interest in teenage girls without evoking censure. As we shall see in a later chapter, Thomas Jefferson's friend James Madison, when in his early thirties, proposed marriage to a girl of fifteen.

Sally may not have been shocked at her master's advances. After all, her mother had entered into a long-term relationship with John Wayles after the death of his third wife. Betty Hemings and John Wayles had six children who survived to adulthood and who had privileges unknown to most slaves. Sally could have expected or at least accepted the same fate for herself.

We do not know much about Betty Hemings's relationship with Sally's father or what she said to Sally or her other children about him, but it seems unlikely that she discouraged relationships across lines of color and class. About the same time the liaison between Sally and Thomas is said to have begun, Sally's older half sister Mary Hemings entered into a sexual relationship with Thomas Bell, a wealthy Charlottesville merchant to whom she had been hired while Jefferson was in France. The two lived together openly as common law man and wife for the remainder of their lives and had two children.

There were other reasons why Sally might have succumbed. She probably believed that she had no choice. There were no laws to protect an enslaved woman in France from rape or other types of sexual exploitation. There were no houses of refuge, no organizations to lend support of any kind. Her brother was there, but his power to intervene on her behalf was limited. Then, too, there was the promise of Paris. Sally learned to speak French, traveled about, and interacted with the city's inhabitants. She had seen the world turned upside down at the Suttons' country inoculation house, where she had been waited on by white people during her period of quarantine. In Paris, she enjoyed a material standard of living that must have appealed. In addition, her master paid her wages, which were higher than those typically paid to Parisian housemaids. She dressed well too. Patsy and Polly wore the latest Parisian fashions, or at least their father's expenditures suggest that they did, especially as Patsy began to make appearances in Parisian society. Sally attended her at these events, and her clothing improved in tandem. At one point her master spent thirty dollars on clothing for Sally, a large sum for the wardrobe of a house servant in Virginia, but not for a lady's maid in Paris.[10]

But Jefferson was not motivated solely by generosity and the demands of high society. His desire for a beautiful, young house servant may have seemed reasonable, even logical to him and others, including Sally. And there was no one in Paris who could check his power to have what he wanted. There was no wife to object, no wife to take out her resentment on the enslaved woman who had become the object of her husband's sexual attention. Back home, gossip sometimes served to curtail a man's behavior, particularly a man who held or aspired to public office, but the dalliance of an unmarried man and a servant girl in Paris would hardly cause a ripple amid the decadence of the *ancien régime*.

A 1995 film, *Jefferson in Paris*, offers a semifictional depiction of this part of the future President's life. Directed by James Ivory and starring Nick Nolte as Thomas Jefferson and Thandie Newton as Sally Hemings, it covers much more than their sexual relationship. Yet the filmmakers were oddly vague about what happened between master and slave. The great film critic Roger Ebert complained that Jefferson is portrayed as so emotionally remote that "you wonder, by the movie's end, if he actually knew he was having sex." Sally becomes pregnant, and Thomas remarks upon it, but "Jefferson seems to talk almost as if she might have gotten pregnant by herself," Ebert wrote.[11] There are no sex scenes on camera. Apparently, the liaison between Thomas and Sally was too hot for Hollywood to handle. Historians, too, have been reluctant to acknowledge what happened, but after two centuries of speculation, DNA and other evidence has convinced the vast majority of scholars and members of the general public that the two maintained an intimate relationship over the course of decades and had four children who lived to adulthood. But evidence about the nature of their liaison is thin in places, particularly in France, where it is said to have begun. And so debate about the matter continues, even among people who do not dispute the existence of the partnership.

For some, the idea that Thomas Jefferson and his slave cared for one another over a period of many years has made the relationship more comprehensible and forgivable, defusing suspicions of sexual abuse. They cite laws and customs that prevented the open acknowledgment of the relationship. They assert that love, or at least affection, characterized the union. Other people scoff at the notion that such a relationship could have been anything other than abusive. Sexual exploitation, including the rape of enslaved women by owners, was not uncommon in the slave states. Although some long-term relationships existed between caring masters and enslaved women, far more were exploitative and cruel.

In *Jefferson in Paris*, Patsy Jefferson resents Sally's relationship with her father. In one scene she slaps Sally across the face to teach Sally to show Polly proper respect. There is no documentary evidence that Patsy Jefferson ever struck Sally Hemings, but she may well have been upset over the liaison between her father and her maid. And we know that Patsy hit at least one slave on another occasion. In 1833, in the basement of her Washington, DC, home, a more mature Patsy beat an enslaved woman whom she suspected of stealing a handkerchief. Her daughter Cornelia said Patsy did not act in the anger of the moment but administered a measured response to the "problem" of theft. Cornelia's account makes clear that her mother was not in the habit of beating slaves with her own hands, but how often would such incidents have to occur before a maid began to fear physical abuse? The beating Patsy administered — singular though it may have been — serves as a dramatic reminder that tension between a lady and her maid could erupt in violence.[12] It could also lead to other types of punishment, ranging from the loss of privileges to sale. Temporary or permanent reassignment to work that was more difficult (i.e., field work) was not always an idle threat. A lady's domestic circle brought together women of unequal power, only one of whom could chastise the others.

Sally and James Hemings certainly understood that they might gain freedom by remaining in Paris when the Jeffersons returned to Virginia. Jefferson scholar Lucia Stanton suggests as much when she says they "*chose* to leave France."[13] Sally's son Madison Hemings also implied that the choice had been theirs to make. Yet they would also have understood that life in France would not be easy. In Madison's account, Thomas Jefferson promised his mother "extraordinary privileges" and freedom for her children when they turned twenty-one. Madison, of course, did not witness the agreement, but Sally Hemings (who was pregnant) did enjoy extraordinary privileges and all of her children did gain their freedom, lending credibility to his account.

It seems that James worked out his own agreement with his master. Upon his return, he worked in New York City and Philadelphia for Thomas Jefferson while he served as secretary of state. During these years, James earned wages comparable to those of a free servant: first six, and later eight, dollars per month, with additional sums for clothing and other necessities. In 1793, James returned with his master to Monticello, but not before securing a written promise that he would have his freedom after teaching another Monticello slave to cook. James was freed, as promised, on 5 February 1796. His younger brother Peter took over as Monticello's head chef and prepared the French food Jefferson found so pleasing. When Thomas became President in 1801, he hoped that James would rejoin him as chef in the President's house, but he and James, who was cooking in a Baltimore tavern, never came to an agreement about James's working conditions. That summer Thomas Jefferson and James Hemings both returned to Monticello, where James was paid twenty dollars a month to cook for the President. James left for good in September when Thomas returned to Washington. A month later, James was dead. An alcoholic, he was said to have committed suicide.[14]

On 22 October 1789, the Jeffersons and the Hemingses had boarded the *Clermont*, which carried them back across the Atlantic. The return of the master to his mountain represented a major change for the domestic servants living there. Many had been rented out while the Jeffersons were in France. Those who remained had carried on absent a master and mistress. Both groups had been separated from the few who traveled with the Jeffersons. Now they were reassembled. Polly's former maid Isabel Hern was among those reunited with family members and friends.

Sally must have faced questions after returning to Monticello. It is likely that James already knew she was pregnant, and by whom, but Sally's mother would have had to be informed, as well as other kin. The promise Thomas made to Sally may have been intended to appease them as much as her. No one appreciates freedom more than one who does not have it, as Martha Washington knew when she decided to treat William Custis Costin as a free person. Just as Martha counted on her promise of freedom for William to temper outrage over the circumstances of his birth, Thomas Jefferson may have counted on his promise of freedom for Sally's children to placate the Hemingses. After all, Hemings family members cooked his food, cared for his clothes, helped him dress, cut his hair, saw to the needs of his daughters, groomed his horses, and managed his household. If they could not come to terms with what had happened, his life might become difficult.

Sally likely had questions for her mother. Her situation was not unusual, and there was protocol to be followed by the concubine, the slaveholder, members of both families, and others who knew about the relationship. First and foremost, social convention dictated that no one acknowledge the affair, even when children were born who closely resembled the father. Flaunting a union across the color line could have serious consequences for everyone. There were exceptions, of course, as in the earlier case of John Custis IV and his enslaved son Jack. But John Custis IV was eccentric and, perhaps more significantly, did not aspire to a political career.

After Paris, Sally Hemings — though expertly trained — never worked as a lady's maid. Instead, she sewed for her master and engaged in other light work.[15] How long her first child lived remains unknown. Apparently, not long. Another child, a daughter born in 1799, died as well, but four more children would survive to adulthood.

Patsy Jefferson married her third cousin Thomas (Tom) Mann Randolph Jr. three months after returning to Virginia. Within another month, she left Monticello in the company of her new husband. Tom's proposal and Patsy's acceptance caught everyone by surprise. The two had known each other since childhood but had been out of touch for years — until the Jeffersons and Hemingses stopped at Tuckahoe, the Randolph family estate, on their way home from France.

At least part of Patsy's attraction to Tom may have been intellectual. Thomas Jefferson had once worried that Patsy might marry a "blockhead."[16] Tom was no blockhead. Instead, he was a well-educated man who, like his wife, had spent years studying abroad. For four years he attended the venerable University of Edinburgh learning about natural philosophy, natural history, astronomy, chemistry, and other subjects.

In some ways, Tom seemed a logical choice for Patsy. The Randolphs had long been prominent in Virginia's social and political circles. The marriage strengthened ties of long standing between the two families. The bride's and groom's fathers (both widowers) had grown up together. Thomas Jefferson's father had acted as guardian to Thomas Mann Randolph Sr. after his father died in 1745. Peter Jefferson had moved his own family to the Randolph home at Tuckahoe to better oversee the estate and care for the orphaned four-year-old. The two young Thomases had become fast friends.[17]

Still, one wonders why Patsy decided so suddenly to marry. Was she infatuated with Tom, or did she wish to escape Monticello? Her mother had died shortly before she left the plantation for France, and

now Sally Hemings was there with her father. Rumors about the relationship between Jefferson and Hemings had begun circulating as
soon as they returned to Virginia.[18] Sally's pregnancy was visible to
everyone.

Patsy's apparent angst over her father's shadow family seems a departure from Virginia custom. Patsy's mother had accepted her own
father's relationship with Betty Hemings. Martha Jefferson relied on
Betty when she was growing up, and after her father's death she incorporated Betty's family into Monticello's staff. Martha Washington
likewise found a way to tolerate her father's extramarital relationship
and the child who came of it: Ann Dandridge. She also found a place
for William Custis Costin. Patsy Jefferson seems to have been less accommodating. Patsy and Tom married at Monticello on 23 February
1790 in a small affair attended by members of their immediate families.
It is impossible to know what she was thinking as she said her marriage
vows before the Reverend James Maury Sr., the Episcopalian minister
who officiated at her father's request.[19] Was she looking forward to a
new life with Tom, or was she glad to escape her old one? The Hemingses were on hand to make the wedding celebration as pleasant as
possible for the Jeffersons and their guests, although where exactly the
very pregnant Sally was we do not know.

Tom was twenty-two years old; Patsy was eighteen. By the standards of his contemporaries, his dark hair and swarthy complexion
precluded his being considered handsome, but he was tall and ath-
letic. Patsy resembled her father: tall, thin, with red hair and blue eyes.
People who knew her commented on her sweet disposition, cheerful
demeanor, and charm, but rarely her looks. Margaret Bayard Smith,
who met Patsy and Polly in Washington in the winter of 1802, described Patsy as "homely," in contrast to her beautiful younger sister.[20]

"Marry in haste, repent at leisure" is an adage that can be applied
to Patsy's adult life. She and Tom raised a large family together, but
the happy times they experienced early on eventually gave way to discontent: the family's fortunes declined, Tom's health deteriorated, and
Patsy clung to her father instead of her husband for stability. We cannot know whether Patsy regretted her choice to marry Tom, but we

Martha (Patsy) Jefferson Randolph.

know she resisted the fate that awaited her as his wife almost from the start.

No matter what type of man a woman married, she was expected to yield to his judgment, even if she possessed the superior intellect or knowledge. Before marriage, a girl submitted to her father's direction, and many parents expected to be involved in the choice of a spouse, but Thomas Jefferson apparently thought his daughter should marry whom she pleased. Of course, by the time she was ready to marry, he had observed her behavior over eighteen years and could be reasonably certain that her choice would meet with his approval. In fact, upon learning that Patsy wanted to marry Thomas Mann Randolph Jr., he wrote that Tom would have been his "own first choice" because of his "talents, disposition, connections & fortune." Thomas Jefferson's listing of these attributes to describe his future son-in-law was in part wishful thinking. Tom was known to be quarrelsome. Other members of his family were as well, causing Patsy to worry years later that her son Jefferson (Jeff) would exhibit "the Randolph character," by which she meant a jealous and suspicious nature.[21] Tom's talents, connections, and fortune were real enough, however. Although he did not complete his studies at Edinburgh, he had applied himself diligently and planned to continue his education upon his return to Virginia. And as a member of one of Virginia's most politically connected and economically secure families, he could count on relatives and their friends to help him succeed in his chosen vocations of planting and politics.

Patsy and Tom began their life together as members of Virginia's elite class. Social, political, and economic standing mattered to young couples because wealth and status passed from one generation to another, although not without effort on the part of parents. In Virginia's agricultural society, status rested in large part on the possession of land and labor. Whatever scruples about slavery Patsy had developed in Paris had vanished by the time she married. The same can be said for her father, who had once entertained the idea of ending slavery in Virginia. Now he and Patsy set about to ensure that she and her husband had sufficient land and slaves to maintain a prominent position in Virginia society. Historians have offered disparate explanations for why Thomas Jefferson became less willing to question slavery over time. Part of the answer lies in his ambitions for his daughters. Giving them slaves was a way to ensure their future wealth and happiness.

Thomas Jefferson worked quickly to ensure that Patsy and her husband had enough land and slaves to count themselves among the state's grandees. (He had accepted the post of secretary of state in George Washington's administration and would soon leave for New York.) The groom's father gave his son a plantation known as Varina, comprising 950 fertile acres along the James River near Richmond, as well as livestock, two dwellings, and forty slaves. The father of the bride deeded over to his daughter an additional thousand acres of farmland in Bedford County, along with twenty-seven slaves, about half of them children. The Jefferson slaves consisted of six families, most of whom already lived on the Bedford County plantation known as Wingo. Thus, the newlyweds began married life with nearly two thousand acres and sixty-seven slaves—assets that placed them squarely within Virginia's small class of wealthy slaveholders.[22]

Five years later, when his younger daughter married her first cousin John Wayles Eppes, Thomas Jefferson deeded over a similar marriage settlement. To ensure the "fair" treatment of each daughter, he listed the names of the slaves he had given Patsy (thirty-one altogether, including some he had transferred later) and matched them with the names of thirty-one slaves designated for Polly, who by then had changed her name to Maria. Four children, ages ten to fourteen, were separated from parents in the process, and other families were split up.[23]

The majority of the slaves given to Patsy and Tom Randolph were expected to produce the market crops that would allow the young couple to prosper, but some were domestic servants who would keep the house running. Still, Patsy found herself without a maid to meet her personal needs. Not long after her wedding, she asked her father to send her one. Sally Hemings would have been the logical choice since she had served Patsy in this capacity while in Paris. Perhaps Patsy intended her request to end the relationship between master and maid and, just as important, to tamp down the gossip that linked Thomas Jefferson and Sally Hemings. But Thomas did not send Sally. Instead, he chose fourteen-year-old Molly, daughter of Mary Hemings and granddaughter of Betty Hemings.[24] Molly had no biological ties to Patsy, which may have been one reason she was chosen. Her mother Mary had been born before John Wayles and Betty Hemings became intimate. Sally remained at Monticello.

Tom wanted to move to Varina, at least temporarily, where he could both farm and continue his legal studies. Patsy was not pleased with the prospect. But instead of voicing her concern to her new husband, she told her father that she was "very much averse to it." It was not a woman's place to contradict her husband's choice of residence, a social convention upheld by Thomas Jefferson in principle. In a letter written shortly after Patsy's marriage, he assured her that henceforth her happiness depended on her ability to please her husband: "To this all other objects must be secondary; even your love for me." But fathers played a key role in settling a daughter into marriage, and he apparently saw nothing untoward in negotiating to ensure his daughter's happiness. He began planning for Tom and Patsy to acquire another plantation, Edgehill, a Randolph property conveniently located just three miles from Monticello, across the Rivanna River.[25]

Tom was reluctant to take on the responsibility of running a larger plantation. More acreage would take time away from his studies. It would also require more labor, and Tom held an "aversion" to increasing his slaveholdings. "To increase the number of my negroes would be an insurmountable objection," he insisted. Like other men who had come of age in the Revolutionary War era, he was willing to question Virginia's continued reliance on slavery, but also like his contemporaries, his reservations were easily overcome. He soon acquiesced to pressure from his father-in-law to secure more land and human property. Within a few years, Tom would become one of the largest slaveholders in Albemarle County.[26]

Father and daughter's cause had been helped when Tom journeyed to Varina and found conditions not quite as favorable as he had hoped. He became ill and blamed his discomfort on the climate. But when he agreed to purchase Edgehill from his father, he said it was "to Gratify Patsy."[27] The negotiations did not go smoothly. Thomas Mann Randolph Sr. had other plans for the property, and Tom Jr. quarreled with his father, complicating the matter further. Dogged insistence by Thomas Jefferson gradually wore them both down. Tom Jr. apologized and paid his father two thousand dollars for approximately fifteen hundred acres of property and the slaves who lived there.

Patsy had gotten what she wanted without confronting her husband directly. Instead, she had convinced her father to intervene on her behalf. The acquisition of Edgehill showed that Patsy had her own ideas about where and how she wanted to live. She maneuvered within Virginia's patriarchal society to advance her own welfare and happiness. She continued to do so throughout her lifetime, sometimes acting in her own best interest and sometimes in the interest of her children. Her decisions also, of course, affected the lives of her family's slaves.

Patsy had obtained an excellent academic education in Paris but little training in the practical skills expected of a Virginia planter's wife. The preservation of meats and the management of slaves were not part of the Abbaye Royale de Panthemont curriculum. Patsy had received instruction in "arithmetic, geography, history, and modern languages" from the best instructors in Paris, her daughter Ellen Randolph Coolidge wrote years later, though she was "destined to become wife, mother and mistress in a Virginia family." Her convent schoolmates had been the "daughters of wealthy and considerable persons [who] were considered as above the necessity of attention to such homely matters." Learning to run her own home, Ellen said, had proven "painful" for her mother.[28]

Establishing herself as the mistress in a new household posed significant challenges for any young bride. A remark by one of Patsy's daughters about Betty Brown suggests the particular difficulty Patsy had in assuming the management of slaves formerly associated with Monticello. The maid for years had satisfied Patsy's mother, who had brought her to Monticello when she married Thomas. When the Jeffersons relocated to Richmond during the Revolutionary War, Betty Brown had gone along. She and her children had been captured by British troops and taken to Yorktown, but they had been returned at the conclusion of the fighting. The war tested Betty Brown, and Martha and Thomas Jefferson had found her trustworthy. Yet Ellen Randolph Coolidge remembered Betty Brown, who had come to work for Patsy, as bad tempered and domineering.[29]

Family events like marriage and the establishment of a new household had the potential to roil relations between owners and slaves whose families were torn apart. The nearness of Edgehill and Monticello, however, meant that the Hemings slaves separated by Patsy's marriage to Tom would be able to visit one another, minimizing any disruption. Even though the Randolphs would not move to Edgehill for some time, the slaves who worked the land would have family nearby. Randolph slaves, too, gained a degree of family security. When Tom purchased Edgehill from his father, he also bought the slaves whose families lived on the plantation.[30]

Would Sally Hemings have borne Thomas Jefferson's children if Martha Jefferson lived? It hardly seems likely. Although some white men flaunted their relationships with black consorts in front of wives, most did not. Wives could and did make demands on their husbands, which were supported by relatives and friends. It was not uncommon for enslaved women to be sold at the insistence of a wife or her kin, along with any children resulting from the relationship. The dissension caused by such a sale was reason to think twice about sexually abusing enslaved women, particularly among men like Thomas Jefferson who were public figures. When gentlemen engaged in extramarital liaisons across the color line, they tended to be circumspect. The relationships were almost always open secrets within the man's neighborhood or close circle of acquaintances, yet elite Virginians maintained a "cultural code of silence," preventing their being publicized.[31] The relationship between Thomas Jefferson and Sally Hemings did become public, but Sally was not sold, no doubt in part because no white wife was present to insist. Patsy was newly married and focused on her own household, and Maria was too young to assert herself as mistress of Monticello, which left Thomas Jefferson on his own to work out his relationship with Sally Hemings and her family.

CHAPTER 14

First Lady

Patsy Jefferson Randolph's housekeeping responsibilities were heavy for one so young and inexperienced. Soon after she married Tom Randolph, her father began his years of government service, first as secretary of state, later as vice president, finally as President. The appointments kept him away from Monticello for long stretches of time. Patsy tried during these years to supervise her father's domestic staff as well as her own. Tom was also doing double duty, managing Monticello's farming operations as well as his own. Although it took ten years to build a house at Edgehill, Patsy and Tom did not live full-time at Monticello. They spent part of the summer there and visited periodically, but they lived at Varina, and — for a brief time — Belmont, a property belonging to one of Tom's kinsmen.[1] Edgehill's proximity to Monticello made it easier for Patsy to supervise her father's staff once the Randolphs moved there, but she nevertheless found it difficult to keep her father's house in order. According to the standards of the day, it was the job of white mistresses to ensure that no scandalous behavior tarnished a family's reputation, but her father's continuing relationship with Sally Hemings caused tongues to wag. At first, only locals paid attention, but eventually the entire country became embroiled in talk about Thomas Jefferson's sexual indiscretions.

When Thomas Jefferson left Monticello in the late winter of 1801 to begin his first term as President, neither Patsy nor her sister Maria (who had married John Wayles Eppes four years earlier and was living in Chesterfield County) expected to go to Washington to serve as their father's hostess. Yet the following winter they were in Washington doing exactly that, although both had young children at home. Patsy was by then the mother of five. Maria had a son born the year before. An erupting scandal prompted them to travel to the nation's capital in aid of their father. It was Patsy's time in Washington in the winters of 1802–1803 and 1805–1806 that has earned her a place in the First Ladies exhibit in the Smithsonian Institution.

President Jefferson had been satisfied at first to serve without a First Lady. He thought white women, like enslaved people, had no place in politics. He had educated Patsy and Maria, but he did so to ensure that they would be good companions to their husbands and competent teachers for their children. He did not anticipate that either would play a public role in his administration. Members of Congress often left their families at home and lived in hotels or boardinghouses while doing the nation's business. There were other women in Washington, of course. A small cadre of elites lived in the city year round, and others came for the social season, which closely corresponded with the congressional session. But the new President expected to have little to do with them as he went about governing.[2]

The President left nearly all of his slaves in Virginia, as well as his daughters. Objection to slavery had increased in the North, where states were dismantling the institution. Slaves could be difficult to manage in a city, where it seemed easier to disappear than in the country. And bringing slaves from Monticello would mean disrupting routines at home.

The lack of a First Lady and slaves in Washington did not crimp President Jefferson's efforts to entertain. In fact, he hosted events more frequently and extravagantly than did either of his predecessors. During the three to five months that Congress was in session, he held three dinners a week for members of Congress and other government officials. A woman's presence was neither required nor desired at these all-male gatherings, where conversation centered on politics and policy.[3] A hostess seemed necessary only when dinners, receptions, or other social events included guests of both sexes. On the rare occasions when women were invited to the President's house, the wife of the secretary of state, Dolley Madison, was only too happy to step in, but it was the President who determined protocol. In an effort to appear democratic, he did not always give precedence to high-ranking guests but allowed everyone to enter the dining room and be seated in somewhat random order. The practice became a minor scandal when the first British minister to the United States, Anthony Merry, and his wife Elizabeth complained about the breach of protocol.

The "pall mall" approach to dinner seating contrasted sharply with the President's more ordered system for serving food. He preferred to dine *à la française*, which required an even number of dishes arranged symmetrically on the table. Each was classified according to a set hierarchy, with the most important as the centerpiece. The orderly presentation of dishes showcased the President's abundant resources and sophisticated culinary knowledge, but it also diminished the need for a wait staff. Further, a revolving dumbwaiter installed in the wall of the dining room meant food could appear without the entrance of a servant. At times, President Jefferson served the food himself to avoid having footmen in his dining room. If one was required, he could be summoned through a system of bells the President had installed in the executive mansion soon after his arrival.[4] As long as he had his French chef and maître d'hôtel, the President could entertain without waiters or hostesses.

President Jefferson believed that political matters were best discussed out of the hearing of servants and women. The partisan politics of the era seemed to know no bounds, and he hoped to avoid gossip about the political maneuvering that went on in Washington. He feared leaks of information concerning matters pending before Congress and related to foreign affairs. Servants (both free and enslaved) and women were notorious for spreading rumors. Jefferson once told a visitor that he could speak freely in the dining room without lowering his voice since *"our walls have no ears."*[5]

The President could not run the executive mansion without help, of course, but he decided from the start to rely on free servants. He hoped to bring former slave James Hemings to Washington as his cook, but when the plan fell through, he hired Honoré Julien, who had served as cook in the last months of the Washington administration and whose stellar reputation for combining southern and French cooking styles held appeal. Etienne Lemaire, another Frenchman, performed the role of maître-d' for most of the years Jefferson spent in the capital. Irishman Joseph Dougherty, who had worked in the President's house during John Adams's presidency, stayed and took charge of Jefferson's coach and stables. The rest of the staff consisted of men and women of various ethnic backgrounds.[6]

An apprentice cook was the exception to the rule against Monticello slaves in Washington. Because the President was still keen to have a French-trained chef, he brought fourteen-year-old Ursula Granger, the granddaughter of Ursula and George Granger Sr., to Washington so she could learn to cook from Honoré Julien. Ursula, who was paid two dollars per month, lasted only a year. She was pregnant when she arrived in the capital. Her child—the first ever born in the President's house—died before the young mother returned to Monticello, but in June 1802, when the President contemplated a trip back home, he reasoned that it would be "next to impossible to send Ursula and her child home and bring them back again." He apparently expected Wormley Hughes and perhaps other slaves to object to Ursula's return to Washington. Wormley, one of the President's gardeners and the son of Betty Brown, was apparently the father of the baby.[7]

Edith (Edy) Fossett, age fifteen, replaced Ursula in the kitchen. The daughter of one of Monticello's housemaids (Isabel Hern Fossett) and one of its carpenters (David Hern), Edy stayed until the President retired in 1809. Her husband Joseph (Joe) Fossett, Monticello's blacksmith, was a member of the Hemings family, the son of Mary Hemings—Betty Hemings's oldest child. The President seems not to have worried about separating Edy and Joe for long periods; when he returned home to Monticello, usually twice a year, he tended to leave her in Washington, a situation that did not sit well with Joe. In 1806, as the President headed for Monticello, Joe headed in the opposite direction to see his wife. Jefferson feared he had lost Joe for good, but a slave catcher he employed soon apprehended him near the President's house. Joe managed only a brief visit with Edy before he was whisked away to jail, then returned to Monticello.[8]

Eighteen-year-old Fanny Hern, the daughter of Monticello farm workers, joined the household in 1806 and stayed through 1809. Fanny was Edy's sister-in-law and the wife of Monticello's wagoner, David (Davy) Hern Jr. Fanny and Davy saw one another on occasion because he transported goods back and forth between Monticello and Washington. Still, their separation proved difficult. Davy had only recently left Washington for home in fall 1808 when their baby died of whooping cough. Grief-stricken upon learning the news, Davy begged to return to Washington. The President permitted a five-day visit at Christmas,[9] perhaps having learned a lesson from his experience with Edy and Joe.

One other slave worked at the President's house. John Freeman was not from Monticello but from nearby Maryland. Soon after his arrival in Washington, Jefferson hired the young man's services, paying his owner eight dollars per month.[10] Such arrangements were not uncommon, but if the President thought he would avoid disgruntlement among the help at Monticello by employing his services rather than bringing another slave from home, things did not work out as he hoped. In summer 1803 when he returned home, John Freeman came along and fell in love with Melinda Colbert, granddaughter of Betty Hemings. The couple pledged to marry, but they belonged to different people. (Melinda belonged to the President's daughter Maria.) Freeman asked the President to purchase them both. Jefferson refused on the ground that he already had too many domestic servants. He warned Freeman that he could not expect to see Colbert every time they returned to Monticello. Yet, a few months later the President relented and purchased Freeman for a term of eleven years, after which he was to be freed.[11]

John Freeman was the closest the President came to having a personal valet while in Washington. Freeman traveled with the President and attended at table when he dined alone. He may have performed other personal services. The President clearly trusted Freeman, as he had the Hemings brothers James and Robert, but John Freeman appeared less often in public than had the Hemingses.

The three enslaved women who worked in the kitchen learning to make the custards and other desserts the President favored stayed out of the public eye. None of them conducted the President's business in the city streets. Black people were a conspicuous presence in Washington when Jefferson took office, making up almost a quarter of the city's population.[12] Enslaved and free blacks alike could be seen laboring along the roads, buying and selling produce at the market, accompanying owners on errands, delivering merchandise to homes and businesses, and unloading goods at the wharves. Slaves helped to build the structures that made up official Washington, and coffles of slaves made their way through the city streets, some to jobs within the city limits and others to points south, victims of the slave trade that still operated within the United States. But at 1600 Pennsylvania Avenue, chores like purchasing food for the table were left to free white men. None of the enslaved women ventured off the grounds.

President Jefferson took pains to present himself as a man of the people while in Washington, usually riding his horse about town unattended by Freeman or any other servant. The practice shocked some of the city's inhabitants, who were accustomed to seeing important personages with maids and manservants. An unkempt appearance was part of his effort to appear democratic. By greeting guests in shoddy clothing and slippers worn down at the heel, he hoped to anchor the republic in the principle that all men are created equal. By emulating the formalities of behavior and dress styles of the European courts, George Washington and John Adams had jeopardized the republic's survival, or so Jefferson thought. British minister Anthony Merry in particular took umbrage when the President greeted him "in slippers down at the heels" and clothes "indicative of utter slovenliness and indifference to appearances." Merry himself was dressed in full diplomatic regalia. Irish poet Thomas Moore was equally appalled at the President's dress upon his introduction to Jefferson, although his response did not threaten the already fragile relationship between Britain and the still fledgling United States, as Merry's had.[13]

If Jefferson had employed an enslaved valet, his wardrobe might have improved, but the valet's presence would have carried a political message that apparently the President did not want conveyed. Although slavery was legal in Washington, the decision to move the capital from Philadelphia to a southern, slave-friendly city had proven controversial among citizens living above the Mason-Dixon line, including certain congressmen with abolitionist leanings. Slavery had the potential to divide the nation, as the President well knew.

On 1 September 1802, the *Richmond Recorder* carried a page-two article by James T. Callender claiming that the President had for years kept an enslaved woman as a concubine: "Her name is SALLY," Callender proclaimed. He had some of the details wrong, but the substance of his charge was true. Sally was intimately involved with the President and had given birth to his children. Callender, a political writer with a reputation for scandalmongering, had been rebuffed by the President when he sought help in securing a government job. He kept up his attack in the Richmond newspaper into the following year, when he apparently drowned in the James River.[14] By then, other Federalist opponents were regularly lampooning the President with doggerel, cartoons, letters, news articles, and gossip.

The *Virginia Gazette*, in Lynchburg, took the President to task for humiliating Patsy and Maria: "These daughters, who should have been the principal object of his domestic concern, had the mortification to see illegitimate mulatto sisters, and brothers, enjoying the same privileges of parental affection with themselves. Alas!" The President, the writer declared, should have "married some worthy woman of [his] own complexion."[15]

Other political enemies ridiculed the President in verse and song. One rhyme, sung to the tune of "Yankee Doodle," began this way:

> Of all the damsels on the green,
> On mountain, or in valley,
> A lass so luscious ne'er was seen,
> As Monticellian Sally.

Yankee doodle, who's the noodle?
What wife were half so handy?
To breed a flock of slaves for stock,
A blackamoor's the dandy.

This poem first appeared in the Boston *Gazette*, but it was picked up by the Philadelphia *Port-Folio* on 2 October 1802.[16] Through such means, the story of Sally Hemings was widely disseminated — and widely believed. Political opponents who were reluctant to speak out publicly pondered the situation privately. In Massachusetts, John Adams (who had experienced Callender's malice firsthand while he was President) put pen to paper as a means of reassuring his children that despite their father's fondness for women in his youth, "no illegitimate Brother or Sister exists or ever existed."[17]

In the months before Sally Hemings's name appeared in print, poems had already circulated in the vulgar press lampooning the President for having sex with enslaved women. The subject was widely talked about "by Virginia Gentlemen," as the *Gazette of the United States* acknowledged, even as it took a stand against publishing such charges without corroboration. One reason the story caught on and spread so quickly was that aversion toward interracial sex had been growing. Relationships that had been tolerated in the eighteenth century came under greater scrutiny at the start of the nineteenth. Sex across the color line had a long history in Virginia, but around the time Callender's accusations appeared, some people were pressing to end the practice. A Norfolk newspaper in 1803 published a petition asking legislators to enact a law preventing "any white woman from haveing a black husband and to prevent white men from haveing black or yellow wifes or sleeping with them."[18]

In the midst of mounting scandal, Patsy and Maria came to Washington. Neither wanted to visit, but they relented when the President pressed them. The sisters were unaccustomed to — even uncomfortable with — being thrust into the limelight, but they wanted to help their father, who hoped their presence would encourage the public to see him as a family man rather than a slaveholder cavorting with his

"African Venus"—one of the terms Callender used to describe Sally Hemings. This is not to say that the President wanted his daughters in Washington solely to serve a political purpose, but in fall 1802 it seemed urgent to demonstrate his devotion to them. Ironically, the President who wanted women kept out of politics and public life inserted his daughters into the middle of both.

Elaborate preparations had to be made before the Jefferson daughters could be presented to Washington society. Although the President showed disdain for fashion in diplomatic and social circles, he told his daughters to purchase whatever they needed to make themselves stylish, instructing his kinsman George Jefferson (who handled his business transactions in Richmond) to pay for whatever Patsy and Maria needed to mingle in Washington's highest social circles. He also sent his daughters cash, at one point enclosing one hundred dollars in a letter to Patsy. Both daughters protested his extravagance, but their father insisted. Before leaving for the capital, Patsy requested the help of Dolley Madison in securing two wigs (one for her and one for Maria) from Philadelphia to "relieve us of the necessity of dressing our own hair." Hairdressing was time-consuming and required a level of skill beyond the ability of either of the women. Lady's maids knew how to style a mistress's hair, but apparently the President's daughters were not bringing a capable maid with them, possibly because neither of them had a highly trained one at the time. Patsy sent samples of her and her sister's hair so the new wigs, "of the most fashionable shapes," could be matched in color.[19]

Despite the frenzied preparations, one thing after another delayed their trip, which left the President frustrated. On 18 October he still had not heard when they would be coming, although he had expected word "daily." One of the reasons he had sent the cash was to ensure that want of money would "occasion no delay." In earlier correspondence, he had made sure they had detailed instructions on how to get from Edgehill to Washington. Patsy, feeling pressured, assured her father in late October that she and her sister were doing everything they could to set off soon. "We recieved your letter and are preparing with all speed to obey its summons," she wrote. She hoped they could set a firm date for departure by the following Friday.[20]

Maria apologized in early November that the traveling party still had not left home: "I Lament sincerely that it has not been possible for us to go sooner, as the visit will be scarcely worth making for so short a time." Because of the lateness of the season, she preferred to wait until spring, although her sister thought they should carry on with their plans. Four days later Patsy reported another delay, this one "of 2 days only." In this letter, she describes the journey as "a flying visit only to shew that we are in earnest with regard to Washington."[21]

Patsy and Maria arrived in Washington in late November and stayed almost six weeks. Patsy brought two of her children: Ellen, who had just turned six, and Jeff, who had recently turned ten. Patsy's youngest and oldest daughters were left at home with their father, as was Maria's infant son Francis. An enslaved nursemaid, Priscilla Hemings, came along to care for Ellen and Jeff,[22] a job that would keep her behind the scenes.

Margaret Bayard Smith, a chronicler of social life in the capital city, wrote delightful descriptions of Patsy's visit without ever mentioning Priscilla Hemings. On one visit to the President's house, Smith found the President and Patsy sitting together, playing with Ellen and Jeff. On another occasion, she found Ellen so charming that she extended an invitation to the young girl to visit without her mother. Patsy dropped Ellen off at Smith's house one morning and left her until seven in the evening.[23] Smith does not say whether the enslaved nursemaid came too. She was the President's friend and married to the founder of the *National Intelligencer*, a Republican newspaper that supported the President, and certainly understood the purpose of the family visit. She did what she could to make it successful by presenting the President as a man devoted to his charming family.

The President continued to host frequent dinners while his daughters were in Washington, only now Patsy and Maria served as hostesses. They had been in the city only a month when they pronounced themselves "heartily tired" of entertainments. Patsy and Maria much preferred the morning visiting engaged in regularly by Washington ladies to the larger and more elaborate events at the President's house.[24]

While in Washington, Patsy and Maria, at their father's insistence, continued to spend freely on clothing and accessories of the type deemed suitable for high society. Shortly after their arrival their father gave them each twenty dollars for this purpose. Not since Paris had Patsy and Maria worn the latest fashions. City and country attire was so different that one of Patsy's children, Virginia, was said not to have recognized her mother upon her return home until Patsy changed from her traveling dress into a more familiar calico.[25]

The Washington visit weighed heavily on Maria's conscience because she thought she had let her father down. She was socially awkward compared to Patsy and thought she had left a poor impression on Washington's fashionable, wealthy, and influential people. The expense of the visit only added to her distress. It "made my heart ache," she told her father later, to think of the cost. Thomas Jefferson reassured Maria that her visit had been worth the money: "Your apologies my dear Maria on the article of expense, are quite without necessity. You [Maria and Patsy] did not here indulge yourselves as much as I wished." Her "backwardness" in Washington had been the result of his own "ignorance" in placing her in a situation for which she was unprepared.[26] Her father's reassurance notwithstanding, Maria knew she had done little to dampen the scandal that surrounded her father.

Although Patsy apparently made a better impression in Washington, she must have shared her sister's misgivings because she was reluctant to return. In 1803, when both her husband, Tom, and Maria's husband, John Wayles Eppes, were elected to the House of Representatives and went to Washington to serve in the Eighth Congress, the two men moved into the President's house without their wives.[27] Remaining in Albemarle County, Patsy cared for her family, monitored farming operations, and reported events to her husband and father. The overseer at Monticello (Gabriel Lilly) consulted her about important labor issues, such as what to do with a disgruntled slave who ran away (Kit) or another (John) who fomented discontent among the hands. At one point, Patsy complained that "Lilly's business has taken up so much of my time and paper" that she had none left to report on the family except they were "all remarkably healthy." No wonder she felt hurried. In 1803, she had given birth to Mary Jefferson Randolph, bringing the number of children at home to six.[28]

When Tom returned to the capital for the start of the Ninth Congress, Patsy went with him despite the impending birth of another child. The Randolphs arrived in Washington on 1 December, just in time for the start of the congressional session. As before, Priscilla Hemings came as a nursemaid. Other slaves came too, although it is not clear which ones.[29]

Once again, Thomas Jefferson asked Dolley Madison to procure fashionable items for Patsy in advance of her arrival.[30] It may seem odd today that the President of the United States would ask the wife of the secretary of state to do his family's shopping, but it was customary in that time for elite Virginians who had access to goods and service to help friends obtain them. Earlier in the year, Dolley had bought earrings, a pin, and other things for the President's family. "Nothing more is wanting," he assured her at that time, except for his four-year-old granddaughter Virginia, who could use "a sash or something of that kind."[31] The President's expenses in bringing Patsy and her family to Washington were again considerable. He paid for wigs and fashionable accessories like combs, shawls, and veils, as well as a carriage for the Randolphs to use while in Washington. There was another outlay of one hundred dollars to cover the expenses they incurred in traveling from Virginia.[32]

Once Patsy arrived, the question arose whether she should be regarded as the wife of a congressman or as the daughter of the President. This was no moot point: etiquette required congressional wives to call on the wives of diplomats, while the wives of diplomats would be expected to call on the President's daughter, especially one living in the executive mansion and serving as hostess. Elizabeth Merry, the wife of the British minister, tried to clarify the situation by writing Patsy to ask her preference. Patsy's response only confused the matter more: she wished to be treated with no more courtesy than would be extended to any stranger. At her father's request, Patsy then asked to make the first call in the manner of the wife of a congressman, but Elizabeth Merry was uncomfortable with the situation and no visits occurred.[33]

As before, Patsy presided at some (perhaps most) dinners at the

President's house, which were largely for male guests, including one that had the potential to be particularly contentious. The dinner was for a Tunisian diplomat in town to negotiate payment for a ship seized by the American navy during the intermittent fighting between the United States and Barbary pirates off the coast of North Africa. John Randolph of Roanoke, one of the President's harshest critics, was to be at the dinner. Thomas Jefferson probably hoped Patsy's presence (along with that of her daughter Anne) would help tamp down animosities that might otherwise surface.[34]

The scandal over the President's relationship with his enslaved maid had not died down in the years between Patsy's first and second trips to Washington. If anything, it had intensified. In 1806 William A. Burwell, who had recently served as the President's secretary, showed Patsy a particularly offensive bit of doggerel penned by Irish poet Thomas Moore. The most accusatory lines did not mention Sally by name but made fun of the fact that the champion of freedom kept an enslaved lover:

> The weary statesman for repose hath fled
> From halls of council to his negro's shed,
> Where blest he woos some black Aspasia's grace,
> And dreams of freedom in his slave's embrace!

Patsy and Burwell together confronted her father with it, but he laughed and refused to discuss it.[35] He did not deny the charge, nor did he offer Patsy any comfort or advice on how to cope with the constant derision that marred his presidency. He seems never to have acknowledged Patsy's difficult position. She was humiliated by the gossip and unable to respond. And it was not only the rumors that upset her.

Patsy bore witness to her father's intimate relationship with Sally Hemings whenever she traveled to Monticello. Patsy's mother and Martha Washington may have accepted their fathers' extramarital liaisons with enslaved women with more composure than Patsy, but they did not have to endure the barrage of ridicule Jefferson's political opponents poured forth. The partisan political arena did not subscribe to the gentleman's code of conduct that said what a man did in the privacy of his own home could be ignored. On the contrary, the political environment of the early republic emboldened newspapermen, poets, and political enemies to exploit what would previously have been seen as a private matter. Jefferson's personal life had become part of the public conversation. Thinking back on these days, an older Patsy recalled the campaign as constant and cruel. The attacks, she said, were "slander," although she surely knew the truth.[36] From Patsy's point of view, the Hemingses, who had long been a personal asset, had become a public liability. Her father's reputation (and that of the entire Jefferson family) was at stake.

It is difficult to know what upset Patsy more: her father's behavior or what was said about it. She could do nothing to change either. Instead, like many other slaveholding women of her era, she pretended not to know the paternity of the children of mixed ancestry born at home. It is inconceivable that Patsy did not know, however, for — as we shall see — she deliberately set out to distort the truth. She insisted that someone else in the family had fathered Sally's children. She shared that story with her children, some of whom, long after Thomas Jefferson and Sally Hemings had died, would point to other family members they said had been intimate with Sally.

In the moment, published accounts mocked the President mercilessly. The *Boston Gazette* printed the following verse:

> Dear Thomas, deem it no disgrace
> With slave to mend thy breed,
> Nor let the wench's smutty face
> Deter thee from the deed.[37]

Joseph Dennie, a major literary figure in early America, reprinted this verse, along with a twist on a classic English metaphor: "If . . . 'a man may *kiss his cow*,' surely a *Philosopher* may *kiss his wench*."[38]

Though he was then only thirteen, William Cullen Bryant mocked the President in a bit of verse that called for his resignation (albeit not on account of the liaison):

And thou, the scorn of every patriot's name,
Thy country's ruin and thy country's shame! . . .
Go, wretch! Resign the Presidential chair.
Disclose thy secret measures, foul or fair. . . .
Go scan, philosophist, thy Sally's charms,
And sink supinely in her sable arms;
But quit to abler hands, the helm of state.[39]

Amateurs of all stripes tried their hand at verse, alongside established poets. Senator John Quincy Adams penned more than one rhyme lampooning the President and his "Dusky Sally." The *Port-Folio*, a literary and political magazine that published anonymously the poems and musings of many Federalists, printed the senator's "Ode to Xanthias Proceus." The racially offensive poem likened the President to a Roman nobleman who fell in love with a slave girl, although Adams felt Jefferson suffered by comparison since the slave who attracted Xanthias had been white.[40] Political cartoonists weighed in, too. Around 1804 James Akin depicted Thomas as a rooster, Sally as a hen. The caption read, "A Philosophic Cock."

The President's sex life became fodder for gossip as well as published attacks. Outraged—and perhaps hypocritical—elites saw his relationship with Sally Hemings as an affront to white women. Louisa Catherine Adams, wife of the Massachusetts senator, took umbrage when President Jefferson entertained important Indian chiefs and their wives in Washington. His action seemed to elevate the Native American women to a respectable status, which she found offensive. "Perhaps," she speculated, it was "the first *step* toward the introduction of *the incomparable Sally*" into Washington society.[41]

Abigail Adams took up the theme that the President had done a disservice to his daughters. In a letter written to Jefferson in 1804, she accused him of forcing them to compete for his affection with a black woman and her children. In a veiled reference to the matter, she pronounced him neither an "affectionate father" nor a "kind master."[42]

Rumors of sexual misconduct at the President's house went beyond his relationship with Sally Hemings. One charged Jefferson with keeping an enslaved harem at 1600 Pennsylvania Avenue. The fact that he brought young slave women to Washington to learn to cook may have fueled the rumor. As late as 1832, Frances M. Trollope resurrected the story with embellishments in her *Domestic Manners of the Americans*. In this version, Jefferson fathered children by not one but "a numerous gang of female slaves." The births of enslaved babies in the Presidential mansion gave credence to the accusations. The gossip circulated long and far. Hemings descendants continued to discuss the rumors for generations.[43]

Patsy could not shut out her father's critics. Most of the scandal-mongers were Federalist adversaries, known to both the President and Patsy. They included prominent members of Washington society. Patsy, like Louisa Catherine Adams, must have wondered where it would all lead.

Around the time that James T. Callender was writing about Sally Hemings, he also resurrected another sex scandal involving the President. Other journalists took up the story too. As a young man, Thomas Jefferson had fallen for Elizabeth Moore, the future wife of his best friend and Virginia grandee John Walker, and pursued her even after she married John. The public revelation put Elizabeth's reputation in jeopardy. Her husband charged the President not only with attempting to seduce his wife but also with "efforts to destroy my peace." In an attempt to put the matter to rest, Thomas Jefferson acknowledged in a letter to acting U.S. attorney general and secretary of the navy Robert Smith the "incorrectness" of his behavior toward Elizabeth Moore and referenced other "allegations against me," without specifying what they were. Possibly he hoped to quell rumors about Sally Hemings, although the reference may have been to other, untoward overtures involving Elizabeth. The President apologized for offering "love to a handsome woman" when he was "young & single." His behavior had been nothing more than adolescent injudiciousness.[44]

Patsy probably played a role—albeit inadvertently—in the public disclosure of her father's transgression. Early in his presidential term, she and Maria had been interrogated at a family gathering about the President's relationship with the Walkers. Patsy repeated what her father had told her shortly after their return from France: the Jeffersons and Walkers had fallen out over money. Her response suggested that John Walker had behaved dishonorably with regard to a debt. Word of her response spread. The aspersion on Walker's financial integrity helped fuel his outrage at the President and bring the seduction to public attention.[45]

Patsy surely realized later that her father had lied about why the Walkers and Jeffersons no longer visited, and the President must have understood the role his lie to Patsy had played in the unfolding of events. Perhaps that is why he said nothing when she confronted him with Thomas Moore's verse about his relationship with Sally Hemings.

Patsy had been embroiled earlier in another scandal that rocked her family and Virginia society for decades. In the 1790s Tom's sister Judith Randolph had married her distant cousin Richard Randolph and established a home aptly, as it turned out, named Bizarre. Judith's sister Ann Cary Randolph (called Nancy) lived with them. Rumors soon flew that Richard and Nancy had conceived a child whom Richard murdered at birth. Responding in part to public outrage, two Cumberland County magistrates had Richard arrested in April 1793. He was exonerated in court, but further rumors circulated, including charges leveled by John Randolph of Roanoke (Richard's brother) that Nancy had sexual relations with one of the family slaves. Patsy's father encouraged her to stand by her husband's sisters.[46]

Thomas Jefferson's encouragement of Patsy's support for Nancy Randolph, and Patsy's willingness to defend her sister-in-law, requires explanation. A lady's reputation was everything, after all, and Patsy risked exposing herself to scorn. Part of the answer may lie in societal expectations that a woman stand by her man — first her father and later her husband, and by extension his relatives. Obedience was said to be an important womanly attribute. But Thomas's encouragement of his daughter's loyalty may have roots as well in the era's ideas of masculinity and sexuality. Predators then (as now) do not see themselves as engaged in unacceptable behavior.[47] Thomas Jefferson, with his own experiences in seducing forbidden women, may have convinced his daughter (as well as himself) that there was nothing untoward about what happened at Bizarre. In Richard's case and his own,

Thomas Jefferson expected Patsy to lend a measure of propriety to men accused of sexual misconduct.

The scandal at Bizarre reveals something about ladies and their slaves, as well as about contemporary conceptions of gender and sexuality. The rumors about Nancy Randolph and Richard Randolph had their origins in the circle of slaves who served the ladies in an elite household, slaves who had access to intimate details of gentry life. In this case, Richard, Judith, and Nancy were visiting the home of Randolph Harrison when Nancy—a young, single woman—reportedly went into labor. Two slaves witnessed the birth and may have assisted with it. Slaves also knew what had happened to the baby after it was declared dead and disposed of.[48]

Virginia law barred slaves from testifying against a white person in court, but their words found their way into the proceedings against Richard nevertheless. Randolph Harrison testified that he saw and heard nothing of the birth until a "negro-woman" told him that Nancy had miscarried. He investigated and learned from other slaves that the infant's body had been "deposited on a pile of shingles between two Logs." The slaves were able to show Harrison the spot, which he found stained with blood. Mary Page, a white woman, who had eavesdropped on a conversation between Nancy and her maid, reported the maid's description of Nancy as "larger" than usual before the alleged miscarriage. Nancy had seemed concerned about her size and asked her maid whether she looked bigger than before. The maid answered yes. No one in the courtroom questioned the hearsay, even though the original witnesses were enslaved.[49]

No wonder Thomas Jefferson preferred to leave his slaves at Monticello rather than bring them to Washington. They had access to secrets that were better confined to rural Albemarle County than broadcast about the nation's capital.

In the midst of scandal and the Washington social season, Patsy gave birth on 17 January 1806 to a second son, James Madison Randolph, the second child to be born in the executive mansion.[50] The name "James Madison" had been given to another member of the President's family the year before. James Madison Hemings (called Madison) had been born to Sally Hemings when James and Dolley Madison—frequent visitors—happened to be there. Dolley promised Sally a gift for naming her second son after James. The promise—which Dolley apparently never kept—probably reflected her knowledge that the infant was an important member of Jefferson's household, albeit one who was enslaved.[51]

The births of Madison, on 18 January 1805, and his brother Thomas Eston Hemings (called Eston), on 21 May 1808, are remarkable because they show that the public scandal involving the President and his slave had done nothing to cool the relationship between Thomas Jefferson and Sally Hemings. Eston was said from birth to have closely resembled his father. The DNA testing that now bolsters the claim that Thomas Jefferson fathered Sally Hemings's children was done on Eston's descendants, and it is he who scientists and historians most confidently declare to have been the son of Thomas Jefferson.

Thomas Jefferson had won reelection to the presidency by a landslide the year before Madison's birth, carrying fifteen of the seventeen states that at the time constituted the nation. Voters obviously cared no more about the scandal than they did about the hypocrisy inherent in his claiming to be a champion of liberty while staking a claim to human property—another favorite theme of his Federalist opponents. Given his overwhelming victory in 1804, the President may have been dismissive of any suggestion that he alter his personal behavior, but Patsy would have assessed the situation differently. For her and her children, more was at stake than the outcome of a political contest.

Patsy stayed in Washington the entire winter of 1805–1806. She left in the spring and did not return during the remainder of her father's presidential term, even though her husband continued to serve in Congress until 1807. Her father retired from the presidency and left Washington in 1809, with Edy Fossett. John Freeman had six years left of servitude. His wife, Melinda Colbert, was now free and living in Washington with the couple's children. Rather than insist that Freeman join him at Monticello, Jefferson sold the remainder of Freeman's years of service to incoming President James Madison for $181.81. He may have been concerned about having a man slated for freedom mixing with his slaves who did not share that good fortune.[52]

Patsy Jefferson Randolph never served as First Lady in the manner of Martha Washington or Abigail Adams or Dolley Madison. Nevertheless, the Smithsonian Institution has bestowed the title of First Lady upon her on the basis of the time she spent in Washington in 1802–1803 and 1805–1806.

The First Ladies featured in the Smithsonian exhibit are known for advancing particular causes. Louise Catherine Adams promoted women's rights, Lucy Hayes promoted temperance, Mary Todd Lincoln promoted services for freed slaves and wounded soldiers. Eleanor Roosevelt stood for African American equality and human rights. Lady Bird Johnson led a "beautification" initiative to clean up blighted neighborhoods and highways. Rosalynn Carter's cause was improving healthcare for the mentally ill. Nancy Reagan embarked on a campaign called "Just Say No" to curb substance abuse. Laura Bush, a trained librarian, promoted literacy and reading. Michelle Obama's focus was on fitness through better eating and exercise and on supporting military families (an initiative referred to as "Joining Forces").

If one were to identify Patsy's "cause," what would it be? Certainly she advanced her father's agenda. Even when she was home in Virginia, Patsy did what she could to support her father. She watched over the Monticello household in his absence, and she kept abreast of his political fortunes. She took an interest in his election to office. She also backed his embargo. When President Jefferson signed into law a controversial act restricting trade with Britain and France (in effect from December 1807 to March 1809) in an effort to stop their interference with American shipping, Patsy—along with many other elite women—turned her attention to making fabric and clothing rather than importing it. In the months after the measure went into effect, she oversaw the manufacture of 160 yards of homespun and clothed her children with it.[53] Patsy also lent the President her respectability in the face of scandal. She avoided confronting the issue of her father and Sally Hemings head on, appearing publicly by her father's side and denying privately within the family what had happened.

Patsy Jefferson Randolph has not been the only child of a President to bear the discomfiture of her father's sex scandal. There have been others. But she — along with her sister Maria — may have been the first. Her situation was complicated by the fact that she bore witness to these events while fulfilling the duties of First Lady. She can be counted as the first of a number of First Ladies who have stood by a President in the face of public allegations of personal misconduct. The role of First Lady has evolved since Patsy's time, but the experience of a political wife or child standing by a husband or father in the face of scandal remains all too familiar.

Attitudes have changed since Patsy's time. What made President Jefferson's conduct with Sally Hemings so disgraceful in the eyes of his critics was her race and class. Class played a role as well in the scandal that erupted over his pursuit of Elizabeth Walker, for Thomas Jefferson had wronged a gentleman and sullied the reputation of a lady. None of his critics worried about the reputation of Sally Hemings because they shared the racist assumption that she had none to lose. There is no reason to think that Patsy Jefferson Randolph did not share the prevailing attitudes about race and class, which makes her situation all the more troubling to ponder.

CHAPTER 15

Mistress of Monticello II

As we have seen with Martha Washington, a First Lady's duties did not end when the President left office. After Thomas Jefferson retired, Patsy Jefferson Randolph moved with her children to Monticello so that she could help her father entertain large numbers of family members, friends, and political allies, as well as dignitaries and curious citizens. The visitors proved friendly, making Patsy's life more pleasant than it had been in Washington. She was confident of her ability to manage her father's complex household, including his slaves. He had once considered asking his sister Anna Scott Marks to take on housekeeping duties at Monticello, but Patsy advised against it, in part because she judged her aunt incapable of handling the help. They "have no sort of respect for her and take just what they please before her face," Patsy wrote.[1]

From 1809 until her father's death in 1826, Patsy called Monticello home. Her husband, Thomas Mann Randolph Jr., had a room at Monticello and spent much time there, but he also established a separate residence in a wood-frame home close by.[2] The marriage later collapsed as financial troubles drove Tom into a downward spiral of drinking and depression, but his insistence on a separate home had more to do with Virginia law than with his troubled relationship or personal demons. Tom was unwilling to give up the status of homeowner because only property holders and taxpayers could vote or hold public office. Tom and Patsy had four more children after she moved to Monticello.

Tom did not go back to Congress after his second term ended in 1807. Instead, he devoted his attention to planting. He was widely admired for devising a method of contour plowing that helped curb erosion. Still, he could not make ends meet. Brief stints in the military (during the War of 1812) and as a federal revenue collector hardly helped. In 1819 he turned again to politics, serving three years as Virginia's governor and three more as a member of the House of Delegates, positions that took him to Richmond. Patsy and the children remained at Monticello, except for the 1821–1822 legislative session when his daughters Virginia and Cornelia and their enslaved maids joined Tom in the state capital.[3]

At Monticello, Patsy focused on raising her children and managing the household. Thomas Jefferson had begun during his presidency to remodel the house with the goal of making it more distinguished and showcasing his exalted status. Patsy's job was to assemble a domestic staff that in number and comportment reflected the mansion's new grandeur. The remodeling went on throughout the former President's lifetime, but the full complement of wait staff lent the place a sense of wealth and luxury notwithstanding the constant construction.

Despite the disorder (or perhaps because of it), Patsy ran the house like clockwork. One guest from Boston—somewhat taken aback at the punctuality—remarked, "Everything is done with such regularity, that when you know how one day is filled, I suppose you know how it is with the others." Bells signaled guests to prepare for breakfast and dinner and rang again to signal they should sit down at the table. Thomas Jefferson usually retired early, but bedtime for others at Monticello tended to be around 10:30 p.m. A slave made sure a fire and a candle were lit for each guest who stayed overnight. Bostonian George Ticknor found a slave awaiting him at night to take his orders for the morning. The same slave returned the next morning to awaken him and light a fire.[4]

When Patsy moved to Monticello in 1809, she and Tom had seven children, ages one to eighteen. By 1818 she had given birth to another four: Benjamin Franklin (1808), Meriwether Lewis (1810), Septimia Anne (1814), and George Wythe (1818). Other relatives lived at Monticello too. To manage this large and complicated household, Patsy enlisted the help of her older daughters. She needed their assistance, but she also wanted them to learn to keep house. Patsy's oldest daughter, Anne, had married Charles Bankhead in September 1808, but Ellen, Cornelia, Virginia, and Mary were at home and of an age to learn the everyday responsibilities of a plantation mistress. The girls took turns, each managing Monticello for a month at a time. The one on duty "carried the keys," an expression that referenced the necessity of locking up supplies and keeping accounts of their use to ensure sufficient stocks on hand and to prevent pilfering. The housekeeper kept track of goods ranging from needles and thread to molasses and rum. Rare, expensive items like sugar and spices and vanilla beans necessitated especially close scrutiny. Some Monticello dishes called for wine. Other forms of alcohol were used in a variety of dishes, including brandied peaches.[5] Spirits of all types had to be carefully accounted for.

The Randolph daughters complained about the time they devoted to housekeeping. Mary thought the functions she performed "are exactly such as a machine might be made to perform with equal success, locking and unlocking doors, pouring out tea and coffee and in the interim plying my needle."[6] But of course the Randolph daughters were not like machines. Each performed the tasks differently. Mary came in for a bit of doggerel on the part of her father for being stingy with meal preparation:

> While frugal Miss Mary kept the stores of the House
> Not a rat could be seen, never heard was a mouse
> Not a crumb was let fall
> In kitchen or Hall
> For no one could spare one crumb from his slice
> The rations were issued by measures so nice
> When April arrived to soften the air
> Cornelia succeeded to better the fare
> Oh! the boys were so glad,
> And the Cooks were so sad,
> Now puddings and pies everyday will be made,
> Not once a month just to keep up the trade.[7]

Monticello's kitchen. © Thomas Jefferson Foundation
at Monticello. Photo by Philip Beaurline.

The thoughts and actions of white mistresses have been written about more often than those of enslaved women. Tom Randolph was one of a small number of white writers in the period to acknowledge the latter's feelings. The cooks that he refers to in the poem were enslaved, but Tom no doubt captured their attitude. Extra sweets might have made the white occupants and visitors happy, but the women in the kitchen had to work all the harder.

Tom Randolph aside, the labor of cooks and other enslaved people who put food on Monticello's table was all but invisible to most family members and guests, but not to the Randolph woman. In Thomas Jefferson's retirement years, the kitchen was left largely in their hands. The former President went into the kitchen daily to wind the clock he had installed, but planning and preparing meals fell under the purview of Patsy, her daughters, and Edy Fossett.

The Randolph girls, who began housekeeping at Monticello in their teens, may have experienced some difficulty in managing the kitchen.

Pleased with the English muffins she tasted while residing temporarily in London in the 1830s, Ellen remarked on their similarity to those she had eaten years before at Monticello "when the cook happened to be sober." Ellen would have had in mind either Peter Hemings, who served as head cook at the plantation from 1796 to 1809, or Edy Fossett, who took over from him. Cooks, as Ellen knew, could be difficult to manage, whether enslaved or free. At least once, she reprimanded her London cook for preparing several dishes for a small dinner party without authorization.[8]

Cooking was more labor-intensive than it is today. Food processors, electric mixers, and modern leavening agents have reduced the time cooks spend chopping, grinding, kneading, and beating. Scullions at Monticello probably rubbed solids through perforated colanders to puree them since they had neither blenders nor food mills. Mashed potatoes were made by pushing cooked potatoes through a colander with a wooden spoon. One culinary historian calls the work of making almond paste in Jefferson's kitchen "grueling." The superfine sugar called for in many Monticello desserts was made by pulverizing granulated sugar using a mortar and pestle. Cooks today can use a food processor to turn stale or toasted bread into crumbs in short order, but the kitchen helpers at Monticello would have made them the old-fashioned way, by rubbing stale bread across a grater.[9]

Open-hearth cooking was still common in most Virginia homes, and only wealthy families or commercial restaurants had enough staff to make the time-consuming dishes served at Monticello. Ordinary Americans—and certainly not enslaved Americans—applied no glazes to boiled meat to give it "an elegant, glossy finish," as was done at Monticello. Sausage meatballs served at Monticello required tedious chopping of the veal and beef suet by hand. The mixture was then beaten in a mortar until it was almost turned into paste. In the days before packaged gelatin could be purchased, jelly making began by boiling bones from veal or other livestock. The process had to be started a day or two before the wine, fruit, or other flavorings were added.

Food preparation also posed dangers. Working around stoves and boiling water were obvious hazards. Making vinegar posed another risk. Fumes from the pepper vinegar served at Monticello were strong enough to inflict pain on anyone who stood over the pot. For this reason, the recipe, updated for a modern cook, recommends making the vinegar only if the kitchen is well ventilated. At Monticello, as in many Virginia homes, cider was a beverage of choice at meals. Apples had to be pressed and processed and the final product bottled and corked carefully to prevent spoilage or worse. In 1793 most of the 140 bottles that had been put up exploded. Glass, cider, and corks "flew in such a manner as to render it dangerous," Patsy reported to her father. "Of the 140 bottles . . . you will hardly find 12," such was "the havoc."[10]

Mistresses were not involved in most mundane kitchen tasks, although most probably learned to make fancy desserts. The dearness of certain ingredients helps explain why. Plus, fancy desserts were considered a womanly art and a marker of elite status. It was also assumed that the young women would one day supervise their own cooks. The few existing references to members of the Jefferson family engaged in cooking suggest that Patsy's daughters learned to make cakes and puddings (likely custards baked in a crust).[11] But most food preparation was left to the cook and her helpers.

The Randolph girls sat in the kitchen with recipes in hand, in the manner of their grandmother. Since Martha Jefferson's day, the location of the kitchen had changed, as well as the cook. Martha Jefferson had read recipes unfamiliar to Ursula Granger in the cramped kitchen under the South Pavilion. Granddaughter Ellen Randolph did the same, except the cook was Edy Fossett and the site was a larger, well-equipped structure connected to the main house by a passageway.[12] Patsy and two of her daughters wrote out numerous recipes for tomatoes, which in the early nineteenth century were only beginning to be popular, ranging from gumbo soup to green pickles and omelettes.[13]

Today, visitors to Monticello can see recreated versions of Edy's kitchen, first used in 1808, and of the room next door that she shared with her eight children. The restoration of the kitchen, complete with brick floor, stew stove, and French cookware, is based in part on one inventory completed by James Hemings in 1796 and another in Patsy's hand from 1826. The stew stove had eight openings and incorporated a kettle. The constant source of hot water allowed the cook better control over the heat, which was necessary for the production of French sauces and certain other dishes. (A stew stove was a precursor to the cast-iron range.) The recreated kitchen includes a collection of French copper cookware as described in the inventories. Copper pans were considered ideal for use on a stew stove and for French cooking. The Monticello collection included not only saucepans of various sizes but specialized pans for cooking fish, tarts, and other foods. The French-styled kitchen would not have been considered unusual in many elite French and English homes, but it was unfamiliar elsewhere, including rural Albemarle County.[14]

Virginia described her seat in the kitchen as "my *throne*" in a letter to her fiancé, Nicholas P. Trist, a wording that staked her claim as the one in charge.[15] But Virginia knew that Edy was the better cook. Edy Fossett, after all, had trained for years under a renowned French chef. The cook's helpers, too, probably knew more about food preparation than Virginia. Yet text on display in the recreated kitchen at Monticello suggests that the Randolph women were the skilled cooks, rather than Edy Fossett: "Martha Randolph and some of her daughters kept handwritten recipe books that they used to select menus and instruct the cooks."

A recipe in hand was no guarantee of success. Culinary historian and food writer Damon Lee Fowler has noted shortcomings in a number of the recipes compiled by Jefferson family members. Patsy's recipe for chicken fricassee is "problematic," in part because it "sacrifices flavor left and right." A recipe for macaroons written in Jefferson's own hand has been pronounced "hopeless" by another food writer because of errors in the proportion of ingredients as well as the baking directions. Nor would a recipe for sponge cake, also in Jefferson's hand, have produced an acceptable cake if the listed ingredients were used as written.[16] It was up to Edy to turn out delectable dishes despite such flawed instructions.

When Ellen married into a Boston merchant family in 1825, her mother gave her a French cookbook (*Le Cuisinier Royal*) that included five pages of familiar, handwritten recipes. Still, Ellen wrote home requesting directions for making other favorites, including "gingerbread such as Edy makes." It is not known whether anyone fulfilled her request. Directions for making many of the dishes served at Monticello existed only in the cook's head. No written recipe exists for the bread served there during Jefferson's time, but historians know it was served regularly. Vegetables, a favorite of the President, were also served regularly, yet family records say little about their cooking. And some types of cooking, such as the making of macaroni noodles, are hard to quantify, since they require the cook to mix ingredients based on their feel or consistency rather than an exact measure.[17]

Any good cook knows that tasting is part of the process. If a mistress was on hand, she could do the sampling, but at times it was only the cook and helpers in the kitchen. It is hard to imagine cooks like Ursula Granger, Peter Hemings, or Edy Fossett sending a dish to table without judging its seasoning for themselves. Okra soup, a favorite at Monticello, relies in part on salt pork, which can vary considerably in saltiness. A quick taste could make the difference between a delicious and a disastrous dish. Many foods had to be adjusted at the last minute with salt and pepper. A Monticello recipe for brown onion sauce — a type of gravy — reminds the cook to "taste and add salt and pepper as needed" before serving.[18] When black cooks like Edy were left to adjust the seasoning on their own, they claimed in effect an ability to pass judgment on white food ways and entertaining styles — an action that in other circumstances might have been considered a violation of racial etiquette.

The color line was breached regularly in the kitchen. Saying that white mistresses reading recipes sat upon a throne reinforced plantation hierarchy, but in fact girls like Virginia read recipes to learn some of what their black cooks already knew. They could recite a step in the process of making a fancy dish and watch as the cook showed them how to do it. In this way, they learned to cook well enough to supervise their own kitchens after they married.

Edy could no doubt have decided on her own what to prepare in her master's kitchen, but Patsy or Virginia or another Randolph daughter entered the kitchen daily, sometimes to read recipes but always to decide what was to be served. Between planning menus, authorizing and paying for small purchases, unlocking and locking storage areas, taking inventory, watching food preparation, and tasting and adjusting the finished product, the preparation of a meal could command a lot of a mistress's time even when enslaved women performed the actual labor. It comes as no surprise, then, that Ellen Randolph once apologized to a correspondent for having so little time to write. It was her month to act as Monticello's housekeeper, she explained, and she had no time to "think of any thing but beef and pudding."[19]

Many of the recipes prepared at Monticello were extravagant, even wasteful by modern standards. The original recipe for oyster soup called for a quantity of oysters to be boiled, then discarded. Other oysters were then poached in the broth before the soup was served. Oysters were cheaper and more plentiful in Jefferson's time, but these and other directions suggest cost was not an important consideration in meal planning. One of Patsy's recipes for chicken fricassee, for example, called for disposing of the cooking broth.[20] Such extravagance suggests that Patsy and her daughters were complicit in the overspending that characterized her father's life.

Monticello's elaborate dinners offered opportunities for slaves to acquire material goods and small amounts of cash. Although slaves worked long hours for the Jeffersons, they managed nevertheless to raise vegetables and animals that made their way to the master's table. Account books show payments to slaves for ducks and fish, cabbages and sweet potatoes, apples and chestnuts, and much more. Although they lived on an outlying plantation, Bagwell Granger and his wife Minerva were among the slaves who on Sundays brought poultry, animal skins, cucumbers, squash, and whatever else they had on hand to sell or trade. Patsy at least once purchased catfish from Madison Hemings for fifty cents. She or her daughters regularly bought not only food but items ranging from beeswax, brushes, and brooms to animal skins and buckets from more than seventy slaves. People who could not get to the mansion house farm could sell through an intermediary. Husband and wife Wormley and Ursula Hughes, for example, appear to have sold items for others as well as themselves.[21] Through such interactions, Patsy and her daughters came to know a large number of Jefferson slaves who never worked in the house.

Both slaves and mistresses benefited from the exchange of goods, but the interchanges were about more than access to needed or wanted items. On Sundays, as Monticello's enslaved people paraded before Patsy in hope of selling produce and handmade items, they might also seek favors or share grievances. The ritual, repeated throughout the South, involved children as well as adults and was helpful for teaching youngsters—especially those who otherwise did not spend time around the owner's home—how to behave in an owner's presence. No one was born knowing how to carry out the subservient behavior expected of slaves. It had to be taught. The ongoing interchanges were fraught with danger for slaves, since mothers whose children did not behave according to an owner's notions of proper subservience could be held accountable. Yet enslaved women readily participated in the hope of ingratiating themselves and their children with the mistress and thereby earning favors ranging from extra food or clothing to a reprieve from work to care for a sick child. As a girl, Patsy may have seen her mother engaging in similar behavior with Monticello's slaves.[22]

Slaves did not always bring all of their produce and homemade items to owners because it could be peddled elsewhere. Nearby Charlottesville held an open market each Sunday. The slaves used the money they received to purchase better or more varied food and clothing there or elsewhere. John and Priscilla Hemings managed to accumulate enough cash through the slave economy that Patsy, on more than one occasion, borrowed small sums from them.[23] The transactions speak to Patsy's comfort in making requests of slaves. Whether the enslaved joiner and nursemaid were happy to lend the money is difficult to know. It is hard to imagine a situation in which they would have felt comfortable saying no.

Patsy sought cucumbers, cabbages, and other vegetables from slaves in part because Monticello's terraced garden, though large, grew experimental plants in the main rather than food for the table. Also, large numbers of unexpected guests could leave the cook short of supplies. In winter, sweet potatoes or pickled cucumbers hoarded by slaves in root cellars beneath their cabins proved appealing. The same was true of hominy, beans, and apples in April.[24] Having these items on hand year round required initiative and planning on the part of the enslaved men and women who grew and preserved them.

Through their actions, slaves improved their own diets as well as those of their owners and guests. Hunting, trapping, and gathering gave slaves access to foods like possum and duck, as well as honey, nuts, and berries. Patsy's son Thomas Jefferson Randolph (Jeff) joined some of the slave men on forays to hunt possum or fell a bee tree. After a successful hunt, he and the men would return to the slave cabins to eat whatever the enslaved women had cooked. Jeff pronounced the activities great fun. The enslaved hunters probably enjoyed the hunts too, only more was at stake for them than a good time. Their efforts supplemented the meager rations supplied by the master. Thomas Jefferson was neither more nor less generous toward his slaves than other planters in the area. At Monticello, food rations were distributed weekly: each adult received a peck of cornmeal, a half pound of meat, and four fish. Breastfeeding mothers received an extra quarter peck of cornmeal.[25]

Slaves who worked closely with owners in the home did not necessarily have the same opportunity to engage in the so-called slave economy. Nevertheless, they earned small bits of cash from time to time when visitors handed them tips for services rendered. Edy Fossett, working in the kitchen, might not have garnered tips for her services, and she earned the same rations as everyone else, but she probably had access to certain foods through her work, perhaps the discarded oysters used in making soup. Her husband, Joe, worked from dawn to dusk overseeing the mechanical needs of the plantation and operating its blacksmith shop, but with his master's permission he managed to make small sums of money. Joe spent some of his time laboring for local saddle makers. Thomas Jefferson collected a dollar for each saddle Joe worked on, out of which Joe was allowed a small portion.[26]

Once the food was secured and cooked it had to be plated and served. As he had in Washington, the former President employed dumbwaiters and revolving shelves to cut back on the number of servants in the dining room. Dishes were placed on warming plates filled with hot water or sand, and carried through a passageway into a behind-the-scenes staging area. The food was then put on plates and garnished before being carried upstairs to the revolving service door. Afterward, the servants would use the same shelves to remove the dishes. Even so, the need for servants in the dining area was not eliminated. The butler, who in Jefferson's retirement years was Burwell Colbert, announced the dinner and stood nearby in case his services were required.[27] The position of butler was held by Hemingses from the time the family arrived at Monticello. Burwell was the grandson of Betty Hemings. His mother was Betty Brown, the first of the Hemingses to arrive on the mountain after Martha Wayles Skelton and Thomas married. Martin Hemings had served as butler before his nephew Burwell took over in 1809.

Dinner was served in the French style, accompanied by beer and cider. After the main course, servants removed the top tablecloth and arranged a second course of what today would be called desserts: cakes, custards, puddings, and such. The second tablecloth would be removed to make way for nuts and fruits and sweetmeats, which were served along with wine.[28] The Randolph women were on hand to ensure that the service matched the quality of the food.

As the Jeffersons well knew, the right sort of food and service was crucial to the maintenance of social standing in both country and city. When noted author and socialite Margaret Bayard Smith decided to give a dinner party in 1835, she consulted "the most experienced and fashionable waiter in the city," who not only pushed her toward a more elaborate menu than she first envisioned but told her what types of dishes were out of style. Plum pudding was old-fashioned, while ice cream, grapes, and oranges would help to make her party a success. "Pies, partridges and pheasants" were ordered from a French cook especially for the occasion.[29] The food Patsy and her daughters approved for the table had to be stylish as well as sumptuous.

Patsy seemed to come into her own at Monticello during her father's retirement years. As a young woman, she had married soon after her return from France and left the plantation to establish a home with her husband. Despite the land and slaves she and her husband received as gifts from their parents, she struggled to establish a tranquil and prosperous home. In the nation's capital, she seemed helpless to change a political and social environment that pilloried her father. She escaped Washington after the winter of 1805–1806. But in 1809, a more mature Patsy emerged to take control of the household at Monticello. She had a purpose and newfound confidence. Her father needed her, and she was determined to succeed as mistress of Monticello.

CHAPTER 16

The Hemingses

What was Thomas Jefferson thinking when he agreed to have his daughter, Patsy Jefferson Randolph, keep house at Monticello? Was he worried about how she and Sally Hemings would get along? And what about the rest of the family? Patsy's seven youngest children would come with her to Monticello. Sally's four youngsters were already living there. Patsy's children ranged in age from one to thirteen, Sally's from one to eleven.[1] The Hemingses could hardly be kept apart from the Randolphs.

Sally must have viewed Patsy's arrival at Monticello with trepidation. Her future and the future of her children depended on a promise — one that was not legally binding. She was accustomed to Patsy's presence at Monticello, especially in summer, but when Patsy assumed full-time duties as mistress, she was bound to make changes. What new demands might she impose? At one time, Sally's mother and older brothers had been there to defend her, but they were now gone. Betty Hemings had died in 1807. Thomas Jefferson had sold Martin years earlier as the result of a dispute, and his whereabouts were unknown. James was dead, and Robert had found a path to freedom.[2] Other Hemingses remained, but Sally surely felt keenly the loss of Betty and her brothers.

Oddly enough, the Randolphs and the Hemingses seem to have gotten along by pretending not to know the truth about who had fathered Sally's children — or who had fathered Sally Hemings, for that matter.

It must have been difficult. The dissonance of living a lie takes a toll on those who practice it, but the taboo against acknowledging interracial liaisons was powerful, and the principal players proved disciplined enough to keep secrets. Although Monticello's visitors noted the resemblance between Sally's children and the Jeffersons, they carried on as if their only relationship was slave and slaveholder, albeit slaves with privileges and slaveholders willing to indulge them. Still, more than one visitor to Monticello remarked on the resemblance of servants to family members and called them "white."[3] Patsy's son Jeff admitted that in the twilight, one could easily mistake one of Sally's sons for his grandfather. And it was not solely a physical resemblance — although this was striking. Comportment and conversation also made the Hemingses resemble Jeffersons.

Sally's sons learned to play musical instruments and performed for the Jefferson family and guests. The oldest, Beverly, and Eston fiddled on Saturday nights while Jefferson's granddaughters danced with young men from the neighborhood. Madison and other Hemingses — Sally's children and their extended relatives — learned to read or at least to recognize their ABCs. Some learned to write. Literacy, Thomas Jefferson had once said, was the last step in "civilizing" Indians and presumably other people who had not been steeped previously in European-American ways. "Letters," he wrote in 1808, "are not the first, but the last step in the progression from barbarism to civilization." It was dangerous, he said, to teach slaves to write because they could use the skill to forge freedom documents and might refuse to be "kept in subjugation."[4] Yet the Hemingses were allowed to take this last step toward "civilization" with the help of Thomas Jefferson's grandchildren.

After Patsy moved to Monticello, Sally Hemings had no more children. The relationship between the former President and his maid appears to have remained cordial, but it may no longer have been intimate. Thomas Jefferson was nearly sixty-six years old when he retired, but Sally was thirty years younger. Her mother Betty had given birth to her last child at the age of forty-one. Patsy was forty-five when she had her last baby in 1818. Sally was young enough at thirty-six to have borne another.

Any number of reasons could explain why Sally bore no more babies. Many women in her day experienced complications of childbirth that left them unable to conceive, though no record suggests that Eston's birth was difficult. And Sally may have developed other health problems; Thomas Jefferson's own health was in decline. It is also possible that the sexual attraction between master and slave diminished, particularly once his daughter and grandchildren were in residence. Or Patsy may have convinced her father to discontinue a relationship that had already caused her angst and sullied the family's reputation. It is equally possible that Sally found a way to use Patsy's disapproval to end a relationship she did not want. There is no way to know for certain what happened, but the timing of Sally's end to childbearing is suggestive.

Thomas Jefferson's grandson Jeff said that he never saw or heard evidence to make him think that his grandfather and Sally Hemings were anything other than master and chambermaid: no "motion, or . . . look, or . . . circumstance" hinted otherwise.[5] Jeff took over the management of Monticello in 1815, at age twenty-two. He married that same year, and by 1817 had moved to nearby Tufton plantation. He had been born at Monticello, but his residence there was sporadic since his parents split their time between several plantations while he was growing up. And for much of this time he was too young to serve as a reliable witness to adult affairs. He had not even been born when Sally had her first child, and he was only sixteen when she gave birth to Eston. Still, his statement may have reflected knowledge that the sexual relationship between Thomas Jefferson and Sally Hemings came to an end around the time the President retired from office.

Yet the major part of Jeff Randolph's testimony about the relationship between his grandfather and Sally Hemings, we now know, was false. Addressing the matter long after Thomas and Sally had died, he told his grandfather's biographer Henry S. Randall that his cousin, Peter Carr, confessed to fathering Sally's children. DNA testing has now ruled out Peter's paternity. Jeff also told Randall that his grandfather's account book proved that Thomas Jefferson had not been at Monticello when one of the Hemings children was conceived. This too has proven false. Jeff based his story on seemingly irrefutable evidence — a confession and a written record — which helps explain why people believed it for so long.

The fact that Jeff cited "evidence" to pronounce his grandfather "not guilty" indicates that someone in the family still wanted to refute the charge that Thomas Jefferson fathered children with Sally Hemings. Historian Jan Ellen Lewis makes a convincing case that it was Patsy. She urged Jeff to search his grandfather's papers for proof exonerating him, and she took the stories about "Dusky Sally" — in Jeff's words — "much to heart."[6] Patsy and Jeff were not, however, the only members of the family to deliberately deceive on this subject. Patsy's daughter Ellen falsely accused Peter Carr's brother Sam of fathering Sally's children.[7] Patsy, Ellen, and perhaps elite white women more generally appear to have been determined to establish, or restore, racial order within the household, if only in retrospect.

Despite efforts by elite white women to police sex across the color line, slaveholding men continued to sexually exploit enslaved women. The vast majority of these interactions are understood as rape, but men like Thomas Jefferson understood at least their own cases differently. Interracial sex seemed to many an acceptable way for single and widowed white men to satisfy their sexual appetites, provided the relationships were not blatantly abusive. John Wayles's relationship with Betty Hemings seems to fit into this category. Thomas Bell had no white wife when he began living openly with Mary Hemings. Thomas Jefferson's son-in-law John Wayles Eppes formed a relationship with Betsy Hemings, who had been nursemaid to his and Maria's son, after his wife died.[8] And Thomas Jefferson's relationship with Sally Hemings occurred after he had been widowed.

Bachelors and widowers appear to have entered into interracial relationships fairly often in Virginia during the colonial and early national periods. George Calvert of Prince George's County, Maryland, established a shadow family before marrying a white woman, Rosalie Stier. His sister Eleanor married Martha Washington's son, Jacky

Custis. Jefferson's friend John Hartwell Cocke recalled that many of Virginia's batchelor slave masters had children with slave mistresses.[9]

We do not know a lot about how Patsy interacted with her half siblings, but we know that she supervised Harriet Hemings's vocational education. Patsy's housekeeping role extended beyond the kitchen and dining room to include the many tasks mistresses undertook to clothe family members and slaves. Cloth production had been dormant for a time after Martha Jefferson's death, but Thomas Jefferson revived it after taking notice of the textile industry emerging in the North. In the mid-1790s, he decided to purchase some of the new machines that were revolutionizing textile manufacturing. He had once owned a skilled weaver, Nance Hemings (Betty Hemings's third daughter), but in 1787 he had given her and her children (Critta and Billy) to his youngest sister Anna when she married Hastings Marks. Now he bought Nance back for sixty pounds. Nance wanted to be purchased with her children, but Billy remained in Louisa County with Anna, though Tom Randolph bought Critta for seventy pounds to work as Patsy's maid.[10]

Growth in textile manufacturing had been spurred in part by the embargo on imported goods Jefferson enacted while President and in part by the disruption in trade caused by America's second war with Britain. By the time war was declared in 1812, Thomas Jefferson was speeding up and expanding Monticello's textile production. Enslaved women had once made cloth using hand-operated spinning wheels and looms; now they learned to operate multispindle spinning frames and looms with flying shuttles. A new building at a Jefferson farm located near Shadwell housed the operation at first, but by 1815 the "factory" had been moved to Monticello's Mulberry Row. Jefferson hired a white weaver to set up the shop and teach enslaved girls to use the machines,[11] but once the enterprise was up and running, he put Patsy in charge.

His choice of Patsy was logical. She had practiced needlework from a young age, at his insistence. "Without knowing to use it herself," he asked, "how can the mistress direct the work of her servants?"[12] Patsy had become a skilled seamstress. She had experience supervising the manufacture and distribution of slave clothing at her own home, and while her father was in Washington, she had supervised the manufacture of clothes at Monticello. Patsy's new role was thus simply an extension of an old one.

Six or seven teenage girls and four teenage boys spun and wove wool, cotton, and a mixture of cotton and hemp under Patsy's direction. Patsy was charged with determining the efficiency and honesty of each worker, as well as the profitability of textile manufacturing overall. By measuring, counting, and recording, Patsy (and her father) could learn quickly who was performing adequately and who was not, who might be taking or wasting raw materials and who could be trusted to do neither.[13] The fourteen-year-old daughter of Sally Hemings was one of the workers Patsy supervised.

Putting Harriet Hemings in the textile factory may have been the former President's attempt to teach her useful skills by which she might earn a living in freedom. Or the idea may have been Patsy's. Patsy, who as an adult tended to think of slaves as assets, was uncomfortable having white or nearly white slaves who looked like the Jeffersons around. Patsy's mother had incorporated her father's concubine and their children into her household, but Patsy would not have to do the same for her father's children, at least not for long. Her father was willing to free Sally's children and have them leave Monticello as they came of age, although he refused to send Sally away, as Jeff later said Patsy wanted.[14] By teaching Harriet, Beverly, Madison, and Eston trades, he could prepare them to support themselves as freed people, just as James and Robert Hemings had.

Beverly, Madison, and Eston learned woodworking. Madison became a skilled wheelwright as well. Opportunities for women were more limited, but women of all social classes worked with textiles in some capacity. Martha Jefferson's thread case was among the few personal items Thomas kept after his wife passed away.[15] She and other elite white women decorated clothing and household furnishings with ornate needlework. Lady's maids learned this type of sewing, but Harriet Hemings and other women of the working class (both enslaved and free) labored to produce more practical items. Thomas

Jefferson and Patsy Randolph both may have considered work in the needle trades suitable for a daughter who by law and custom had no father or other freeman legally bound to support her.

Although Thomas Jefferson surely believed he had the right to decide Harriet's fate, he would have considered the wishes of Harriet and her relatives because they dominated jobs that were essential to the operation of his household. The Hemingses and other Monticello slaves were accustomed to negotiating with the master about matters ranging from an overseer's authority to their living arrangements. In fact, one historian has described the slaves as engaging in "persistent petitioning, and artful negotiation."[16] There is no reason to think that the decision about Harriet Hemings's occupation unfolded differently.

Another possible occupation for Harriet might have been as a maid in the house, but training maids took years and Harriet's training would have fallen to Patsy. No lady wanted to put this level of effort into training a maid who would someday leave. Besides, Patsy already had maids, some of whom were Hemingses. Patsy's father had given Mary Hemings's daughter Molly to Patsy shortly after she married Tom, and Tom had purchased Nance Hemings's daughter Critta from a family member to work as a maid for Patsy. Clearly, the mistress of Monticello did not want to be rid of all Hemingses. She placed some in key household posts, but unlike Harriet, these Hemingses neither evoked memories of scandal nor ignited more gossip. Patsy probably helped decide Harriet's fate.

Was it difficult for Harriet to work under a sister who played the role of mistress? Surely she worried about crossing Patsy and earning her wrath, but Harriet had come from a line of women who learned early on how to please both master and mistress. She apparently was up to the task.

Each of Sally's children grew up knowing that he or she would not be enslaved for life, which Madison said freed them from dread and allowed them to be "measurably happy."[17] But Harriet must have experienced her father's promise of freedom as both exhilarating and disquieting. Unlike her mother, Harriet had never left Monticello. She heard stories, surely, about life in places as far away as Paris and as nearby as Charlottesville, but she had no firsthand experience of cities.

Freedom opened opportunities, but it also meant missing family and friends. The future was full of promise but also loss for the young girl learning to operate multispindle spinning frames and looms with flying shuttles.

Harriet Hemings left Monticello in 1822. No one pursued her, and her fate remains unknown. The documentary record last places her in Philadelphia or Washington, DC. Overseer Edmund Bacon said he put her on a stage bound for Philadelphia with fifty dollars plus the amount of the fare. He did so on orders, although he did not say whose. Harriet's older brother Beverly left Monticello around the same time. No effort was made to recapture him either. No advertisement announced his disappearance, and no reward was offered for his return. The promise made to Sally had been that her children would be freed when they reached the age of twenty-one. Beverly was older—about twenty-four—when he left Monticello, but Harriet was twenty-one. Beverly's departure was no doubt delayed so that he could accompany his sister. Neither Madison nor Eston had reached the age of twenty-one in 1822, which explains why they did not leave with their siblings.

It seems likely that Beverly and Harriet left together, or joined one another soon after they disappeared, and entered into white society. Patsy's daughter Ellen Randolph Coolidge apparently believed the two were passing as white. When such people disappeared, "it was called running away," she said, but certain slaves "were never reclaimed" because they "were sufficiently white to pass." Madison Hemings later said both Harriet and Beverly had gone to Washington, where they lived as white people, married into respectable families, and raised children.[18]

The former President wrote in his farm journal that Harriet Hemings and her brother Beverly had run away, although it is clear— especially in the case of Harriet—that they were aided. Harriet must have had some say in what happened. She could hardly have been sent off to pass as a white woman against her will. Her brother Madison said "she thought it in her interest . . . to assume the role,"[19] implying that she had given the matter thought and exercised a degree of choice.

The decision to leave and pass as white could not have been easy.

People who crossed racial lines sacrificed family connections in the process. Although testimony by Madison Hemings suggests that Harriet and Beverly remained in touch with one another and with their mother and brothers, infrequent and secret communications were a poor substitute for interactions that had once occurred daily and openly.

Skilled in the use of textile machinery, Harriet may have joined the stream of farmers' daughters who were flooding into Philadelphia in the 1820s. Once away from Monticello, she would have been able to present herself as an educated white woman. Madison specifically noted that by "dress and conduct" Harriet looked the part. As Peter Fossett (the son of Joe and Edy Fosset) once observed, anyone associated with "such a family as Mr. Jefferson's," knew many things others did not. The former President was a collector, and his home boasted a library, a museum, and an art gallery. He owned an eclectic mix of curiosities, ranging from bows and arrows made by Indians to maps and portraits of famous politicians and scientists. The wonders hanging on the wall included a painting depicting the surrender of Cornwallis at Yorktown, a portrait of Diogenes, and a bear's claw brought from Missouri.[20] A statue of Cleopatra, mammoth bones, the horns and antlers of various animals and the like were incorporated into formal lessons and informal discussions with the Randolph children, as well as guests. The Hemingses could not have helped but absorb lessons in natural history, history, geography, and art. All four of the children had stayed around the mansion in their youth doing light chores and running errands. When they got old enough, they would have been made to understand the importance of the education they received in the mansion as well as in the manufactories. Harriet and Beverly could have passed for white not only by virtue of their looks, but also by virtue of their education.

Patsy, like her father, had probably concluded that Sally's children were white and thereby deserving of freedom. Ellen and her other children may have agreed, having been influenced by their grandfather's thinking. Until 1910 Virginia law proclaimed that people with no more than one black grandparent (and three white grandparents) were not black. The law applied only to free people, but Thomas Jefferson had long maintained that the law should apply to enslaved people too. He was troubled by unions between white and black people that resulted in the enslavement of persons who looked to be or were in fact (by legal definition) white. The issue had come before him, literally, early in his legal career in the form of indentured servant Thomas Howell. Howell was obligated to serve his mother's master for a term of thirty-one years because his mother was indentured and one of her parents had been either black or of mixed ancestry. The law that kept mother and son enslaved had been adopted to punish people whose sexual relationships crossed the color line. Jefferson, appalled at Howell's plight, proposed legislation to allow Virginians to manumit slaves without legislative approval. The Howells were not the only white or nearly white people ensnared in bondage. The existence of white slaves prompted Jefferson to argue before the highest court in Virginia that "under the law of nature, all men are born free, every one comes into the world with a right to his own person, which includes the liberty of moving and using it at his own will." Jefferson termed this "personal liberty."[21] His promise to release Sally's children from slavery after they reached the age of majority was consistent with his belief that legally white people should have the right to their own persons.

Subsequent generations of Americans have wondered how Thomas Jefferson justified in his own mind making Sally Hemings his paramour, given the virulent racism that he shared with his white contemporaries. The explanation is that he did not think of Sally or her children as black. When he wrote in Notes on the State of Virginia that blacks were inferior in "body and mind," that they were not as good looking as whites, that they did not have the mental capacity for producing poetry of good quality, he did not have the Hemingses in mind.[22]

For Jefferson, the question of race came down to a mathematical formula. He determined through an algebraic calculation "that a third cross clears the blood" of "negro" taint. In other words, if a black women had a child with a white man (like Betty Hemings's mother) and the daughter (i.e., Betty) had a child with a white man (i.e., John Wayles), the resulting child (i.e., Sally) would give birth to a pure white child provided the father was white. Jefferson likened the process to breeding sheep. As any farmer knew, crossing a merino ram with another type of ewe would result in the birth of a merino ram in the fourth generation provided all of the crossings after the original were with merino sheep. The problem as Jefferson saw it was not that Harriet, Beverly, Madison, and Eston were black. (They were not black by law.) The problem was that they were enslaved, and the law did not allow him to free them without pleading his case before the state legislature. Even if he had been willing to do so, what would he have said? Most planters who manumitted slaves did so in recognition of years of faithful service or for heroic acts. Jefferson could hardly have made a convincing case for manumitting all four of Sally's children on this basis. And presenting the case before the legislature would have fed the gossip and embarrassed the family (especially Patsy) all the more. Better to have them go quietly than to follow legal procedure.[23]

Virginia law at the time required freed slaves to leave the state unless granted an exemption by the state legislature, because many white Virginians, not just slaveholders, feared uncontrolled blacks in their midst. Freed slaves' self-control, many feared, would prove inadequate to maintain the social order. Even northern abolitionists shared this concern.[24] By sending Harriet and Beverly out of the state, the former President may have considered himself in compliance with at least part of the law.

As Harriet Hemings matured, the Hemingses and the Jeffersons must have worried that she would have a child in bondage. Most women—enslaved or free—had given birth by the time they were twenty-one. If Harriet had a child in slavery, her status would have passed to another generation of Hemingses. Someone must have watched Harriet carefully to prevent this from happening. In *Notes on the State of Virginia*, Thomas Jefferson went so far as to claim that black men were "more ardent" and "eager" in lovemaking than white men, which might have caused worry on his part that Harriet would be the target of their sexual advances. Black men failed to provide the "tender delicate mixture of sentiment and sensation" that made sex between whites superior, he said.[25] We can only conclude that Thomas Jefferson was describing the type of relationships he had with his wife, Martha, and his concubine, Sally. For her part, Harriet Hemings must have recognized the difficulty early marriage to a free black or enslaved man would pose because she waited to start a family until she left Monticello.

By crossing the color line with Sally Hemings, Thomas Jefferson has seemed hypocritical to modern people. He wrote about the repulsiveness of black people in *Notes on the State of Virginia*, while taking one to bed. But people who charge Jefferson with hypocrisy are wrong on Jefferson, even as he was wrong on race. He never subscribed to the belief that everyone with any African ancestry whatsoever was black. Instead, he believed that black people of mixed ancestry with enough white "crossings" could become white and deserving of life free from bondage. His thinking was flawed. For one thing, people are not merino sheep. But the idea allowed him to rationalize—even quantify—freedom for his children. The same train of thought would have allowed Patsy to do the same. She could supervise Harriet's education in the needle trades and see her off with her brother to freedom while keeping other people (including other Hemingses) enslaved. In the future, Patsy would have decisions to make about what to do with Harriet's mother and youngest brothers, but after 1822 she no longer had to worry about Harriet and Beverly. Meanwhile, financial troubles were mounting for the Randolphs and the Jeffersons—a development that threatened to dismantle Monticello and render the keeping of other promises uncertain.

CHAPTER 17

Death of Thomas Jefferson

Thomas Jefferson died on July 4, fifty years to the day after the colonies adopted the Declaration of Independence. His health had been declining for years, but in June he took to his bed with what may have been prostate cancer. For several weeks Patsy Jefferson Randolph sat with her father during the day, aided by family members and slaves. At night her son Jeff and her son-in-law Nicholas Trist took turns keeping watch, again with the help of slaves. Burwell Colbert, trusted valet and butler, slept on a makeshift bed in the room. Sally Hemings and her sons Madison and Eston were surely among the people who came and went. By the night of July 3, it was clear to everyone that Thomas Jefferson was dying. At one point, he rallied enough to summon and speak with his servants, but neither their names nor his words have been preserved. In midmorning the next day, Burwell realized his master was uncomfortable and adjusted his pillow. Thomas died soon after and was buried the next day in the rain. Family, friends, and servants attended the graveside service, presided over by Episcopalian rector Frederick Hatch. Slaves made the coffin and dug the grave.[1]

Afterward, Patsy attached great importance to a small book of verse her father wrote shortly before he died. "A death-bed adieu" asked Patsy not to weep and assured her that Thomas would carry her love to her deceased mother Martha and sister Maria. Thomas Jefferson's youngest sons also attached great importance to a document demonstrating a father's affection. His will bequeathed them freedom. The wills of white men rarely mentioned their sons or daughters born to enslaved woman.[2] Jefferson did not acknowledge Madison and Eston as kin, but he singled them out—along with three older, longtime servants—for emancipation.

The death of a father represents a personal loss for his family, of course, but it also prompts a financial reckoning. Such was the case following the death of Thomas Jefferson, whose fortune had been spent. For years, the Jeffersons and Randolphs had been struggling to maintain an elite style of life and concocting schemes to stave off financial ruin. In 1820 Maria's widowed husband John Wayles Eppes had offered to trade Jefferson "United States bank stock for Negro men—say 12." Eppes would use them to clear land for a couple of years before deeding them over to his son Francis. Meanwhile, his father-in-law could use the bank stock to shore up his finances. Desperate for more funds, the former President proposed a lottery, which was illegal at the time, but the state legislature approved an exception. Tickets were printed and sold for ten dollars each, but not enough money came in to save the estate. The downward spiral ended only with the former President's death and the dissolution of his holdings. On the day Thomas Jefferson died, he owed creditors more than a hundred thousand dollars. His 130 slaves were appraised at thirty thousand dollars.[3] The home so closely associated with him would have to be sold, and those who lived there—black and white alike—would have to leave. Everyone suffered, but most of all the slaves. It was a sad and stressful time.

The family's financial woes began long before Thomas Jefferson's death. By the time Patsy and her children moved to Monticello in 1809, Thomas Mann Randolph Jr. was in need of cash and willing to sell Varina and its slaves to raise it. When no suitable buyer could be found, Tom instead sold the thousand-acre Bedford County plantation that his father-in-law had given him at the time of his marriage to Patsy. The Randolph debts continued to mount. In 1823, facing certain financial ruin, Tom turned to his eldest son for help. Jeff had earlier assumed management of his grandfather's estate, which was also financially distressed. Now the young man shouldered his father's $23,000 debt in return for a deed of trust for Varina, Edgehill, and the forty-nine slaves who lived and worked on the two plantations. To discharge the debt (which by 1825 had grown to $33,500) and salvage his own financial position, Jeff decided to sell everything. Tom was satisfied to see Varina go but not Edgehill. Jeff's plan produced a rift between father and son, especially after it became clear that Jeff intended to sell the slaves apart from the property.[4] Selling land and labor together was a way to avoid one of the worst of slavery's features: the breaking up of families.

The idea that Edgehill would be dismantled and the slaves Tom had "raised" parceled out to different buyers was too much for Tom. He was already distraught at having sold slaves to pay debts. In 1815 he had sold a number of slaves, including nineteen-year-old Betsy, the spouses George and Jenny together with two of their daughters, and a man named Mason. Tom's papers make clear that the slaves had done no wrong to warrant sale. Financial "necessity" was the culprit. "I part from [them] with very great regret," he said. He claimed to have formed an attachment, particularly to Mason. In 1818 Tom again succumbed to pressure and sold a slave named Maria to one of Monticello's overseers, who presumably would at least keep her near family and friends. But Maria's sale, like the sale of Mason and the others, did little to staunch the family's losses, and other slave sales followed. At one point Tom sold a four-year-old girl away from her mother.[5]

Under the terms of Edgehill's sale, set for 8 August 1825, the slaves were to be sold first, then the land (divided into parcels). Tom went before the Virginia Superior Court of Chancery to stop the sale, arguing that Jeff's approach would jeopardize the crop and make the land less valuable. The court agreed, but its injunction only delayed the transactions. By the time the Edgehill slaves and lands were sold, Tom had all but ceased living at Monticello.[6] Patsy had sided with her son, and the marriage seemed all but over.

Tom was ruined financially, but Patsy still had a means of support. She and her unmarried children lived with her father, and she owned eleven domestic servants who were hers in fee simple, so not subject to sale for her husband's debts. They included Betsy and Priscilla Hemings, who were now in their fifties, another older servant, and eight young girls, three of them the daughters of Burwell Colbert and his deceased wife Critta.[7] The girls were especially valuable since Patsy could hire them out and live on the income they generated, give them away to her heirs, or sell them as needed.

Tom was not the only Virginian, or the only member of his family, whose financial position was deteriorating. The situation was distressing not only for the Randolphs but also for their slaves. When the sheriff came to seize property belonging to Tom's brother William, some of his slaves barricaded themselves in the house in a fruitless effort to ward off sale. Tom sympathized and wanted to help his family, but Patsy objected. "With my *urgent entreaties* [I] have kept him clear of all *new* engagements," she told her father.[8] The young woman who had hesitated to tell Tom that she did not want to move to Varina had become more assertive as she aged.

For Tom, the loss of his land and slaves was as much about his manhood as about money. A man without property could neither vote nor run for public office. The way the sale was conducted distressed him further. Tom prided himself on his fair treatment of bonded laborers and had once bragged that in thirty years of planting, few of his slaves had run away.[9]

Tom was no abolitionist, but he was willing to entertain the idea of freeing at least some slaves. As governor he had once proposed freeing a certain number of young slaves (two-thirds of them female) each year to reduce the number of slaves in the state. Like most other white Virginians of his day, Tom did not want freed people to remain in the state, and he proposed sending them to Haiti with funds raised through a tax on slaveholders. The move, which would have separated families, hardly seems progressive today. Yet the proposal drew the ire of many simply for broaching the subject of emancipating slaves. Martha Washington's granddaughter Eleanor (Nelly) Custis Lewis thought his fiery speeches on the subject encouraged slaves toward disobedience. Thomas Jefferson withheld support for his son-in-law's plan, although he pronounced him courageous for advancing it.[10] Patsy, like most other white Virginians, was not keen on plans for diminishing slavery's importance. She seems to have accepted a style of life that pledged slaves as collateral to secure loans and sold them for the best price when the bill came due, even if it meant selling them out of the neighborhood. Edgehill's and Monticello's slaves had been mortgaged to the hilt, and most would be sold wherever buyers could be found.

The Jefferson debt was a long time in the making. No one event explains it, although Thomas's willingness to cosign loans for other gentlemen helped trigger the crisis that led to Monticello's sale. Patsy blamed her father's financial troubles on Virginia's economic woes, his generous hospitality, his neglect of personal finances while in public service, and his slaves. Ellen Randolph Coolidge explained the problem this way: her grandfather had run up debt because he did not wish to overwork his slaves. Jeff Randolph said much the same: his grandfather had allowed his feelings for his slaves as people to outweigh his concern for their status as property.[11] Presumably he could have worked them harder or sold them to avoid financial ruin. The Randolphs evidently found it more palatable to blame the victims of Virginia's economic system than the former President or themselves.

Thomas Jefferson's extravagant way of living had contributed to his debts. His remodeling of Monticello was but one example of overspending—albeit a significant one. At the same time, he had constructed an elaborate retreat known as Poplar Forest. Jefferson's homes were no doubt valued for their own sakes, but ostentation was a means of marking their occupant as a man of wealth and power; the hospitality that greeted visitors there went beyond the welcome Virginians typically extended to guests.

Thomas Jefferson and his family found it difficult to curb their spending even in the face of looming financial doom. In dire need of cash nine years before his death, the former President arranged to sell his library to the U.S. Congress. Most of the twenty-four thousand dollars he received went to pay his obligations, but soon after arranging the sale, he purchased a bay horse on credit, which increased his debt by a hundred dollars. He also began purchasing books to reconstruct a library at Monticello, and there seemed to be no end to his gifts for grandchildren. When ten-year-old Cornelia complained that she did not have a silk dress like her older sister, her grandfather purchased three, one for her and two for other granddaughters. Other gifts included elaborate saddles, exciting vacation trips, and musical instruments of the best quality. Even when all hope was lost that Monticello might be saved, except perhaps through a lottery, the family continued to spend. Thomas Jefferson ordered a new pianoforte, which afforded so much pleasure that he made plans to order another as soon as the lottery money came in.[12]

Thomas Jefferson's lavish gifts also included human property. By the mid-1790s, he had given Patsy and other family members almost eighty slaves.[13] Some were given in groups, such as those he gave Patsy and Tom Randolph at the time of their marriage. Others were transferred individually. In 1812 he made a present of Thruston Hern, brother of Edy Hern Fossett, to his grandson Jeff. Five years later Thruston ran away, probably with the help of Paul Jennings, one of James Madison's slaves. Thruston was never recaptured, and in 1819 Jefferson gave Thruston's brother Moses Hern to Jeff, presumably as a replacement.[14] And so it went.

By the time Thomas Jefferson wrote his will in mid-May 1825, he had already transferred substantial property to his family. The payment of his debts would take most of the rest. Whatever remained would go to Patsy. The funds were to be held in trust for her until after Tom's death, to ensure that her husband's creditors would not seize the assets. Jefferson freed Madison and Eston, along with John Hemings (carpenter), Joseph Fossett (blacksmith), and Burwell Colbert (valet and butler). All three had distinguished themselves as "faithful" servants. Colbert had shown up for work as usual after learning of his wife's death, an act that astounded Jefferson's granddaughter Ellen. "He did not lay by and send us the keys as I expected he would," she marveled, although upon reflection she thought it had probably been for the best: "The want of employment would only leave him more time for the indulgence of his grief, which is so sincere as to excite the greatest degree of sympathy." Apparently it did not occur to her or any other member of the Jefferson family to tell Colbert that he could take time from his duties to mourn his wife. Nor did it occur to them to find a way to free Colbert's children. His master did bequeath him cash, along with a log house on an acre of land for use over his lifetime, but Colbert's children belonged to the Randolphs and remained enslaved.[15]

Joseph Fossett (Joe) and John Hemings were each given an acre of land, a log house, and tools of their trades, in addition to freedom. Joe's wife Edy and their eight children belonged to Thomas Jefferson, but they remained enslaved; Joe worked and saved over his lifetime in order to purchase them. John's wife Priscilla was not Jefferson's to bequeath, since she belonged to Patsy.[16]

Thomas Jefferson took no action to free the majority of his slaves. Like others, he blamed the slaves for his family's predicament. His slaves had not worked hard enough to pay off his debts, which would have allowed him to improve their living conditions and set them free. Yet the debt had not been incurred solely to keep the plantation afloat. Monticello represented a dream Martha and Thomas Jefferson had shared from the time they married: to live as grandees. The master of Monticello kept spending to sustain the dream long after her passing. He did not want to live another way, nor did his daughter, or perhaps they did not know how. Cornelia Jefferson — who seemed at one time to consider taking another path — once remarked: "I suppose not untill we sink entirely will it do for the grand daughters of Thomas Jefferson to take in work or keep a school."[17]

Patsy had encouraged her father's spending. As his term in Washington wound down, the President had hoped his lands would be sufficient to grant Patsy's children independence as they came of age. They would have to live within their means. "The plainest stile of living which keeps them out of debt" is better than living in splendor for a few years and watching "their property taken away for debt," he wrote. Patsy assured her father that he need not worry about her children. They were young and had no expectation of living in a particular style. Besides, her own lands would at least "insure them food and raiment." Her father should look to his own happiness and not worry about her and her children. You should not be "deprived of those comforts which long habit has rendered necessary to you," she wrote.[18]

It fell to Jeff—in consultation with his mother and other family members—to discharge his grandfather's debt through the sale of land and slaves. At length, Patsy and her children debated how to survive without Monticello and its workforce but also which domestic slaves should be kept and by whom. Even Ellen Randolph Coolidge, who had married the son of a wealthy and well-connected northern merchant and lived in Boston, wanted her share of the domestic slaves, despite Massachusetts's ban on slavery.

In one of the peculiarities of slave society, Ellen had continued to own her maid, Sally Conttrell, after she married and moved to Boston—or rather her husband Joseph did, since Ellen's property passed to him upon their marriage. The Coolidges could not keep Sally enslaved in Boston, so they rented the skilled seamstress to a Virginian. Joseph signed a power of attorney allowing Jeff to, in Ellen's words, "dispose" of Sally. In what Ellen must have thought was a show of affection, she directed her brother to give Sally some choice in finding a new owner. It is not clear how much say Sally had in the matter, but the mathematics professor at the newly established University of Virginia hired her as his wife's maid and nurse. Sally Conttrell was more fortunate than most slaves in her situation. The mathematician, having decided to quit the university and return to Europe in 1826, gave the Coolidges four hundred dollars for Sally and declared her free.[19] Any slaves Ellen inherited could expect, like Sally, to be hired out or sold, but the chance that another would follow Sally's path to freedom was effectively nil.

In 1827 the Randolphs put the mansion, furnishings, and most of the slaves up for auction. It took four years to find a buyer for the house, which eventually went for seventy-five hundred dollars, but the other items, including about 130 slaves, sold more quickly. A host of bidders were only too glad to purchase members of the Hemings family, as well as other slaves, and willingly paid 70 percent more for the men, women, and children than the appraisers had expected. The price on certain slaves was set deliberately low to give family members a chance to buy them at bargain prices. Descendants of Thomas Jefferson and Betty Hemings were among the purchasers. The remaining slaves scrambled to find buyers in the neighborhood who would keep them near loved ones.[20] The custom of "allowing" slaves to find their own buyers was said to make them more cooperative, but it also helped relieve an owner's guilt. When local purchasers were not found and slaves were sold away from family and friends, it was because the slaves had failed to find a suitable purchaser.

Patsy and her daughters stayed away from the sale. The Randolph women clearly found the spectacle of selling the slaves they had worked with disturbing. Patsy's middle daughter Mary expressed relief when it was over, even though she was not present. The slaves put up for auction in the bitter cold days of January included Edy Fossett and Fanny Hern, who had worked with Mary and the other Randolph women in Monticello's kitchen. Fanny's husband was also sold, as were Edy's children and Israel Gilette, who had worked as a scullion and waiter. No one knows what happened to most of the Jefferson slaves, not even the ones "saved" from sale by Patsy and her children.[21]

As the sale unfolded, there was much lamenting in certain quarters of the United States. Many wondered why Thomas Jefferson did not follow the example of George Washington and bequeath his slaves freedom. But Jefferson was no Washington. He was not wealthy enough both to live a life of luxury and to free his slaves. He had managed to do only the one.

Sally Hemings escaped sale that cold January day, but she was not legally freed. In order to emancipate her, Thomas Jefferson would have had to petition the legislature to allow her to remain in Virginia. His will included language asking legislators to grant Madison Hemings, Eston Hemings, Burwell Colbert, John Hemings, and Joseph Fossett exemptions from the law that required freed slaves to relocate, but he was unwilling to name Sally, probably for fear doing so would reignite gossip. Perhaps to spare his daughter and grandchildren further humiliation—or maybe at their insistence—he kept silent. Sally

Hemings nevertheless left Monticello and spent her remaining years with her sons Madison and Eston and their wives (free women of color) in Charlottesville.

Madison and Eston were able to support their mother, wives, and children with the woodworking skills they had learned at Monticello under the tutelage of their uncle John Hemings. Eston also began a promising career as a musician. Following the death of their mother in 1835, the brothers moved from Virginia to Ohio, where they believed they would find greater opportunity. Madison worked in the construction trades and lived out his life on a sixty-acre farm in Rosa County. He and his wife associated with the local African American community, but later some of his descendants identified as white. Eston headed a dance band that played in southern Ohio. Frustrated by the lack of opportunities there for free people of color, in midcentury he moved with his wife and children to Wisconsin, where he made a living as a cabinetmaker. The family adopted the surname Jefferson and passed into white society.[22]

Soon after laying her father to rest, Patsy, too, left Monticello. She went briefly to Washington, DC, and then to Boston for a longer stay. There, she and her two youngest children (George Wythe, age eight, and Septimia, twelve) lived with Ellen and Joseph Coolidge. Unwilling to concede his place at the head of the family, Tom Randolph made plans to retrieve his wife and children. Patsy, not wishing to cut all ties with her husband of thirty-seven years, agreed to return to Monticello, where they lived until Tom's death in June 1828.[23]

Patsy spent the remainder of her life in the homes of her children Ellen, Virginia, and Jeff. She and her unmarried children continued to be supported by slaves, at least in part. Jeff launched an effort to raise money on his mother's behalf from the federal government, the state of Virginia, and other government entities. The state of South Carolina and the city of Philadelphia came through with funds, but other places did not. The Randolphs resented especially the failure of Virginia and the United States to recognize Patsy's contributions as her father's First Lady.[24]

Elite women in reduced circumstances sometimes took in boarders or opened schools as a means of making ends meet, but doing so would have cost Patsy status. Because she had slaves, she had other options: she could rent or sell them for cash. Patsy did both. In 1833 Patsy sold two slaves out of what she called "dire necessity." Her youngest sons attended the University of Virginia, their expenses paid for by the work of Lavinia and Charlotte, two slaves Patsy hired out to raise the fees.[25]

Patsy first wrote a will in April 1835. Most of her property consisted of slaves, some of whom went to her children. She was the legal owner of Sally Hemings, Wormley Hughes, and Betsy Hemings, who she said should be allowed to live as free people. The will also singled out two of Burwell Colbert's daughters, Emily and Martha, for freedom. Nine months later Patsy wrote a new will similar to the first, only now she bequeathed Martha Colbert to her son Lewis.[26] Patsy may have succumbed to pressure from Lewis, or perhaps Martha Colbert had done something to displease her. In January, President Andrew Jackson had named Lewis secretary of the Arkansas Territory, and he had married President Jackson's grandniece Elizabeth Martin that spring. Patsy may have considered Martha Colbert a suitable wedding present. She knew that Burwell, Martha, and other members of the Colbert family would be devastated by the change in her will, but she made it anyway. Patsy consistently put her own children first when it came to deciding what to do with slaves.

Patsy Jefferson Randolph's death occurred not long after she revised her will. On the night of 9 October 1836 she went to bed with a severe headache. She died the next morning.[27] She lies buried in the Monticello graveyard beside her husband and her father.

PART 3
Madison

CHAPTER 18

Dolley Payne

Dolley Payne Madison was closer in age to Patsy Jefferson Randolph than to either Martha Dandridge Washington or Martha Wayles Jefferson. Martha Washington, born in 1731, and Martha Jefferson, born in 1748, had married and started families by the time the American Revolution began. Dolley Madison and Patsy Randolph, born in 1768 and 1772, came of age after the declaration of peace. All four were born into slaveholding families and grew up in Virginia, but their upbringing was less alike than one might suppose. Martha Jefferson and her daughter Patsy were raised in families with great wealth and important social connections. The Payne and Dandridge families were both of middling rank, but the childhood experiences of Dolley Madison were nevertheless quite different from those of Martha Washington. Jack and Fanny Dandridge were Anglicans who embraced slavery and the hierarchical society in which they lived. Their goal was to rise in the hierarchy, and owning slaves was a means of doing so. John and Mary Payne were Quakers who questioned the place of slavery in the nation and suffered personal financial loss for their beliefs. Before Dolley was out of her teens, her parents had emancipated their slaves and left Virginia for Pennsylvania and its promise of freedom for all.

Dolley Madison's father, John Payne, was not a Quaker or an abolitionist by birth. He grew up in a family not so different from that of other well-to-do slaveholders. His father, Josias Payne, was a prosperous planter who worked his land in Goochland County with slave labor. Josias's wife Anna has been described as a pretty women who owned beautiful things. Josias and Anna were both Anglicans. He was a vestryman in the church, seeing to it that roads and bridges were maintained, the poor cared for, and criminals punished. He was also a justice of the peace and a member of the House of Burgesses.[1]

John Payne married into the Quaker faith in 1761. His bride, Mary Winston Coles, had been a member of the Society of Friends from birth. The Quaker church, which opposed intermarriage, banished Mary for marrying John but readmitted her three years later after John converted. Their fervent support of Quakerism set the Paynes apart from most in Virginia, where Anglicanism predominated.

At the time of their marriage, John and Mary Payne were slave-holders of modest means, at least compared to the grandees who ruled Virginia, and even compared to John's father. They set up housekeeping on a farm of nearly two hundred acres but, unhappy with their situation in Virginia, left to settle in New Garden, a Quaker community in North Carolina. Dolley was born 20 May 1768 in the North Carolina log cabin the family called home.[2]

The Paynes stayed in North Carolina for about a year. Why they returned to Virginia is unclear, but offers of hospitality, land, and slaves from family members may have been factors, as well as conditions in North Carolina. In 1785 Josias Payne died, and John inherited six hundred acres of land along with the "Negroes, Peter, Ned, and Bob." The Paynes eventually built a farmhouse at Coles Hill plantation in Hanover County on land Mary's father deeded over to her. The farmhouse was a modest frame structure of one and a half stories. Two rooms sat on either side of a large hallway. Bedrooms were located on the upper floor. There were a number of outbuildings, in addition to slave cabins. Young Dolley was cared for by an enslaved woman she called "Mother Amy."[3]

As a youth, Dolley learned the housewifery skills that other girls in similar circumstances were taught, including how to supervise the work of slaves. She cooked, did plain sewing, made soap, and took care of younger siblings. She also studied academic subjects. Dolley's childhood in many ways resembled that of Martha Washington, although the two were born decades apart. But while Martha Washington sat in St. Peter's Anglican church, which reinforced hierarchical society, Dolley attended the Cedar Creek Meeting, where Friends questioned the morality of owning slaves and admonished slaveholding members to set theirs free. John and Mary Payne were among many Quakers increasingly troubled by the contradiction inherent in owning slaves and embracing Quaker principles.

Some members of the Cedar Creek Meeting, John Payne included, began to free slaves in defiance of the Virginia law that prohibited manumission without legislative approval. John and Mary maintained the Meeting's record of slave manumissions from 1778 to 1782 and served as witnesses to at least some of these transactions, including the freeing of "one negro woman named Betty aged about forty" by Thomas Pleasants of Goochland County.[4] Dolley certainly knew and understood what her parents and other members of the Meeting were doing and why.

In 1782 a new law allowed slaveholders to manumit slaves without the legislature's approval and made it possible for freed slaves to remain in the state. The Cedar Creek Meeting marked the change by purchasing a new book to record yet more manumissions. Minutes make clear that the goal of the Friends was not simply the release of slaves held by individual members. They wanted an end to slavery.[5]

John Payne appears to have freed his slaves after the 1782 law went into effect, although the timing is not clear. Neither is the number of slaves who obtained freedom through his actions. He apparently owned five slaves, whom he freed in 1783,[6] but he may have emancipated others on another occasion.

The Cedar Creek Meeting congregants were not the only Virginians freeing slaves at this time. Historian Eva Sheppard Wolf estimates that something like ten thousand slaves were freed in eight of the state's counties by slaveholders, not all of them Quakers. She bases her estimate on 350 deeds and wills recorded from 1782 to 1806. Not all of the emancipators acted from the same motivation. Some were inspired by the ideals of the American Revolution. Others feared the wrath of God. Still others wanted to reward the faithful service of particular slaves or to motivate future service by holding out freedom as a reward.[7]

No matter the inspiration, people who clung to slavery saw the actions of emancipators as subversive because they threatened the labor system upon which economic fortunes rested. Certain members of the Payne family probably fell into this group, and apparently disapproved of other Quaker ways as well. Dolley's grandmother once gave her jewelry despite the Quaker prohibition on dressing in anything other than plain style. The gift surely displeased her parents, which no doubt explains why Dolley did not wear it openly but kept it in a bag tied around her neck.[8]

John and Mary Payne must have kept a strict Quaker home, judging by their actions as members of the Cedar Creek Meeting. Both served on disciplinary committees that called other members to account for their behavior, and recommended exclusion from the community when they thought it warranted. Records from the period when the Paynes were members show "disownments" for a wide range of breaches, including marrying outside the faith, fighting, drunkenness, wearing fashionable dress, and more generally following worldly ways. The church also took disciplinary action against members who supported slavery. Infractions ranged from the sale or purchase of slaves to the supervision or abuse of one.[9]

After freeing his slaves and ceasing to farm, John Payne had to find other means of supporting his family, which by 1783 consisted of husband and wife, Dolley, her five siblings, and one more on the way. He and Mary decided to leave the Virginia countryside for Philadelphia and start over in what they thought of as a free city in a free nation. Philadelphia boasted a market economy, not a slave economy, and John planned to open a business that would make and sell starch. The city's Quakers, who tended to do business with one another, would make for a steady clientele, and they would admire what he and Mary had done. In 1758 the yearly meeting of Friends had voted to ban slaveholders from any of the city's Quaker services.[10] John Payne had every reason to believe that he and his family would be well received.

Philadelphia must have come as a shock to the Paynes. They were accustomed to a quiet rural life of hard work performed by family members and slaves. Now they were bombarded by the noise and bustle of the city. Urban Philadelphia offered opportunities and temptations unknown in rural Virginia, where Quaker neighbors policed one another closely. The Quaker community in Philadelphia tried to do the same, but the city's population was growing and diversifying, which made this difficult. Philadelphia Quakerism was on the wane in the second half of the eighteenth century, losing influence not only because of demographic changes but because their pacifism had kept them out of the army during the American Revolution, a situation that did not sit well with many patriots.[11]

The Paynes soon found that the city offered challenges as well as opportunities. Philadelphia's economy was not as robust as they had supposed. Starch was an item people could do without in a stagnant economy, and John's business did not do well. Mary Payne gave birth shortly after arriving in the city, but the child, named Philadelphia, died soon after birth. John Payne also fell out of favor with the Quaker community, which added to the family's woes and no doubt exacerbated its financial troubles.[12]

The Paynes joined the Northern District Meeting upon their arrival, but the congregants proved less welcoming than expected. By July 1783, members were expressing concern that the Payne children might "be exposed to various temptations." Their worry may have reflected general unease about how youth raised in the country would react to city living, rather than the behavior of the family, but in 1786 the Paynes moved to the Southern District Meeting, where they encountered similar suspicions. In 1788 that meeting disowned Dolley's oldest brother, Walter, for having "absconded from his usual place of abode without satisfying his Creditors." Four years later, her brother William Temple was disowned for joining the army. The following year, brother Isaac was disowned for frequenting houses of ill repute and for gambling. All three young men fled to Virginia. John Payne came under investigation for improper financial dealings, and he too was read out of the Southern District Meeting a short time later.[13]

Dolley later said she was eleven or twelve years old when the family relocated to Pennsylvania, but biographer Catherine Allgor has concluded that she was fifteen. Dolley appears to have been a good

Quaker girl. She dressed in plain style, attended meetings, and avoided the debauchery that was part of city life. She married a good Quaker boy, John Todd Jr., a tall, handsome redhead, whose law practice was thriving. Yet Dolley had been reluctant to commit to him. Her niece Mary Cutts wrote later that Dolley did not want "to relinquish her girl hood." She apparently had a change of heart when her ailing father asked her to reconsider. No one can be certain of John Payne's motives in pressing his daughter to marry, but he probably wanted to ensure her respectability and financial security — two things her parents could not at that point offer her.[14]

John Todd Jr. wanted to make Dolley Payne his wife despite her father's economic misfortune. Dolley accepted his proposal, and the couple married at the Pine Street Monthly Meeting House on 7 January 1790 in the midst of a snowstorm. The following year they purchased a home not far from her parents.[15] The Todds' three-story brick row house was plain, but it stood in one of Philadelphia's finest neighborhoods, at the corner of Fourth and Walnut streets. John's office was located on the first floor. The second-floor parlor faced the street. Furnishings were for the most part plain, but the Todds purchased some luxury items, including mahogany chairs, fine china, and silver-plated serving dishes. In this, they were like certain other Quaker families who were unwilling to spurn all luxuries. The Todd household must have been lively. Dolley's younger sister Anna lived with them, and Dolley gave birth to two sons, John Payne Todd (born 29 February 1792) and William Temple Todd (born 4 July 1793). The family also had a dog, a pet bird, and one of John Todd's law clerks living with them.

In marrying John, Dolley followed the path of all "good" Quaker women, who were expected to marry and raise children within the faith. Her sister Lucy took a different course. Shortly after Dolley married John, Lucy eloped with one of George Washington's nephews. The bride was only fifteen; the groom, George Steptoe Washington, was not much older at seventeen—and he was not a Quaker. The elopement created a scandal, and Lucy was read out of the Society of Friends for misconduct.[16] She accompanied her new husband to Harewood plantation in Jefferson County, Virginia (now West Virginia), where she became the mistress of slaves.

Dolley might have lived out her life as a dutiful Quaker wife, but John Todd Jr. died of yellow fever in the epidemic that struck the city in 1793—the same one that forced the U.S. government to relocate to Germantown. Dolley had left Philadelphia with her children, but her husband remained to care for his parents and tend to his law practice. He was not the only person to brave the great danger. Secretary of state Thomas Jefferson stayed for a time and estimated the number of deaths at thirty per day. U.S. treasurer Alexander Hamilton stayed and contracted the disease, but he survived. For the most part, whites evacuated the city. Blacks did not. Although Philadelphia was progressive for its time, its white citizens expected blacks (free and enslaved) to stay behind to take care of the ill and the dead. As Isaac Heston, legal clerk to John Todd Jr., observed, "I do not know what the people would do, if it was not for the Negroes, as they are the Principal nurses."[17]

William Temple Todd died the same day as his father; the cause is not clear, as the infant had been sickly from birth. In any case, within a matter of hours on 24 October 1793, Dolley lost both her husband and a son. Dolley's father had died exactly a year earlier. For the first time, Dolley was without a man who had a say over her affairs.

A grieving Dolley returned in December 1793 to a city devastated by the epidemic. Thousands had died, and thousands more had moved away. The widow Todd was attractive, healthy, and wealthy. She inherited property from her husband as well as his parents, who had also died in the epidemic. No one expected her to remain single for long.

Although Dolley's father had gone bankrupt and been read out of the Southern District Meeting, he did not give up on Quakerism or the fight against slavery. He joined a society of Free Quakers and signed a petition asking Congress to end the institution throughout the nation. But even within his family, he proved to be alone in his resistance. After the epidemic, Mary sold the Paynes' Philadelphia house and moved with her two youngest children to Virginia where she lived with her daughter Lucy Payne Washington and was waited on by slaves.[18] Eventually, Dolley and her sister Anna would also return to Virginia, Dolley as the wife of a slaveholder. Thus, the cycle of slaveholding continued despite John Payne's best intentions. Family connections with slavery proved difficult to unravel.

When asked in later years by author Margaret Bayard Smith to provide a biographical account of her life, Dolley Madison wrote only about two hundred words. The emancipation of the Payne slaves and the move to Philadelphia were included. She mentioned her marriages and other family milestones. She recounted her move to Washington, DC, but said little about her time as First Lady and mistress of Montpelier.[19] Dolley's choice of what to include and exclude no doubt reflected a presumption that Smith knew about her life as the wife of the fourth U.S. President, James Madison. But the inclusion of her parents' decision to manumit their slaves indicates that it was a signal moment in her life.

CHAPTER 19

Mrs. Madison

After John Payne's starch business failed, Dolley's mother Mary had converted the Payne home on North Third Street into a boarding-house catering to government officials. One of her tenants was Aaron Burr, at the time a U.S. senator from New York. He became such a close friend that Dolley named him guardian of her young son John Payne Todd (called Payne). After glimpsing Dolley on the streets of Philadelphia, James Madison asked his friend Burr to arrange an intro-duction. Dolley, aware that her would-be suitor was an important con-gressman from Virginia and the principle architect of the new govern-ment, wrote a close friend in spring 1794: "The great little Madison has asked [Aaron Burr] to bring him to see me this evening."[1]

Martha Washington was apparently impressed with Dolley because she encouraged the match and extended invitations to her for events at the President's house.[2] Dolley had become a kinswoman though Lucy's marriage. As First Lady, Martha served as the city's premier hostess, gathering in the President's house important visitors to Phila-delphia along with government officials and other city residents.

George Washington had at times expressed frustration with Quak-ers, who were pushing him to act against slavery. He maintained that such agitation only made matters worse. A petition signed by John Payne and other Quakers (including Benjamin Franklin), which sparked heated debate in Congress, particularly vexed him. The Sen-ate took no action, but the House of Representatives — with Madi-son's backing — took up and passed (narrowly) a resolution limiting the power of the federal government over slavery in the states, thereby strengthening the ability of southern slaveholders to fend off attacks on the institution.[3] George Washington must have derived satisfaction from knowing that the daughter of John Payne was showing an interest in a man who had helped thwart her father's efforts to end slavery. And if Dolley married James Madison, she would return to Virginia and become the mistress of slaves.

Before he met Dolley, James had been unlucky in love. In his early thirties, he had fallen for and become engaged to Kitty Floyd, who was only fifteen. Kitty was the daughter of William Floyd of New York, a signer of the Declaration of Independence. She broke the engagement after William Clarkson, a nineteen-year-old medical student, showed her attention. When the first Congress met in New York City, Madison seemed to take an interest in a widow named Henrietta Colden, but nothing came of this relationship either. Now, in Philadelphia, he became infatuated with Dolley. She was young — seventeen years his junior — and not very worldly. One British diplomat described her mind as "uncultivated" and disdained her fondness for gossip. He admitted, though, that she was "a very handsome woman."[4]

James proposed not long after he and Dolley met. She hesitated. That summer, she traveled to Virginia, where she mulled over the matter. She had been a teenager when she left the state for Philadelphia, old enough to recall something of life in the countryside. Was she willing to give up the excitement of city life? James would return to Philadelphia to serve as a member of Congress, but Dolley could expect to spend much time at Montpelier, the slaveholding plantation belonging to James's father and mother. She had grown up with slaves, but in a home of middling means, and she had come of age in Pennsylvania, a state that was moving rapidly toward abolition.

James's proposal presented a moral dilemma for Dolley. Marriage to him would mean greater wealth and higher social status, but she would be spurning the plain living of Quakers for the wealth and ostentatious display of grandees. And James's elite social status depended on slaveholding. The two were linked. One reason Quakers opposed slavery was that it encouraged owners toward a luxurious and slothful life rather than one of simplicity.[5] There was also Payne to consider. He would join her in Virginia and be raised in contradiction to his father's principles.

Yet Dolley said yes. She may have wanted to get away from Philadelphia, the scene of so much heartache. Her husband, son, father, father-in-law, and mother-in-law had died in quick succession. Some of her siblings had died too. Others had been banished from the community or had moved to Virginia. Her mother was in Virginia as well. It is easy to imagine that the home she had shared with her husband on Fourth and Walnut streets now felt large and lonely.

Dolley seems to have felt little connection to the Quaker community of Philadelphia. It had not supported the Payne family, and she seems to have resented the way both it and her father policed her behavior. She once described her father as "strict" and "single-minded," which suggests a tense relationship. One of Dolley's biographers describes John as inflexible, even oppressive. Dolley applied similar words to the Quaker community. A decade later, when she returned to the city in search of medical attention, she complained, in a letter to one of her sisters, that the Society of Friends "used to control me entirely and debar me from so many advantages and pleasures."[6] She had coveted items the Friends disallowed. In girlhood, as we know, she concealed jewelry given to her by her paternal grandmother in a bag worn around her neck and was most sorry when the string came loose and it was lost. On the evening she met James Madison, Dolley, dressed in mulberry-colored satin gown, wore a strand of yellow glass beads.[7]

Dolley may also have resented the limited opportunities Quaker women had to acquire the skills associated with feminine success in secular society. In an unpublished biography of her famous aunt, Mary Cutts wrote that Quakers forbade girls from learning the "ornamental accomplishments which are too generally considered the most important parts of female education." Perhaps this is why she emphasized Dolley's social accomplishments so much. Mary Cutts, like her aunt, used the term "strict" to describe Quaker ways.[8]

Children do not always share their parents' zeal for particular moral causes, and it seems that Dolley (and the other Payne children) did not share their parents' enthusiasm for Quakerism. The Paynes had arrived in the city at a time when the Quaker community was losing influence, which may have been a factor. Some Quaker women were daring to marry outside of the faith. Dolley's good friend Eliza Collins married Richard Bland Lee on 20 June 1794, just months before Dolley and James said their vows. Like James, Richard was a member of the House of Representatives from Virginia and came from a prominent slave-holding family. Dolley was also friends with Sally Bartram, who married a Roman Catholic. Dolley knew personally two other Quaker girls who married out of love, rather than duty, and she romanticized these unions. The young women had, Dolley said, "eloped to effect a union with the choice of their hearts."[9] Clearly, from a young age, Dolley had questioned how much "duty" should play in the decision to marry.

Even before her first marriage, there had been signs that Dolley rejected Quaker strictures on nuptials. Two years before she wed John Todd Jr., she bristled at the reaction of certain Friends to the marriage of Sally Pleasants and Sam Fox. Because of the death of a cousin, the wedding party had been small, but a large number of people paid their respect by visiting anyway — too many, apparently, for the older members of the Society of Friends, who complained about the "parade." Dolley scoffed when older Quakers "talked off" certain marriages of which they did not approve.[10]

On her trip to Virginia, Dolley visited a Quaker aunt and uncle (Lucy and Isaac Winston) before going to Harewood, where she would have had the opportunity to discuss the prospect of matrimony with her mother, sisters, and brother-in-law. Dolley left no record of what was said or what she observed with regard to Lucy's marriage, but in August, on her way back to Philadelphia, she wrote James that she was ready to become his wife.[11]

No one knows for sure why the young widow decided to marry the much older bachelor, but James made sure Dolley knew he would provide for her son. As her husband, James Madison would have been entitled to manage the property Dolley and her son inherited from her former husband, but he relinquished any claim to the Todd estate in deference to young Payne. He also pledged to set aside a generous amount of his own money for Payne's future. Dolley described James

Mrs. James Madison.

as tender toward her son. And James had more to offer than financial security: he would be able to guide Payne as he grew to manhood.[12]

Dolley and James married 15 September 1794 at Harewood plantation, her sister Lucy's Georgian-style limestone home near Charlestown (in what is now West Virginia) that remains even today in the hands of the Washington family. Dolley wore an elegant and expensive white patterned silk lace dress with a low-cut neckline and a fitted waist, along with white silk slippers. Orange blossoms adorned her hair. The man who stood beside her appeared in some ways to be her opposite. She stood tall for a woman of the era at five feet, eight inches. He was short for a man, at five-foot-four. She was outgoing; he was reticent, at least until he got to know someone well. She was young and attractive; he was older and somewhat dour. She liked brightly colored clothes of the latest fashion; he dressed in drab black clothing from an earlier era. People sometimes said she looked like a queen; someone once said he looked like "a schoolmaster dressed up for a funeral."[13] Yet time would show how well suited they were to one another.

There was another important difference: James was Episcopalian. The marriage evoked a swift response from the Philadelphia Quakers. Not only had Dolley married outside of the faith; she had married before the requisite year of mourning passed following the death of her first husband. She had chosen a spouse whose luxurious trappings (elaborate clothing, fine household furnishings, and decadent foods) Quakers renounced. The advocates of plain living had many reasons to worry that Dolley was traveling an ungodly path through life, which is why they read her out of the Meeting.

In response, Dolley spurned her remaining Quaker ways. Although Mary Cutts maintained much later that her aunt never gave up the fundamental tenants of Quakerism, she admitted that the marriage changed Dolley, who dropped the somber colors Quakers wore and donned more elaborate and colorful attire. She acquired other fancy clothing and jewelry. She also abandoned the Quaker style of writing dates, recording her wedding date as "September the 15th" rather than "ye 15th day of ye 9th month." She also shed "enough [Quaker] restraints to allow her to enter freely into a gayer Society" more suited to James Madison's station in life.[14] And of course there were the slaves. Whatever qualms she may have had in marrying James, Dolley did not seem concerned about applying Quaker principles of equality and opportunity to them.

Dolley's decision to return to Virginia and slaveholding probably reflected in part her belief that African Americans were inferior and therefore needed to be controlled. Although Philadelphia Quakers might be termed progressive on the subject of slavery, they were not modern people who embraced multiculturalism. The Society of Friends wanted an end to slavery, but it did not favor freedom from social control for freed people. Rather, its members wanted to remake freed slaves in their own image. By the time of the Madison marriage, Pennsylvania had adopted an emancipation law, and Quakers were monitoring the behavior of former slaves. Colorful dress and party-ing were two ways freed people could attract negative attention from Quaker brethren, whose home visits to former slaves were undertaken, they said, to ensure their "moral and religious improvement."[15]

The newlyweds did not live at Montpelier right away. Instead, the Madisons returned to Philadelphia, where James resumed his con-gressional duties. They moved into a "Neat & good Brick three Story House . . . not far distant from Congress Hall" at 429 Spruce Street, which they furnished with French furniture, a style popular with Thomas Jefferson, George Washington, and others. They brought slaves from Montpelier. Dolley attended Martha Washington's draw-ing rooms. Like other ladies, she and her sister Anna (who continued to make her home with Dolley) followed the latest fashions in hats, dresses, shoes, and hairstyles. They also made friends with the women of important families, such as that of Pennsylvania governor Thomas McKean.[16]

After James retired from Congress in 1797, he and Dolley left Phila-delphia for Montpelier. Despite her prior knowledge of slavery, Dolley must have experienced the move as a shock. Slaves still lived in Phila-delphia, but they were not numerous. The Madisons held more than one hundred in bondage. Most worked in agriculture, but a large con-tingent of them cleaned, cooked, sewed, served meals, answered the door, did the laundry, and performed other domestic tasks around the house. Dolley was spared at first from supervising them all because her mother-in-law, Nelly Conway Madison, was managing the household.

The Madison family had held land in Orange County from the time Ambrose Madison (James's great-grandfather) purchased it in 1723. His plantation (called Mount Pleasant) produced tobacco with slave labor. Ambrose did not live on the land at first, nor did he live long. He arrived in the spring of 1732 and was dead by late summer. Three slaves, it was said, poisoned him. Two, Turk and Dido, were his own; the third, Pompey, belonged to a neighbor. Pompey, said to be the ringleader, was executed. Turk and Dido were whipped and returned to the Madi-son plantation, which was run by the widowed Frances Madison until she died in 1761 and her son James Madison Sr. took over.[17]

Charges that slaves poisoned owners surfaced periodically in the slave states. Five years following Ambrose's death, Thomas Chew, uncle of James Madison Sr., in his capacity as sheriff of Orange County, oversaw the execution of Eve, a slave accused of poisoning her master. Eve was burned at the stake. As Eve's and Pompey's fates suggest, punishment of slaves for capital crimes was harsh and ongoing. When Dolley Madison arrived at Montpelier, she must have heard of Ambrose's fate along with other frightful tales. At least one site in the region bore the name "Negrohead," possibly so named because the head of a slave dismembered for a crime had been put on display there. The local court had at least once ordered that the head of an executed slave be exhibited on a pole.[18]

After his mother's death, James Madison Sr. rebuilt the house his father had constructed at Mount Pleasant and renamed it Montpelier. The plantation prospered and grew, and slaves created the wealth that afforded James Jr. the opportunity to serve in government.

James Madison Jr. continued the home's renovation. Between 1797 and 1800, he added a wing to the mansion house with a dining room and one other room downstairs and two chambers on the upper floor. Workers added a second front door, as well as a portico two stories high that ran the length of the house. The result was a mansion that looked unified but afforded the two Madison families (senior and junior) separate living spaces. Although Dolley and James would share the structure with his parents for many years to come, the two families maintained different schedules and relied on separate wait staffs.[19]

In the process of remodeling, James moved the slave quarters that had once stood within sight of people arriving at the mansion by coach. Now the enslaved staff would live in the back, out of sight of approaching visitors but within call of the master, mistress, and young master. The mansion's south terrace overlooked a detached kitchen, two smokehouses, and yard where household servants worked and lived. From a second-floor window, Dolley could watch the help washing, cooking, and preserving meat. The arrangement was typical of plantations of the upper South in which the domestic workspace was detached from but close to the main house.[20]

3-D virtual reality model of South Yard slave quarter at Montpelier.
Rendering by Chad Keller. Courtesy of the Montpelier
Foundation, James Madison's Montpelier.

The housing for domestic slaves consisted of timber-framed duplexes, sixteen by thirty-two feet, with wooden floors and glazed
widows. As many as ten family members occupied each. The housing
was cold and drafty in winter, hot and humid in summer. Even so, Dolley and James considered it better than the shelter they provided field
slaves elsewhere on the plantation. The housing occupied by domestic
servants was more pleasing to the eye and better furnished, but there
was virtually no privacy, and the thinner wood-frame buildings probably offered less protection from the elements than the sturdier log-
hewn structures that housed the field hands. The buildings could be
entered or repurposed as Dolley or James wished. At one point, James
told men constructing a new stable to put the lumber in the duplexes'
lofts for seasoning.[21]

James did more than remodel the mansion and slave housing. At one time, a blacksmith shop had stood near the mansion house, run by a slave named Moses who had several men working under him. James had slaves move the shop where it could not be seen and where the smoke and smells it produced would not permeate the air. He did other things to rid the landscape near the house of reminders that Montpelier was a working plantation. He directed slaves to move the earth to create a lovely level lawn, which the Madisons used for entertaining, and he had a structure resembling an ancient temple built atop his icehouse to disguise its purpose. A nearby pond (the source of the household's ice) was probably dammed by his slaves. The arrangement allowed Dolley to serve iced tea to guests on the portico throughout the summer.[22]

While James concentrated on the buildings, Dolley took a keen interest in redesigning the Montpelier yard. She hired a French horticulturalist, Monsieur Charles Bizet, who was paid four hundred dollars a year. He supervised the Madison slaves in fashioning a horseshoe-shaped front garden and taught them to maintain exotic plants. Some of them learned French in the process. Nelly Conway Madison may have been unhappy with the more fashionable garden Dolley designed, for she directed her own gardener to preserve the old-fashioned plantings she preferred, but these were in the back of the house. The younger Mrs. Madison could be seen in the garden plucking fruit and flowers from the earth and trees, wearing an apron and wide-brimmed bonnet to protect her clothing and complexion. She was especially fond of the pink blossoms of the evergreen oleander shrubs. A young slave trailed Dolley as she walked about ready to carry whatever the mistress gathered.[23]

Slaves cultivated their own gardens, and some sold produce to Dolley for the Montpelier table, along with chickens and eggs. They supplemented their diets with these foods as well. Some even kept hogs.[24] The transactions with Dolley brought her in contact with slaves who worked some distance from Montpelier's domestic spaces. It also gave Dolley power to affect what the slaves produced on their own time, for she could buy or refuse to buy what they had to offer. The ritual of exchange whereby slaves visited and sold or traded small items was a powerful tool at the disposal of a mistress.

Rituals such as these were part of the façade that kept slavery from appearing overtly cruel—at least to the slaveholding class. Slaves might bring the owner an egg or a vegetable or a flower, a small gift that had to be reciprocated, at least in theory, through the distribution of better clothing or food or efforts to keep enslaved families intact. As long as gifts and kindnesses flowed back and forth, slavery appeared more benign than it ever was. These rituals were part of the rhythm of life common to slaveholding plantations throughout the South.

James and Dolley Madison left Monticello in 1801 for the new capital in Washington, DC. Incoming President Thomas Jefferson had asked his friend and confidant to serve as secretary of state. It was her husband's decision to relocate, but Dolley embraced the opportunities the city had to offer. As subsequent events would show, no role suited her better than that of Washington hostess.

President Jefferson's habit of shunning large entertainments in favor of small dinner parties where men affiliated with a particular political party discussed government business offered an opportunity for Dolley to shine as a hostess. She and James stepped into the social void and invited members of both sexes to their home at 1333 F Street, NW, two blocks from the President's house. Theirs was a handsome, three-story brick home with first-floor rooms well suited for public entertaining. The Madisons lived in the home throughout his term as secretary, except for the first year, when they stayed in one of six row houses on Pennsylvania Avenue between Twenty-first and Twenty-second Streets that collectively were known as the "Six Buildings."

At the Madison home, men and women of different political parties mingled freely, attended by the Madison slaves, who secured, cooked, and served the food and cleaned up afterward. The Madisons brought slaves to Washington for this purpose, but they also purchased or hired help. Dolley became involved in at least one of these transactions. In 1804, for four hundred dollars, James Madison purchased the enslaved David from Eliza Parke Custis Law, the eldest grandchild of Martha

Washington. Like John Freeman, who worked for the President at 1600 Pennsylvania Avenue, David was to be freed after a number of years—five in his case.[25]

While Thomas Jefferson was hosting mostly all-male gatherings and serving food with the use of dumbwaiters in an effort to keep women and attendants (enslaved or not) from carrying state secrets out of the President's house, the Madisons were undermining his efforts. At their F Street home, members of Congress, Jefferson's cabinet, and local gentry, male and female, ate, talked, and gambled away the hours after dinner, bottle after bottle of spirits lubricating the conversation and lowering inhibitions. Dolley's Quaker background did not dissuade her from participating, even in betting games played with cards. When they were not entertaining at home, the Madisons made for convivial guests in the homes of Washington's other distinguished residents.[26]

Dolley rapidly rose to prominence as a Washington hostess, but not everyone was pleased with her efforts. Although Henry Clay famously observed that everyone loved Dolley Madison, in truth she had critics. The mixing of ladies and gentlemen seemed forward to some, and her habit of circulating among her guests brought charges that she paid too much attention to the men. Some found her outfits too daring. Dolley's elaborate wardrobe, meant to draw attention, reflected the latest Parisian fashions, including plunging necklines. Martha Washington had covered her bosom with a kerchief; the tall and buxom Dolley did no such thing. Former First Lady Abigail Adams for one disapproved of ladies who wore "their clothes too scant," deeming them "an outrage upon all decency."[27]

Gossips began to talk not only about Dolley's relationships with men but those of her sister Anna. Scandalous accusations surfaced about various affairs.[28] It is possible that some of the gossip originated because men were visiting Dolley in her private chambers. As the election of 1808 approached, some of these rumors made their way into print in Richmond and Georgetown. Federalists whispered about Mr. Madison's supposed impotence and his wife's unfaithfulness.[29]

All of this took place as Thomas Jefferson was coming under attack for having children with his slave Sally Hemings. As we have seen, the newspapers got some of their facts wrong, and charges against President Jefferson escalated to include an accusation that he kept a harem of enslaved women at 1600 Pennsylvania Avenue. Allegations against the Madisons were part and parcel of the politics of the era. The charge of sexual misconduct was thought to be a powerful weapon that could be wielded for political advantage, although in retrospect it seems doubtful that it altered the opinion of anyone who was not already convinced that a particular person was unfit for public office. It had not hurt Thomas Jefferson's political career, nor did it hurt James Madison's. After serving eight years as secretary of state, James was elected President, as everyone expected. Yet Dolley may have learned a lesson and altered some of her behavior to better comport with societal expectations of a First Lady. She stopped gambling, for example. Guests of the Madisons continued to play betting games like loo, but Dolley no longer participated.[30] Even so, criticism of the Madisons continued after James was sworn in as President, but soon it focused on a different subject: Mr. Madison's War.

CHAPTER 20

First Lady

When her husband was sworn in as President in 1809, Dolley Madison was already a renowned Washington hostess. As First Lady, she continued to bring men and women of different political persuasions together, only now her dinners, parties, and balls took place in a more public setting. Dolley's efforts to bridge political divides through social interactions helped keep the nascent democracy from splintering and furthered her husband's political goals.[1] She was a flamboyant partner to James Madison and used the means available to women of her era to help him. She courted her husband's friends and enemies by counting them among her guests and by keeping up a steady correspondence. But if Dolley Madison's actions furthered democracy, it was a democracy of a peculiar type: one that extended privileges to whites and relegated blacks to minion status. Dolley imposed slavery on her guests and by implication helped to impose it upon the nation.

To entertain on a grand scale, the Madisons required a large staff. Although they could have hired (and occasionally did hire) free workers, they brought slaves to the President's house, most of them from Montpelier. The Madisons made no effort to disguise the fact that they were slaveholders.

The act of bringing slaves to the nation's capital was not as fraught for the Madisons as it had been for George and Martha Washington. Washington, DC, had a substantial free black population, but no law dictated that an enslaved person would become free after a certain period of time, as had been the case in Philadelphia. Still, the Madisons knew that urban environments offered hiding places for escaped slaves; the Washington papers regularly ran advertisements from owners seeking their return.

The Madisons might have followed Thomas Jefferson's lead and brought to Washington only a small number of slaves to work behind the scenes, but their desire for domestic help was not as modest as his, in part because of their habit of entertaining. They wanted servants who could perform with impeccable skill and whom they could trust. Like other slaveholders, they put their trust in "home-grown" slaves with whom they had experience. It was not simply a matter of choosing slaves unlikely to abscond. The Madisons needed staffers who would maintain family and state secrets.

Dolley brought Sukey to Washington to serve as her lady's maid. Sukey was only twelve years old, but she already knew how to provide a variety of personal services for her mistress: how to dress her hair, assist with her bath, and care for her fine clothing. Elite women deemed such help essential for keeping up appearances, with the result that ladies rarely went anywhere without a maid.[2]

Paul Jennings also accompanied the Madisons to Washington. Although he was only ten years old, he was already experienced in waiting on the family, having served for a time as Payne Todd's personal attendant. In Washington, Paul acted as a footman. Eventually he would become James Madison's personal valet.

Each chosen slave had to please Dolley and James both, since they would all live and work closely together. Sukey and Paul would have learned to please the mistress and master from young ages, as each of their mothers had worked in the Madisons' Virginia home. Dolley's niece once observed that her aunt expected unquestioning obedience from all young people, free as well as enslaved. Apparently Paul and Sukey pleased Dolley in this regard.[3]

Despite his youth, Paul Jennings proved to be a close observer of the life of the powerful during the nation's formative period. Later in life, he wrote about his experiences in a memoir that offers a glimpse into how Washington's elite and the Madison's slaves behaved during the War of 1812. Because of his memoir and the diligent work of his biographer Elizabeth Dowling Taylor, we know more about him than about Sukey or any of the other slaves who occupied the President's house during the Madison administration.

Paul Jennings was born in 1799—the year George Washington died. His father was a white English merchant named either William or Benjamin Jennings; his mother (whose name has been lost) was of African and Indian ancestry.[4] The decision to place Paul in the house may have been based on his light skin—evidence of his mixed ancestry.

The imposing building that served as the home of the President faced Pennsylvania Avenue, the main roadway in Washington, DC, which was very much a city under construction. By the time the Madisons arrived with their slaves, office buildings had been constructed in clusters, and boardinghouses dotted the landscape: government workers toiled in the former and lived in the latter. Official Washington was mostly a city of men, although more women were arriving each year. The population had mushroomed since the Madisons first arrived in 1801. When James assumed the duties of secretary of state, it was a sleepy town of about three thousand residents; a decade later the number had risen to more than eight thousand.[5] Washington was no Philadelphia, to be sure, but it was an exciting city in the making.

After eight years of the widowed Jefferson's administration, the arrival of a First Lady created quite a buzz. Dolley Madison began her tenure as the President's hostess with the celebration of her husband's inaugural. Washington's streets were full of carriages and spectators, large numbers of whom flocked to the President's house after the ceremonies. Author Margaret Bayard Smith and her husband Samuel Harrison Smith (founder of the *National Intelligencer*) had to wait half an hour before they could enter, so great was the crush of people. Even the bedrooms were crammed; "high and low" mixed "promiscuously," Smith reported.[6]

The inaugural ball held that evening at Long's Hotel was just as crowded. Four hundred people bought tickets in advance at four dollars apiece. The atmosphere became so oppressive that someone broke windows to improve the ventilation. Dolley stood with her husband near the door to greet the company. She wore a plain dress with a "beautiful bonnet of purple velvet, and white satin with white plumes." Smith described her as dignified yet affable: "She looked like a queen." In both manners and appearance, she "answered all my ideas of royalty."[7]

Dolley was soon entertaining regularly on Wednesdays. Winter (when Congress was in session) was the height of the social season. Thomas Jefferson had held no levees while in office, but now they were back. The First Lady's drawing room drew crowds of two and three hundred, which swelled to five hundred during the war years. The events became so jam-packed that people referred to them as "squeezes." For receptions, various rooms were set up with tables full of wine, punch, and cake, but still it could be difficult to get to the refreshments. Mary Boardman Crowninshield — wife of secretary of the navy Benjamin W. Crowninshield, who attended a New Year's celebration in 1816 — said it took the two of them ten minutes to "push and shove ourselves through the dining-room." Enslaved servants pushed through throngs with food and drink for those who were unable to make it to the tables.[8]

In addition to the regular Wednesday receptions there were balls and other social gatherings. James Madison's secretary (and Dolley's kinsman) Edward Coles was a regular attendee at these events, having concluded that much of the work of governing was done at them, but their frequency wore him out. "I am sick, yes heartily sick with the number of our parties," he once wrote.[9]

Food and drink were abundant at Dolley's gatherings, and she had favorite recipes. Unfortunately, none of them survive, at least not in her hand. She was said to be especially fond of "Jefferson Gingerbread," indicating perhaps its origins. Her recipe for Roman Punch apparently called for sugar, lemons, French brandy, and rum. Sarah Gales Seaton, wife and sister of the proprietors of the *National Intelligencer*, described some of the food served toward the end of a dinner she attended in 1812: "Ice-creams, maccaroons preserves and various cakes are placed on the table, which are removed for almonds, raisins, pecan-nuts, apples, pears, etc."[10]

The servants were expected to do what they could to make everyone feel welcome. At one levee Dolley attempted to put a flustered guest (described as a country bumpkin) at ease by speaking with him and ordering a slave to get him a cup of coffee.[11] One can imagine the servant jostling his way across a crowded room with coffee and cups perched precariously on a tray. Squeezes and dinner parties required a lot of work from the Madison slaves, who were highly visible to guests. Their number at times equaled, even exceeded, the number of diners, for Dolley appointed a servant to stand behind each guest at dinner parties.[12]

Few guests appear to have been surprised or offended when they encountered slaves working in the President's home. Margaret Bayard Smith found the behavior of the women at social gatherings more remarkable than the presence of slaves. Instead of sitting and waiting for men to come to them, modern women (including the First Lady) stood and walked, much like the men. The result was greater "freedom and equality," Smith thought. One guest who was unperturbed by slaves at the entertainments was Martha Washington's granddaughter Eleanor (Nelly) Custis Lewis.[13] She had attended Martha Washington's more formal gatherings in Philadelphia during an earlier era when woman sat and waited for the men to begin conversations. Change had come for women, but not for slaves.

In addition to short-term visitors, the Madisons frequently had family or other people living with them. George Steptoe Washington died in 1809, and his wife, Lucy Payne Washington, lived with her sister at the President's house until she remarried in 1812, for example. Caring for family members and other guests required a large retinue of servants, who did more than serve three meals a day: breakfast at 9:00 a.m., dinner at 4:00 p.m., tea at 8:00 p.m. Dolley saw to it that slaves met her guests' every need. A bell installed in each room enabled occupants to call a slave at any hour. The slaves brought from Montpelier were soon overwhelmed, and Dolley had to hire extra help. Over time, Dolley increased the number of domestic staffers from fourteen to thirty.[14]

The outbreak of a second war with Britain in 1812 did not curtail entertaining. A second inaugural ball, open to everyone who could afford a ticket, was held at the Davis Hotel on Pennsylvania Avenue. The Madisons also celebrated the beginning of the Near Year in 1814 with an elaborate gathering. Dolley appeared "truly regal," according to Sarah Gales Seaton, "dressed in a robe of pink satin, trimmed elaborately with ermine, a white velvet and satin turban, with nodding ostrich-plumes and a crescent in front, gold chain and clasps around the waist and wrists."[15]

Dolley was determined to impress guests not only with food, drink, and service but also with her person. Other elite women spent a lot on wardrobes, but Dolley was extravagant even by their standards. She was accustomed to ordering large quantities of personal items, even before she became First Lady. One order from her years as the wife of the secretary of state requested a dozen pairs of shoes with heels, two dozen pairs of long white kid gloves, four dozen pairs of short gloves in assorted colors, three dozen pairs of stockings, five shawls, and a dozen snuffboxes ("fanciful but very cheap"), along with other items. But during her years as First Lady, her outfits seemed to shine with even more splendor. She placed hundreds of orders for clothing and routinely asked people traveling to urban centers to purchase items for her. One of her orders was for two thousand dollars' worth of clothing from Paris. At the New Year's celebration she staged in 1816, Dolley dressed in a yellow satin gown with a high neck and long sleeves covered by butterflies, a cape, and a turn of white lace with white feathers, trimmed with gold.[16]

Many visitors likened Dolley's appearance to that of a queen, among them British diplomat Sir Charles Bagot, who knew what one looked like. Sarah Gales Seaton used the word "dignified" to describe her hostess at the sit-down dinner she attended in 1812. Dolley's crimson cap was so ornate it reminded Seaton of a crown, but the First Lady's behavior was "far removed" from that expected of royalty, she added, perhaps knowing that not all who described Dolley as regal meant it as a compliment. Frances Few, sister-in-law of Albert Gallatin (secretary of the treasury under both Jefferson and Madison), was one of those who found Dolley's wardrobe distasteful.[17]

Dolley's resemblance to a queen was not accidental. She deliberately wore headgear resembling a crown. One silver headdress was shaped exactly like one. She also had crowns or other symbols of monarchy embroidered on her turbans. Dolley designed some of the headdresses herself,[18] although it would have been Sukey or other enslaved seamstresses who constructed them. Maids would also have been busy behind the scenes making sure Dolley's dresses fit, since garments ordered from abroad had to be tailored.

What was Dolley thinking as she made her purchases and planned her wardrobe? Did she believe the wife of a United States President should be the equivalent of royalty, or did she simply hope to outdo the fashionable women who attended her social events? Elaborate plumed headdresses made her one of the tallest people (if not the tallest) at any gathering. However crowded the room, she was visible at all times to all of her guests. Two things are apparent: she harbored no compunctions about giving up the plain style of clothing associated with her Quaker upbringing, and she used slaves not only in public but also behind the scenes to enhance her physical presence and social status.

Beyond the elaborate costumes, food, and drink, Dolley was determined to turn the President's house into a grand mansion that reflected the exalted status of the office. During the Madison's tenure, Congress made two appropriations, one to repair and improve the mansion ($12,000) and the other for interior decoration ($14,000). Architect Benjamin Henry Latrobe was hired to help, but final decisions about design and purchases were up to the Madisons. Dolley worked closely with Latrobe to make sure he knew what fabrics, furniture, mirrors, and other items she preferred.[19]

A couple of incidents that occurred during the renovations reveal something about the experiences of slaves in the President's house. Among other things, Dolley and her architect decided to replace cut-glass lamps with ones made out of metal. The metal lamps would bear handling by slaves, who Latrobe believed were "clumsy and careless."[20] The First Lady would either have approved the change or suggested it. There is no indication that slaves had actually broken any lamps, but the worry was that they might. In this way, preconceived notions about slaves in the President's house influenced decorating decisions.

In September 1809 word reached Latrobe that the First Lady was dissatisfied with his work. He complained in a letter to Dolley that servants were repeating talk to this effect overheard in the President's house. Dolley immediately assured him that the hearsay was untrue: she was perfectly happy with his efforts on her behalf. But she promised Latrobe she would interrogate her staff to determine who was responsible for the rumor.[21] It was not Latrobe's intention to upset the First Lady. He and his wife worried whether the purchases they made on her behalf would please her. They carefully sought her opinion on all matters, including the color of the lace she wanted on the interior of the Madison carriage and the type and color of fabric she preferred for curtains. They took care that a pianoforte and guitar were of the finest quality.[22] When Latrobe raised his concern about the rumor, he was careful to do so in a way that criticized Dolley's slaves rather than the First Lady. He would have known he was on safe ground because Virginia elites were quick to put the blame on enslaved help for everything.

Dolley's contributions to the success of James Madison's presidency extended beyond entertaining. She actively participated in her husband's political campaigns. During the fall and winter of 1812–1813, when James's secretary Edward Coles was ill, Dolley and her son Payne stepped in to take over his duties. In this capacity, Dolley arranged the President's schedule, decided who he should see and who should be turned away, and met with members of Congress and others involved in the war effort.[23] Moreover, when Madison himself was ill, as he often was, Dolley nursed him and made sure the nation's business did not suffer. Dolley seemed to make up for James's weaknesses, her personality countervailing her husband's perceived shortcomings.

Dolley did not use all of her political power to further her husband's political agenda. She had her own goals and aspirations. She found ways to help members of her family and her friends socially and financially, by securing them government positions, for example, earning their devotion in return.

Dolley took care as First Lady to cultivate friends, give no offense, and protect her own and her husband's reputations. When her correspondence put her or someone else in an unfavorable light, she asked recipients to read and destroy the letter. "Now burn this, & all like it," she once wrote. Her efforts paid off. Writers avoided criticizing her; those who did not praise her tended to take a neutral stance.[24] Especially during the War of 1812, the President came under heavy criticism, but Dolley grew more popular. She supported her husband's policies, but she was not blamed for them. Nor was she criticized (at least in surviving documents) for turning once again against Quaker principles to support the war. The young Dolley, who had once opposed slavery, lived plainly, and embraced pacifism, now directed the work of slaves, lived extravagantly, and advocated combat.

There were many reasons for the onset of the War of 1812. Britain had imposed trade restrictions on the United States, impressed Americans to fight in the British navy, and generally insulted the fledgling nation. In addition, some Americans blamed the British for inciting Indians, who blocked westward expansion by the land-hungry Americans, and others hoped that Canada might through war be persuaded to throw off British rule and join the United States. Yet many Americans were upset with the President for starting what they derisively termed "Mr. Madison's War." Dolley Madison nonetheless grew more popular than ever, thanks in part to her own efforts to tout her heroism.

The story most often told about Dolley has her delaying departure from Washington in the face of a marauding British force in order to remove Gilbert Stuart's portrait of George Washington from its frame and carry it to safety. The painting was more important politically than monetarily. Its possession by the British might have become a symbol of American weakness, especially if they paraded it around or burned it in the street. Dolley understood this and was determined not to allow the portrait to fall into British hands, or so the story goes. Dolley's bravery became the coup in what was otherwise a tale of loss and defeat. The tale has elements of truth, although the salvaged portrait was a copy of the original painting, and Dolley did not personally remove it and carry it away.

Certain details have been verified as fact, or at least seem probable. British troops had entered the Chesapeake Bay, attacked Baltimore, and were moving toward the nation's capital. Before the President left to join troops gathered outside Washington to defend the city, he beseeched Dolley to save the cabinet papers and other public documents. She worked feverishly, most likely with Sukey and possibly other bonded servants, to cram as many as possible into trunks. These in turn were loaded onto a wagon and spirited away. Dolley also saw to it that trunks were loaded with books, silver, clothing, and the red velvet curtains that had hung in the drawing rooms.[25]

By the time the British bore down on Washington the next day, most Washingtonians had fled, but Dolley remained behind with the slaves and other servants, who were busy preparing the 3:00 p.m. dinner, as usual. Members of Madison's cabinet were expected, as well as several military officers and others. Paul Jennings, fifteen at the time, set the table for forty and placed ale, wine, and cider to cool in cut-glass decanters, despite the chaos unfolding outside. Washingtonians continued to flee, hoping to get out with at least some of their valuables. But orders for the dinner had been placed, and preparations would not cease until someone canceled them.[26]

One wonders how Paul managed to maintain his composure. Perhaps he thought he might fare well under British rule. He may have hoped the troops would take the city and liberate its slaves. In fact, about six hundred slaves fled Virginia masters to join the British during this so-called second war for independence.[27] But it is also possible Paul stayed at his post for fear of reprisals from Americans. There was considerable anxiety among white Washingtonians that slaves would join the British assault on the capital. Voluntary associations of white men exempted from military service were formed to patrol the city and protect it from black misbehavior.

Dolley was anxious for her country and fearful for her husband. His capture by the British would have been a major military coup, as would her own. Finally, Daniel Carroll of Georgetown came to warn her of the invading army's imminent approach, and she left the President's house in a carriage with one of the Montpelier slaves, Joe Bolen, in the driver's seat. Sukey went with her. What happened in the moments before her departure is the subject of dispute, in part because a letter Dolley wrote to her sister Lucy—an important source for learning about what happened—may have been altered by Dolley long after the events occurred.[28]

In the letter to Lucy (now remarried), reputedly written as events unfolded, Dolley describes watching for the British through a spyglass and ordering a wagon to be "filled with the plate and most valuable portable articles belonging to the house." About 3:00 p.m., she wrote, "our kind friend, Mr. Carroll, has come to hasten my departure." Carroll, she said, grew frustrated by her delay, "because I insist on waiting until the large picture of Gen. Washington is secured, and it requires to be unscrewed from the wall." When the process proved tedious, "I . . . ordered the frame to be broken, and the canvass taken out." Only then did she leave. Dolley's letter ends: "When I shall again write you, or where I shall be tomorrow, I cannot tell!!"[29]

Daniel Carroll later claimed publicly that he was the one who had rescued the painting, a story that members of his family believed and repeated. Dolley was upset and refuted his statement. In a letter she knew would become public, she called Carroll's version of events "erroneous." He had played no role in saving the portrait, she said. She had directed her servants "in what manner to remove it [the painting] from the wall, remaining with them until it was done." She then enlisted two passersby from New York, Robert G. L. De Peyster and Jacob Barker, "to help me to preserve this portrait," which the two took in a wagon to a "humble but safe roof." Dolley insisted she had remained behind to save the portrait even though it put her "life and liberty" in danger. It would have been unseemly for the former First Lady to tout her role in a newspaper or other public forum, but she could do so in a private letter, confident that its contents would be made public—in that time, a common means of disseminating information the letter writer wanted known. Dolley gave her reason for wanting the portrait saved: "I acted thus because of my respect for General Washington—not . . . to gain laurels," but if there was merit in the act, "the merit in this case belongs to me."[30]

Carroll was not the only person to dispute Dolley's version of events. John Sioussat, the butler in the President's house, recalled that *he* had cut the picture from the frame with a penknife. But the painting itself yields no evidence that anyone (Dolley included) cut the painting from the frame.[31]

Paul Jennings later dismissed the widely circulated story that his mistress removed the painting of Washington as "totally false." In his 1865 memoir, he said she took "what silver she could crowd into her old-fashioned recticule," but she did not take the portrait down. She had too little time and would have needed a ladder to remove it. He recalled that the French doorman and the Irish gardener took it off the wall and "sent it off on a wagon, with some large urns and such other valuables as could be hastily got hold of."[32]

Evidently people on the scene wanted to place themselves at the center of the story: Dolley Madison, John Sioussat, Daniel Carroll, and Paul Jennings each emphasized their own role in saving the portrait and disputed claims by others. Their descendants further embellished the role their forebears had played. Jennings, his granddaughter said, had hidden the portrait for a time under the old Key Bridge. Sioussat's descendants repeated his claim that he had cut the portrait from the frame with a knife, but Sukey's son Ben Stewart said it was his mother who wielded the knife. Dolley's biographer Catherine Allgor comes as close to the truth as we may ever get. The First Lady, she says, "organized herself and her slaves to leave the house." Believing the British would arrive at any minute, she ordered her staff to break the frame (not cut it) and carry the painting out intact. Paul Jennings's biographer Elizabeth Dowling Taylor relates a similar version, but adds that Paul held the ladder that allowed the eight-foot-tall picture to be taken down, and was probably one of the "two colored boys" who helped load it onto the wagon that transported it to a barn in Maryland.[33]

There is no question that Paul Jennings and other slaves helped get the painting to safety. Yet they rarely are accorded any recognition for their role. It was common for slaveholders to take credit for what slaves had done. Masters wrote about a field they had planted or hogs they had raised, and mistresses reported making cloth or preparing sausage, when in fact their slaves had performed the labor. The services of slaves (and other servants for that matter) were taken for granted, but today it seems only right that their actions be acknowledged, especially since they did more than help salvage a painting. After Dolley's departure with Sukey and Joe Bolen, other servants stayed as long as they dared. The enslaved butler, John Freeman, managed to carry out a feather bed while fleeing from the British troops with his wife and child. Paul Jennings and John Sioussat were the last to leave. Sioussat carried Dolley's pet macaw to safety.[34]

Although people thought the British would arrive any minute, hours passed before they came. In the meantime, Paul and some of the other slaves roamed the city. At one point, Paul met the President and some of his friends in Georgetown who were still trying to decide their next move. Paul eventually sought refuge at the home of a Methodist minister, where he could see the flames that engulfed the President's house and other government buildings.[35]

Despite everyone's efforts, much was left behind and lost in the burning. Dolley later lamented that "a part of my clothes, and all of my servants' clothes, etc., etc." are gone. Her words serve as a reminder that the events of late August 1814 posed a personal hardship for the slaves as well as for the Madisons, although in truth not all of the loss can be attributed to the British. In the hours between Dolley's departure and the arrival of British troops, city residents swarmed the house and carried off what they could.[36]

Does it matter if the story of Dolley Madison's heroism during the War of 1812 is part myth? Some myths may not be harmful, but this one seems to have negative consequences. Erasing enslaved blacks from the story implies that black people played no role in forging America. Focusing wholly on free whites suggests that the American story is theirs alone. The repetition of this idea is harmful, not just for the people of color whose contributions are devalued, but for all Americans. History cannot be manipulated without consequences. Absent professional and personal ethics, stories about the past end up as propaganda rather than history. Myths impede our ability to ask questions that can help us expand our understanding of the past.

Why did Paul Jennings, Sukey, John Freeman, Joe Bolen, and possibly other slaves work so hard to save items when the President's house was threatened? Part of the answer may be that they took pride in their actions—as incongruous as that might seem. It is well known that at times enslaved laborers worked slowly or not at all, or performed jobs ineffectively when they could get away with it. This form of protest served to remind owners that mastery had limits. Negotiations were not conducted between equals, and owners could resort to violence to get slaves to do their bidding, but the strategy worked at times to mitigate some of slavery's worst features. Yet at the same time, slaves could and did, like other laborers, take pride in their accomplishments. The slaves chosen to work in the President's house were reliable and highly skilled. It should come as no surprise that they performed impeccably in the face of the British danger.

There may be other explanations for why bonded people worked quickly to save particular items in the President's house. No one knew how the war would end. If the Americans triumphed, there might be hell to pay for those who had not done as expected. But it is also probable that the painting, papers, and other items meant something to the slaves who saved them. There was much talk in the United States of freedom and rights. At the time of the Revolution, American rhetoric had denounced enslavement, albeit that of the colonies by the British. States in the North had employed the same rhetoric to justify ending slavery within their borders, and countries outside of the United States were acting to end slavery. In 1811 Spain had outlawed slavery at home and in some of its colonies; Chile also abolished slavery in 1811. Mexico did the same in 1813. Closer to home, George Washington had freed his slaves in his last will and testament. The painting of the first President and the documents carried out of the President's house may have mattered to the enslaved help more than we have realized.

As to why the actions of slaves and other servants were omitted from the oft-repeated story of Dolley Madison and the rescued painting, we can look in part to Dolley herself. She publicly took credit for what they had done. In doing so, she was simply following conventions of the day. A mistress who wrote in her housekeeping journal, "I killed a turkey," cannot be expected even to have been on the scene when the bird was slaughtered.

The story of a First Lady ordering slaves to take down a portrait or relying on slaves to save presidential papers may not seem as heroic as the more familiar one, but there is still plenty to admire about Dolley Madison. Most accounts of her heroism in the War of 1812 downplay her fears, but she worried about her husband and her country, not

A VIEW of the PRESIDENT'S HOUSE in the CITY of WASHINGTON
after the Conflagration of the 24.th August 1814.

President's house after its destruction by the British, 1814.

just her personal welfare. Rather than save personal belongings, Dolley saved national treasures, including important documents. Margaret Bayard Smith saw the First Lady shortly after she and James returned to Washington. She described Dolley as so "much depress'd, she could scarcely speak without tears."[37] Dolley was not fearless, as some accounts suggest. She was afraid, but she acted anyway, which surely meets the definition of heroism.

When the Madisons returned to Washington, they found the President's house too charred by British arson to be habitable. They stayed briefly with Dolley's sister, then moved temporarily with their slaves into the Octagon House, an elegantly appointed mansion at the corner of New York Avenue and Eighteenth Street owned by fellow Virginian and slaveholder John Tayloe III. The Tayloes were not in residence, having removed to their country estate in Virginia.[38] There, Dolley resumed entertaining as the war raged on.

The treaty ending the war, negotiated in Europe and already ratified by the British, arrived at the Octagon House on 15 February 1815. After President Madison read and signed the document, Octagon House occupants, free and enslaved people alike, celebrated with liberal quantities of wine. The butler John Freeman poured, and Paul Jennings played the "President's March" on his violin.[39]

At the end of James's presidency, Dolley was more popular with the public than her husband. Despite the outcome of the war, his reputation had fallen, reaching a low perhaps with the British sacking of Washington. Dolley was lionized for bravery in the face of the British threat, while Federalist opponents of the war charged the President with cowardice. Yet, not everyone loved Dolley. Rumors of her sexual improprieties resurfaced after the war, thanks to detractors like Gideon Granger, the postmaster general, who had opposed the war. Massachusetts congressman Josiah Quincy used particularly vile language in criticizing the attendees at Dolley's drawing rooms for seeking favors—implying that sex was among them. A mock advertisement for a book insinuated that Dolley and the U.S. attorney general William Pinkney were having an affair. Pinkney was something of a lady's man, and Dolley was among the female admirers who attended court sessions in which he played a role. While there was also gossip about an affair between James Madison and Dolley's sister Anna, most of the sexual innuendo directed at the President charged him with impotence; Dolley, in contrast, was pronounced oversexed.[40]

Some criticism, less scandalous to her contemporaries perhaps, called out her reliance on slaves. In February 1816, Dolley lit up a presidential reception with enslaved men holding pine torches and was roundly criticized for using them as human candlesticks. The abolition press more generally attacked her pro-slavery views.[41] Such disapproval did not deter her commitment to slavery. If anything, it seemed to grow after she retired with her husband and took on the role of mistress at Montpelier.

CHAPTER 21

Mistress of Montpelier

After her husband retired in 1817, Dolley Madison assumed full-time the role of plantation mistress. During James's presidential years, the Madisons had relied on his mother and a plantation manager to oversee Montpelier. James's father had died in 1801. His widow had carried on without him, but at age eighty-eight Nelly Conway Madison had grown frail.

While in Washington, Dolley had kept abreast of what certain slaves were doing at home. She paid attention to the domestic work, including textile production, for example. But now she became more engaged with Montpelier. She did not necessarily supervise its large staff of domestic laborers directly, but early each day she met with those who did. Close supervision was not needed as long as the results were monitored. Like other mistresses, Dolley counted food, linens, and other stores; oversaw the preparation of meals; and inspected rooms to ensure their good order. This was similar to what she had done in Washington, DC, where she also supervised a large contingent of domestic workers. But at Montpelier, Dolley's oversight of slaves extended beyond the domestic help. The plantation was divided into four farms, each with its own labor force and slave quarters. Dolley allocated blankets to the field hands and families living on all of the farms. She also inspected the food that she or James or the overseer procured for them. This work irked Dolley, who once complained that the need to inspect the supply of pork and other housekeeping duties were preventing her from writing poetry, a pastime popular among

Montpelier, artist's rendering, 1818.

ladies. On another occasion, she groused that curing bacon "for our large family" was taking up too much time. "How tired I am of it!" she wrote.[1]

Slavery shaped Dolley's life at Montpelier in much the way it did those of other slave mistresses living on large plantations. For example, the purchase of foodstuff from slaves for the mansion's table fell to Dolley. She bought such large quantities that when someone sent the Madisons a barrel of cabbages, carrots, parsnips, and turnips, Dolley's cousin Sally Coles remarked that it was like carrying "coals to New market [*sic*]."[2]

Mistresses like Dolley were expected to show some interest in the welfare of the youngest enslaved children on the plantation. Owners tolerated the presence of young children—even encouraged them to hang around—because they believed slaves raised at home were more reliable and less dangerous than others. Besides, young children tend to be cute, and enslaved children were no exception. They offered amusement much as if they were pets. After she moved back to Washington, DC, in her later years, Dolley was often seen outside her home with an old cat and a small black boy for company.[3]

Enslaved children were said to have followed Dolley wherever she went at Montpelier. She assigned them chores and rewarded their completion with a favor or "gift." The practice was not uncommon on southern plantations. Children would often gather around owners hoping for an egg or a biscuit or some other small token in exchange for whatever labor or behavior an owner asked of them. In the eyes of owners, the ritual helped establish routines that were important to slavery's functioning. Very young children learned to behave as owners wanted, and they learned the etiquette of race relations while they were young enough to avoid serious consequences for any mistakes.[4]

Slavery demanded that both slaves and slaveholders fulfill prescribed roles. It was not enough for owners that slaves try to avoid punishment. Slavery rested on violence or the threat of violence to be sure, but the constant beating of slaves to enforce compliance would have exhausted everyone. Instead, an elaborate drama was honed over time, in which each side enacted particular parts. Slaveholders wanted to play the part of benevolent stewards rather than of capricious exploiters of other human beings. Slaves played along because they saw in the owner's desire an opportunity to extract better food, shelter, clothing, and protection of person and family than would otherwise have been possible. Slavery was never a benevolent institution, but enslaved people often found it advantageous to pretend that it was. They lived in a dangerous world in which a wrong word or even a look could land children or their parents in deep trouble. For their part, owners were aware that slaves could be easier to manage when they assumed a paternalistic role than when they did not. This is not to say that all owners lived up to the ideals embedded in the concept of "good" mistress or master, but from the slave's perspective, it was better to have one who wanted to be good than one who did not.

Virginia slaveholders like the Madisons (and the Jeffersons and Washingtons) accepted the drama of race relations as evidence of love and loyalty on the part of the enslaved people — particularly children. Dolley's kinswoman Mary Cutts used the term "love" to describe how the enslaved children felt about her aunt. But the children and their parents likely used a different vocabulary to describe their attachment to the mistress.

It was not only enslaved children who engaged in ritualistic dramas intended to demonstrate a bond of reciprocity between slaves and slaveholders. Adults too shaped their behavior to act out the idea that slavery was a set of mutual obligations. The Marquis de Lafayette saw such a demonstration on a visit to Montpelier in 1824. Leftovers from breakfast were taken from the mansion to "Granny Milly," who lived with her daughter and granddaughter at Walnut Grove, one of Montpelier's slave quarters. In return for the leftovers, Milly gave an egg or potato from her small garden. The Madisons hoped the exchange would demonstrate that slavery (at least at Montpelier) was not the evil institution abolitionists made it out to be. Lafayette — an opponent of slavery — said he was impressed, but the incident failed to convince the Revolutionary War hero that slavery was anything other than a terrible injustice.[5] Patterns of reciprocity offered proof of slavery's benevolence only to those who wanted to believe.

After sixteen years at the center of Washington's social scene, Dolley found life in rural Virginia to be dull and sequestered.[6] Visitors helped relieve the monotony, and Dolley welcomed them in large numbers. She and James once hosted ninety people for a Fourth of July dinner. More commonly, a dozen or so people sat at the table. Some stayed for dinner only, but others remained overnight or for extended periods. Guests included friends, political allies, and strangers who ranged from the celebrated to the obscure. Family members also came and went. The number of guests varied with the season: in winter fewer people braved the poorly maintained roads to reach the Madison home.[7]

Montpelier was well suited for entertaining. Its public spaces included a drawing room described by one visitor as "a museum of the arts." Private spaces were well appointed and well staffed. When Margaret Bayard Smith visited on 4 August 1809, she was one of twenty-three people staying at the plantation house. Even so, she was assigned her own attendant, an enslaved woman who helped her undress and prepare for bed. Nancy not only tucked her in for the night but woke her for breakfast the next morning, brought her ice and water, and helped her dress for the day's activities. Margaret described Nancy as "attentive" and "talkative," much like her mistress. When Margaret returned in August 1828, another well-trained maid waited on her and her husband. British abolitionist Harriet Martineau visited Montpelier in February 1835 and described the slaves as indefatigable and in constant attendance. There was truth in one guest's observation that Dolley and James Madison enjoyed company because neither of them had to carry out the work of entertaining. They had only to act hospitable. "Thoroughly-trained and most mannerly servants" did the rest.[8]

It required at least two dozen slaves to serve the Madison's visitors. Whether they acted as personal attendants, cooks, gardeners, housekeepers, or servers, all contributed to the comfort of Montpelier's guests. Everyone seems to have made a herculean effort. The dinner party for ninety people required that four kitchens be kept going at once. The numerous smaller affairs could be just as taxing for the slaves involved. After a dinner party, some of the help might be called upon to entertain the guests with music. Command performances extended the hours of what was already a long working day.[9]

Dolley continued to rely on Sukey during these years, although the relationship between lady and maid was marked by tension and distrust. Dolley was sure Sukey stole from her. It was common for mistresses to blame household help when an item could not be found or when the need to reorder supplies came around sooner than expected. Once when a letter did not arrive within the time Martha Washington's granddaughter Nelly Custis Lewis expected it, she and the other white members of her household assumed a slave had taken it, only to have it show up by regular post shortly after. The entire system by which mistresses became the keeper of the keys was built around the premise that slaves would take items if given the chance. In 1818 Dolley banished Sukey from the mansion for taking things behind her back. The exile was intended to get Sukey to mend her ways, not to get rid of her. Finding a new maid would have been costly and time-consuming. A trained lady's maid sold for eight or nine hundred dollars, but they rarely came up for sale, and there was no guarantee a replacement would prove satisfactory. Dolley preferred a maid brought up to the occupation at home, but at age fifty, she felt "too old to undertake to bring up another."[10] Dolley soon brought Sukey back from exile. She, like many other slaveholders, convinced herself that a propensity for theft was intrinsic to slaves. A certain amount had to be tolerated in exchange for the services slaves rendered. A lady's reliance on her maid, then, gave the slave a degree of leeway in deciding whether to help herself to small items.

It is impossible now to know whether Sukey appropriated items for her own use. Many slaves did take from owners without authorization. Owners—even owners like the Madisons who spent lavishly on friends and family—did not always provide adequately for their slaves. In addition, some slaves saw "taking" as a protest against slavery and its conditions of depravity. But whether Sukey actually took things is beside the point. Dolley thought she did and punished her accordingly. Yet despite Sukey's shortcomings, Dolley considered her "my most efficient House servant." She complained in August 1833 about the difficulty of doing without Sukey while caring for James, who was very ill, because the maid had come down with "billious fever."[11] At times, owners charged slaves with faking illness to avoid work, but not in this case. The symptoms of "bilious fever" included severe diarrhea, fever, and nausea or vomiting. Dolley could, of course, recruit other slaves to wash the bed linen and carry out the other grubby chores involved in nursing James, but they would have been less familiar with the way she liked things done.

Yet Dolley did not always find Sukey reliable. Once when Dolley sent Mary E. E. Cutts some chestnuts, she felt compelled to explain that she had packed them herself: "Sucky had nothing to do with any of them I assure you."[12] Apparently Sukey's packing of chestnuts had been found wanting on a previous occasion. As we have seen with Martha Washington's maid Charlotte, even the most trusted of slaves might sometimes garner a mistress's disapproval.

It is hard to tell in retrospect what behavior constituted resistance to the conditions of slavery—or even retaliation—and what was plain carelessness. Consider the death of Dolley's pet macaw. The bird, which had accompanied the family home from Washington, was ill disposed toward anyone other than Dolley and James. Children in particular found it frightening, and more than one was threatened into better behavior by the cry "Polly is coming!" When a nighthawk brought an end to the bird's tyranny, one of the Madison slaves took the blame for failing to bring her "to her perch in the hall."[13] We cannot know what exactly happened. Domestic slaves were often scapegoated for anything that went wrong in the house. But it is easy to imagine a slave charged with the bird's care becoming fed up and letting the bird go. In this case, the Madisons preferred to chalk up the loss of the bird to the carelessness of slaves than to a deliberate act.

Because domestic slaves worked closely with family members and guests, they were a constant topic of discussion among family and friends. Dolley took a keen interest when her sister Anna acquired a new lady's maid in 1818. If I were you, she offered by way of advice, "I'd try to attatch her to me & my children."[14] It seems ironic that Dolley was full of advice for Anna about how to foster a good relationship with a lady's maid given the difficulty of her relationship with Sukey. Dolley wrote about her banishment of Sukey to a distant farm in the same letter.

Good relationships had to be forged not only with lady's maids but also with other slaves who interacted with family members. The slave Sam, for one, was dispatched to the Cutts home to bring Anna and her children to Montpelier. In December 1829, Dolley offered her brother John C. Payne the services of a weaver: "I insist on Hariots weaving for you—or Amey's doing it whichever you like best." John lived nearby and was familiar enough with the Madison slaves that Dolley expected him to have a preference. Mistresses took special care to nurture good relationships between servants and loved ones in letters. They mentioned greetings sent from slaves and told slaves of greetings sent from afar. When Dolley wrote her nephew Richard D. Cutts in the late 1820s, she offered remembrances from family members "& even the black faces." Anticipating a visit from her sister Anna and family in 1826, Dolley wrote Anna's daughter: "even the Negroes, young and old, want to see you."[15]

The pretense that slaves and owning family members cared for one another persisted despite slaveholders' constant worry that slaves would retaliate for what was being done to them. Every slaveholder knew on some level that slaves desired freedom. During the American Revolution and the War of 1812, some had demonstrated a willingness to fight against their owners on the side of the British. In the late eighteenth and early nineteenth centuries, slaves in French Saint Domingue (now Haiti) had waged a successful war for independence and freedom against their colonizers. In 1800 a plot masterminded by the slave Gabriel to overthrow slavery had been uncovered in Richmond.

Even so, a particularly brutal slave rebellion in Southampton, Virginia, seems to have come as a shock. In 1831 the enslaved Nat Turner led a revolt that resulted in the death of about sixty white people — as well his own death and those of his followers and other uninvolved slaves. Although Southhampton County was far southeast of Orange, the rebellion had enormous consequences for all of Virginia and for the rest of the South. Ever after the slaveholding class looked with greater suspicion on its bonded people, lest another attack follow closer to home. In nearby Albemarle County, Jane Randolph, wife of Thomas Jefferson's grandson, was so frightened she tried to persuade Jeff to move to a place that had outlawed slavery. Dolley expressed similar fears throughout the fall and winter of 1831–1832, although she apparently never expressed the desire to relocate to an area where slavery was illegal.[16]

In the aftermath of Nat Turner's rebellion, Virginia legislators enacted new restrictions on slaves and free blacks. No one could teach slaves to read or write: literate slaves might write their way to freedom by forging free papers. Nor could slaves assemble for religious services without a licensed white preacher: an assemblage of blacks alone offered an opportunity to plot another rebellion. The new laws were supposed to allay fear of another rising, but anxiety remained.[17]

Slaveholders, including Dolley Madison, lived with two contradictory ideas: slaves might retaliate against the people who held them in bondage, but their own slaves were content and not likely to engage in vicious behavior. Although they clung with all of their might to the second belief, they were vaguely aware that there was much they did not understand, or even discern, about the men, women, and children they held in captivity—field hands certainly, but even those who worked in their homes.

Slaveholders knew slaves had their own ways of doing things, their own preferences in clothing, hairstyles, and foods, for example. James Madison told guests at Montpelier not to expect service from the wait staff on Sundays because they had the day to themselves. He knew they went to church because he saw them coming and going, but he did not know how they acquired fancy attire for Sunday wear. They even carried umbrellas when it rained. Dolley was probably more aware than her husband of how the Madison slaves came to own a bit of finery. She, not he, paid them small sums for vegetables and other foods, which they used to purchase coveted items ranging from caps and calico to coffee and sugar, even umbrellas.[18] Yet, even she might have been surprised to learn the extent of the Madison slaves' economic activities.

A burgeoning market economy characterized the years 1815–1860. The increased amount of cash and goods available made it possible for bondmen and -women to accumulate small sums of money by buying and trading agricultural products as well as home-crafted items. Slaveholders tended to tolerate this type of activity because it was thought to ease discontent on the plantation and cut the cost of maintaining slaves. Slaves with a crop in the ground or poultry in the yard not only supplied food for their families but were less likely to run away or otherwise disrupt plantation routines than those without. Yet slaveholders who were not careful could find the slave's economic activities working to their disadvantage. Once slaves gained expertise in market practices, they might sell, trade, and consume goods without an owner's approval. For this reason, slaveholders tried to control their mundane, everyday economic transactions, as Dolley did when she offered to purchase eggs, chickens, and vegetables herself rather than to have the slaves sell them elsewhere.[19] But masters and mistresses were never in complete control.

Slaves' purchases did more than meet subsistence needs. When enslaved people donned clothing of their own choosing, they were constructing an identity that went beyond that of slave. On other days, slaves wore the uniform clothing prescribed by owners, but on Sundays they could dress more to their liking. So important was the need to maintain a separate identity that even slaves who had no money found ways to adorn their bodies. They dyed clothing with bark or berries, carved jewelry from wood or shells, and refashioned discarded clothing obtained from owners or others. At times, some slaves appropriated clothing without an owner's permission. One Virginia woman "borrowed" a dress from her mistress by sneaking it out of the house under her petticoat. The young woman wanted finery to wear to a dance and was willing to risk punishment to have it.[20] James and Dolley Madison may have believed that a slave's most important duty was to an owner, but slaves knew better. On Sundays and at other times when they were not forced to do their owners' bidding, they fulfilled such roles as mother or father, aunt or uncle, brother or sister, friend, leader, preacher, healer, tinkerer, hunter, gatherer, or gardener.

Church attendance was important for reasons beyond religious observance. Just as free whites might attend church to do business and learn the price of tobacco or hear the latest neighborhood gossip, enslaved blacks might go to learn what was happening in the community. There could be news of relatives and friends living on distant plantations or of opportunities to trade and sell on the black market. There could even be advance notice that a planter was migrating from the area or selling slaves to pay a debt.

At Montpelier, as elsewhere, slaves gathered at night as well as on Sundays — sometimes clandestinely — to worship, tell stories, or enjoy music and dance. Paul Jennings, who learned to fiddle as a boy, played on such occasions. Some slaves fashioned their own instruments from what was at hand, but others saved small bits of money (perhaps tips from the guests) to purchase them.[21] At times slaves belonging to Montpelier's visitors joined them. Some came often, others seldom or only once, but all shared news about a world beyond the confines of Montpelier plantation.

Domestic slaves no doubt knew more about owners than owners knew about them. Margaret Bayard Smith spent most of her time at Montpelier in Dolley's bedchamber reminiscing with her friend. Like other women, they did not so much sit and chat as talk while keeping busy at domestic tasks such as needlework. Women like Margaret and Dolley did not limit their conversations to private matters but rather covered a host of subjects, including politics. Dolley's help heard it all. Harriet Martineau, on a visit to Montpelier, reported that the former President spoke in favor of freeing slaves and sending them to Liberia, and noted the irony of his speaking against slavery in a room inhabited by two or three slaves. Whatever the topic of conversation, domestic servants were trained to show no response. Paul Jennings's biographer Elizabeth Dowling Taylor explains that slaveholders viewed slaves "like part of the wallpaper."[22] Perhaps, but unlike wallpaper, slaves listened.

The Madisons had difficulty understanding even the slaves who worked closest to them, including Paul Jennings, who was promoted to valet in 1820. Except for Sundays and holidays, Paul's day began before dawn and continued until James went to bed, usually around 10:00 p.m. Paul bathed, dressed, and shaved his master, took care of his clothing, and waited on him throughout the day.[23] He was trusted enough to run such errands for the master as retrieving books lent to Thomas Jefferson's granddaughters, who lived twenty-eight miles away. On one of these excursions, Paul met Fanny Gordon on the plantation of Charles and Jane Taylor Howard; Jane was James Madison's first cousin, and Fanny was her lady's maid, one of about thirty-five slaves on the plantation.[24] Paul and Fanny fell in love and hoped to marry.

Marriage between slaves living on different plantations was not considered ideal by slaveholders. The owner of the man had to give permission for the husband to travel to his wife's plantation, and the woman's owner had to allow a man from another plantation to mingle with his slaves. Many slaveholders thought "abroad" marriages, as they were called, increased opportunities for theft, since purloined goods might go undetected when stowed with a wife's belongings. Also, husbands expended energy to help their families living on another plantation. They hunted food, fashioned furniture, and taught skills to children. Perhaps more important, any children born of a union between an enslaved couple living on separate plantations belonged by law and custom to the owner of the wife. These might prove obstacles enough, but the problems multiplied if one of the owners decided to relocate some distance away. In the 1820s an increasing number of Virginia slaveholders were moving west and southwest, where more fertile soils held the promise of profit for planters who could supply enough labor. It was customary in these circumstances for one owner to sell a spouse to the other. Some did not want to be bothered, but James Madison once sold a slave named Jesse in such a situation.[25]

Still, James did not endorse abroad marriages. He believed slaves preferred abroad marriages because, when they visited their families on Sundays and holidays, they could not be asked to perform "a share of the little calls to which those at home are liable." Slaveholders, the Madisons included, expected their household help to be at their beck and call even during "off times." Familial relationships abroad were seen as both a nuisance and a ruse concocted by slaves to avoid rightful duties. For this reason, planters with large slaveholdings preferred that men and woman find spouses on the home plantation. Thomas Jefferson offered rewards for couples who married at home rather than abroad.[26]

The Madisons were thus reluctant to grant Paul permission to marry. In fact, James Madison had difficulty understanding why his valet wanted a family. When slaves like Paul found wives and became fathers, he chalked it up to a defect in their moral character—an inability to restrain their sexual urges. Nonetheless, Paul Jennings and Fanny Gordon were wed in 1822 after gaining permission from his and her owners. The Howards gave them a special supper to mark the occasion.[27]

Paul and Fanny eventually had five children together. The Madisons knew of Paul's family but paid them little attention and seldom gave permission for Paul to visit. His children belonged to Charles Howard, but this explains only part of their indifference. James Madison was never able to see Paul Jennings and Fanny Gordon, or any other slaves, as people with the same wants and desires as himself. In this and other matters pertaining to the men, women, and children he held in captivity, James Madison proved to be "a garden-variety slaveholder."[28]

Americans have tended—perhaps wished is a better word—to remember the Presidents and First Ladies who owned slaves as good masters and mistresses—though it is not always clear what is meant by "good." Was Dolley Madison a "good mistress"? Her domestic slaves appear to have fared no better and no worse than others in Virginia. They were subject to the same indignities and cruelties that were the lot of every person held in servitude.

Dolley's contemporaries and modern-day historians have lauded her acute social skills. She reportedly put people at ease and made everyone feel at home. She has been credited with averting diplomatic crises and bridging partisan divides, but her relationships with slaves demonstrate the limits of her social skills. We do not know whether she shared or endorsed the language her brother John C. Payne used when he wrote that he was looking for a new place to live out west that would be free of "the annoyances of insects and free blacks," both of which he found "very objectionable."[29] But it is clear that, like her husband, she did not understand her slaves as fellow beings. To the people she held in bondage, she was less the socially adept hostess of historical lore than a socially inept mistress who had trouble empathizing or sympathizing with them.

Rather than express sympathy for enslaved women, James Madison felt sorry for white mistresses, whom he thought had to exert too much energy directing slaves: "They cannot trust their slaves in the smallest particulars, and have to superintend the execution of all their own orders." To make matters worse, mistresses in Virginia lived "surrounded by vicious free blacks" who keep their "owners in a state of perpetual suspicion, fear, and anger."[30] There is no reason to think Dolley was an especially weak or ineffective manager of slaves compared to other slaveholding women. Harriet Martineau found her to be "strong minded" and as "fully capable" as her husband. James Madison told Martineau that he believed men and women could be trained to use their heads and hands equally,[31] which suggests he agreed with Martineau's assessment of his wife's capabilities. But like mistresses throughout the South, Dolley discovered time and again that her household help had wills of their own that could not be expunged.

Dolley did exhibit the conventional behaviors of a "good mistress." For example, when she and a number of slaves accompanied James to the Virginia Constitutional Convention in Richmond in the winter of 1829–1830, she wrote dutifully, sending greetings to Paul's wife and children and assuring Sam's wife that he was "well and sober." She sent Ralph's love to his mother and said that he would bring her a gift when he came home. She informed Sarah's husband that his wife hoped to hear from him. Paul Jennings was literate, so he wrote his family in his own hand,[32] but he required his owner's permission to take the time and resources necessary for writing and posting a letter. Today these actions might seem small, but they were meaningful to people separated by distance and unable by virtue of their enslaved status to do anything about it.

The constitutional convention occurred at a time of rising antiblack sentiment in Virginia. Dolley never explicitly wrote about race — or if she did, the document has not survived — but a letter she composed in July 1831, around the time of her sister Anna's death, is revealing. Anna Payne Cutts suffered from a condition referred to as dropsy of the heart. Dolley expressed gratitude for the kindnesses shown her sister by many lady friends. I "could love the blackest Indian," she wrote, conjuring up an image of the person she could least love, if that Indian had acted compassionately toward her sister.[33] Like other southern ladies of her day (and many northern ones), she compartmentalized people by race or ethnicity and found Indians and blacks lacking. They were each, in her eyes, species apart.

A rumor circulated during James's retirement years that he had fathered a child by an enslaved woman. No historian or biographer has been able to confirm the birth, though such liaisons were plainly not unusual. (Dolley, like other white people of her day, used the term "yellow" in correspondence to describe the children born of such unions.)[34] Dolley must have heard the rumor, but neither she nor James discussed such matters in any written material that has survived. Nor did they acknowledge Thomas Jefferson's relationship with Sally Hemings, although surely they knew about it. Dolley Madison and other mistresses coped with extramarital relationships in the slave quarters through silence. Acts unspoken and unacknowledged could be ignored and seemed not to factor into assessments about whether someone was "good" to their slaves.

For Dolley Madison's contemporaries, a common meaning of "good mistress" (or good master) was one who did not sell or otherwise sever the family ties of slaves. The troublesome fact about the Madisons is that Dolley and James had begun to do exactly that.

CHAPTER 22

Decline of Montpelier

A casual observer of Montpelier in the late 1820s or early 1830s would probably have concluded that all was well. The former First Lady and President were entertaining large numbers of guests in grand style with the help of an abundant and attentive wait staff. Their son Payne Todd had grown into a handsome and debonair young man who lived nearby and came over to help his parents when he could. Enslaved laborers could be seen and heard working in the yard, playing music, dancing, and telling stories. The slaves gardened and sold their excess produce to the mistress for small sums that they used to purchase finery and other items in local stores. On Sundays they walked to church, carrying umbrellas when it rained.

But behind the scenes, another story was unfolding. James Madison's health was poor, and Payne Todd had become a major disappointment. The family's financial position was deteriorating rapidly and threatening the stability of life for the Madison slaves. Yet hope persisted that Payne would mend his ways, that the plantation could be made profitable, and that the former President, like George Washington, would find a way to emancipate his slaves, if not upon his own demise, at least upon Dolley's.

After his stepfather retired from the presidency in 1817, Payne Todd returned to Virginia with his parents. He was still young (twenty-six), and the Madisons assumed he would settle down, marry, and make a place for himself among Virginia's gentry. At least for a time, Payne attempted to live up to their expectations. He established a plantation on land given to him by James, but he had a hard time making Todds-berth (as he dubbed it) profitable. Virginia farming had changed since James Madison's youth. Tobacco was less profitable, and successful farmers had diversified their crops. Never one to be out of fashion, Payne too diversified, though instead of tried-and-true crops he in-vested in silkworms. No one in the region had done well with them, but some—Payne included—hoped for a breakthrough. Payne also made an effort to court a suitable bride.

Unfortunately, silkworms cannot thrive in Virginia's climate, and Payne botched the courtship. And there were other signs of trouble. Like other grandees, he sought to put his personal stamp on his coun-try seat, but Payne was no Jefferson (or even Washington or Madi-son) when it came to architecture. At Toddsberth, smaller buildings, including cabins for slaves, surrounded a central tower that served as the main house, an eccentric arrangement that elicited derision from those who saw it.[1]

Perhaps the only thing conventional about Payne's life was his reli-ance on slaves. They too had been a gift from his stepfather. Separat-ing slave families through sale was frowned upon in certain circles, but giving slaves to family members, especially to help them get a start in life, seemed acceptable to slaveholders, if not to slaves. In this case at least, the slaves were relocated only a couple of miles.

It is difficult to know what to make of Payne Todd from this dis-tance in time. He was an addict. He drank, smoked, and gambled to excess. He disappeared for months at a time and was unable to account for where he had been or what he had done. In November 1825 James wrote to Payne's last known address: "Your last letter to your mother made us confident that we should see you in a few days. Weeks have passed without even a line explaining the disappointment." The former President begged his stepson to get in touch with his mother no mat-ter what the cause of his absence: "Let the worst be known, that the best may be made of it." Three months later, James was still pleading for news.[2]

Payne was more womanizer than family man, and he was incon-stant in business as well. He toyed with the idea of establishing a gold mine and later a marble quarry. He failed at these endeavors, as he had with the silkworms.[3] His finances were a disaster. In 1816, at the age of twenty-four, Payne had inherited the Todd home in Philadelphia, along with other property that had belonged to his father. He soon sold the house, and the proceeds quickly disappeared. Payne became embroiled in legal problems stemming from financial misconduct. Time and again he looked to his parents to bail him out. When he could borrow no more from them, he turned to other relatives and friends, including his uncle Richard Cutts and the merchant and investor John Jacob Astor. His requests strained kinships and friendships. Even so, he ended up in jail more than once. In June 1829 Dolley wrote to her sister Anna that Payne was incarcerated for a debt of two or three hundred dollars: "It almost breaks my heart to think of it." She wanted to help, but it was up to her husband to decide what to do.[4] James again helped.

Historians and biographers have found it difficult to understand why Dolley kept coming to her son's aid. Some have called her an enabler, or blamed Payne for the financial train wreck that (in their telling) eventually squandered the Madison fortune.[5] But the story is more complicated.

Payne could be aggravating, but he was also charming. Tall, dark, and handsome, he was well educated, capable, and helpful. During his stepfather's presidency, Payne filled in as secretary when he was needed and served in diplomatic posts. He helped his mother bring people from different political parties together at social functions. His charm, good looks, political connections, and knowledge of a vast array of subjects made him a favorite at her social gatherings. After his parents retired to Montpelier, Payne wrote letters on their behalf, ran their errands, and pitched in to help with farming operations. When he traveled, Payne purchased important works of art for their home as well as other wanted items.

Payne Todd was Dolley's only surviving child and the only child James Madison ever had, and family was the sole social support available to help men with problems like Payne's. In the early republic, elite men and women did not rely on the public dole or private charity. The Madisons, who cared deeply about public opinion, were not about to subject Payne to debtor's prison. They felt the same about other family members, whom they helped weather difficult circumstances. These included Dolley's brother, John C. Payne, who like Payne Todd was an alcoholic and botched business dealings and diplomatic appointments.[6]

It some ways, Payne's situation was similar to that of Martha Washington's son Jacky Custis. Both had lost fathers at young ages, and both had become the stepsons of rich and powerful men. But Jacky, through his father, inherited a place in a rich and aristocratic family. Payne's paternal inheritance was incomparably smaller, but he nevertheless lived as a grandee; he was well aware that his style of life was one his Quaker relatives rejected. Years later, on his deathbed, Payne proclaimed faith in Quaker ideals even though he had not lived up to them.[7] It seems that Payne never grew entirely comfortable as a member of Virginia's elite.

There was another man in young Payne's life besides his father and stepfather: Aaron Burr. After the death of Payne's father, Burr—an up-and-coming politician and devoted father to his own daughter—had stepped in as Payne's guardian. Payne was twelve years old when Burr fatally shot former U.S. treasurer Alexander Hamilton in a duel. Burr then went west looking for business and political success, but his pursuits led to charges of treason. He was never convicted, but the indictments (there were three) and trial (there was one, in 1807) left his reputation in ruins. Burr avoided imprisonment, but he hardly turned out to be the model of manhood Dolley once hoped he would be.[8]

Payne's life was characterized by great loss but also by incredible opportunities. His appointment as an attaché to Albert Gallatin took him to Europe from 1813 to 1815. Gallatin had undertaken a diplomatic mission to end the war with Britain, but Payne, whose appointment was unofficial, had treated his time in European capitals more like a grand tour. He spent lavishly ($8,000) on leisure, art, and gambling.[9] Orange County, Virginia, must have seemed insipid by comparison. Alcohol, tobacco, gambling, and disappearing for months on end (to more exciting places like New York City and Philadelphia) relieved the tedium of life on a remote country estate in Virginia. It also distanced him from the slaves who made gentry life possible, not only through their work but through their persons. As Payne Todd's finances deteriorated, he took out more and more loans secured by human property.

Payne was not the only member of the Madison family spending more than he could afford. In 1826 James told Thomas Jefferson that he and Dolley were living on borrowed funds, and just months before he died, James admitted to his friend Charles J. Ingersoll that they were living beyond their means. A lavish lifestyle coupled with poor harvests and falling prices for commodities put the Madisons in debt. James took out a mortgage on Montpelier, sold land he owned in Kentucky, and began to sell slaves.[10]

Montpelier was one of many Virginia plantations experiencing financial difficulties in those years. Disease and harsh weather plagued farmers large and small.[11] Virginia planters like Thomas Mann Randolph Jr. were selling "surplus" slaves as a means of paying off debts that had been decades in the making. Slave sales had occurred previously within the neighborhood, but the new sales sent enslaved people far away, to emerging states in the West and South where the cultivation of market crops reaped large profits for anyone who could secure land and labor.

James sold sixteen slaves in 1834 to a family member who wanted them for his Louisiana sugar plantation. William Taylor of Point Coupée, according to Dolley, was making "a great deal of money" through the enterprise. The sale was intended to pay off a debt Dolley owed to her niece Mary E. E. Cutts. The sale has come to light because of a letter Dolley wrote asking Mary for a receipt for the interest paid on the loan. James, she said, had hoped to pay the entire amount due, but the proceeds from the "sale . . . of his Negroes . . . did not enable him to do so." It is not clear what happened to all of the funds raised in the sale, but Dolley explained why it had not yielded more. Only the slaves "who wanted to go with Taylor" had been sold. Presumably others had objected to relocation, and James had respected their wishes. It is unclear from Dolley's letter whether she approved of her husband's decision. The tone of the passage is apologetic for failing to raise the sum needed to pay Mary, not for selling slaves.[12]

In the same letter, Dolley asked Mary to send "a whole peice of pritty 12 1/2 cent Calico," which she would pay for "directly."[13] Dolley probably wanted the cloth for her maids. It would not do for them to appear in shabby dress, no matter how strapped the Madisons were for cash. In the same letter, Dolley asked Mary to forward a copy of another letter to Margaret Bayard Smith—the one Dolley thought proved her heroism in the War of 1812. Dolley's letter to Mary ended with the phrase "Now burn this, & all like it." Scholars have long believed Dolley wanted the letter destroyed because it offered proof that she tried after the fact to shape the story of her actions as the British bore down on Washington, DC, but Dolley had more than one reason to keep this letter from the light of day. The Madisons could not meet their financial obligations, and they were selling slaves in consequence.

Little is known about the slaves who were sold, but one of them (a woman named Betty) was ill. The kinsman who purchased her complained and sought a refund, and when one was not forthcoming, he filed suit. The sale did not yield enough funds to retire James's debt. Moreover, he was left with too few adults to cultivate his crop and had to hire extra temporary help. James soon sold twelve more slaves.[14]

Harriet Martineau visited Montpelier in 1835, a week after the last transaction. The former President seemed eager to absolve himself of any blame while assuring her of his objection to bondage. He would not have sold slaves, he said, if they had been willing to relocate to Africa—specifically, Liberia. In 1833 James had become president of the American Colonization Society, an organization founded in 1816 to promote the idea that people whose ancestors originated in Africa should be moved there, even if they had been born in the United States.[15] (The congressional ban on the importation of slaves beginning in 1808 meant that fewer and fewer people enslaved in the United States had ever set foot in Africa, and of course few, if any, had lived in Liberia.)

Few slaves embraced colonization. Relocation required a long and dangerous journey far from kin and community to a place that was largely unknown. It was unclear whether advocates of the venture would provide sufficient resources to ensure the new colony's prosperity. It was not even clear if there would be funding sufficient to

pay for transport. The reluctance of slaves to go along with colonization offered its advocates a ready excuse to do nothing about ending
slavery. James Madison's claim that he would have sent slaves to Africa
had they not objected seems particularly hollow given that he was selling slaves in order to pay debts.

The former President also blamed his economic woes on the licen-
tiousness of Montpelier's enslaved women, who he said gave birth to
too many babies, resulting in a slave population too big for him to
support. Superfluous slaves could not be set free because they would
be unable to live peacefully with whites, he asserted, although, as Martineau noted later, Madison offered no proof of this. But as historians
know, slaveholders pushed enslaved girls into sexual relationships as
early as possible to increase the slave population. Thomas Jefferson
remarked in 1820 that a woman who had a child every two years was
more profitable than any man — even the best field hand: "What she
produces is an addition to the capital, while his labors disappear in
mere consumption." Slaveholders were not so much forcing women
into sexual relationships (although that did happen) as rewarding
those who had children (e.g., with better housing, food, or clothing)
and punishing those who did not (e.g., through sale). They also turned
a blind eye toward the sexual abuse of enslaved women — even girls —
by travelers, neighbors, and owners. James Madison mentioned none
of these factors to his visitor. Instead, the former President pointed
to perceived shortcomings of the enslaved women, which not inci-
dentally had the effect of excusing slaveholders for sexually exploiting
them.[16]

Montpelier's financial decline presented an obstacle to freeing the
Madison slaves, but this did not stop visitors from pressuring the
former President on the subject. People with different motives were
eager to observe and discuss the emancipation of Madison's slaves,
as well as race, slavery, and abolition in general. Such was the case
when the Marquis de Lafayette came in 1824, accompanied by his private secretary and the young social reformer Frances (Fanny) Wright.
Lafayette's secretary took it upon himself to interview the Madison
slaves about whether they were happy. (They said they were.) Wright

spoke to Dolley and James about her desire to found a utopian community that would emphasize equality without regard to sex or race.[17]

The Madisons welcomed to Montpelier people who held views antithetical to their own, even when the resulting conversations made them uncomfortable or challenged their assumptions. Author Jesse Torrey, notorious for writing about the horrors of slavery and the slave trade, visited, and Dolley and James once sat down to dinner with a freed slave named Christopher McPherson, a man of mixed ancestry who had been introduced by none other than Thomas Jefferson. According to McPherson, he enjoyed an agreeable conversation over a pleasant dinner followed by breakfast the next morning. Discussions, at least while James's health was good, could be both lively and provocative. Abolitionists and other reformers—hoping to convince the former President and First Lady to champion a cause or take action as a means of influencing others—routinely added Montpelier to their itineraries. Dolley's cousin Edward Coles was particularly fervent in urging James to free his slaves. He visited frequently and kept up a steady correspondence with both Madisons.[18]

Edward had grown up in an elite family whose wealth stemmed from slaveholding. Having decided as a young man that slaveholding was immoral, he made up his mind to free any slaves he inherited, but he kept the decision to himself. If his father suspected that Edward would emancipate any inherited slaves, he could have (and probably would have) bequeathed his youngest son another type of property.[19] John Coles II died in 1807 when Edward was twenty-one. As he had anticipated, Edward's family raised a storm of protest when he told them of his decision. Freeing some but not all of the Coles slaves could roil relations on the other Coles properties, they said.[20] It would also deprive the slaves of the governing authority they required. The arguments were typical of those used by elite Virginians, who acted as though slaveholding benefited everyone involved.

A decade passed before Edward Coles could free his slaves. In addition to his family's opposition, there was the matter of debt. He had inherited a dozen slaves along with a debt-ridden plantation in Albemarle County. While Edward's financial obligations were modest in comparison with those of James Madison and Thomas Jefferson—

Edward owed five hundred dollars—he found it difficult to raise the sum even after he accepted a government position. It was hard enough to keep from going further into arrears. When he tried to sell his farm, there were no takers. Eventually Edward Coles bought land in Illinois, and in spring 1819, he headed west with seventeen slaves, whom he freed along the way.[21]

In late summer, James Madison expressed admiration for Edward's act of manumission. He had not only freed his slaves but provided the land and tools, instruction, and employment they would need to succeed as freed people. It was too bad, James wrote, that he could not change "their colour as well as their legal condition," for without that change the former slaves would never be fully free. Race doomed them, he said, to "privation" that robbed freedom of half of its meaning.[22]

Edward Coles's commitment to abolitionism was lifelong and national in scope. As governor of Illinois from 1822 to 1826, he advocated keeping slavery out of the state. He also maintained personal and professional acquaintances with the leading lights of Virginia, including Thomas Jefferson and his grandson Jeff Randolph, and urged them toward emancipation.[23] When Coles visited the Madisons in December 1831, he helped James lay out a plan for manumitting the Madison slaves. Coles was close to his cousin Dolley. The two kept up a lifelong correspondence, but it was to James that Edward turned when he discussed manumission. Gender and legal conventions placed husbands in control of marital property, which seemed to dictate that Coles direct his efforts toward him rather than toward her. Dolley was close to her Coles relatives who had opposed Edward's efforts to emancipate his own slaves, and this may also help explain why he dealt with James rather than Dolley.

If anyone could convince the Madisons to free their slaves, it was Edward Coles, for whom they held great affection. His portrait hung on their dining room walls along with portraits or engravings of George Washington, Thomas Jefferson, John Adams, James Monroe, Andrew Jackson, Martin Van Buren, the Queen of Denmark, the Queen of Holland, and a "likeness of a Negroes Head." After James died, Edward was among the small number of people who received as a memento a lock of the former President's hair. The bequest included money to have it mounted in a piece of jewelry to be handed down in the Coles family. Around the same time, Edward wrote Dolley a heartfelt letter in which he claimed the status of her "nearest & dearest friend." Coles was not naïve on the subject of emancipation. No one knew better than he the obstacles. Like George Washington, James Madison had to figure out what to do about slaves who were too young or too infirm to support themselves. There was also the question of how to handle marriages between Madison slaves and partners on other plantations. Moreover, the law of 1806 requiring freed slaves to leave the state raised questions of cost, since the former slaves would need to be relocated.[24] And James worried about Dolley. He had to provide for her were he the first to die, which seemed likely given his advanced age and poor health. Madison's debts would need to be paid. Still, Coles thought, emancipation could work if he granted freedom only to slaves born after a certain date. Any slaves remaining after the payment of debts could be left to James's heirs.

Coles emphasized manumission's importance for the former President's legacy. George Washington's will had been widely celebrated by much of the public. Thomas Jefferson had not followed Washington's example, but even he had managed to free some slaves. Coles acknowledged each obstacle and proposed solutions. What could be done about slaves who had spouses on another plantation? Let them choose between attaining freedom and remaining with loved ones, Coles said. Before moving west, he had exchanged two elderly women who did not want to go for slaves belonging to his mother who did. One of the women who stayed would have had to leave behind an only child, the other a husband.[25]

There remained the problem of what should happen to the slaves once they were freed. When Coles presented a proposal for ending slavery to Jeff Randolph, he suggested placing a tax on black people for the purpose of raising money to move them out of the state. He expected children as well as adults to contribute toward their own emancipation and banishment. The ownership of any babies born in bondage after a certain date would be transferred to the state, which could put them to work as soon as they were able to earn money for their transport.[26] It seems likely Coles made the same or a similar proposal to Madison. He hoped the state would step in to facilitate manumission within its borders.

Madison and Coles agreed that the best place for former slaves would be Africa. The U.S. Congress in 1819 had allocated a hundred thousand dollars for the relocation of illegally imported slaves, and some of the funds had been used to establish the colony of Liberia on the coast of West Africa. The American Colonization Society had begun relocating former slaves there, but the process of resettlement was slow, both because free blacks did not want to leave family and friends in the United States (the only homeland they knew) and because it was proving difficult to raise enough cash to cover expenses. Coles remained optimistic nevertheless. The Madison slaves would raise the money themselves if they were paid for the work they performed before or after being emancipated.

Coles was liberal-minded for his time. He did not, like many members of the American Colonization Society, lace his language with racist slurs of the type that regularly appeared in the group's literature, nor did he make statements that maligned blacks, but he agreed that expecting blacks to live among people prejudiced against them would hardly be freedom at all. His thinking fell in line with that of James Madison and other leading politicians, including James Monroe of Virginia, William Crawford of Georgia, Henry Clay of Kentucky, Richard Rush of Pennsylvania, Robert Finley of New Jersey, and Daniel Webster of Massachusetts. And Coles was not the only emancipationist to express a belief that blacks and whites could not live together. Fanny Wright also believed that the two races would need to be separated geographically.[27]

When Coles left Montpelier in December 1831, he thought he had been successful. No specific plan to free the Madison slaves had been laid out, but he was certain James would write a new will with an emancipation clause. In a follow-up letter dated 8 January 1832, Coles reiterated his arguments and reminded his kinsman of the harsh judgment of history should the former President fail to release his slaves from bondage.[28] James Madison's declining health made the matter of writing a will urgent. Incredibly, the relentless visiting continued. Dolley, who until then had enjoyed entertaining. complained in 1832 to

Anna about the demands the public put upon her husband: "He reces. letters, & visitors as if he was made of Iron—to his great disadvantage & mine." On this occasion the secretary of state and his family were expected shortly. Dolley and James did not know them well. "I am sick at the very idea of seeing *such* strangers, in our condition," she wrote. James was so ill at the time that he could not sit up, and it would fall to Dolley to meet and greet them.[29]

James Madison died in his study on 28 June 1836 at the age of eighty-five. His health had been poor for five years. His care during the last months was directed by Robley Dunglison, the doctor who had attended Thomas Jefferson on his deathbed. Paul Jennings and Sukey waited on him the morning of his death. Paul shaved him about 6:00 a.m. then stood by—as he had done for many years—ready to do whatever his master required. Sukey brought his breakfast, but he was unable to swallow.[30]

The former President was buried in the family cemetery at Montpelier two days later. A large procession that included family, friends, dignitaries, and slaves helped lay him to rest, but like Martha Washington, Dolley did not attend her husband's funeral. Instead, she stayed indoors with James's niece Nelly Willis.[31] Everyone wondered what she would do without her beloved husband of forty-one years. They also watched to see what would happen to the Madison slaves.

The death of a master—whether George Washington, Thomas Jefferson, James Madison, or anyone else—was unsettling for enslaved people. They understood that a financial accounting would follow and that they would figure, literally, in it. Change would come, particularly if slaves were sold or parceled out to heirs. Daily routines would alter for those who remained at home, particularly those who had offered personal service to the master. No wonder the slaves who attended the funeral service for James Madison were visibly upset. One of Dolley Madison's descendants took their sobs as evidence of genuine "bereavement in the loss of a kind and benevolent master."[32] As we know, James Madison was no kinder or more indulgent than other slaveholders; yet, the tears shed by his slaves were real enough. Rumors were already circulating that the President's widow would sell at least some of them. This fear was sufficient to account for all of the tears, but slaves who cried and carried on at the burial of an owner were also participating in a ritual of long standing. Race relations in Virginia and throughout the South required slaves and slaveholders to maintain the appearance that they cared about one another. Family members expected outward expressions of grief from slaves at the death of an owner, and slaves rarely disappointed. Breaking the implied paternalistic contract at such a moment could have disastrous consequences. People who did not demonstrate the proper demeanor could expect to be among the first sold if it came to that. Appearances mattered, particularly to public figures like Dolley Madison, who worried about her reputation and her husband's legacy.

The fate of the Madison slaves rested in Dolley's hands. The death of a husband transferred a certain amount of power to his widow, especially when she was made executrix in a will, as Dolley was. And James had given her his slaves.

CHAPTER 23

The Widow Madison

People who hoped James Madison would follow George Washington's lead and free his slaves upon his or Dolley's death were greatly disappointed. The fourth President freed no one through his will, not even his longtime valet Paul Jennings. Like George Washington, James Madison left the bulk of his estate to his wife. But while George bequeathed his slaves to Martha for her use during her lifetime, arranging for them to obtain freedom upon her death, James left his slaves to Dolley as a transfer of property.

When Edward Coles learned in July what James had done, he was outraged: "His (Mr. Madison) Slaves are not emancipated!" he informed his sister. Conversations and correspondence with the former President had left him certain that at least some of the Madison slaves would be freed. Someone, Coles thought, had changed Madison's mind, but who? Unable to pinpoint a culprit, he soon drew a different conclusion: there had to be a second will. "I cannot divest myself of the belief that he has made a secret Will, by which his slaves will be free at the death of his wife," Coles wrote in late July 1836. The Madison slaves reached the same conclusion: their master intended to grant them freedom, but the document was missing.[1]

A secret plan to free the Madison slaves was conceivable. It would have avoided the problem Martha Washington faced after her husband died—namely, that she feared for her life. A fire of mysterious origin seemed to suggest that someone wanted her gone sooner rather than later. Dolley apparently shared Martha's fears. Some years after

Martha Washington died, Dolley was still writing about the fires (she said five) that had been set at Mount Vernon, even after Martha Washington had let her husband's slaves go sooner than he intended.[2] One can easily imagine Dolley and James discussing Martha Washington's experience and what it implied for Dolley's safety as they pondered whether or when or how to free the Madison slaves. Of course, no one knew how long—or if—Dolley would outlive her husband, but he was considerably older than she and in poor health when he wrote his will.

In addition to the Madison slaves, Dolley inherited Montpelier, a house in Washington, and her husband's papers, including his notes on the Constitutional Convention, thought to be quite valuable. But James and Dolley Madison had miscalculated the worth of the papers and the ease with which they could be sold. When Dolley felt the need for cash, she soon turned to the slaves.

There was a clause in James's will restricting the sale of slaves except in cases of misconduct. This seems incongruous with the facts of slaveholding. The law required slaves to go wherever an owner directed. When slaves balked, violence or the threat of violence usually turned the situation around. Yet it had been relatively common in James Madison's lifetime for slaves to request a sale for specific reasons, for example, to keep spouses together. In the early nineteenth century, many planters were on the move, and slaves whose husbands or wives lived on another plantation would plead with owners to either sell them to a spouse's owner or purchase a loved one. Planters liked to honor these requests insofar as possible. Doing so placated slaves and helped ensure their cooperation. It helped cement ties between slaveholders, whose political and financial fortunes rested on maintaining solidarity as a class. And it helped slaveholders hold themselves out as stewards of slaves, no small matter for men and women who traded in human property. For these reasons pleading by slaves for particular sales could produce the desired result—not always, but often enough for slaves to hope.

Virginia slaveholders looking to sell human property often took into consideration, as well, a slave's preference for a particular owner. Granting slaves some say in accepting one purchaser or declining another eased tensions at difficult moments. Although this customary practice had no basis in law, enslaved people took advantage of it as they could to keep families together. James Madison may have thought that if sales became necessary, his slaves would scour the countryside and locate places for themselves, saving Dolley the distress of doing so.

It was wrenching to separate slaves from kin and community, and slaves threatened with sale and miserable at the thought of leaving family and friends sometimes did desperate things, like running away or damaging property or refusing to work no matter the punishment. The worst fate, from the slave's perspective, was to be sold at auction. When planters went bankrupt, creditors could force a sheriff's sale of assets to recover at least a portion of the debt. Slaves sold by the sheriff never knew where or with whom they would end up. James seemed determined not to have it come to that. His will sanctioned slave sales, as long as the slaves had some measure of control over where they would live.

It was a lot to put on Dolley. Montpelier was unprofitable, and she would have to either make it profitable or sell slaves to new owners acceptable to the bondmen and -women on the plantation. For help, Dolley turned to her son Payne Todd, who—as we have seen—had trouble managing his own farm and finances. Her choice did not bode well for Dolley or for the Madison slaves.

When Dolley began selling Montpelier slaves without their consent within two months of her husband's death, the slaves and others reacted with shock and revulsion. Not much is known about who was sold that summer, but in at least one case, a young family was separated. The husband, wife, and child at least remained in the same neighborhood, but no slaves living at Montpelier could be sure they were safe from sale to distant places. Edward Coles wrote in horror following an August visit to Montpelier: "Every day or two . . . a Negro trader would make his appearance . . . like the hawk among the pigeons."[3]

Whenever traders appeared, slaves ran to the house to complain, citing the language of James's will. They voiced objections even in the presence of company, which may have been a deliberate strategy.

Growing up in a Quaker community and later as a political wife, Dolley had learned to avoid controversy. She had once advised a niece to sustain "a sweet and gentle character" always because "contention in any form, either political or civil," was distasteful. "Our sex are ever losers, when they stem the torrent of public opinion, she observed."[4] Dolly would have understood all too clearly that the situation with the slaves was bound to evoke debate ending in condemnation.

Much of the disapproval surrounding the slave sales at Montpelier centered on Dolley's disregard of James's wishes, but critics soon took aim at him as well. It was the former President who had put the slaves in a situation where they could be sold at all. Even Edward Coles blamed James and sympathized with Dolley: "His poor widow is compelled, it is said, to sell." If slave sales had to occur, the former President ought to have done it before he died, sparing her the necessity.[5]

The criticism apparently gave Dolley pause. After indicating that she would sell a substantial portion of the Madison workforce to U.S. senator George Waggaman for his Louisiana lands, she backed off, attributing her change of heart to the pleas of slaves who did not want to leave the neighborhood. Dolley wrote Waggaman a polite letter declining his offer. She did not change her mind about selling slaves, however. She still hoped to sell a quarter of them (about twenty-five slaves) to a local buyer.[6]

The widow Madison faced other decisions as well. At age sixty-eight, she was in charge of her own fate for the second time in her life. The first had been after her first husband died. Dolley Todd had chosen then to marry an elite slaveholder from Virginia. Now Dolley Madison made another life-changing decision. She left the Virginia countryside for Washington. Montpelier would be sold. James had liked life in remote Orange County, but Dolley found it tedious, particularly during winter and rainy weather, when the number of visitors slacked off. Her niece said Dolley "felt very lonely at Montpelier,"[7] which was true, but there were other reasons for the move.

Acting as mistress of a large slaveholding plantation was both time-consuming and aggravating. Monitoring the health of Montpelier slaves in fall 1842 left Dolley feeling anxious and fatigued. An enslaved family had come down with an ailment, a doctor had left orders, and Dolley had assumed responsibility for seeing that they were carried out. But as at Monticello, Montpelier's enslaved people had their own ideas about how to handle illness. To ensure compliance with a white doctor's instructions, a "good mistress" had to monitor patients diligently. Dolley was particularly concerned with the fate of this family because she had "previously lost a man, and a woman Cook of great value to me." And more Montpelier slaves were complaining of symptoms, including members of Dolley's domestic staff. After three weeks, the illness, whose symptoms included a sore throat, still lingered in the neighborhood. Dolley had spent many hours watching over her husband as his health declined in the 1830s, and she seems not to have minded the duty, but tending slaves was a different matter. She was inclined to think of slaves in terms of what they did for her, rather than as sentient human beings. Following the death of her cook, Dolley mourned the loss of her services while expressing no sympathy for the woman's family and friends.[8]

Dolley's move to Washington excused her from exercising direct supervision over the healthcare of slaves. It also relieved her of day-to-day responsibilities for feeding, clothing, and supervising a large labor force. It was better to close the mansion in Orange County and leave its farming operations under the care of overseers who would be supervised by her son. Although Dolley expressed sorrow at leaving Montpelier, she certainly felt relief as well. Her absence would shield her from the turmoil that erupted as more and more slaves were sold and Montpelier was put up for sale. The undoing of the slave community that had begun under her husband could be completed by Payne, who would oversee both Toddsberth and Montpelier. It would be Payne who would bear the brunt of the discomfiture posed by the sale of the estate, including its human property.

Other people besides the slaves bristled at the idea that Montpelier was to be dismantled, its slaves scattered. Members of the Madison clan resented Dolley's control of James's assets (assets that would be passed on to her son and not to them). James bequeathed to his nieces and nephews nine thousand dollars, an amount that approximated the worth of Montpelier at the time. Dolley, as executrix, could pay it or not. If she did so, she would inherit Montpelier in fee simple, which meant it would be hers to pass onto her son or someone else of her choosing. If she could not come up with the cash, she would still retain the use of Montpelier over her lifetime, but upon her death the property would be sold and the proceeds divided among James's other heirs.[9]

Dolley decided to pay. By mid-September 1836, she had already turned over the nine thousand dollars, even though the will gave her three years to make the payment and contained language forgiving her should she fail to come up with the money even then. Her haste in distributing the funds, as well as other bequests, left her short of cash. She sold slaves to raise more.

Members of the Madison family were not happy. They argued over exactly who should receive the nine thousand dollars, while simultaneously arguing they were entitled to more. James Jr.'s youngest sister complained bitterly that she had never received her fair share of her father's personal property, including his slaves. His brother William filed suit over the distribution of assets as specified in the wills both of James Madison Jr. and of James Madison Sr.[10] Part of the problem was the resentment James's siblings felt over the substantial resources he had turned over to Payne Todd and other of Dolley's relatives during his lifetime. The bequest of nine thousand dollars had been intended to appease the Madisons, but it did not achieve its purpose.[11]

Although Dolley was said to have charmed all types of people, including James's political opponents, it is an understatement to say that she never charmed the Madisons, whose antipathy could only have been exacerbated by the agitation of the Madison slaves. Montpelier's dismantlement would have riled slaves living on the plantations of James's siblings and other kin since the slave populations on the family properties were interrelated. One can easily imagine frantic slaves pleading with Frances, William, and other Madisons for help in keeping relatives and friends together or at least close to one another as Dolley's plan to dismantle Montpelier began to unfold. In short, the large number of James's relatives in the vicinity of Montpelier offered Dolley yet another reason to head for Washington.

The Washington that awaited Dolley in 1843 was different in important respects from the one she had left in 1817. For one thing, the population had tripled. The District of Columbia now claimed 23,364 residents.[12] Neighbors lived close to one another, and patrols roamed the streets in an effort to deter disorder.

Dolley's two-story house stood on the northeast corner of Lafayette Square, an area known for its rich and influential residents.[13] Built in the colonial style, the gray-stucco home had a gabled roof, dormer windows, and a cellar where Dolley's domestic slaves lived. (Cellars served as sleeping quarters for many of the city's slaves, including those who worked in the President's house.)

Sukey and Paul Jennings were among the domestic slaves who accompanied Dolley to Washington, a move that separated families. Paul, for one, had to part from his wife, Fanny Gordon, and their five children. The pending sale of Montpelier must have left them wondering whether they would ever see home and loved ones again. And it was not only the slaves in Virginia at risk of sale. No one was safe, and those who were not sold might be rented out to work for others. President James K. Polk and his wife Sarah, who occupied the President's house from 1845 to 1849, paid Dolley for the hire of Paul Jennings.

Sukey was fortunate at first to have some of her children working with her in Washington, but Dolley did not like Sukey's son Ben Stewart, whom she considered loud and rambunctious. At times in the past he had been banished to a distant quarter. (Dolley was said to love children, but apparently not everyone's.) In 1843 Dolley sold Ben to a Georgian for five hundred dollars. Ben, who was around eighteen at the time, made clear that he did not consent to the sale and that it had not been to a kinsmen. His wording suggests not only that he was familiar with the contents of his master's will but that he considered his sale to be a breach of customary practice. It did not matter. Soon all of Sukey's children were gone except for her daughter Ellen.[14]

Slave sales were never far from the minds of the Madison slaves in Washington. Dolley's home stood across the corner from a redbrick home belonging to slave trader John Gadsby. An addition to the back of his house held slaves who had been sold and were awaiting transport to new owners in the South. The structure's barred windows and the nighttime howls and cries of the captives must have served as a grim reminder to Dolley's enslaved help of their possible fate.[15]

Washington nevertheless held certain attractions for Sukey, Ellen, Paul, and other of Dolley's slaves. City slaves had more opportunities to form friendships outside the confines of an owner's home. In rural Virginia, only a few trusted slaves were allowed to travel beyond the plantation. In the city, domestic slaves of both sexes had opportunities to meet outsiders. Dolley Madison's active social life made it possible for her slaves to get to know other people working and living in similar circumstances, especially the maids and drivers who traveled the city with their ladies. Those who did not know it before they arrived in Washington surely recognized that the city held out the prospect of freedom for those willing to risk everything. The possibility worried Dolley, but for a time her focus continued to be on the sale of Montpelier.

CHAPTER 24

Sale of Montpelier

Payne Todd helped his mother manage and eventually sell the Montpelier estate. Even before Dolley Madison moved to Washington, Payne supplied his mother with bacon, paid her debts, handled Montpelier's wheat harvest, and much more. In fall 1842 Dolley dismissed her overseer, after accusing him of paying more attention to his own crops than to hers. Payne searched for a new one to meet her specifications. Like many other planters, she preferred a single man, or at least one without a large family because "they want less provision." She was willing to pay $150 a year.[1]

The roiled relations at Montpelier occasioned by slave sales and rumors of more to come made it hard to find someone for the job. Payne was unwilling to turn the Montpelier slaves over to a "slave breaker," a man who employed especially harsh tactics to manage a slave force. Dolley approved Payne's decision to turn down two applicants known as "whipper[s] of Negroes." Hiring an overseer with a reputation for using corporal punishment might have made a bad situation worse. When pushed too far, slaves could and did resist, sometimes by ruining crops or destroying buildings or occasionally harming an overseer or manager. One of Thomas Jefferson's slaves, Billy Hubbard, in 1819 attacked an overseer at Poplar Forest because the overseer ordered him to work on a Sunday—a day slaves normally had to themselves.[2] The incident and others like it were discussed among Dolley's circle of friends and acquaintances.

After Dolley moved to Washington, DC, in 1843, her reliance on

Payne increased, but he never assumed complete control of his mother's affairs. Instead, he reported regularly on the situation at Montpelier, and she made decisions from afar. Dolley wrote Payne frequently and grew frustrated when he did not answer right away. For his part, Payne usually waited for his mother's approval before acting. When he did not, she still let him know what she thought.

To meet his mother's expenses, Payne began selling pieces of the Madison furniture as well as some of his stepfather's papers. In winter 1843, he offered to sell two enslaved youths (Paul and George) to Henry W. Moncure. The Richmond merchant, who owned land in Orange County, was interested, if the boys — said to be fifteen and sixteen — were strong enough to plow. After having his plantation manager look them over, Moncure offered five hundred dollars for both. Payne had asked three hundred dollars for each, but Moncure justified the lower price because neither could handle a plow. "I am told such Boys command in this Place about $250," he wrote in his counteroffer.[3]

While Payne was assisting his mother, he was trying — unsuccessfully, it would seem — to fight alcoholism. In "Letters and Memorandum," which he compiled from 1844 to 1847, Payne wrote of ordering brandy, rum, and wine because the want of them made him sick. In one entry, he admitted that he had drunk whiskey all day. But he also reported efforts to improve. He drank ice water because he believed it would break his dependence on spirits, and he wrote of his determination to do better in the future.[4]

Dolley knew of Payne's alcoholism, but she relied on him anyway, in part because she did not like to share her financial woes with others, but also because she saw her finances and her son's as intertwined. From time to time she sent him small sums, as he did her. Unfortunately, neither made sound decisions based on their economic circumstances. If Payne was forever in a fog of unreality grounded in drink, Dolley was forever in a fog of unreality grounded in miscalculations about the worth of her husband's estate and her own proclivity for spending.

Certain biographers and historians have been quick to blame Payne for the demise of the Madison fortune. One says that Payne "managed to single-handedly drive Montpelier into bankruptcy." But such an assessment assumes that Payne was solely in charge of his mother's property. Letters between mother and son make clear that the two held ongoing discussions of financial matters. She, not he, made most decisions. Dolley Madison (along with many scholars) appears to have expected that Payne—who had never shown any real interest in Virginia farming—could make a go of his stepfather's estate, a feat the former President himself had been unable to pull off in his retirement. And it was James Madison who miscalculated the worth of his estate, especially the value of his papers. Meanwhile, Dolley kept borrowing funds to sustain a style of living beyond her means. All the while, Payne had his own financial woes. "I am now as low on finances as well can be," he wrote during these years.[5] Given all of this, it is difficult to conclude that Dolley Madison's financial problems were all Payne's fault.

For Payne, one solution to his mother's financial troubles was for her to live with him at Toddsberth. He did his best to structure the plantation to please her, going so far as to eliminate stairs as much as possible since she had difficulty climbing them. She never came, not even to visit.

It was Dolley, not Payne, who decided to sell Montpelier to Henry Moncure, although her son handled most of the complicated and protracted negotiations. Dolley agreed to sell the "dwelling house, springs, overseers house, sawmill and pond," along with slaves, horses, cattle, sheep, hogs, furniture, farming utensils, and personal property. The contract allowed Dolley to repurchase Montpelier within five years, provided she paid for any improvements Moncure made to the property.[6]

Why was the latter clause included? Given the state of her finances, Dolley could scarcely have expected to accumulate enough funds to repurchase the estate. But evidently it served an important purpose. As Dolley knew all too well, the slaves were upset at the prospect of sale and separation from kin and community. Indeed, one of them arranged to have a letter written informing Dolley of the discontent just in case her mistress did not hear about it from other sources.[7] The repurchase clause may have been intended to ease disgruntlement and reassure slaves that there would be no further sales of human property, since the new owner would need to keep the estate intact for at least five years. The wording also may have been intended to calm critics who wanted Dolley to set the Madison slaves free, as they imagined James had wanted. The clause gave hope that the President's widow might yet find a way to free the Madison slaves, though in the end, Dolley declined to buy back Montpelier.

Before the sale was finalized, Dolley transferred to her son more than twenty slaves, including six or more children too young to be considered working hands. Eight of the adults were at least age forty. Their ages suggest that they belonged to families who had been with the Madisons for a while. Nicholas, age thirty-six, and Nicholas Junior, age thirteen, were likely father and son. We can imagine Dolley's dilemma as she contemplated which slaves to keep with her family and which ones to convey with the land. While her agreement with Moncure offers no clue as to which slaves stayed at Montpelier, we do have a list of the slaves she gave to Payne in mid-June 1844, which includes their ages:

Tydal (65)
Willoughby (about 60)
Gabriel (about 50)
Matthew (about 45)
John (about 40)
Nicholas (36)
Raif Junr (about 33)
Jerry (about 32)
Charles (about 30)
Joshua (about 22)
Nicholas Junr (about 13)

Sarah (about 50)
Winny (about 45)
Milly (about 40)

Sylvia (about 33) with four children
Caty (about 22) with young children
Charlotte (about 20)[8]

A month later, Dolley gave Payne an additional twenty slaves. No ages are listed, nor any children designated as such, which suggests that they were all working hands. At one time, Dolley had hoped Payne would inherit the Madison plantation and all of its slaves. That was out of the question now, but at least Payne would have a substantial part of the labor force to add to the slaves he already owned:

Lewis
Stephen
Ralf Junr
Gery
Randall
Ellick
Blind John
Sam
Tom
Ben Senr
Abraham
William

Julia
Amy
Sucky
Harriet
Becca
Nancy
Fanny
Ellen[9]

The deeding of slaves to her son circumvented the law that would have forced their sale for the payment of Dolley's debts, an indication that her finances were in greater disarray than his. Around the same time Dolley was transferring slaves to Payne the enslaved Sarah Steward wrote her mistress with "bad news." (She did not pen the letter herself but rather asked "a young lady" to write on behalf of herself and the other Madison slaves.) "The sheriff has taken all of us and says he will sell us at next court unless something is done before to prevent it—We are afraid we shall be bought by what are called negro buyers and sent away from our husbands and wives," she wrote. Sarah wanted her mistress to find a local buyer who would purchase at least the husbands and wives so they could stay together. The matter was urgent—the next sheriff's sale was only a little more than two weeks away. "We are verry sure you are sorry for this state of things," Sarah said, "but think my dear misstress what our sorrow must be." Sarah asked in particular about Caty and her children: "What is to be done" about them?" Caty's husband was in Washington with Dolley. When she penned her letter, Sarah did not know that Dolley had already devised a solution, which was to deed them over to Payne. Caty and her children were listed among those transferred to Payne just weeks before Sarah wrote her letter.[10]

The next month, Dolley and Payne entered into an agreement with Moncure. The deed of sale listed the outbuildings on the plantation as including a kitchen, a smokehouse, and a stable. It mentioned orchards as well: peach, pear, apple, cherry, and other trees unspecified, the fruit of which was to be split equally between buyer and seller.[11]

Negotiations over the division of Montpelier's human inhabitants were more complex than those that split up the fruit. "I wish . . . to retain some few of the black people," Dolley wrote on 12 August 1844, but she had not yet decided who. Dolley admitted that the subject was troubling, but she expressed hope that the matter could be settled soon. Instead, negotiations dragged on. In early September, Dolley asked Montpelier's purchaser whether she could "choose some few, of the Negroes, and some of the furniture—and to retain the family Burial Place." Payne took issue with the supplicant tone of his mother's letters. Moncure had "not the slightest authority over either furniture or Slaves except such as he bought some time ago," Payne wrote. "None since I saw you." Yet, "the tone of your letters would seem to give him authority he never possessed."[12]

The transactions were time-consuming and frustrating for everyone involved. At times Payne was overwhelmed by the need to manage his mother's and his own affairs. "I am working morning & night," he assured his mother in fall 1844, as details of the sale were still being hammered out. On top of everything else, "the negroes is a source of trouble of the most onerous kind." His letter came to sudden stop: "I am interrupted."[13] Brief as it is, the document hints at the difficulties Payne confronted. It was not simply the financial details that needed to be sorted out but the human "problems" created by the sale. The slaves did not acquiesce quietly, and it was Payne, not Dolley, who experienced the chaos and unrest of a slave community in dissolution.

The transfer of close to fifty slaves from Montpelier had also increased chaos and confusion at Toddsberth, which was not ready for them. The main house at Toddsberth had burned in March 1841, along with valuable artwork, papers, and furnishings brought from Montpelier. The outbuildings were spared, but the mansion had to be rebuilt. The reconstruction apparently had been completed only recently, and now time and resources had to be found to build housing and procure food for an influx of slaves. In late November 1844, Payne assured his mother that the needs of the slaves were being met and that they were being put to use, but things were not going as smoothly as he implied. Some of the slaves had been pledged as collateral on debts that Dolley had incurred earlier. This meant that the turmoil of sorting out who would go and who would stay remained unresolved. Payne advised his mother to keep Raif, Caty, and her children. He judged Sarah "very valuable indeed." A number of other slaves were "under a levy": Milley and her children, Elizabeth and her children, Tom, and Nicholas, whose hand had been burned sometime previously, were among those serving as surety.[14] Gradually the slave population upon which the Madisons had depended financially was being scattered to pay creditors and meet the need for labor at Toddsberth and at Dolley's home in Washington.

Things got so bad at Montpelier that Moncure complained about the Madison slaves who remained there as he attempted to take control of the property. In fall 1844 he told Payne to remove "your People." They were making it impossible for him to hold his plantation manager accountable because the man blamed the Madison slaves for all missing and damaged property. "I could not make him responsible for the preservation of any thing that was left on the Premises," Moncure grumbled.[15]

Eventually Dolley sold about a quarter of the Madison slaves with the property. About half were sold away from the plantation. She and Payne retained the rest, most of whom lived at Toddsberth.[16]

In the midst of these negotiations, Dolley questioned whether she had the right to sell a woman who was giving her trouble in Washington. Particular slaves were slated for sale because of her huge debts and the agreement with Moncure, but she hoped to sell this one because of her disposition. Payne responded, "In answer to your enquiry whether you could dispose of a bad girl I have only to say that you are free to sell or put in pledge or otherwise *any of the Slaves with you*, in Washn. or here, to neighbours who would take One or more as you please." Payne went on to assure his mother that she could also dispose of the slaves she had transferred to him.[17] Payne's response indicates that he and his mother regarded the Madison slaves at Toddsberth (transferred by deed and fact in recent months) as still Dolley's property. She, not he, would decide their fate.

The sale of Montpelier did not go through until late 1844. There was a problem with the deed and Moncure would not pay until it was cleared up. The sale was further complicated by the debts — more than ten thousand dollars — that Dolley had incurred and that were secured by the property.[18]

Dolley's sale of her husband's estate provoked criticism, especially from people who continued to believe that her husband wanted his slaves to go free. William Lloyd Garrison's abolitionist newspaper *The Liberator* lambasted the widow. So did Horace Greeley's *New York Tribune*, which could not fathom why she would have to sell slaves. In 1837, Congress had paid her thirty thousand dollars for James Madison's notes on the Constitutional Convention and the Confederation Congress. Was that not enough? The *Rochester Evening Star* reported Dolley's sale of a daughter away from her mother, lamenting not only the sale but Dolley's failure to act in an acceptable female fashion. Dolley was a mother herself, the *Star* noted, and should have known better than to separate a mother from a child.[19]

It is difficult today to reconcile popular images of Dolley Madison with the slaveholding woman who resorted to selling slaves. One does wonder why she could not live more modestly. But truth be told, she was acting in the manner of other wealthy Virginians of her day. An older generation of slaveholders had taken pride in its reluctance to sell family slaves, but in an economic crisis, many planters of the antebellum era found selling slaves to be a quick way to raise cash.[20] Besides, this was not the first time Madison slaves had been scattered. Montpelier slaves had been divided among family members at the death of James Madison Sr. in 1801 and again when his wife Nelly Conway Madison passed away in 1829. Further divisions of property occurred when Madison family members came of age and settled plantations of their own. Payne Todd had taken a share of the Madison slaves at the time he established Toddsberth. Quite possibly, Dolley Madison did not see herself as deviating substantially from the behavior of her predecessors. The slave community attached to the Madisons had long been in a state of flux as Madison family members married and died, built up and tore apart plantations, and reallocated slaves accordingly.

From the slave's perspective, however, there was a difference. Family ties among the Madisons, most of whom lived in the vicinity of Orange County, had helped ensure that slaves could stay connected with relatives. And the previous estate sales had been considered friendly: Madison family members more or less cooperated to divide property equitably while minimizing disruption to the slaves. When James's mother died 11 February 1829, she held nineteen slaves in captivity to be divided among her heirs. By the terms of her will, the slaves had a say in how they would be distributed. Only the three oldest stayed at Montpelier: Sawney, Violet, and Lucy. No value was ascribed to them in the estate inventory. In fact, it was estimated that each would cost the owner sixty dollars for food and clothing over the remainder of his or her life. James's sister Sarah Madison Macon and her husband Thomas, who lived not far from Montpelier, took six of the nineteen slaves, estimated to be worth $825. Nine other slaves, valued at $2,425, went to James's youngest brother, William Madison, whose plantation,

Woodberry Forrest, was located in Madison County, abutting Orange. One slave went to James's nephew Ambrose Madison (Moses, valued at $375), who had a plantation in Orange County.[21] It was this type of "friendly sale" James Madison had in mind when he specified in his will that slaves should not be sold without their consent except for misconduct. It was the shift to a different sort of transaction that prompted Ben Stewart's complaint that Dolley had auctioned him without his consent and to someone who was not a kinsman. The slave sales that followed the death of James Madison Jr. were decidedly not friendly.

From Washington, Dolley Madison kept abreast of events in Orange County as best she could. Reports came from Payne, of course, but the desire of the Madison slaves in Virginia to share information with the occupants of the Lafayette Square house and to seek the mistress's help prompted some to send reports of their own. Sarah Steward was one of the slaves Dolley had deeded over to Payne shortly before Montpelier's sale. Sarah wrote about matters of interest to both Dolley and the Madison slaves in Washington and included solicitous declarations of fealty and friendship for "Dear Mistris." A letter dated 24 April 1847 carried news not only of Sarah's health but also the health of people in the neighborhood, a marriage, the death of a woman in childbirth, and the progress of work at Toddsberth. Sarah had obtained medicine from Doctor Slaughter. Miss Ellen and her groom John Myers were married at the home of Doctor Slaughter and dined the next day at their brother's home. They visited Mrs. Willis, then left for Norfolk. Silvey had gone into labor on Friday and died Sunday night. Neither Doctor Slaughter nor Grymes was able to save her. The work hands were busy planting corn.[22]

Sarah asked her mistress to pass certain information on to others. "Tell Susan that Rebecca has a fine daughter named Susan Ellen after her Mother." "Tell Susan that little Betty is verry unwell" and suffering from "fitts." "Her son Thomas has bad risens on both of his armes." "Winney is tolerable well." Sarah sent Caty, Ralph, Mathew, and Caty's three children her love and related Winney's wish to be remembered to Matthew and the rest of the slaves in Washington.[23] For such a short letter, Sarah Steward managed to convey quite a bit of news.

Following the standard conventions of letter writing, Sarah sent "love & respects to all" and love specifically to "Miss Anny and your self," as well as an apology for not writing sooner, which she blamed on her poor health. Her letter reveals slavery to have been more than an abstract labor system. It was also a set of personal relationships that crossed class boundaries and in this case geography. The etiquette of letter writing allowed Sarah to act the part of the faithful and respectful slave and at the same time help dispersed family and friends stay in touch. For their part, mistresses like Dolley took comfort in a slave's expressions of fealty and fondness and were only too glad to share information they believed would make slaves more content. Such conventions of behavior helped ease the tensions intrinsic to the relationship between mistress and slave.

CHAPTER 25

In Washington

In Washington, Dolley Madison kept up appearances. She maintained a steady correspondence and rounds of visiting. She did her best to comply with requests from all types of people who wanted a copy of the President's autograph or her own.[1] The completion of such mundane tasks and routine entertaining gave the appearance of normality. But the situation was far from calm. Dolley's slaves in the District of Columbia were as restive as those back in Virginia.

Washington society welcomed Dolley Madison as a celebrity upon her return. She entertained and was entertained frequently and in high style. She once made sixty-five social calls in a single month.[2] Her visitors, to whom she served cake and wine and punch, were numerous and not limited to ladies. Washington's important men (President Polk included) were part of Dolley's circle. Because life among the elite was expensive, Dolley borrowed money. Although she sold Montpelier and undid its slave community, the proceeds proved insufficient to pay all of her debts.

Life in Washington posed challenges not only for Dolley but for her slaves. Her legendary entertaining required constant work, and she put them in danger of sale by spending beyond her means. As Dolley's niece Mary Cutts delicately put it, James Madison had served as "a check upon her liberality," but after he died, there was no one to rein in her spending or that of another niece, Annie Payne, who lived with her.[3]

Dolley's financial situation worsened over time. She had mortgaged her Lafayette Square home in 1842 to obtain three thousand dollars from financier John Jacob Astor. The Library of Congress holds papers that demonstrate the extent of Dolley's debts, which were greatly entangled with the finances of her son. She borrowed where she could: a hundred dollars here, two hundred there. A bank lent her sixteen hundred dollars, but many of the loans were from individuals, including the well-to-do William W. Corcoran.[4] Such loans carried high interest rates.

Dolley's deteriorating finances were reflected in her wardrobe. When she got to the point where she could no longer obtain credit, she stopped purchasing new gowns and had her maids refashion clothing from previous years. But there were limits to what even a skilled seamstress could do, especially once Dolley could no longer scrape together the means to purchase new trimmings. After a while, Washingtonians began to remark on her old-fashioned clothing. Long, colorful shawls had once been the fashion, but Dolley continued to wear them, along with once-popular turbans and caps with black curls trailing out. Dolley did not lose interest in being fashionable. On 15 July 1845 she joined St. John's Episcopal Church in Washington because it was popular with the city's elite,[5] but she could no longer afford all of the material trappings of grandee life.

Dolley's slaves must have watched the lavish spending during her first days in Washington with foreboding. Her willingness to sell or mortgage slaves and homes to underwrite an elite lifestyle must have struck them as both foolish and cruel. And of course there was the behavior of her son. Madison slaves both in Washington and in Orange County would have been well aware that Payne Todd's alcohol consumption and gambling debts posed threats to their well-being and that of their friends and families.[6] Dolley's finances were tightly interwoven with his even after the sale of Montpelier.

Paul Jennings's wife became gravely ill in spring 1844. He asked for, and Dolley granted him, permission to make a short visit to Virginia to check on Fanny. Paul wrote his mistress soon after his arrival to express appreciation for her kindness. Fanny too, he said, was "vary thankful to you." When Paul did not return or send further word, Dolley grew alarmed. If he stayed away too long, he might lose his position in the President's house; she would not only forfeit the income from his job but also lose the eyes and ears that kept her apprised of what went on in the nation's highest political and social circles. Dolley regularly attended dinners and parties hosted by President James Polk and First Lady Sarah Polk at the presidential mansion, including those otherwise attended by cabinet members only. The previous month Dolley had spent a pleasant day with the Polks visiting Mount Vernon. But domestic servants like Paul were in a position to learn household — and in this case, government — secrets.[7]

The relationship between Dolley Madison and Paul Jennings was already tense. The two had worked closely for decades, but proximity did not mean slaves and owners developed an affection or even respect for one another. Five years after James died, Dolley had written a will granting Paul Jennings freedom at the end of her life. Even so, she did not seem to hold any special affection for him. Manumission of individual slaves could have the effect of strengthening slavery rather than undermining it. Promising freedom to a particular slave encouraged cooperation from someone who might otherwise take matters in his own hands by running away,[8] as Oney Judge and Hercules had done in an earlier era. Perhaps James had asked her to free Paul at her passing, or perhaps she believed that this was what the public expected and wanted.

Whether he intended it or not, Paul's absence — coupled with his silence — demonstrated a determination not to be controlled. He was well connected and respected in Washington, and if Dolley tried to bring him back forcefully, word of her action would spread quickly. His friends and slavery's foes might once again raise the issue of James Madison's will and Dolley's seeming refusal to follow his instructions. Many people still believed that James intended to free his slaves, especially Paul Jennings. There was, however, a solution to Paul's defiance other than having him hauled back to Washington in chains. He could be sold or allowed to purchase his freedom. Dolley would forfeit the money President Polk paid for his services, but she would at least have his purchase price. She would also be free of the worry that Paul might prove unreliable henceforth. He was in his late forties, and no one knew how many years he had left to carry out his duties anyway.

In summer 1846 Paul proposed purchasing his freedom. Dolley said yes. They agreed upon a price of two hundred dollars. Paul, who had saved only eighty dollars, approached Senator Daniel Webster of Massachusetts for the rest. Webster, though sympathetic, was strapped for cash, but he was able to secure $120 from a local insurance agent named Pollard Webb. Jennings would pay off Webster who in turn would reimburse Webb. Legally, Paul remained enslaved, but as of September 1846 he was free of Dolley. A few weeks later, Paul was back in Orange County with his family. Fanny had died, but Paul had children and other relatives in the area. The former slave continued to report to his former mistress about matters of interest, including her son and the Madison slaves, but he traveled where he wished and acted as a free man. He soon returned to Washington, where he secured a job in the U.S. Pension Office, a position that allowed him to pay off his debt to Webster at the rate of eight dollars per month.[9]

As Paul Jennings's financial situation improved, Dolley Madison's deteriorated further. The former First Lady sometimes found herself short of food. Payne, too, was strapped for cash. In mid-September 1847 Payne apologized for being unable to send a wagon of supplies expected by his mother and Sukey. He hoped certain payments would "fall into my hands" by October, when he planned to visit his mother in Washington. In response, Dolley stressed the urgency of her situation. "I have borrowed as you *must* know," she wrote and "am at a stand, until supplies come from you."[10]

Paul Jennings was sympathetic to the inhabitants of Dolley's home and sometimes brought them food. On occasion he went with Daniel Webster to the farmer's market. Webster purchased vegetables for Dolley and sent them to her by way of Paul, who sometimes shelled out small sums of cash to her himself.[11] In this way Paul managed to curry favor with his former mistress while simultaneously looking out for his enslaved friends at Lafayette Square. When Dolley was short of supplies, she was not the only one to suffer. Paul's grasp of racial and class etiquette, honed over decades of service, was impeccable. Dolley never suspected him of anything other than devotion to her.

For many years, historians thought of Paul Jennings as a loyal member of the Madison household. He described himself as such and expressed sympathy for Dolley's deteriorating financial condition. But Jennings was more complex than his account lets on. He may have maintained the outward demeanor of a loyal and trustworthy slave, but in truth he was neither. While impressing James and Dolley Madison with flawless service, he worked behind the scenes to chip away at slavery whenever he got the chance. At great risk to himself, he forged papers and served as a go-between for people who wanted to escape slavery, including (as mentioned earlier) one of Thomas Jefferson's bondmen. Paul Jennings valued freedom as much as James Madison and the other founding fathers who did so much to enshrine the concept of liberty in the documents that established the United States.

Almost immediately after securing his freedom, Paul became involved in the largest escape attempt by slaves in the nation. In 1848, seventy-seven slaves boarded the schooner *Pearl*, docked just south of Pennsylvania Avenue, and bound for free territory. Paul Jennings not only helped plan the escape attempt but also helped Sukey's daughter Ellen get on board.[12]

Ellen Stewart, age fifteen, had learned months before that she was to be sold. Dolley had called Ellen to the parlor ostensibly to do an errand but in fact to give a slave trader an opportunity to assess her value. Satisfied that Ellen would suit his purpose, the trader and Dolley laid plans for him to snatch the girl from a nearby public square. Dolley would send Ellen to the public pump for water at an agreed-upon time; the trader would be there to capture her. The element of subterfuge suggests that Dolley expected resistance, perhaps from Ellen but also from her mother. Other slaves would have been upset as well. Dolley and the trader clearly hoped that Ellen would be long gone before Sukey and the others learned what had happened.

The tableau did not unfold as Dolley planned. Ellen learned of the plot and fled before the scheme could be set in motion. She had the help of Paul Jennings and others who hid her for five months until the *Pearl* set sail.

On Saturday, 15 April 1848, Ellen joined seventy-six other slaves aboard the *Pearl*. Calm waters delayed departure; then a strong wind prevented the *Pearl* from entering the Chesapeake Bay as planned. An informant sounded an alarm, a posse formed, and the ship was over-taken. The refugees, including Ellen, were pulled from the ship's hold and paraded to jail through the city streets. Dolley or her representa-tive joined other owners of the *Pearl*'s human cargo at the jail the next day to reclaim their property. Most owners arranged for the sale of the slaves who had been involved; few wanted to keep the renegades in their midst. The episode touched off three days of rioting by proslavery Washingtonians, which only added to owners' fears of a society out of control. Although the ship captain and supercargo were convicted of stealing and transporting slaves illegally,[13] Washington slaveholders worried that the city had become a center of abolitionist activity.

Dolley once again made plans to sell Ellen. Payne evidently thought the sale should wait until some of the fervor surrounding the escape attempt died down, but Dolley was impatient. She had not seen Ellen since her capture, but had "heard a bad acct. of her morals & con-duct." Nevertheless, she would follow Payne's advice provided the delay was no more than a week. Dolley Madison sold Ellen Stewart for four hundred dollars shortly after she wrote Payne. She pocketed three hundred dollars and sent Payne the remaining hundred to "put your clothes in order." Despite her strained finances and all that had gone on, Dolley was concerned that her son's wardrobe befit a member of the elite class. She lamented that Ellen had enjoyed "6 months dissi-pation" at the hands of "Abolitionists."[14] She apparently believed Ellen would not have run off without their encouragement. She refused to acknowledge her own role in prompting the crisis, nor did she enter-tain the idea that someone close to her like Paul Jennings had been involved. Ellen managed to make a second getaway while being trans-ported to Baltimore, this time for good, severing all past relationships.

Ellen and Sukey held positions in Dolley's household that were assigned to the most trustworthy of slaves. But Ellen's escape demonstrated that her loyalty (and possibly her mother's) was no more real than the pretended paternalism of slaveholders, who wanted to be seen as good stewards even as they used or sold slaves to suit their interests. The well-ordered slaveholding household was a façade covering up tensions inherent in a system that deemed some people to be the property of others.

Dolley took her frustration and anger out on Sukey, then in her fifties. Although some people believed Sukey knew of her daughter's whereabouts and hoped some day to join her, there is no evidence that she did. An account written after the capture of the *Pearl* and before Ellen made her second getaway described Sukey as "overwhelmed with grief at the fate of this, the last child of five that slavery has snatched from her arms."[15] Whether or not she knew the whereabouts of her daughter, she would have worried and grieved her loss.

Unable to find and punish Ellen, Dolley sold her lady's maid of forty years to a "family in the city in want of a capable woman like herself." Her new owners purchased Sukey for a particular term of years rather than for life. By buying her services for a set period, her purchaser could avoid having to support Sukey in old age, should she live beyond the time when she could carry out domestic tasks. It also gave Sukey an incentive to work placidly for a few more years. Sukey had "the prospect of freedom *some time*," in the words of someone knowledgeable about her situation.[16]

Disorder seemed to characterize life at Lafayette Square in late 1848. One night in May a fire broke out that was thought to have been deliberately set. Someone had put matches between the home's shutters and window sashes. All might have been lost, had not a neighbor spotted the fire and alerted the enslaved Ralph, who was asleep in the cellar. Ralph rushed to wake his mistress and Annie Payne, both of whom were sleeping upstairs. Because Dolley slept with her door locked from within, he had some trouble rousing and rescuing her. After Ralph saw Dolley and Annie safely outside to the garden, Dolley sent him back inside to retrieve trunks filled with James's papers. Afterward, Dolley seemed relatively calm. She assured Payne that steps were being taken to protect her and other Washington inhabitants: "the Watch is nightly around the City."[17]

Dolley's brave front may have been a mother's way of reassuring her son that all was well. In truth, the fire was Dolley's worst nightmare. She had worried about the possibility of arson from the time she heard of the fires breaking out at Mount Vernon following George Washington's death, and her locked bedroom door suggests that she feared more than fire. Slaves in Washington also posed dangers.

Ralph acted quickly to save Dolley's life, her home, and part of her husband's legacy. Slaveholders liked to point to such selfless acts of courage by slaves as proof that slavery satisfied all parties involved. Presumably Ralph would not have awoken his mistress or reentered a burning building for reasons other than love and loyalty. But Ralph had many reasons to act as he did. If Dolley or the night watch or her neighbor suspected him of arson or if he had failed to save his mistress's life or the former President's papers, he could have faced retaliation. Moreover, he would have known the importance of the papers for his mistress's financial well-being and thus for the well-being of her slaves. If Dolley's finances could be put in order, there was less chance that more slaves would be sold. In more immediate terms, the sale of the papers would help secure food and other necessities for the struggling occupants of Dolley's Washington home. Ralph's wife and children survived the fire, apparently without his assistance. They, like Ralph, would have understood the consequences had Ralph not gone to Dolley's rescue.

Later that year, the U.S. Congress paid Dolley twenty-five thousand dollars for the publication rights to the papers Ralph saved. This was in addition to the thirty thousand dollars Congress had paid Dolley the year after James died for his notes from the Constitutional Convention of 1787 and other papers. The second congressional payment proved controversial. Certain opponents of the measure, like John C. Calhoun of South Carolina, noted that James had bequeathed money to the American Colonization Society and argued that Congress, through its purchase of the papers, was thus supporting an antislavery society. The measure passed nevertheless. Dolley was to receive only the interest from the twenty-five thousand dollars. The principal was to be kept intact and distributed upon her death to whomever she named in her last will and testament.[18] As it turned out, the naming of an heir proved controversial.

CHAPTER 26

Death of
Dolley Madison

Dolley Madison died, at the age of eighty-one, Thursday, 12 July 1849, at her home on Lafayette Square in Washington, DC. Four days later her body was carried across the square to St. John's Episcopal Church, opposite the President's house. After the eulogy, she was laid to rest in Washington's Congressional Cemetery. A printed program lists the order of the dignitaries who made up the funeral procession: family members, followed by President Zachary Taylor and members of his cabinet, the diplomatic corps, members of the U.S. Congress, justices of the Supreme Court, officers of the army and navy, and Washington's mayor and city council. "Citizens and strangers," including Dolley's slaves, brought up the rear. It took forty-eight carriages to carry everyone, including one designated for Dolley's household servants. People attending the funeral or reading about her death had a sense that they were participating in a major historical event. Mourners in Washington wore badges and stars of black in her honor. A reader of the *Richmond Whig* called on the ladies of Virginia to wear black armbands for thirty days to commemorate Dolley Madison's passing.[1]

The slaves who attended Dolley in her final days and who watched as their mistress was laid to rest remained in bondage. Dolley wrote numerous wills over a period of years. None of them freed any of the Madison slaves with the exception of Paul Jennings. A will made out in February 1841 had granted him freedom, but as we know, he had already purchased it by the time his mistress died. Each of Dolley's wills left most of her assets (slaves included) to Payne. The 1841 will bequeathed enslaved girls ages ten to fifteen to her nieces Mary E. P. Allen and Mary E. E. Cutts and her sister Lucy Payne Washington Todd. Presumably the girls would serve as maids and offer the recipients a measure of financial security through their ability to work and bear babies in bondage. Dolley left a more substantial bequest to her niece Annie Payne: "my negro Woman and her children," along with one-third of Dolley's clothing, a piano, bedroom furniture, and papers that Annie was instructed "to *burn*." Dolley's "negro Woman" at the time was Sukey. She also left money to her brother John C. Payne and his two sons, funds for two marble monuments to mark her husband's grave and her own, portraits of herself and of James, and her books — although it is unclear whether she intended the portraits and books for Annie or Lucy. Subsequent wills altered these terms, but each left everything or nearly everything to her son.[2]

After she died, Dolley's heirs fought over her bequests. Dolley had signed two new wills shortly before she passed away. Each had the backing of different family members. A will dated 11 June 1849, said to have been written by Payne, left everything to him.[3] Another will, drawn up a month later by Dolley's nephew J. Madison Cutts, divided about twenty thousand dollars (the money left from the sale of James's papers to Congress) between Payne Todd and Annie Payne. Everything else went to Payne. Dolley had been roused from a coma and given opium three days before she died and urged to sign the latter will.[4] The two wills had this in common: Dolley had written neither.

Payne challenged the Cutts will in court. He lost, and what remained of the twenty thousand dollars was split between the two disputants. Each got about five thousand dollars, after the deduction of legal expenses. The family feud continued, the settlement notwithstanding. Charges and countercharges flew between Annie and members of her family, on the one side, and Payne, on the other, as they battled over Dolley's papers and other belongings. In the process, valuable documents were confiscated and destroyed by Annie and her sister Mary.[5]

James C. McGuire, the administrator of Dolley Madison's estate, found himself caught between Payne and Annie. Payne was adamant that his mother's debts should be paid from the sale of her assets.

Dolley Madison and her niece Anna (Annie) Payne.

Annie and her allies blamed Payne for the debts and sought a way to keep Dolley's property in the family. At one point the estate administrator had to ask Annie to return silver she had taken from her aunt's home; she claimed it had been a gift from Dolley prior to her death.[6]

Although the family fought bitterly over Dolley's personal items, no one questioned who should assume ownership of Dolley's remaining slaves. Payne inherited them all. How many is unclear, but by then only a small number were left.

In a memoir she wrote of her aunt, Mary Cutts described the slaves transferred to Payne upon his mother's death as "with him, and faithful to the last."[7] Her phrasing suggests a smooth transition. Dolley's domestic help knew Payne, of course, and they might have welcomed a chance to reunite with family and friends on his Virginia plantation, but it is uncertain where they went after Dolley died. We do not know, for example, whether they remained in Washington for any length of time or whether any were sold. But while the details of what happened to Dolley's domestic slaves have been lost to history, criticism of her failure to free them has not.

The disposition of the slaves shocked people who had hoped that at last some of James Madison's slaves would go free. The idea of a second, secret will had never been debunked. And even people who did not much care whether the slaves were liberated railed against her decision to pass them to Payne. Critics had already been complaining that she was selling slaves to maintain an elite style of life, and now they feared more might be sold to ensure a life of privilege for her son. Dolley's supporters had defended previous slave sales by citing her impoverishment, which many found implausible.[8] Perhaps ironically, it was Payne who satisfied at least some of his mother's critics.

Upon his death of typhoid fever on 16 January 1852, Payne did what his mother could not bring herself to do: free the remaining Madison slaves. His will bequeathed two hundred dollars to each. Payne left all of the Madison papers in his possession—some his mother's and some his stepfather's—to the executor of his mother's estate. He also bequeathed a flute to a Dr. Bogle. Any remaining proceeds from his estate were to go to the American Colonization Society. Payne's decision to let his slaves go was no doubt made easier by his lack of close relationships with family members. Who was there for him to bequeath the slaves to? He had no children, and he was estranged from most of his mother's and stepfather's relatives. Quaker family members in Philadelphia and his cousin Edward Coles had long been advocates of abolition and would hardly have countenanced a gift of slaves.

The terms of Payne's will greatly displeased certain relatives. Annie's husband James H. Causten, scoffed at the possibility that Payne had sufficient funds to free the slaves given the number of creditors to be satisfied. Causten offered Payne's will as evidence that he had been a man of poor character.[9]

Fifteen people awaited their freedom while Payne's debtors contested his will. They were all that remained of the Madison slaves, including those he had received as gifts from his stepfather and mother. The slaves, frustrated by the delay, petitioned the estate administrator for their freedom the following year. It was granted, but the slaves never received Payne's monetary bequest. The American Colonization Society probably never received any money either.[10] In the end, the debts of Dolley Madison and her son Payne Todd wreaked havoc on the slaves and their families in the same way that Thomas Jefferson's debts had devastated his slaves. Out of hundreds of people held in bondage by James Madison and his heirs, a mere fifteen gained freedom by will and one (Paul Jennings) through self-purchase. Except for Ellen Stewart, who ran away, the rest disappeared into the marketplace as commodities sold or pledged as collateral to cover living and other expenses.

Payne's will implies that he shared his famous stepfather's wish to end slavery and to relocate former slaves outside of the country. His plan differed from James Madison's in one important respect: Payne refused to link the two. For him, freedom could occur absent colonization. The two hundred dollars he designated for each slave may have been intended to allow the slaves to relocate to Africa but could also be used to go wherever else they might wish.

No one knows where the freed slaves went. Virginia law required them to leave the state, but that law was not always enforced. It is possible that at least some of them made their way to Washington, where they had friends or family to help them. Others may have stayed in Virginia, and still others could have set out for parts unknown.

The question lingers: could James Madison have had a second, secret will that would have freed more slaves earlier? Certain evidence suggests he might have written one or composed a codicil that would free his slaves upon the death of his wife. Or he may have written a nonbinding letter expressing the wish that she arrange to let them go. There is no way to know for sure, and it may seem now not to matter.

After all, if another will or letter surfaced, it could not alter the past: Montpelier was sold and its slaves scattered. But while the discovery of such a document would not change history, it could change how we remember Dolley and James Madison.

Certain historians and biographers have seen in George Washington, Thomas Jefferson, and James Madison a nascent abolitionism that, if realized, could have set the nation on a path that would have avoided the Civil War. This school of thought regrets the nation's embrace of slavery and postulates that the founders might have done more to rid the nation of slavery if only the time had been right, if only such action did not threaten the unity of the nation, if only they had not had so much else to do, if only slavery had not proven so financially lucrative or politically advantageous, if only (as in the case of Thomas Jefferson) debts had not been so large or estate law so clearly written on the side of creditors, if only (as in the case of James Madison) white Americans had been more willing to accept black Americans living freely in their midst. For these scholars, inaction on the part of the early Presidents represented a colossal failure of leadership, a lack of political courage. But what if it were not James Madison who failed the test of leadership, but rather Dolley? Would knowledge that she thwarted her husband's plan to free his slaves change our opinion of him or of her?

The question is troubling. The traditional picture of elite slaveholding women—particularly the wives of powerful men like the Presidents—has been one of dutiful women following the dictates of a patriarchal society. But what if they were not so dutiful and instead made independent decisions? Women of the early republic are said to have exerted a moral influence that made both men and the nation better. What if the independent decisions made by women were not always nobler than those made by men and sometimes were worse?

There is strong but inconclusive evidence suggesting that Dolley Madison ignored a second will or other instructions from her husband. During a happenstance conversation at Warm Springs, Virginia, in 1849, William Taylor—the Madison kinsman who purchased sixteen slaves from James in 1834—told Edward Coles that James Madison had left instructions for Dolley to free his slaves but that Dolley had ignored them. Taylor claimed to have discussed the matter with

James's niece Nelly Willis, who told him the lawyer who helped James Madison prepare his will came away with the understanding that the former President wanted to free his slaves, but not while his wife was living. James expressed confidence that Dolley knew and would find a way to carry out his wishes. Subsequently, Henry Clay told Coles that Dolley had told him that the former President expected her to free his slaves upon her death. In December 1855, Edward Coles wrote Nelly Willis to ask what she knew. Her son John Willis replied on his mother's behalf that James Madison wanted to free his slaves and entrusted his wife to carry out his written wishes. Nelly had witnessed Dolley opening a letter from her husband on the subject the very day of his burial, a letter that was never seen again.[11]

If the document described by Nelly Willis ever existed, it has been lost or destroyed. Did Nelly Willis or her son lie? The Madisons were not fond of Dolley, but Nelly was closer to her than the rest of James's family. Nelly lived near Montpelier and visited with the Madisons. She also stayed with Dolley while James was laid to rest. Although some members of the Madison family resented the terms of James's will, Nelly was probably not among them, since she had received special consideration. Besides, she would have derived no benefit from the emancipation of James's slaves.[12]

It would have been in character for James Madison to leave the particulars of freeing his slaves to Dolley (whether he left written instructions or not). He had trusted her judgment throughout their marriage. But if James expected his widow to find a way to free his slaves, he misjudged her inclinations.

We have seen instances in which Dolley altered documents to put her actions in a better light. One was the letter to her sister in which she took credit for saving the portrait of George Washington that hung in the President's house as British troops bore down on the nation's capital during the War of 1812. In another letter, she insisted that "the merit in this case [saving the portrait] belongs to me." She was also matter of fact about her efforts to alter her husband's political correspondence to put everything (and everybody) in the best possible light. And Dolley did ignore James's instructions in the matter of selling slaves without their consent. It is not inconceivable that she destroyed a document or ignored other of her husband's expressed wishes.

Like the bequests of other prominent Virginians, James Madison's identified people and institutions that he deemed to be of particular importance. There was Dolley, of course, and other relatives. Three colleges also received funds: the University of Virginia ($1,500, along with a portion of Madison's library), the College of New Jersey (now Princeton, $1,000), and Madison College in Pennsylvania (now defunct, $1,000), as well as the American Colonization Society ($2,000). Certain bequests, such as the one to the ACS, were to be paid only if sufficient funds were raised by the sale of his papers, but Dolley went ahead and honored the bequest. She may have believed the society's work was an essential component of abolition and that James's support of it was more important to his reputation than the emancipation of his slaves. She may have shared the hope of ACS supporters that the United States would become a nation freed of slaves rather than a nation whose slaves were freed. Historians have called her husband delusional for linking colonization and abolition. They have described his plan to send freed slaves overseas as "fantasy."[13] The same can be said of Dolley's efforts to guard her husband's legacy on slavery—if that's what they were—while dismantling the slave community at Montpelier.

Leaving Dolley's intentions aside, it seems unlikely that James would have left his slaves for Dolley to pass along to Payne. James, by his own estimate, had already spent tens of thousands of dollars on his stepson. He had given Payne a farm and slaves and paid off numerous of his creditors. In his will, James left Payne a collection of medals and a walking staff carved from the timber of the frigate *Constitution*, suggesting a belief that Payne had already received his inheritance.[14]

James Madison was keenly aware that what he did about slavery at the end of his life would shape how others thought of him, as it had the reputations of his predecessors. George Washington had in large part been hailed a hero for freeing his slaves. Thomas Jefferson, in contrast, freed only a few slaves upon his death. The majority of Jefferson's slaves had been sold at auction, a spectacle no one wanted to see repeated. For the slaves, it had been a heart-wrenching sundering of family ties. For the Jeffersons, it represented an end to a way of life as well as a public humiliation.

The sale of Jefferson's slaves had occurred in 1827 and 1829. Monticello had been sold in 1831. What happened at Monticello must have been on James Madison's mind when he wrote his last will and testament in 1835. He may well have written out instructions that he hoped would free his slaves and avoid a similar tragedy unfolding at Montpelier. Whether he did or not, a tragedy unfolded. There was no auction, but rather a slow and steady scattering of slaves as they were picked off one by one or in groups, sold for cash or relinquished to satisfy creditors who had accepted them as collateral for loans that were never paid.

There may not have been a second will or any additional document. Even so, it is difficult to believe that Dolley was not involved in deciding what to put in and what to leave out of James's will. As her husband's health declined, Dolley began to assume more responsibility for helping him make decisions. During the former President's last years, she acted as his personal secretary, helping him with correspondence and other matters. She had always enjoyed a great deal of influence over James, and as he grew weaker her power to sway him grew stronger. Yet, Edward Coles directed all of his powers of persuasion at James, not Dolley. It was perhaps the greatest flaw in his scheme to emancipate the Madison slaves: he tried to convince the former President that his legacy depended on what he — not she — did about them.

Inside and Outside

To be a slaveholder or a slave was to be in a dynamic human relationship. Slaveholders held enormous power over the people they claimed as property, but masters and mistresses were never able to exercise complete control over the men, women, and children they held in captivity. The First Ladies discussed in this book knew that human property was not like other chattel. The help was harder to manage. Oney Judge, Betty Hemings, Sukey, and other maids were not like sticks of furniture that could be placed in the house exactly as owners wanted. The enslaved domestic servants of the Washingtons, Jeffersons, and Madisons found ways to live, love, pray, play, and protest despite the very real constraints and cruelties imposed by a slaveholding regime.

For historians, curators, archivists, archeologists, preservationists, and others who want to depict slaveholding and enslavement as a lived experience, rather than as a tableau frozen in time, the fraught and dynamic nature of the relationship between First Ladies, Presidents, and slaves poses a challenge. Educators charged with teaching about slavery at sites like Mount Vernon, Monticello, and Montpelier exemplify the problem. The presidential homes, which I visited in spring 2015, have all been preserved and restored to resemble the ones George Washington, Thomas Jefferson, and James Madison knew after they retired from the presidency, but the central and dynamic role of slaves and slavery does not get displayed inside the houses. Although professionals, students, and volunteers are working hard (and successfully) to find out about the slaves who lived and worked at the historic sites, enslaved women, men, and children are largely absent from the tours that aim to show millions of visitors what life was like inside the homes of the Virginia grandees.

Let me walk you through my recent tours to show why representing and teaching slavery poses such a problem. It is not my intention to criticize the volunteer guides who work hard year-round to ensure that people who want to see the historic homes can do so. They have limited time; groups must move quickly from one room to another to avoid a logjam. At Monticello and Mount Vernon, during peak times of year, groups enter the houses as close as five minutes apart, and the pace at Montpelier is only slightly less frantic. (The homes are such popular tourist destinations that Mount Vernon remains open 365 days a year. Monticello closes only on Christmas, Montpelier on Christmas and Thanksgiving.)

Nor is it my purpose to question the work of the scholars and students who are trying to uncover the stories of the Washingtons, Jeffersons, and Madisons—including their slaves—at these historic sites. I applaud the efforts of everyone involved, and I am grateful for their generosity in sharing their knowledge about the Presidents, their families, and their slaves with anyone willing to listen.

But I do want to ask and help answer a deeper question about why Americans have been reluctant to portray the founding families and slaves in the same spaces.

I begin my visits of the presidential homes in the Virginia piedmont so beloved by Jefferson and work my way east to Mount Vernon. When I arrive at Monticello, it is pouring rain, and like the other tourists in my group, I am glad to be inside when I enter the Great Hall. Our guide tells us that if we had come during Thomas Jefferson's retirement years, Burwell Colbert—Jefferson's enslaved butler—would have greeted us at the front door. I am pleased to hear him mentioned. She goes on to explain that those of us with letters of introduction would have awaited the appearance of our host on one of the room's twenty-eight Windsor chairs. The rest, she says with an enthusiasm for artifacts that should have been a warning to me, would have been allowed to marvel at the Indian art, fossils, bones, calendar clock (which tells the day of the week as well as the time), art, and other objects in the room before being shown the door. But the guide also takes the time to mention Jupiter Evans, who grew up with Thomas Jefferson and found a bride at the same time and in the same place as his master. She explains that while Thomas Jefferson courted Martha Wayles Skelton at her father's plantation, Jupiter courted Suck, which is accurate and interesting. But Jupiter's and Suck's enslaved status does not come up. In that moment, I wonder whether other members of the tour group—mostly older adults and a family with two children—know Jupiter and Suck were enslaved. Their first names provide a clue in that they are typical of the curious appellations slaveholders sometimes bestowed on slaves, especially without the surname Evans, which the guide does not mention.

The guide goes on to say that many of Monticello's guests stayed overnight and were waited on by Critta. I assume she means Critta Hemings Colbert, one of Betty Hemings's grandchildren, who worked as Patsy's maid, but again she does not use a surname. On any given day, she continues, Critta could be seen carrying the linens across the balcony that connects the living spaces upstairs. We all look up at the balcony as if Critta might appear at any moment. Naming Critta makes her seem real, but the following day, when I again take the tour, a different guide does not mention Jupiter and Suck Evans or Critta Hemings Colbert.

On both tours, domestic slaves are mentioned in a small room off the Great Hall. After pointing out the double doors that helped to keep heat in the South Square room; Patsy Jefferson Randolph's writing desk; paintings of Patsy, her father, and her daughter Ellen; and silhouettes of other family members, the guide mentions that Patsy met with Burwell Colbert here each day to plan the work of the household. Then, almost as an afterthought, she says that Thomas Jefferson fathered Sally Hemings's children. There were six children; four lived to adulthood. I wonder if she will remark on the peculiarity of the relationships within the household. Patsy and her children lived intimately with her father's shadow family, and the Randolphs gave orders to relatives who were expected to obey because Virginia law decreed that they inherited the enslaved status of their mothers. But nothing is said about the relationship between the Randolphs and Hemingses, and we move on as a group into Thomas Jefferson's book room. There is no further mention of slaves at Monticello on the remainder of either of my two tours. Instead we learn about the President's books, artwork, gadgets, and household furnishings.

Slaveholders and slaves came together in the mansion, but today's visitors to Monticello learn far more about inanimate objects than about the maids, valets, and other domestic slaves who worked here. As our group stands in the room where Thomas Jefferson slept, the guide points out his bed and water closet without mentioning the slaves who came in and out to change the linens and empty the chamber pot. She also directs our attention to the storage area at the top of the alcove that divides the bedchamber from Jefferson's study and holds his bed. Later on we see an octagonal bedroom where James and Dolley Madison slept when visiting. The predominantly green and white wallpaper with a trellis design, our guide notes, is a replica of the original.

As I head back outside and into the rain, I cannot help but wonder why it seems more important to know what material possessions surrounded members of the Jefferson family than who they interacted with daily. Part of the problem no doubt relates to the purpose of preservation efforts. The homes of Jefferson, Washington, and Madison have been maintained precisely because the Presidents lived there; consequently, the stories of the First Ladies and the enslaved help they supervised have been supposed less important. Yet, furnishings, building plans, art, and other objects are pointed out on the tours and scrutinized for what they reveal about the great men. Logic would tell us that the relationships the Presidents maintained with the women and slaves who lived with them reveal at least as much about them as chairs, calendar clocks, and pieces of china.

What explains our reluctance to make slavery and women more central to our understanding of the Presidents? It is a problem not only at the presidential homes but at other historic sites and museums and in written histories and biographies. Even painters have been reluctant to depict the Presidents and First Ladies with slaves — or the Presidents with First Ladies, for that matter — despite the centrality of both ladies and slaves to elite status in Virginia. Is it because we do not know how to reconcile the paradox of living in a nation founded on principles of freedom and democracy yet accepting of subordination and enslavement for particular people? Do we simply feel more comfortable celebrating our founders as champions of freedom than as exploiters of slaves? Is it that we—the public—would rather not know what slaveholding was really like, particularly slaveholding by revered public figures? Or perhaps it is because we would rather not see the ideas of slavery and gender inequality as foundational to our nation. It would seem that the relationships of the people inside the presidential houses were fraught not only when the Presidents lived in them but still today as we walk through and contemplate our nation's early history.

The public tour at George and Martha Washington's Mount Vernon is similar to the one at Monticello in that guides briefly acknowledge certain slaves in passing. The tour begins in the servant's hall, a one-and-a-half-story outbuilding to the left of the main house that accommodated the coachmen, valets, lady's maids, and other "servants" who accompanied the Washingtons' many visitors. I want to ask the docent how lady's maids and valets were summoned when needed, but the crowd moves too quickly to allow for questions. Having waited nearly an hour on this unseasonably warm day in April, the people behind me are in no mood to linger, especially not the young children, who surge ahead despite parental admonitions. Inside the house proper, docents mention four slaves by name: William Lee, who would have answered the door during George Washington's retirement years; Christopher Sheels, who was with the President when he died, and the enslaved women Molly and Caroline, who we are told took care of the many overnight guests who came to Mount Vernon. It takes less than fifteen minutes to wind through the rooms on the first and second floors of the mansion. Guides point out, among other things, family portraits, a mahogany table and sideboard, china and silver table settings, a terrestrial globe, George Washington's presidential chair, and the bed where he died, but references to human inhabitants are mainly to renowned visitors, although Martha Washington and her grandchildren Nelly Custis Lewis and Wash Custis are mentioned.

I expected Montpelier's two-hour tour called "Dolley Madison and the Women of Montpelier" to include more information about the house slaves. A printed brochure promises information on the "diverse, dynamic, and strong women—enslaved and free" who "managed and maintained Montpelier over . . . 300 years" and "navigated the oppressive boundaries of gender, race, and class." Yet this tour, too, makes scant mention of Montpelier's domestic slaves or Dolley's role in overseeing them, although Dolley's reputation as hostess extraordinaire comes up, as does the notion that everyone loved Dolley. Efforts by members of our small group to elicit more information about Montpelier's domestic slaves produce vague answers. "We don't really know," the guide says more than once. Moving through the house, she points out furnishings, a table with cards set for a game of loo (one of Dolley's favorites, I know), paintings, and sculptures. Paul Jennings makes an appearance in the dining room in the form of a life-size cutout figure. In the room where James Madison died, our docent tells us that Paul Jennings slept here to care for the former President as he was dying and that Sukey brought him breakfast that morning. But rather than explain Sukey's role in the household and her importance to Dolley, the guide turns our attention to the remodeling that James Madison undertook at Montpelier. Given that the only two men in our group do not seem particularly interested in the tour's subject and keep asking questions about other matters (James Madison's chess set, the maps on the walls, the type of shingles on the roof), I can see that it is not entirely her fault that the subject keeps drifting away from the women who lived and worked here. Afterward, one of the cashiers tells me that the "Dolley Tour" appeals to women who have a hard time convincing their husbands to come along.

Fortunately, the house tours are not the only way to learn about the Washington, Jefferson, and Madison slaves. Outside the mansions, visitors can learn a lot about the slaves who lived and worked at the sites, either by exploring the grounds, exhibits, and galleries on their own or by joining tours specifically about slaves. Outside the mansion at Mount Vernon, visitors can view refurbished slave quarters and reproductions of personal items that belonged to the slaves, including clothing, furniture, ceramics, cookware, and toys. Archeological digs on the south lawn at Montpelier—where the Madisons' domestic slaves lived—are ongoing and visible whether or not visitors sign up for the slavery tour, and some tour groups focus specifically on the efforts of archeologists to uncover evidence of slave life and culture. Monticello's slavery tour focuses on Mulberry Row, the street where the Jefferson family's domestic slaves lived and worked.

There are obvious and good reasons for moving the tours focused on slavery outside of the presidential homes. This allows more time to discuss the people who labored to make the trappings of Virginia gentry life possible. I cannot help but wonder, though, how this compartmentalization affects our understanding of who the Presidents and First Ladies were, who the enslaved people were, and how slavery shaped the nation from its creation. The inattention to both First Ladies and slaves inside the homes seems at once to oversimplify and misrepresent life there. By rendering the slaves largely invisible on the inside, we lose the idea that slavery entangled everyone involved in a dynamic and complicated relationship that needs to be understood if we are ever to know who made America. By thinking about the slaves only when we are outside of the house, we seem to perpetuate the idea that slavery can be understood as a thing apart from owners. Yet slavery not only supported the Washingtons, Jeffersons, and Madisons economically but also defined their day-to-day experiences.

As citizens, parents, teachers, historians, curators, archivists, archeologists, preservationists, and tourists from inside and outside the United States, we all know the weight of history and the weight of the perceptions and misperceptions that shape it. We also understand that we have the ability to redress history's inaccuracies and reveal the complexities of the human condition. We can hope that future generations will do a better job of telling the full story of the nation's founding. Maybe this is why on my first day at Monticello I am particularly interested in the groups of fifth graders from regional schools. I find a place to stand sheltered from the rain while I await the start of my own tour. Groups of students are met on the front porch by a succession of guides. What do you know about Thomas Jefferson? the guides ask. I am impressed by what I hear in response. Obviously, teachers have prepared the youngsters well for the field trip. Thomas Jefferson was the third President of the United States, governor of Virginia, author of the Declaration of Independence, secretary of state, vice president, a member of Virginia's House of Burgesses, minister to France, founder of the University of Virginia, an inventor, a planter. He loved technology. With each response I keep hoping that before reaching the end of the list, someone will mention something else key for understanding Thomas Jefferson. As the rain comes down, I perk my ears desperately wanting someone — a guide or a teacher if not one of the children — to say he was a slaveholder.

No one does.

Acknowledgments

I owe a debt of gratitude to many people, especially my husband, Ronald M. Schwartz. He not only encouraged the project from the start but read and commented on a draft of the manuscript. A sabbatical from the University of Rhode Island allowed time to begin the project, and a fellowship from its Center for the Humanities provided research funding. Jody Lisberger, Rae Ferguson, Karen Markin, Gale Eaton, Melissa French, Paula Grey, and Gigi Edwards gave helpful feedback on parts of the book and offered inspiration by sharing their own excellent writing. Thanks especially to Jody for teaching me the importance of scene and to Rae for inspiring me to keep writing despite a personal setback. My sister Lisa Jenkins also read and commented on parts of the manuscript. Thanks to her and to other family and friends for engaging in countless conversations about First Ladies and slaves. Staff, including volunteers, at Mount Vernon, Monticello, and Montpelier generously shared their time and ideas. In particular, I thank Mary V. Thompson, John Marshall, Emilie Johnson, Christian Cotz, Grant Quertermous, and Lydia Neuroth. Sandra Dijkstra and Elise Capron of the Sandra Dijkstra Literary Agency offered advice on pulling the book proposal together. Elise put me in touch with Timothy Mennel at the University of Chicago Press, whose editorial advice has been spot on. Two readers selected by the University of Chicago Press gave detailed and helpful advice for bringing the project to completion, and Joel Score, also of the University of Chicago Press, gave the manuscript a close reading and suggested improvements. Whatever flaws remain in the book are mine, not theirs.

Notes

Abbreviations

DMDE   *Papers of Dolley Madison*, Digital Edition, ed. Holly C. Shulman. Charlottesville: University of Virginia Press/Rotunda, 2004.

FLTJ   *The Family Letters of Thomas Jefferson*, ed. Edwin Morris Betts and James Adam Bear Jr. Charlottesville: University Press of Virginia, 1986.

LRGW   *Letters and Recollections of George Washington*. Garden City, NY: Doubleday, Doran, and Company, 1932.

MWSJ   Martha Wayles Skelton Jefferson, 1772–1782, Part B: Household Accounts. Library of Congress, Manuscripts Division, http://hdl.loc.gov/loc.mss/mtj.mtjbib026572.

PTJ   *Papers of Thomas Jefferson*, vol. 10, *22 June–31 December 1786*, ed. Julian P. Boyd (1954); vol. 38, *1 July–12 November 1802*, ed. Barbara B. Oberg et al. (2011); vol. 39, *13 Nov. 1802–3 March 1803*, ed. Barbara B. Oberg (2013). Princeton, NJ: Princeton University Press.

SLDPM   *The Selected Letters of Dolley Payne Madison*, ed. David B. Mattern and Holly C. Shulman. Charlottesville: University of Virginia Press, 2003.

WPPMW   *"Worthy Partner": The Papers of Martha Washington*, ed. Joseph E. Fields. Westport, CT: Greenwood Press, 1994.

Introduction

1   The survey asked historians, political scientists, and other scholars which of the First Ladies had been of greatest value to the Presidents they loved. On the separate question of which First Ladies and Presidents constituted the most

powerful couples, Martha and George Washington came in second, behind Eleanor and Franklin Roosevelt. Dolley and James Madison ranked fourth. The poll has been conducted five times since 1982. Dolley Madison ranked in the top six in each of the surveys. Martha Washington held ninth place in three of the five polls. In 1993 and 2003, her ranking fell to twelfth and thirteenth respectively. Martha Jefferson was not included in the 2014 survey. See https://www .siena.edu/centers-institutes/siena-research-institute/social-cultural-polls/ first-ladies-study/ (accessed 02/03/2016).

2   The second President of the United States, John Adams of Massachusetts, neither grew up in a slaveholding household nor owned slaves of his own. His wife Abigail, also from Massachusetts, grew up in a household with four slaves. See Fritz Hirschfeld, *George Washington and Slavery: A Documentary Portrayal* (Columbia: University of Missouri Press, 1997), 230n15.

3   According to one of Martha Washington's biographers, she "always treated the slaves in her power well," although the basis for this assertion is a comparison to another mistress with a reputation for egregious abuse of her slaves. Patricia Brady, *Martha Washington: An American Life* (New York: Penguin, 2005), 39. See also Ron Chernow, *Washington: A Life* (New York: Penguin, 2010), 118. Ellen McCallister Clark says Martha "displayed genuine concern and even affection for certain individuals who were bound to her in servitude." Clark, *Martha Washington: A Brief Biography* (Mount Vernon, VA: Mount Vernon Ladies' Association, 2002), 23–24.

4   Most of this literature has focused on George Washington and Thomas Jefferson, for example, François Furstenberg, *Name of the Father: Washington's Legacy, Slavery, and the Making of a Nation* (New York: Penguin, 2006); Hirschfeld, *George Washington and Slavery*; Kenneth Morgan, "George Washington and the Problem of Slavery," *Journal of American Studies* 35 (2000): 279–301; Philip Morgan, "'To Get Quit of Negroes': George Washington and Slavery," *Journal of American Studies* 39 (December 2005): 403–29; Gary B. Nash, *The Forgotten Fifth: African Americans in the Age of Revolution* (Cambridge, MA: Harvard University Press, 2006); Philip Schwarz, ed., *Slavery at the Home of George Washington*, 2d ed. (Mount Vernon, VA: Mount Vernon Ladies' Association, 2009); Mary V. Thompson, "And Procure for Themselves a Few Amenities: The Private Life of George Washington's Slaves," *Virginia Cavalcade* 48 (1999): 178–90; Henry Wiencek, *An Imperfect God: George Washington, His Slaves, and the Creation of America* (New York: Farrar, Straus, and Giroux, 2003) and *Master of the Mountain: Thomas Jefferson and His Slaves* (New York: Farrar, Straus, and Giroux, 2012); Dorothy Twohig, "'That Species of Property': Washington's Role in the Controversy over Slavery," in *George Washington Reconsidered*, ed. Don Higginbotham (Charlottesville: University Press of Virginia, 2001): 114–39; Annette Gordon-Reed, *The Hemingses of Monticello: An American Family*

(New York: W. W. Norton, 2008); Jan Ellen Lewis and Peter S. Onuf, eds., *Sally Hemings and Thomas Jefferson: History, Memory, and Civic Culture* (Charlottesville: University Press of Virginia, 1999); essays by Lucia Stanton, republished in *"Those Who Labor for My Happiness": Slavery at Thomas Jefferson's Monticello* (Charlottesville: University of Virginia Press, 2012); Clarence E. Walker, *Mongrel Nation: The America Begotten by Thomas Jefferson and Sally Hemings* (Charlottesville: University of Virginia Press, 2009); Gary Wills, *"Negro President": Jefferson and the Slave Power* (Boston: Houghton Mifflin, 2003). Less attention has been given to James Madison and slavery, but see Elizabeth Dowling Taylor, *A Slave in the White House: Paul Jennings and the Madisons* (New York: Palgrave Macmillan, 2012), and Douglas B. Chambers, *Murder at Montpelier: Igbo Africans in Virginia* (Jackson: University Press of Mississippi, 2005).

5 Stanton, "Free Some Day: The African American Families of Monticello," in *"Those Who Labor,"* 166.

6 The National First Ladies Library in Canton, Ohio, an archive devoted to all of the First Ladies, acknowledges both mother and daughter in its collections.

7 Lisa Kathleen Graddy and Amy Pastan, *The Smithsonian First Ladies Collection* (Washington, DC: Smithsonian Books, n.d.), 12, 100.

8 For a discussion of the importance of historical objects to visitors at the boyhood home of George Washington, see Seth C. Bruggeman, *Here, George Washington Was Born: Memory, Material Culture, and the Public History of a National Monument* (Athens: University of Georgia Press, 2008), esp. chap. 1.

9 Catherin Allgor, *A Perfect Union: Dolley Madison and the Creation of the American Nation* (New York: Henry Holt, 2006), 372, 392–95.

Chapter 1

1 Jacky's two oldest daughters remained with their mother, Eleanor Calvert Custis, who remarried in 1783.

2 See Tobias Lear's account of the President's death in Peter R. Henriques, *The Death of George Washington: He Died as He Lived* (Mount Vernon, VA: Mount Vernon Ladies' Association, 2000), 72–74.

3 In addition to Lear's report, Washington's physicians James Craik and Elisha Cullen Dick left a brief account, and George Washington Parke Custis told what he knew in a memoir written well after the fact: *Recollections and Private Memoirs of Washington*, 1859 ed. (n.p.: Bibliobazaar, n.d.). See also Mary V. Thompson, *"In the Hands of a Good Providence": Religion in the Life of George Washington* (Charlottesville: University of Virginia Press, 2008), 169–70.

4 Lear's account, in Henriques, *Death of George Washington*, 71.

5 On the importance of attendants at the deathbed of Virginia gentry, see Lauren F. Winner, *A Cheerful and Comfortable Faith: Anglican Religious Prac-*

tice in the Elite Households of Eighteenth-Century Virginia (New Haven, CT: Yale University Press, 2010), 146–47.

6   Lear's account, in Henriques, *Death of George Washington*, 73–74, also 49.

7   *The Last Will and Testament of George Washington, Including Martha Washington's Will, Genealogy, Family Trees and a Complete Index of Beneficiaries*, 7th ed., ed. John C. Fitzpatrick (Mount Vernon, VA: Mount Vernon Ladies' Association, 2003), 27.

8   Patricia Brady, *Martha Washington: An American Life* (New York: Penguin, 2005), 219.

9   Winner, *Cheerful and Comfortable Faith*, 146; *Last Will and Testament of George Washington*, 22.

10 On elite Virginians' use of bequests to define boundaries of family and class, see Winner, *Cheerful and Comfortable Faith*, 161–67.

11 *Last Will and Testament of George Washington*, vii, 2–4, 29, 40n58; Henry Wiencek, *An Imperfect God: George Washington, His Slaves, and the Creation of America* (New York: Farrar, Straus, and Giroux, 2003), 354; Dorothy Twohig, "'That Species of Property': Washington's Role in the Controversy over Slavery," in *George Washington Reconsidered*, ed. Don Higginbotham (Charlottesville: University Press of Virginia, 2001), 132n2.

12 List of George Washington's Slaves, 1799, Retirement Series [1797–1799], vol. 4, *The Papers of George Washington Digital Edition*, ed. Theodore J. Crackel et al. (Charlottesville: University of Virginia Press, Rotunda, 2007–); http://gwpapers.virginia.edu/documents/list-of-george-washingtons-slaves-1799/ (accessed 02/04/2016).

13 Wiencek, *Imperfect God*, 339.

14 Henriques, *Death of George Washington*, 54.

15 Ron Chernow, *Washington: A Life* (New York: Penguin, 2010), 810; Scott E. Casper, *Sarah Johnson's Mount Vernon: The Forgotten History of an American Shrine* (New York: Hill and Wang, 2008), 4.

16 *Last Will and Testament of George Washington*, 28.

17 George Washington had one of the largest distilleries in the country. Its construction in 1796 was part of his effort to diversify his plantation economy. Dave DeWitt, *The Founding Foodies: How Washington, Jefferson, and Franklin Revolutionized America Cuisine* (Naperville, IL: Sourcebooks, 2010), 94–97; Henriques, *Death of George Washington*, 56; Winner, *Cheerful and Comfortable Faith*, 151–53.

18 Winner, *Cheerful and Comfortable Faith*, 166; Henriques, *Death of George Washington*, 56.

19 Chernow, *Washington*, 810.

20 Winner, *Cheerful and Comfortable Faith*, 166.

21 *George Washington's Mount Vernon: Official Guidebook* (Mount Vernon, VA:

Mount Vernon Ladies' Association, n.d.), 107–9; Fritz Hirschfeld, *George Washington and Slavery: A Documentary Portrayal* (Columbia: University of Missouri Press, 1997), 217–18; James C. Rees, "Looking Back, Moving Forward: The Changing Interpretation of Slave Life on the Mount Vernon Estate," in *Slavery at the Home of George Washington*, ed. Philip J. Schwarz (Mount Vernon, VA: Mount Vernon Ladies' Association, 2009), 158, 165, 166–69.

22 *Last Will and Testament of George Washington*, 2–4; Wiencek, *Imperfect God*, 5–6.

23 *Last Will and Testament of George Washington*, 2.

24 Wiencek, *Imperfect God*, chap. 9, esp. 321; Philip D. Morgan and Michael L. Nicholls, "Slave Flight: Mount Vernon, Virginia, and the Wider Atlantic World," in *George Washington's South*, ed. Tamara Harvey and Greg O'Brien (Gainesville: University Press of Florida, 2004), 197–222.

25 "Freeing Washington's Slaves," http://www.mountvernon.org/george-washington/martha-washington/the-deaths-of-george-martha/ (accessed 04/15/2016).

26 Hirschfeld, *George Washington and Slavery*, 214.

27 Ibid.

28 From James Anderson, 21 July 1800, and To Mary Stillson Lear, 11 November 1800, in *WPPMW*, 391, 394.

29 Suzanne Lebsock, *The Free Women of Petersburg: Status and Culture in a Southern Town, 1784–1860* (New York: W. W. Norton, 1985).

30 Elizabeth Dowling Taylor, *A Slave in the White House: Paul Jennings and the Madisons* (New York: Palgrave Macmillan, 2012), 26–27; Andrew Burstein and Nancy Isenberg, *Madison and Jefferson* (New York: Random House, 2010), 272–73.

31 Anita Wills, "In the Planter's House: Three Generations of Servants in George Washington's Family," African American Genealogical Society of Northern California, http://www.aagsnc.org/columns/jan99col.htm (accessed 02/03/2016); Spotswood quoted in Wiencek, *Imperfect God*, 57; Washington quoted in Alan Gilbert, *Black Patriots and Loyalists: Fighting for Emancipation in the War for Independence* (Chicago: University of Chicago Press, 2012), 86.

32 Morgan and Nicholls, "Slave Flight," 204, 206.

33 Marfé Ferguson Delano, *Master George's People: George Washington, His Slaves, and His Revolutionary Transformation* (Washington, DC: National Geographic, 2013), 53.

34 Quoted in Hirschfeld, *George Washington and Slavery*, 214.

35 The Virginia slave population had been growing through enslaved women's reproduction since about 1710 or 1720. The trend was obvious by 1790, when the national census put the slave population at 39 percent of Virginia's total. François Fustenberg, *In the Name of the Father: Washington's Legacy, Slavery, and the Making of a Nation* (New York: Penguin, 2006), 17.

36 *Last Will and Testament of George Washington,* 12–13.

37 Joanne Pope Melish, *Disowning Slavery: Gradual Emancipation and "Race" in New England, 1780–1860* (Ithaca, NY: Cornell University Press, 1998), 122.

38 Hirschfeld, *George Washington and Slavery,* 214.

39 Delano, *Master George's People,* 54, 55.

40 *Last Will and Testament of George Washington,* 62n1.

41 "The Will of Martha Washington of Mount Vernon," in *Last Will and Testament of George Washington,* 61.

Chapter 2

1   James Oakes, *The Ruling Race: A History of American Slaveholders* (New York: Vintage, 1983), 9–10.

2   "Family Background," http://www.mountvernon.org/george-washington/martha-washington/early-life-birth-family-of-origin/ (accessed 04/15/2016); Rosemarie Zagarri, ed., *David Humphries' "Life of General Washington" with George Washington's "Remarks"* (Athens: University of Georgia Press, 1991), 6.

3   Patricia Brady, *Martha Washington: An American Life* (New York: Penguin, 2005), 20–21, 25.

4   Ibid., 17, 21–22; Oakes, *Ruling Race,* 11. Fanny grew up in a household much like the one she and Jack established. Her father, Orlando Jones, grew tobacco with slave labor on a plantation near Williamsburg.

5   See for example Patricia Brady Schmit, ed., *Nelly Custis Lewis's Housekeeping Book* (New Orleans: Historic New Orleans Collection, 1982), 13; Bruce Chadwick, *The General and Mrs. Washington: The Untold Story of a Marriage and a Revolution* (Naperville, IL: Sourcebooks, 2002), 48.

6   Brady, *Martha Washington,* 24.

7   Ibid., 23–24.

8   Ibid., 22–23.

9   See "Slave Insurrections in the United States: An Overview," compiled by Joseph E. Holloway, http://slaverebellion.org/index.php?page=united-states-insurrections (accessed 04/15/2016).

10 Numbers have been rounded. Philip D. Morgan and Michael L. Nicholls, "Slave Flight: Mount Vernon, Virginia, and the Wider Atlantic World," in *George Washington's South,* ed. Tamara Harvey and Greg O'Brien (Gainesville: University Press of Florida, 2004), 205; Lathan A. Windley, comp., *Runaway Slave Advertisements: A Documentary History from the 1730s to 1790,* vol. 1 (Westport, CT: Greenwood Press, 1983).

11 Rhys Isaac, *The Transformation of Virginia, 1740–1790* (Chapel Hill: University of North Carolina Press/Institute of Early American History, 1982), 58–68.

12 Joshua D. Rothman, *Notorious in the Neighborhood: Sex and Families across the*

Color Line in Virginia, 1787–1861 (Chapel Hill: University of North Carolina Press, 2003), 4; also Clarence L. Walker, *Mongrel Nation: The America Begotten by Thomas Jefferson and Sally Hemings* (Charlottesville: University of Virginia Press, 2009). On young slaves not being told the identity of their fathers, see Marie Jenkins Schwartz, *Born in Bondage: Growing Up Enslaved in the Antebellum South* (Cambridge: MA: Harvard University Press, 2000), 42–47.

13 Martha Washington's granddaughter Eliza Custis Law inherited and, with her husband, freed Ann Dandridge upon Martha's death. See Henry Wiencek, *An Imperfect God: George Washington, His Slaves, and the Creation of America* (New York: Farrar, Straus, and Giroux, 2003), 84.

14 *Mary Chesnut's Civil War*, ed. C. Vann Woodward (New Haven, CT: Yale University Press, 1981), 29, 31.

Chapter 3

1 Patricia Brady, *Martha Washington: An American Life* (New York: Penguin, 2005), 27–28; *WPPMW*, xx, 421.

2 Brady, *Martha Washington*, 31.

3 Editor Joseph E. Fields does not acknowledge the relationship between Jack and his father, but he discusses the marriage between John Custis IV and Frances Parke Custis and John's various wills in appendix 1 of *WPPMW*, esp. 421–42.

4 Henry Wiencek, *An Imperfect God: George Washington, His Slaves, and the Creation of America* (New York: Farrar, Straus, and Giroux, 2003), chap. 3.

5 For an explanation of the Dunbar case, see *WPPMW*, 7n4 and appendix 1, 424–25.

6 Benson John Lossing, *Mary and Martha, the Mother and the Wife of George Washington* (1886; Danvers, MA: General Books, 2009), 47; Brady, *Martha Washington*, 39.

7 Brady, *Martha Washington*, 40–41; Lossing, *Mary and Martha*, 47–48. According to hearsay recorded in "Martha Custis's Watch," in *American Historical Record*, vol. 1, ed. John Benson Lossing (Philadelphia: Chase and Town, 1872), 358, the watch—which Martha had before she married George—was more likely a gift from George, but it is more plausible that Daniel presented it to her.

8 Sarah Fatherly, *Gentlewomen and Learned Ladies: Women and Elite Formation in Eighteenth Century Philadelphia* (Bethlehem, PA: Lehigh University Press, 2008), chap. 2; *WPPMW*, appendix 1, 435.

9 The books, transcribed by Karen Hess, were published as *Martha Washington's Booke of Cookery* (New York: Columbia University Press, 1981).

10 Wiencek, *Imperfect God*, 76–77.

11 Brady, *Martha Washington*, 34, 39.

12 Wiencek estimates the value of the Custis estate in *An Imperfect God*, 81–83.

13   *WPPMW*, appendix 1, 437, 3–60 passim; Brady, *Martha Washington*, 52; Ellen
      McCallister Clark, *Martha Washington: A Brief Biography* (Mount Vernon, VA:
      Mount Vernon Ladies' Association, 2002), 12.

14   Brady, *Martha Washington*, 50.

15   From Dr. James Carter, [28 November 1757]; From Elizabeth Vaughan, [31 Au-
      gust 1757]; From George Heath, December 1757, and From Lain Jones, 7 April
      1758, in *WPPMW*, 8, 15, 24, 38.

16   To Robert Cary and Company, 20 August 1757, in *WPPMW*, 5–6.

Chapter 4

1   A. L. Bassett, "Reminiscences of Washington: From Unpublished Family Rec-
      ords," *Scribner's Monthly*, May 1877, 79.

2   http://stpetersnewkent.org/About_Us_Mission_and_Ministries/History/
      (accessed 02/07/2016).

3   Cynthia A. Kierner, *Beyond the Household: Women's Place in the Early South,
      1700–1835* (Ithaca, NY: Cornell University Press, 1998), 45.

4   "The Dower Slaves of Martha Dandridge Custis Washington," in *WPPMW*,
      105–7; Marfé Ferguson Delano, *Master George's People: George Washington, His
      Slaves, and His Revolutionary Transformation* (Washington, DC: National Geo-
      graphic, 2013), 56.

5   Philip D. Morgan and Michael L. Nicholls, "Slave Flight: Mount Vernon, Vir-
      ginia, and the Wider Atlantic World," in *George Washington's South*, ed. Tamara
      Harvey and Greg O'Brien (Gainesville: University Press of Florida, 2004), 197;
      From John Dandridge, 29 February 1788, in *WPPMW*, 207.

6   Patricia Brady, *Martha Washington: An American Life* (New York: Penguin,
      2005), 68.

7   "The Estate of Daniel Parke Custis," in *WPPMW*, 126. For a list of the dower
      slaves working at each Custis property, see "Dower Slaves," 132–34.

8   Sundry Goods for a Bride, in *WPPMW*, 86–92.

9   Kierner, *Beyond the Household*, 46; To Mrs. Shelbury, August 1764, and To Mrs.
      S. Thorpe, [15 July, 1772], in *WPPMW*, 148, 151; Ellen McCallister Clark, *Martha
      Washington: A Brief Biography* (Mount Vernon, VA: Mount Vernon Ladies' As-
      sociation, 2002). 22–23.

10   Records are available for only 295 days in 1768. Mary V. Thompson, "'That hospi-
      table mansion': Welcoming Guests at Mount Vernon," in *Dining with the Wash-
      ingtons*, ed. Stephen A. McLeod (Chapel Hill: University of North Carolina
      Press/Mount Vernon Ladies' Association, 2011), 12.

11   To Hector Ross, 8 October 1770, in *WPPMW*, 149–50; Kierner, *Beyond the
      Household*, 50, 58.

12   Complete Inventory, by Counties, of the Estate, in *WPPMW*, 61–76; Fritz

Hirschfeld, *George Washington and Slavery: A Documentary Portrayal* (Columbia: University of Missouri Press, 1997), 12.

13 Douglas R. Egerton, *Death or Liberty: African Americans and Revolutionary America* (New York: Oxford University Press, 2009), 3–5.

14 Brady, *Martha Washington*, 70. On the separation of enslaved families at Mount Vernon, see Henry Wiencek, *An Imperfect God: George Washington, His Slaves, and the Creation of America* (New York: Farrar, Straus, and Giroux, 2003), 122–23. The story of Harry Washington is told in Egerton, *Death or Liberty*, chap. 8.

15 Hirschfeld, *George Washington and Slavery*, 13–14.

16 Morgan and Nicholls, "Slave Flight," 197, 200; Allen Kulikoff, *Tobacco and Slaves: The Development of Southern Cultures in the Chesapeake* (Chapel Hill: University of North Carolina Press, 1986).

17 Morgan and Nicholls, "Slave Flight," 198–99.

18 From John Parke Custis, 5 July [1773], in *WPPMW*, 152–53.

19 Henry Wiencek, piecing together the thin documentary evidence with the circumstances of William Custis Costin's birth and life, makes the case that Jacky Custis fathered the boy. Wiencek, *Imperfect God*, 285–90. No one denying Jacky's paternity has yet to offer another convincing explanation for why William Custis Costin was treated as free, even though his mother was enslaved, or why the famed Civil War spy Elizabeth Van Lew (who had other knowledge of Costin's descendants) wrote privately that Harriet Park Costin, granddaughter of William Costin, was the "great grand daughter of Mrs. General Washington" and granddaughter of "Washington's son Jno. Park Custis." Ibid., 286.

20 Ann Dandridge was formally emancipated after Martha's death by the Custis family member who inherited her. Wiencek, *Imperfect God*, 84.

21 Lucia Stanton discusses Jefferson's attitude toward people with African ancestry who remained enslaved even though Virginia law defined them as white in "Those Who Labor for My Happiness: Thomas Jefferson and His Slaves," in *"Those Who Labor for My Happiness": Slavery at Thomas Jefferson's Monticello* (Charlottesville: University of Virginia Press, 2012), 8. See also Wiencek, *Imperfect God*, 160, 161.

Chapter 5

1 Nancy K. Loane, *Following the Drum: Women at Valley Forge Encampment* (Washington, DC: Potomac Books, 2009), 12.

2 Alan Gilbert, *Black Patriots and Loyalists: Fighting for Emancipation in the War for Independence* (Chicago: University of Chicago Press, 2012), 137–38.

3 Ibid., 86.

4 Douglas R. Egerton, *Death or Liberty: African Americans and Revolutionary America* (New York: Oxford University Press, 2009), 69.

5   Andrew Burstein and Nancy Isenberg, *Madison and Jefferson* (New York: Random House, 2010), 21.

6   Quoted in Gilbert, *Black Patriots and Loyalists*, 245.

7   Richard S. Dunn, *A Tale of Two Plantations: Slave Life and Labor in Jamaica and Virginia* (Cambridge, MA: Harvard University Press, 2014), 49; To Mercy Otis Warren, 7 March 1778, and From John Parke Custis, 21 August 1776, in *WPPMW*, 177 and 171.

8   Orlando Patterson discusses the concept of dishonor with regard to slaves in *Slavery and Social Death* (Cambridge, MA: Harvard University Press, 1982), esp. 1–13.

9   Burstein and Isenberg, *Madison and Jefferson*, 18, 25. Harry Washington was one of the slaves who sailed to Nova Scotia with the British after the troops evacuated New York City. His story is told in Egerton, *Death or Liberty*, chap. 8.

10   Gilbert, *Black Patriots and Loyalists*, 156.

11   Philip D. Morgan and Michael L. Nicholls, "Slave Flight: Mount Vernon, Virginia, and the Wider Atlantic World," in *George Washington's South*, ed. Tamara Harvey and Greg O'Brien (Gainesville: University Press of Florida, 2004), 200–201; Ron Chernow, *Washington: A Life* (New York: Penguin, 2010), 419.

12   Loane, *Following the Drum*, 4.

13   Ibid., 11, 12, 13, 168n8. After Valley Forge came encampments in Middlebrook, New Jersey; Morristown again; New Windsor, New York; and, for the final two winters of the war, Newburgh, New York. Loane discusses conditions at camps other than Valley Forge in chap. 3.

14   Ibid., 110.

15   Ibid., 19–22.

16   Ibid., 106–8.

17   Ibid., 19, 111.

18   Ibid., 108.

19   To ——, [31 May 1781], in *WPPMW*, 186.

20   Loane, *Following the Drum*, 106, 113–14, 127.

21   Ibid., 132, chap. 7.

22   Ibid., esp. chap. 9 and appendix.

23   Ibid., 106; "Life Guards," http://mountvernon.org/digital-encyclopedia/article /life-guards/ (accessed 02/03/2016).

24   Loane, *Following the Drum*, 38.

25   On George Washington's evolving attitude toward black soldiers, see Henry Wiencek, *An Imperfect God: George Washington, His Slaves, and the Creation of America* (New York: Farrar, Straus, and Giroux, 2003), chap. 6. On the Greenes, see Loane, *Following the Drum*, chap. 4.

26   From John Parke Custis, 12 October 1781, in *WPPMW*, 187.

27   To Mrs. John Parke Custis, [15 May 1779], in *WPPMW*, 182.

28   To Fanny Bassett Washington, 24 May 1775, in *WPPMW*, 287.

29   From John Dandridge, 18 January 1788, in *WPPMW*, 203–4, also 208n15.

30   From John Dandridge, 29 February 1788, in *WPPMW*, 207. The scheme did not work out as expected. See 234–35.

Chapter 6

1   Marfé Ferguson Delano, *Master George's People: George Washington, His Slaves, and His Revolutionary Transformation* (Washington, DC: National Geographic, 2013), 53; Miriam Anne Bourne, *First Family: George Washington and His Intimate Relations* (New York: W. W. Norton, 1982), 127.

2   To Fanny Bassett Washington, 3 December 1792, and 22 April 1792, in *WPPMW*, 241, 237; Bourne, *First Family*, 132.

3   To Hannah Bushrod Washington, 22 June 1784, in *WPPMW*, 194.

4   To Fanny Bassett Washington, 15 June 1794, and To Fanny Bassett Washington, 24 May 1795, in *WPPMW*, 269, 288.

5   To Fanny Bassett Washington, [8 June 1789], in *WPPMW*, 215–16; Mary V. Thompson, "Different People, Different Stories: The Life Stories of Individual Slaves from Mount Vernon and Their Relationships with George and Martha Washington," unpublished paper given at symposium, "George Washington and Slavery," Mount Vernon, VA, 3 November 2001, slightly revised 22 April 2002, p. 25, as shared by the author. George Washington wrote the overseer on Martha's behalf regarding Charlotte's health and punishment.

6   To Fanny Bassett Washington 24 May 1795, in *WPPMW*, 287.

7   To Fanny Bassett Washington, [Summer 1789], in *WPPMW*, 217.

8   To Fanny Bassett Washington, 4 August 1793, in *WPPMW*, 250.

9   Charles Francis Jenkins, *Washington in Germantown* (Philadelphia: William J. Campbell, 1905), 149; To Tobias Lear, 7 October 1791, in *LRGW*, 54–55.

10   Thompson, "Different People, Different Stories," 26.

11   Ibid., 27.

12   Ibid., 27.

13   Ibid., 28; Delano, *Master George's People*, 39.

14   Quote from plaque in the Donald W. Reynolds Museum and Education Center at Mount Vernon.

15   Jenkins, *Washington in Germantown*, 155.

16   Delano, *Master George's People*, chap. 1, p. 27; Thompson, "Different People, Different Stories," 29; To William Pearce, 27 October 1793, in *LRGW*, 149.

17   Andrea Wulf, *Founding Gardeners: The Revolutionary Generation, Nature, and the Shaping of the American Nation* (New York: Alfred A. Knopf, 2011), 33, 36.

18   To William Pearce, 6 October 1793, in *LRGW*, 145, 147.

19   To Fanny Bassett Washington, 22 October, 11 November, and 30 November 1794, in *WPPMW*, 278, 280, 281.

20   To Fanny Bassett Washington, 10 May [1795] and 24 May 1795, in *WPPMW*, 286, 287, 288.

21   To Fanny Bassett Washington, 10 May [1795] and 24 May 1795, in *WPPMW*, 286, 287, 288; Jenkins, *Washington in Germantown*, 150.

22   To Tobias Lear, 12 July 1795, in *LRGW*, 88–89.

23   To Fanny Bassett Washington, 13 April 1794, in *WPPMW*, 264.

24   To Fanny Bassett Washington, 1 July 1792 and 22 April 1792, in *WPPMW*, 238, 237.

25   To Fanny Bassett Washington, 29 August 1791 in *WPPMW*, 233.

26   To Fanny Bassett Washington, 4 August 1793, in *WPPMW*, 250.

27   To Fanny Bassett Washington, 2 June 1794 and 15 June 1794, in *WPPMW*, 267, 268.

28   To Fanny Bassett Washington, 1 July 1792 and 24 May 1795, in *WPPMW*, 239, 288.

29   To Tobias Lear, 15 and 19 June 1791, in *LRGW*, 43, 45.

30   To Fanny Bassett Washington, 4 August 1793, in *WPPMW*, 250; Thompson, "Different People, Different Stories," 19.

31   To Fanny Bassett Washington, 4 August 1793 and 5 June 1791, in *WPPMW*, 250, 231; Robert B. Dishman, "Ona Maria Judge Takes French Leave of Her Mistress to Live Free in New Hampshire," *History of New Hampshire* 62 (Spring 2008): 44.

32   To Fanny Bassett Washington, 19 April 1792, in *WPPMW*, 230.

Chapter 7

1   Catherine Allgor, *Parlor Politics, In Which the Ladies of Washington Help Build a City and a Government* (Charlottesville: University Press of Virginia, 2000), 19–20; Carl Sferrazza Anthony, *First Ladies: The Saga of the Presidents' Wives and Their Power, 1789–1961* (New York: Quill, William Morrow, 1990), 46–47; Carol Borchert Cadou, "'An excellent table': The Art of Dining at Mount Vernon," in *Dining with the Washingtons*, ed. Stephen A. McLeod (Chapel Hill: University of North Carolina Press/Mount Vernon Ladies' Association, 2011), 69.

2   To Fanny Bassett Washington, 23 October 1789; To Janet Livingston Montgomery, 29 January 1791, in *WPPMW*, 220, 230.

3   To Fanny Bassett Washington, [8 June 1789], in *WPPMW*, 215–16.

4   Ron Chernow, *Washington: A Life* (New York: Penguin, 2010), 574, 616; Miriam Anne Bourne, *First Family: George Washington and His Intimate Relations* (New York: W. W. Norton, 1982), 135.

5   Mary V. Thompson, "Different People, Different Stories: The Life Stories of Individual Slaves from Mount Vernon and Their Relationships with George and Martha Washington," unpublished paper given at a symposium, "George Washington and Slavery," Mount Vernon, VA, 3 November 2001, slightly revised 22 April 2002, 21–22, as shared by the author; Chernow, *Washington*, 114 (quote), 474.

6   The eight Presidents who held slaves while serving were Washington, Jefferson, Madison, Monroe, Jackson, Tyler, Polk, and Taylor. Martin Van Buren and William Henry Harrison grew up in slaveholding homes, but they did not hold people in bondage while in office.

7   "Oney Judge," http://www.mountvernon.org/digital-encyclopedia/article/oney -judge/ (accessed 04/17/2016).

8   Robert B. Dishman, "Ona Maria Judge Takes French Leave of Her Mistress to Live Free in New Hampshire," *History of New Hampshire* 62 (Spring 2008): 41.

9   Jonathan Blagbrough, "'This Is Nothing but Slavery': Child Domestic Labor in the Modern Context," in *Child Slaves in the Modern World*, ed. Gwyn Campbell, Suzanne Miers, and Joseph C. Miller (Athens: Ohio University Press, 2011), 194. The study of child domestic workers in eight countries was undertaken in 2004.

10 Ibid., 203.

11 Thompson, "Different People, Different Stories," 14–20.

12 Marfé Ferguson Delano, *Master George's People: George Washington, His Slaves, and His Revolutionary Transformation* (Washington, DC: National Geographic, 2013), 53; Charles Francis Jenkins, *Washington in Germantown* (Philadelphia: William J. Campbell, 1905), 103. William Lee came to New York a month after the other slaves, but it was to help Christopher Sheels. His days as George Washington's full-time valet were over, and he was eventually sent back to Mount Vernon. Patricia Brady, *Martha Washington: An American Life* (New York: Penguin, 2005), 163.

13 Fritz Hirschfeld, *George Washington and Slavery: A Documentary Portrayal* (Columbia: University of Missouri Press, 1997), 72.

14 To Tobias Lear, 22 November 1790, in *LRGW*, 31.

15 Ibid.

16 To Tobias Lear, 17 November and 22 November 1790, in *LRGW*, 30, 31; http:// www.ushistory.org/presidentshouse/history/references.htm (accessed 02/03/ 2016).

17 *Heads of Families: First Census of the United States, 1790: Pennsylvania* (Washington, DC: Bureau of the Census, 1908), 5.

18 Thompson, "Different People, Different Stories," 20–21.

19 To Tobias Lear, 12 April 1791, in *LRGW*, 38.

20 Ibid.

21 To Fanny Bassett Washington, 19 April 1792, in *WPPMW*, 230; Thompson, "Dif-

ferent People, Different Stories," 21. George once told a slave he was sending him on an errand when in fact he was returning the slave to an owner from whom he had run away.

22   Thompson, "Different People, Different Stories," 19–20.

23   Ibid., 22–24.

24   Daniel Kilbride, *An American Aristocracy: Southern Planters in Antebellum Philadelphia* (Columbia: University of South Carolina Press, 2006), 2, 5, 7.

25   Ibid., 8, 18.

26   http://www.ushistory.org/presidentshouse/slaves/slavequarters.htm (accessed 02/03/2016); To Tobias Lear, 5 September 1790, in *LRGW*, 3–4.

27   http://www.ushistory.org/presidentshouse/slaves/slavequarters.htm; To Tobias Lear, 5 September 1790, in *LRGW*, 5.

28   To Tobias Lear, 27 March 1791, in *LRGW*, 34.

29   Much of this account of Oney Judge's escape is drawn from Henry Wiencek, *An Imperfect God: George Washington, His Slaves, and the Creation of America* (New York: Farrar, Straus, and Giroux, 2003), chap. 9. See also Hirschfeld, *George Washington and Slavery*, chap. 10, and other sources mentioned in the notes that follow. Historian Richard S. Newman raises the possibility that Richard Allen, former slave and founder of the African Methodist Episcopal Church, aided Oney in her escape. See Newman, *Freedom's Prophet: Bishop Richard Allen, the AME Church, and the Black Founding Fathers* (New York: New York University Press, 2008), 141–42.

30   From Betty Washington Lewis, 9 February 1794, Founders Online, National Archives, http://founders.archives.gov/documents/Washington/05-15-02-0152 (source: *Papers of George Washington*, Presidential Series, vol. 15, 1 January–30 April 1794, ed. Christine Sternberg Patrick [Charlottesville: University of Virginia Press, 2009], 200–201).

31   Wiencek, *Imperfect God*, 330; Dishman, "Ona Maria Judge," 49–51.

32   Wiencek, *Imperfect God*, 290.

33   Ibid., 292–99.

34   Ibid., 323.

35   To Fanny Bassett Washington, 10 February 1794, in *WPPMW*, 256.

36   Wiencek, *Imperfect God*, 272, 321.

37   Dishman, "Ona Maria Judge," 45. The sale of families long held in the Custis family upset George Washington, who looked without success for a way to stop the practice. Wiencek, *Imperfect God*, 337–39; To Tobias Lear, 7 February 1796, in *LRGW*, 194–95.

38   The Staines had at least two daughters. The youngest was called Nancy. They may also have had a son named William. Dishman, "Ona Maria Judge," 59–60. Quoted in Wiencek, *Imperfect God*, 332, 333.

39 Wiencek, *Imperfect God*, 332–33.

40 James Hemings's situation is discussed more fully in chap. 13. See also Dave DeWitt, *The Founding Foodies: How Washington, Jefferson, and Franklin Revolutionized America Cuisine* (Naperville, IL: Sourcebooks, 2010), 139–40.

41 Delano, *Master George's People*, 31.

42 Wiencek, *Imperfect God*, 316–17.

43 Delano, *Master George's People*, 31.

44 A runway advertisement for Oney Judge appeared in the 24 May 1796 edition of the *Pennsylvania Gazette*. See http://www.mountvernon.org/research-collections/digital-encyclopedia/article/oney-judge/ (accessed 02/03/2016).

45 To Tobias Lear, 13 November 1797, in *LRGW*, 250–51.

46 Hirschfeld, *George Washington and Slavery*, 15; Lucia Stanton, "'A Well-Ordered Household': Domestic Servants in Jefferson's White House," in *"Those Who Labor for My Happiness": Slavery at Thomas Jefferson's Monticello* (Charlottesville: University of Virginia Press, 2012), 42.

Chapter 8

1 To Lucy Flucker Knox, [1797], in *WPPMW*, 303; To Tobias Lear, 10 September 1797, in *LRGW*, 120; Mary V. Thompson, "'That hospitable mansion': Welcoming Guests at Mount Vernon," in *Dining with the Washingtons*, ed. Stephen A. McLeod (Chapel Hill: University of North Carolina Press/Mount Vernon Ladies' Association, 2011), 12.

2 Mary V. Thompson, "The Cooks' Day, 1790s," in McLeod, *Dining with the Washingtons*, 51–52; To Elizabeth Powel, 20 May 1797, in *WPPMW*, 302.

3 To Elizabeth Powel, 20 May 1797, in *WPPMW*, 302.

4 Ibid. Modernized recipes for dishes typically served at Mount Vernon can be found in McLeod, *Dining with the Washingtons*, e.g., 153–55 (Yorkshire Christmas Pie) and 187–89 (Martha's Great Cake).

5 To Elizabeth Powel, 1 May 1797, in *WPPMW*, 301.

6 To Fanny Bassett Washington, 25 May 1794; To Elizabeth Willing Powel, 14 July 1797, in *WPPMW*, 265, 305; Charles Francis Jenkins. *Washington in Germantown* (Philadelphia: William J. Campbell, 1905), 147.

7 *WPPMW*, 306n2; From Lawrence Lewis, 24 July 1797, and To Lawrence Lewis, 4 August 1797, Founders Online, National Archives, http://founders.archives.gov/documents/Washington/06-01-02-0227 (source: *Papers of George Washington*, Retirement Series, vol. 1, 4 March 1797–30 December 1797, ed. W. W. Abbot [Charlottesville: University Press of Virginia, 1998], 270, 288–89).

8 To Elizabeth Dandridge Henley, 20 August 1797 in *WPPMW*, 307; Thomson, "That hospitable mansion," 29.

9 To Colonel Richard Varick, 15 December 1801, in *WPPMW*, 398.

10 Patricia Brady, *Martha Washington: An American Life* (New York: Penguin, 2005), 228–29.

11 Robert H. Gudmestad, *A Troublesome Commerce: The Transformation of the Interstate Slave Trade* (Baton Rouge: Louisiana State University Press, 2003): 6–8; Scott E. Casper, *Sarah Johnson's Mount Vernon: The Forgotten History of an American Shrine* (New York: Hill and Wang, 2008), 6, 15, 17.

12 See Karen Hess, *Martha Washington's Booke of Cookery* (New York: Columbia University Press, 1981), 3.

13 Patricia Brady Schmit, ed., *Nelly Custis Lewis's Housekeeping Book* (New Orleans: Historic New Orleans Collection, 1982), esp. 106, 112.

14 Patricia Brady, ed., *George Washington's Beautiful Nelly: The Letters of Eleanor Parke Custis Lewis to Elizabeth Bordley Gibson, 1794–1851* (Columbia: University of South Carolina Press, 1991), 265.

15 Marfé Ferguson Delano, *Master George's People: George Washington, His Slaves, and His Revolutionary Transformation* (Washington, DC: National Geographic, 2013), 55.

Chapter 9

1 As she lay dying, Martha copied these lines from Laurence Sterne's novel: "Time wastes too fast: every letter I trace tells me with what rapidity life follows my pen. The days and hours of it are flying over our heads like clouds of a windy day never to return." Thomas finished the passage, adding "and every time I kiss thy hand to bid adieu, every absence which follows it, are preludes to the eternal separation which we are shortly to make!"

2 "The Forest Chas: City C 2 Jan when Mr. Jefferson was married to Mrs. Martha Skelton," Manuscripts, Mss1 P1827 b 163–97, Palmer family, Papers 1782–1894, Sect. 11, Virginia Historical Society.

3 To avoid confusion, I refer to Martha Wayles by her first name and to her mother by her full name, Martha Eppes Wayles.

4 Virginia Scharff, *The Women Jefferson Loved* (New York: Harper, 2010), 63.

5 "Memoirs of a Monticello Slave," in *Jefferson at Monticello: Recollections of a Monticello Slave and of a Monticello Overseer*, ed. James A. Bear Jr. (Charlottesville: University Press of Virginia, 1967), 4.

6 Betty Hemings had two more children after John Wayles died. John was born in 1776, Lucy in 1777. Both were likely fathered by Joseph Neilson, a white man who worked as Thomas Jefferson's head carpenter. See Annette Gordon-Reed, *The Hemingses of Monticello: An American Family* (New York: W. W. Norton, 2008), 126.

7   Scharff, *Women Jefferson Loved*, 74.

8   Ibid., 75.

9   Jon Kukla, *Mr. Jefferson's Women* (New York: Alfred A. Knopf, 2007), 64.

10   Scharff, *Women Jefferson Loved*, 87.

11   Ibid., 91; Kukla, *Mr. Jefferson's Women*, 64–65; Sarah N. Randolph, *The Domestic Life of Thomas Jefferson* (New York: Harper and Brothers, 1871), 48.

12   Scharff, *Women Jefferson Loved*, 92–93.

13   Ibid., 107–8, 113; Elizabeth Cometti, *Social Life in Virginia during the War for Independence* (Williamsburg: Virginia Independence Bicentennial Commission, 1978), 13–14.

Chapter 10

1   Merrill D. Peterson, ed., *Visitors to Monticello* (Charlottesville: University Press of Virginia, 1989), 11–12. In *Monticello: A Guidebook* (Charlottesville, VA: Thomas Jefferson Foundation, 2008), chapter 1 by Susan R. Stein includes floor plans of the house as Martha likely knew it toward the end of her life, and of the expanded Monticello that is more familiar today (pp. 20, 24).

2   Sarah Nicholas Randolph, *The Domestic Life of Thomas Jefferson*, 3rd ed. (Cambridge, MA: University Press, 1947), 27.

3   "Betty Brown," http://www.monticello.org/getting-word/people/betty-brown (accessed 02/03/2016); Lucia Stanton, "Free Some Day: The African American Families of Monticello," in *"Those Who Labor for My Happiness": Slavery at Thomas Jefferson's Monticello* (Charlottesville: University of Virginia Press, 2012), 108. Thomas had been admitted to the bar in 1767 and continued to practice law after marrying Martha. He also oversaw farming operations on four plantations: Elk Hill in Goochland County, Shadwell and Monticello in Albemarle County, and Poplar Forrest in Bedford County. (He helped his mother with farming operations at Shadwell until she died in 1776, at which time he inherited the property along with the slaves who worked on it.) His responsibilities kept him away from home a good bit.

4   Stanton, "Free Some Day," 118.

5   Ibid., 118; To Martha Jefferson Randolph, 26 October 1792, in *FLTJ*, 105. In this letter, written long after Patsy's birth, Thomas Jefferson not only recalled Patsy's recovery from "a good breast of milk" but recommended the same for Patsy's newborn daughter Anne.

6   Justin A. Sarafin, "Like Clockwork: French Influence in Monticello's Kitchen," and Elizabeth V. Chew, "Carrying the Keys: Women and Housekeeping at Monticello," in *Dining at Monticello*, ed. Damon Lee Fowler (Chapel Hill: University of North Carolina for the Thomas Jefferson Foundation, 2005), 21, 33.

7   Dave DeWitt, *The Founding Foodies: How Washington, Jefferson, and Franklin Revolutionized American Cuisine* (Naperville: IL: Sourcebooks, 2010), 94, 181–82; Fowler, *Dining at Monticello*, 184.

8   Peterson, *Visitors to Monticello*, 58, 98; Stanton, "Free Some Day," 118.

9   Annie L. Barton, "Memories of Childhood's Slavery Days," in *Six Women's Slave Narratives* (New York: Oxford University Press, 1988), 37. On the difficulty enslaved parents faced in nurturing their own children, see Marie Jenkins Schwartz, *Born in Bondage: Growing Up Enslaved in the Antebellum South* (Cambridge, MA: Harvard University Press, 2000), esp. chap. 2. On Ursula's breastfeeding Patsy and the death of Archy, see Stanton, "Free Some Day," 118.

10   Stanton, "Monticello to Main Street," in *"Those Who Labor,"* 216.

11   On John Wayles's will, see Gordon-Reed, *Hemingses of Monticello*, 79.

12   John Wayles's Will, *Tyler's Quarterly Historical and Genealogical Magazine* 6 (1924): 268–70.

13   Stanton, "Those Who Labor for My Happiness: Thomas Jefferson and His Slaves," 4, and "Jefferson's People: Slavery at Monticello," 56, both in *"Those Who Labor."*

14   Eston Hemings acknowledged both John Wayles and Thomas Jefferson as forebears, naming his son John Wayles Jefferson.

15   Stanton, "Those Who Labor," 7; Stanton, "Jefferson's People," 58; Stanton, "Free Some Day," 169. The Hemingses did not all arrive at Monticello immediately after John Wayles died. Betty Hemings and her youngest children went first to Elk Hill. See Annette Gordon-Reed, *The Hemingses of Monticello: An American Family* (New York: W. W. Norton, 2008), 140.

16   Stanton, "Those Who Labor," 7; Stanton, "Free Some Day," 169; William Cohen, "Thomas Jefferson and the Problem of Slavery," *Journal of American History* 56 (December 1969): 503.

17   Stanton, "Jefferson's People," 58; Stanton, "Free Some Day," 181.

18   Stanton, "Free Some Day," 107, 108, 135.

19   Brian Steele, "Thomas Jefferson's Gender Frontier," *Journal of American History*, 95, no. 1 (June 2008): 31, 38.

20   MWSJ, images 24, 37.

21   Ibid., image 36; Stanton, "Free Some Day," 113.

22   MWSJ, images 26, 31.

23   Virginia Scharff, *The Women Jefferson Loved* (New York: Harper, 2010), 111; MWSJ, image 24.

24   Stanton, "Free Some Day," 171.

25   MWSJ, image 28.

26   The Works Progress Administration narratives from Virginia have been published as Charles L. Perdue Jr., Thomas E. Barden, and Robert K. Phillips, eds.

Weevils in the Wheat: Interviews with Virginia Ex-Slaves (Charlottesville: University Press of Virginia, 1976).

27 MWSJ, image 33.

28 Ibid.

29 Scharff, *Women Jefferson Loved*, 125.

30 MWSJ, image 31.

31 Ibid., image 29.

32 http://www.monticello.org/site/house-and-gardens/privies (accessed 11/02/2014).

33 Scharff, *Women Jefferson Loved*, 105.

34 "Housing for Slaves on Mulberry Row," http://www.monticello.org/site/plantation-and-slavery/housing-slaves-mulberry-row (accessed 11/02/2014). See also Stanton, "Jefferson's People," 63.

35 Scharff, *Women Jefferson Loved*, 94; MWSJ, image 27.

36 MWSJ, image 32.

37 Ibid., image 27.

Chapter 11

1 Jon Meacham, *Thomas Jefferson: The Art of Power* (New York: Random House, 2012), 115.

2 Reproduced in Virginia Scharff, *The Women Jefferson Loved* (New York: Harper, 2010), 134–36.

3 The Executive Mansion that stands today on Richmond's Capitol Square (one of the oldest governor's residences in the nation) was not built until 1813.

4 Meacham, *Thomas Jefferson*, 126.

5 Annette Gordon-Reed, *The Hemingses of Monticello: An American Family* (New York: W. W. Norton, 2008), 133; Meacham, *Thomas Jefferson*, 134; "Memoirs of a Monticello Slave," in *Jefferson at Monticello: Recollections of a Monticello Slave and of a Monticello Overseer*, ed. James A. Bear Jr. (Charlottesville: University Press of Virginia, 1967), 6, 10; Stanton, "Free Some Day: The African American Families of Monticello," in *"Those Who Labor for My Happiness": Slavery at Thomas Jefferson's Monticello* (Charlottesville: University of Virginia Press, 2012), 109, 170.

6 Stanton, "Jefferson's People: Slavery at Monticello," 59, and Stanton, "Free Some Day, 132–33, in *"Those Who Labor"*; Andrew Burstein and Nancy Isenberg, *Madison and Jefferson* (New York: Random House, 2010), 81.

7 Scharff, *Women Jefferson Loved*, 132–33; Stanton, "Free Some Day," 108–9, 132–33; Stanton, "Jefferson's People," 59.

8 Stanton, "Jefferson's People," 59; Stanton, "Free Some Day," 132–33.

9 Gordon-Reed, *Hemingses of Monticello*, 135.

Chapter 12

1. Thomas Jefferson wanted these accomplishments listed on the monument that marked his gravesite. Serving as the third President of the United States was conspicuously missing from the list.

2. Virginia Scharff, *The Women Jefferson Loved* (New York: Harper, 2010), 126–27.

3. Ibid., 94; Merrill D. Peterson, ed., *Visitors to Monticello* (Charlottesville: University Press of Virginia, 1989), 12, 13, 17.

4. Lucia Stanton, "Free Some Day: The African American Families of Monticello," in *"Those Who Labor for My Happiness": Slavery at Thomas Jefferson's Monticello* (Charlottesville: University of Virginia Press, 2012), 109.

5. Scharff, *Women Jefferson Loved*, 126–27.

6. Stanton, "Free Some Day," 110; Scharff, *Women Jefferson Loved*, 126–27.

7. For a discussion of how the ministrations of white midwives differed from those of black healers, see Marie Jenkins Schwartz, *Born in Bondage: Growing Up in the Antebellum South* (Cambridge, MA: Harvard University Press, 2000), chap. 5, and Schwartz, *Birthing a Slave: Motherhood and Medicine in the Antebellum South* (Cambridge, MA: Harvard University Press, 2006), chap. 1.

8. From Martha Jefferson Randolph, 30 January 1800, in *FLTJ*, 182–83; Stanton, "Free Some Day," 112–13, 130.

9. Sharla M. Fett, *Working Cures: Healing, Health, and Power on Southern Slave Plantations* (Chapel Hill: University of North Carolina Press, 2002).

10. Annette Gordon-Reed, *The Hemingses of Monticello: An American Family* (New York: W. W. Norton, 2008), 684n35; "Room in Which Martha Jefferson Died," http://www.monticello.org/site/house-and-gardens/room-which-martha -jefferson-died (accessed 02/03/2016).

11. Stanton, "Free Some Day," 167.

12. Overseer Edmund Bacon heard the Hemingses speak of these events multiple times and deemed them credible enough to include in his memoir of life at Monticello. Quoted in Gordon-Reed, *Hemingses of Monticello*, 145. Israel Jefferson, one of Jefferson's former slaves, also heard about Thomas Jefferson's promise from the Hemingses. See Stanton, "Free Some Day," 167.

13. Lisa Wilson, *A History of Stepfamilies in Early America* (Chapel Hill: University of North Carolina Press, 2014), loc. 123.

14. Gordon-Reed, *Hemingses of Monticello*, 144.

15. http://www.monticello.org/site/jefferson/martha-wayles-skelton-jefferson (accessed 02/03/2016).

16. Thomas Jefferson did not write much about this painful time, but much later he sympathized upon learning that one of his former overseers, Edmund Bacon, had lost his wife of many years. "He did not wonder that I felt completely bro-

ken up," Bacon recalled. "He had passed through the same himself; and only time and silence" could provide relief. See "The Private Life of Thomas Jefferson," in *Jefferson at Monticello: Recollections of a Monticello Slave and of a Monticello Overseer*, ed. James A. Bear (Charlottesville: University Press of Virginia, 1967), 117.

17 Stanton, "Free Some Day," 135, 173.

18 Cynthia A. Kierner, *Martha Jefferson Randolph: Daughter of Monticello* (Chapel Hill: University of North Carolina Press, 2012), 39–49.

19 Stanton, "Free Some Day," 184.

20 Kierner, *Martha Jefferson Randolph*, 50.

Chapter 13

1 From Martha Jefferson, 3 May 1787, in *FLTJ*, 39.

2 On Bridgetower, see Cynthia A. Kierner, *Martha Jefferson Randolph: Daughter of Monticello* (Chapel Hill: University of North Carolina Press, 2012), 68.

3 Sue Peabody, *"There Are No Slaves in France": The Political Culture of Race and Slavery in the Ancien Régime* (New York: Oxford University Press, 1996).

4 From Thomas Jefferson to Paul Bentalou, 25 August 1786, Founders Online, National Archives, http://founders.archives.gov/documents/Jefferson/01-10-02 -0216 (source: *PTJ*, 10:296). See also Annette Gordon-Reed, *The Hemingses of Monticello: An American Family* (New York: W. W. Norton, 2008), 183–85.

5 Lucia Stanton, "Free Some Day: The African American Families of Monticello," in *"Those Who Labor for My Happiness": Slavery at Thomas Jefferson's Monticello* (Charlottesville: University of Virginia Press, 2012), 172.

6 Kierner, *Martha Jefferson Randolph*, 61–62; Stanton, "Free Some Day," 173.

7 Gordon-Reed, *Hemingses at Monticello*, chap. 10; Stanton, "Free Some Day," 173.

8 Gene Zechmeister, "James Hemings," http://www.monticello.org/site/planta tion-and-slavery/james_hemings (accessed 08/02/2014).

9 *Jefferson at Monticello: Recollections of a Monticello Slave and of a Monticello Overseer*, ed. James A. Bear Jr. (Charlottesville: University Press of Virginia, 1967), 4; Gordon-Reed, *Hemingses of Monticello*, 194–95; Winthrop D. Jordan, "Hemings and Jefferson, Redux," in *Sally Hemings and Thomas Jefferson: History, Memory, and Civic Culture*, ed. Jan Ellen Lewis and Peter S. Onuf (Charlottesville: University of Virginia Press, 1999), 48.

10 On wages, see Gordon-Reed, *Hemingses of Monticello*, 236; on clothing, see Stanton, "Free Some Day," 174.

11 "Jefferson in Paris," http://www.rogerebert.com/reviews/jefferson-in-paris -1995 (accessed 07/28/2014).

12 On Patsy's whipping of the slave, see Kierner, *Martha Jefferson Randolph*, 253.

13   Stanton, "Free Some Day," 175; emphasis mine.

14   "James Hemings," 11 July 2012, http://www.monticello.org/site/plantation-and
      -slavery/james-hemings (accessed 08/02/2014); Stanton, "Free Some Day,"
      185, 186. James was not the only slave to receive wages while Thomas Jefferson
      served as secretary of state. His man Thomas also received eight dollars per
      month. See To Mary Jefferson, 17 November 1793, in *FLTJ*, 126n1.

15   Gordon-Reed, *Hemingses of Monticello*, 425, 608; Andrew Burstein and Nancy
      Isenberg, *Jefferson and Madison* (New York: Random House, 2010), 304.

16   William H. Gaines Jr., *Thomas Mann Randolph: Jefferson's Son-in-Law* (n.p.:
      Louisiana State University Press, 1966), v.

17   Ibid., 5.

18   Kierner, *Martha Jefferson Randolph*, 119.

19   "Marriage Settlement for Martha Jefferson, in *FLTJ*, 50n1. Philip D. Morgan
      uses the term "shadow family" to describe the families slaveholders created with
      enslaved women. Morgan, "Interracial Sex in the Chesapeake and the British
      Atlantic World, c. 1700–1820," in Lewis and Onuf, *Sally Hemings and Thomas
      Jefferson*, 55.

20   Gaines, *Thomas Mann Randolph*, 26; Margaret Bayard Smith, *The First Forty
      Years of Washington Society*, ed. Gaillard Hunt (New York: Charles Scribner's
      Sons, 1906), 34.

21   Gaines, *Thomas Mann Randolph*, 25 (quote), 26, 57, 61–63, 109; From Martha
      Jefferson Randolph, 18 November 1808, in *FLTJ*, 360.

22   "Marriage Settlement for Martha Jefferson," in *FLTJ*, 49–50; Gaines, *Thomas
      Mann Randolph*, 29, 37. During Tom's years in Edinburgh, his father had run
      short of cash; he had mortgaged Varina, in Henrico County, to meet press-
      ing financial obligations and help pay for the Scottish education Tom and two
      brothers were receiving. Tom would be expected to pay off a debt of $2,900.

23   Stanton, "Perfecting Slavery: Rational Plantation Management at Monticello,"
      in *"Those Who Labor,"* 77.

24   Kierner, *Patsy Jefferson Randolph*, 105–6.

25   To Martha Jefferson Randolph, 4 April 1790; From Martha Jefferson Randolph,
      25 April 1790, in *FLTJ*, 51, 52–53; Gaines, *Thomas Mann Randolph*, 31–34.

26   Kierner, *Martha Jefferson Randolph*, 84–89.

27   Gaines, *Thomas Mann Randolph*, 33.

28   Ann Lucas Birle and Lisa A. Francavilla, eds., *Thomas Jefferson's Granddaughter
      in Queen Victoria's England: The Travel Diary of Ellen Wayles Coolidge, 1838–1839*
      (Charlottesville: University of Virginia Press for the Massachusetts Historical
      Society and the Thomas Jefferson Foundation, 2011), 159–60.

29   She called her a "virago." See Gordon-Reed, *Hemingses of Monticello*, 563.

30   From Martha Jefferson Randolph, 20 February 1792, in *FLTJ*, 94.

31   Joshua D. Rothman, *Notorious in the Neighborhood: Sex and Families across the Color Line in Virginia, 1787–1861* (Chapel Hill: University of North Carolina Press, 2003), 31, 43.

Chapter 14

1   Cynthia A. Kierner, *Martha Jefferson Randolph: Daughter of Monticello* (Chapel Hill: University of North Carolina Press, 2012), 86, 97–98, 106; William H. Gaines Jr., *Thomas Mann Randolph: Jefferson's Son-in-Law* (n.p.: Louisiana State University Press, 1966), 44–45. The Randolphs' domestic slaves (six or eight, including Patsy's maid Molly Hemings) moved with their owners wherever they made their home.

2   For a discussion of women in Washington during Jefferson's presidential years, see Catherine Allgor, *Parlor Politics, In Which the Ladies of Washington Help Build a City and a Government* (Charlottesville: University Press of Virginia, 2000), chap. 1.

3   Lucia Stanton, "Nourishing the Congress: Hospitality at the President's House," in *Dining at Monticello*, ed. Damon Lee Fowler (Chapel Hill: University of North Carolina for the Thomas Jefferson Foundation, 2005), 11–12.

4   Stanton, "Nourishing the Congress," 14; Stanton, "'A Well-Ordered Household': Domestic Servants in Jefferson's White House," in *"Those Who Labor for My Happiness": Slavery at Thomas Jefferson's Monticello* (Charlottesville: University of Virginia Press, 2012), 51. The "pall mall" style died out quietly. See Allgor, *Parlor Politics*, 46.

5   Margaret Bayard Smith, *The First Forty Years of Washington Society*, ed. Gaillard Hunt (New York: Charles Scribner's Sons, 1906), 388.

6   Stanton, "Well-Ordered Household," 41–45, 316n47.

7   To Martha Jefferson Randolph, 18 June 1802, in *FLTJ*, 229. After Ursula Granger returned to Monticello, she and Wormley Hughes raised a large family together. See Annette Gordon-Reed, *The Hemingses of Monticello: An American Family* (New York: W. W. Norton, 2008), 569.

8   The President kept Edy in Washington, DC, until he retired from office— another three years. She somehow managed to see Joe at times, because they had more children. An infant born in January 1803 did not survive, but James Fossett (b. January 1805) and Maria Fossett (b. October 1807) lived to adulthood. After being reunited at Monticello, Edy and Joe had six more. Stanton, "Those Who Labor for My Happiness: Thomas Jefferson and His Slaves," in *"Those Who Labor,"* 17, 309n58; Gordon-Reed, *Hemingses of Monticello*, 573–74.

9   Stanton, "Well-Ordered Household," 44, 46–47, and Stanton, "Free Some Day: The African American Families of Monticello," 139, in *"Those Who Labor."*

10 *PTJ*, 38:108n.

11 Ibid.; Stanton, "Well-Ordered Household," 47.

12 Its population numbered 2,464 whites, 746 blacks. Of the latter, 623 were enslaved and 123 free. Catherine Allgor, *A Perfect Union: Dolley Madison and the Creation of the American Nation* (New York: Henry Holt, 2006), 46.

13 Stanton, "Looking for Liberty: Thomas Jefferson and the British Lions," 27–30 (quotes 27–28), and Stanton, "Well-Ordered Household," 49–50, in *"Those Who Labor."*

14 For Callender's articles in the *Richmond Recorder*, see http://digital.lib.lehigh .edu/trial/jefferson/resources/recorder/ (accessed 11/30/2015).

15 Quoted in Fawn M. Brodie, *Thomas Jefferson: An Intimate History* (New York: Bantam, 1974), 470.

16 Brodie reproduces the entire poem, ibid., 472–73.

17 Quoted ibid., 471.

18 Joshua D. Rothman, "James Callender and Social Knowledge of Interracial Sex in Antebellum Virginia," in *Sally Hemings and Thomas Jefferson: History, Memory, and Civic Culture*, ed. Jan Ellen Lewis and Peter S. Onuf (Charlottesville: University of Virginia Press, 1999), 94; Philip D. Morgan, "Interracial Sex in the Chesapeake and the British Atlantic World, c. 1700–1820," in Lewis and Onuf, *Sally Hemings and Thomas Jefferson*, 60, 67 (quote).

19 To George Jefferson, 6 October 1802; To Mary Jefferson Eppes, 7 October 1802; To Mary Jefferson Eppes, 18 October 1802; To Thomas Jefferson Randolph, 18 October 1802; From Martha Jefferson, 29 October [1802], in *PTJ*, 38:458–59, 600.

20 To Mary Jefferson Eppes, 18 October 1802; To Thomas Mann Randolph, 22 October [1802]; From Martha Jefferson Randolph, 29 October [1802], in *PTJ*, 38:514, 533, 533n, 600.

21 From Mary Jefferson Eppes, 5 November [1802]; From Martha Jefferson Randolph, 9 November [1802], in *PTJ*, 38:649, 655–656.

22 Kierner, *Martha Jefferson Randolph*, 115. Priscilla was the wife of John Hemings, a skilled woodworker who lived and practiced his trade at Monticello. He was the youngest son of Betty Hemings, born after the death of John Wayles.

23 Smith, *First Forty Years*, 35, 49–50.

24 Ibid., 34.

25 *PTJ*, 39:136n; From Mary Jefferson Eppes, 11 January [1803], in *PTJ*, 39:309.

26 From Mary Jefferson Eppes, 11 January [1803], in *PTJ*, 39:309; To Mary Jefferson Eppes, 18 January 1803, in *FLTJ*, 241.

27 Gaines, *Thomas Mann Randolph*, 51.

28 From Martha Jefferson Randolph, 30 November 1804, in *FLTJ*, 264; Kierner, *Martha Jefferson Randolph*, 123. Mary was Patsy's seventh child, but one daughter had died in infancy.

29 Kierner, *Martha Jefferson Randolph*, 127.

30 To James Madison, [3 November 1805], in *DMDE*, http://rotunda.upress.vir ginia.edu/dmde/DPM0114 (accessed 02/24/2014).

31 Ibid.; From Thomas Jefferson, 10 July 1805, in *DMDE*, http://rotunda.upress .virginia.edu/dmde/DPM0729 (accessed 02/24/2014).

32 Kierner, *Martha Jefferson Randolph*, 127.

33 Smith, *First Forty Years*, 404–5; Gaines, *Thomas Mann Randolph*, 59.

34 Kierner, *Martha Jefferson Randolph*, 131.

35 Stanton, "Looking for Liberty," 29–30; Jan Ellen Lewis, "The White Jeffersons," in Lewis and Onuf, *Sally Hemings and Thomas Jefferson*, 138.

36 Kierner, *Martha Jefferson Randolph*, 128–29.

37 Quoted in Andrew Burstein and Nancy Isenberg, *Madison and Jefferson* (New York: Random House, 2010), 412.

38 Ibid. "A man may love his cow though he kiss her not" was the classic saying.

39 From *The Embargo: Sketches of the Times* (1808), quoted in William Aspenwall Bradley, *William Cullen Bryant* (New York: Macmillan, 1905), 18.

40 Elise Lemire, *"Miscegenation": Making Race in America* (Philadelphia: University of Pennsylvania Press, 2002), 18–22.

41 Quoted in Gordon-Reed, *Hemingses of Monticello*, 585; emphasis in original.

42 Quoted ibid., 584.

43 Stanton, "Looking for Liberty," 37, and Stanton, "The Other End of the Telescope: Jefferson Through the Eyes of His Slaves," 97–98, in *"Those Who Labor"*; Gordon-Reed, *Hemingses of Monticello*, 570.

44 From Thomas Jefferson to Robert Smith, 1 July 1805," Founders Online, National Archives, http://founders.archives.gov/documents/Jefferson/99-01-02 -2005 (source: *PTJ*, "early access document"); Jon Kukla, *Mr. Jefferson's Women* (New York: Alfred A. Knopf, 2007), 54–63. Kukla terms the President's behavior "predatory sexuality." He reproduces the letter on pp. 194–95.

45 Kukla, *Mr. Jefferson's Women*, 62.

46 Kierner, *Martha Jefferson Randolph*, 93. Nancy ended up marrying Gouverneur Morris of New York, one of the nation's more aristocratic founding fathers, who authored much of the U.S. Constitution and had a reputation as a rake. Thomas A. Foster, *Sex and the Founding Fathers: The American Quest for a Relatable Past* (Philadelphia: Temple University Press, 2014), chap. 6.

47 Foster discusses attitudes of predators in *Sex and the Founding Fathers*, 159.

48 Christopher L. Doyle, "The Randolph Scandal in Early National Virginia, 1792–1814: New Voices in the 'Court of Honor,'" *Journal of Southern History* 69 (May 2003): 296.

49 Ibid.

50 To Martha Jefferson Randolph, 27 January 1803, *PTJ*, 39:405.

51 Ibid.; Stanton, "Other End of the Telescope," 96.

52   Stanton, "Well-Ordered Household," 53; "Deed of John Freeman's Indenture to James Madison," *PTJ*, Retirement Series, vol. 1, *4 March to 15 November 1809*, ed. Jefferson Looney (Princeton, NJ: Princeton University Press, 2004), 156.

53   Gaines, *Thomas Mann Randolph*, 69–70.

Chapter 15

1   Jon Meacham, *Thomas Jefferson: The Art of Power* (New York: Random House, 2012), 440.

2   William H. Gaines Jr., *Thomas Mann Randolph: Jefferson's Son-in-Law* (n.p.: Louisiana State University Press, 1966), 156–57.

3   Ibid., 92, 112–13, 122, 135.

4   Merrill D. Peterson, *Visitors to Monticello* (Charlottesville: University Press of Virginia, 1989), esp. 64; Susan R. Stein, "Dining at Monticello: 'The Feast of Reason,'" in *Dining at Monticello*, ed. Damon Lee Fowler (Chapel Hill: University of North Carolina Press for Thomas Jefferson Foundation, 2005), 76.

5   Elizabeth V. Chew, "Carrying the Keys: Women and Housekeeping at Monticello," in Fowler, *Dining at Monticello*, 29–31, and, in the section of the same volume headed "The Recipes," 161, 177.

6   Chew, "Carrying the Keys," 30–31.

7   Quoted ibid., 29.

8   Ann Lucas Birle and Lisa A. Francavilla, eds., *Thomas Jefferson's Granddaughter in Queen Victoria's England: The Travel Diary of Ellen Wayles Coolidge, 1838–1839* (Charlottesville, VA: University of Virginia Press for the Massachusetts Historical Society and the Thomas Jefferson Foundation, 2011), 21, 23, 184.

9   "Recipes," 149, 155, 161, 163.

10   Ibid., 107, 184.

11   Ibid., 159.

12   Justin A. Sarafin, "Like Clockwork: French Influence in Monticello's Kitchen," in Fowler, *Dining at Monticello*, 20.

13   Peter J. Hatch, "Thomas Jefferson's Favorite Vegetables," in Fowler, *Dining at Monticello*, 57.

14   Sarafin, "Like Clockwork," 24–26.

15   Virginia J. Randolph (Trist) to Nicholas P. Trist, 21 July 1823, http://tjrs.monticello.org/letter/960 (accessed 11/30/2015).

16   "Recipes," 126, 155, 170.

17   Birle and Francavilla, *Thomas Jefferson's Granddaughter*, xxiv; "Recipes," 94, 102.

18   "Recipes," 106, 142.

19   Ellen W. Randolph (Coolidge) to Nicholas P. Trist, 30 March 1824, http://tjrs.monticello.org/letter/970 (accessed 11/30/2015).

20 "Recipes," 105, 126.

21 Chew, "Carrying the Keys," 33–34; Dianne Swann-Wright, "African Americans and Monticello's Food Culture," 39, 41; "Recipes," 104—all in Fowler, *Dining at Monticello*. At one time, agricultural workers like the Grangers had been allowed to grow a small amount of the staple crop for sale. Jefferson ended the practice because he had difficulty distinguishing "between what is theirs and mine." See Lucia Stanton, "Free Some Day: The African American Families of Monticello," in *"Those Who Labor for My Happiness": Slavery at Thomas Jefferson's Monticello* (Charlottesville: University of Virginia Press, 2012), 126.

22 Stanton, "Free Some Day," 113–14, 126; Marie Jenkins Schwartz, *Born in Bondage: Growing Up Enslaved in the Antebellum South* (Cambridge, MA: Harvard University Press, 2000), 83–84.

23 Stanton, "Free Some Day," 115; Chew, "Carrying the Keys," 34.

24 Hatch, "Thomas Jefferson's Favorite Vegetables," 63.

25 Stanton, "Those Who Labor for My Happiness: Thomas Jefferson and His Slaves," 21, and Stanton, "Free Some Day," 114, in *"Those Who Labor."*

26 Stanton, "Those Who Labor," 20.

27 Swann-Wright, "African Americans and Monticello's Food Culture," 42.

28 Stein, "Dining at Monticello," 76.

29 Margaret Bayard Smith, *The First Forty Years of Washington Society*, ed. Gaillard Hunt (New York: Charles Scribner's Sons, 1906), 359–60.

Chapter 16

1 The Hemings children were Beverly (b. April 1798), Harriet (b. May 1801), Madison (b. January 1803), and Eston (b. May 1808). The Randolph children who moved to Monticello with their mother were Thomas Jefferson (b. September 1792); Ellen Wayles (b. October 1796); Cornelia Jefferson (b. July 1799); Virginia Jefferson (b. August 1801); Mary Jefferson (b. November 1803); James Madison (b. January 1806); and Benjamin Franklin (b. July 1808). Patsy had given birth in August 1794 to another child named Ellen, who died the following year. By 1809 Anne Cary Randolph Bankhead (b. January 1791) was married and living elsewhere. Three more Randolph children would be born at Monticello: Meriwether Lewis (b. 1810), Septimia Anne (b. 1814), and George Wythe (b. 1818).

2 Robert Hemings, who had been hired out in Richmond, took a wife and convinced her owner to purchase him and allow him to buy his freedom by reimbursing the purchase price. Thomas Jefferson had agreed to the arrangement reluctantly, but his resentment lingered. See From Martha Jefferson Randolph, 15 January 1795, in *FLTJ*, 131.

3   Joshua D. Rothman, "James Callender and Social Knowledge of Interracial Sex in Antebellum Virginia," in *Sally Hemings and Thomas Jefferson: History, Memory, and Civic Culture,* ed. Jan Ellen Lewis and Peter S. Onuf (Charlottesville: University of Virginia Press, 1999), 87.

4   Lucia Stanton, "Those Who Labor for My Happiness: Thomas Jefferson and His Slaves," 21–23, Stanton, "Free Some Day: The African American Families of Monticello," 166, Stanton, "Jefferson's People: Slavery at Monticello," 68, and Stanton, "The Other End of the Telescope: Jefferson through the Eyes of His Slaves," 97, in *"Those Who Labor for My Happiness": Slavery at Thomas Jefferson's Monticello* (Charlottesville: University of Virginia Press, 2012); Madison Hemings's Memoir, in Lewis and Onuf, *Sally Hemings and Thomas Jefferson,* 257.

5   Quoted in Rothman, "James Callender," 106.

6   Jan Ellen Lewis, "The White Jeffersons," in Lewis and Onuf, *Sally Hemings and Thomas Jefferson,* 144–47.

7   Clarence E. Walker, "Character and History, or 'Chloroform in Print,'" in *Mongrel Nation: The America Begotten by Thomas Jefferson and Sally Hemings* (Charlottesville: University of Virginia Press, 2009), 79–80.

8   Eppes's relationship with Hemings may have continued beyond his remarriage in 1809. Betsy was nursemaid as well to the children John fathered with his second wife. She was buried in the family cemetery next to her master.

9   Philip D. Morgan, "Interracial Sex in the Chesapeake and the British Atlantic World, c. 1700–1820," in Lewis and Onuf, *Sally Hemings and Thomas Jefferson,* 62–63.

10 Gordon Langley Hall, *Mr. Jefferson's Ladies* (Boston: Beacon Press, 1966), 188. When Patsy moved to Monticello in 1809, Critta came with her. Stanton, "Free Some Day," 183.

11 Stanton, "Free Some Day," 159.

12 To Martha Jefferson, 28 March 1787, in *FLTJ,* 35.

13 Stanton, "Free Some Day," 159–60, and Stanton, "Jefferson's People," 66, in *"Those Who Labor"*; From Martha Jefferson Randolph, 6 May 1813, *Papers of Thomas Jefferson,* Retirement Series, vol. 6, ed. J. Jefferson Looney (Princeton: Princeton University Press), 106.

14 See Annette Gordon-Reed, *The Hemingses of Monticello: An American Family* (New York: W. W. Norton, 2008), 605.

15 The Manuscript Division of the Library of Congress holds personal items belonging to Martha Wayles Skelton Jefferson. See http://www.loc.gov/exhibits/treasures/tri033.html (accessed 12/01/2015).

16 Stanton, "Jefferson's People," 67.

17 Madison Hemings's Memoir, 256, 258 (quote).

18 http://www.monticello.org/site/plantation-and-slavery/harriet-hemings (accessed 02/03/2016); Stanton, "Those Who Labor," 8.

19 Madison Hemings's Memoir, 256–57.

20 Ibid., 257; Stanton, "Other End of the Telescope," 99; Merrill D. Peterson, *Visitors to Monticello* (Charlottesville: University Press of Virginia, 1989), 68–70.

21 The Bowdens who worked for the Washingtons were entrapped in similar circumstances. Henry Wiencek, *An Imperfect God: George Washington, His Slaves, and the Creation of America* (New York: Farrar, Straus, and Giroux, 2003), 160–61.

22 Query XIV, Laws, excerpted in Lewis and Onuf, *Sally Hemings and Thomas Jefferson*, appendix D, 265–66.

23 Thomas Jefferson to Francis Gray, 4 March 1815, in Lewis and Onuf, *Sally Hemings and Thomas Jefferson*, appendix C, 262–63. Jefferson was not the only Virginian interested in the "product" of amalgamation; John Wayles was as well. See, in the same volume, Madison Hemings's Memoir, 255.

24 Joanne Pope Melish, *Disowning Slavery: Gradual Emancipation and "Race" in New England, 1780–1860* (Ithaca, NY: Cornell University Press, 1998), 120.

25 Query XIV, Laws, excerpted in Lewis and Onuf, *Sally Hemings and Thomas Jefferson*, appendix D, 265–66.

Chapter 17

1 "Jefferson's Cause of Death," http://www.monticello.org/site/research-and-col lections/jeffersons-cause-death (accessed 12/02/2015); "Jefferson's Funeral," http://www.monticello.org/site/research-and-collections/jeffersons-funeral (accessed 12/02/2015); Andrew Burstein and Nancy Isenberg, *Madison and Jefferson* (New York: Random House, 2010), 599; Ralph Ketcham, *The Madisons at Montpelier: Reflections on the Founding Couple* (Charlottesville: University of Virginia Press, 2009), 129; Cynthia A. Kierner, *Martha Jefferson Randolph: Daughter of Monticello* (Chapel Hill: University of North Carolina Press, 2012), 202–4.

2 Margaret Bayard Smith, *The First Forty Years of Washington Society*, ed. Gaillard Hunt (New York: Charles Scribner's Sons, 1906), 316; Philip D. Morgan, "Interracial Sex in the Chesapeake and the British Atlantic World, c. 1700–1820," in *Sally Hemings and Thomas Jefferson: History, Memory, and Civic Culture*, ed. Jan Ellen Lewis and Peter S. Onuf (Charlottesville: University of Virginia Press, 1999), 67–68.

3 James H. Bailey, "John Wayles Eppes, Planter and Politician," MA thesis (University of Virginia, 1942), 86; Lucia Stanton, "The Other End of the Telescope: Jefferson through the Eyes of His Slaves," in *"Those Who Labor for My Happiness": Slavery at Thomas Jefferson's Monticello* (Charlottesville: University of Virginia Press, 2012), 98.

4 William H. Gaines Jr., *Thomas Mann Randolph: Jefferson's Son-in-Law* (n.p.: Louisiana State University Press, 1966), 77, 78, 95, 101–2, 103, 142, 148, 155–56.

5   Ibid., 77 (quote), 104; quoted in Virginia Scharff, *The Women Jefferson Loved* (New York: Harper, 2010), 359–60. Overseer Edmund Bacon may have taken Maria to Kentucky in 1822. Stanton, "Free Some Day: The African American Families of Monticello," in *"Those Who Labor,"* 130; "Jefferson at Monticello: The Private Life of Thomas Jefferson," in *Jefferson at Monticello: Recollections of a Monticello Slave and a Monticello Overseer,* ed. James A. Bear (Charlottesville: University Press of Virginia, 1967), 91–93.

6   Gaines, *Thomas Mann Randolph*, 159–62.

7   Kierner, *Martha Jefferson Randolph*, 196.

8   From Martha Jefferson Randolph, 2 January 1808, in *FLTJ*, 318; emphasis in original.

9   Gaines, *Thomas Mann Randolph*, 76.

10   Ibid., 124–25.

11   Stanton, "Other End of the Telescope," 103–4.

12   Alan Pell Crawford, *Twilight at Monticello: The Final Years of Thomas Jefferson* (New York: Random House, 2008), 119, 136, 233; From Ellen Randolph Coolidge, 8 March 1826, in *FLTJ*, 473, 474.

13   Stanton, "Jefferson's People: Slavery at Monticello," in *"Those Who Labor,"* 59.

14   Ibid. Jefferson believed that Thruston had left for Washington where friends of Edy Fossett were hiding him. Stanton, "Free Some Day," 139, 141. Thruston and Moses were children of David and Isabel Hern, who Jefferson inherited from his father-in-law, John Wayles.

15   Mr. Jefferson's Will, in Bear, *Jefferson at Monticello,* 118–22; Ellen W. Randolph (Coolidge) to Virginia J. Randolph (Trist), 31 August [1819], Family Letters, Monticello, http://tjrs.monticello.org/letter/829 (accessed 12/02/2015); Stanton, "Free Some Day," 183–84.

16   Stanton, "Free Some Day," 195. The Fossett family was eventually reunited. See Stanton, "Those Who Labor for My Happiness: Thomas Jefferson and His Slaves," 24, and Stanton, "Free Some Day," 198, 201–4, in *"Those Who Labor."*

17   Stanton, "Those Who Labor," 19; Cornelia Randolph to Ellen W. Coolidge, 24 November 1825, Family Letters, http://tjrs.monticello.org/letter/1019 (accessed 12/03/2015).

18   To Martha Jefferson Randolph, 5 January 1808; From Martha Jefferson Randolph, 16 January 1808; From Martha Jefferson Randolph, 2 March 1809—all in *FLTJ*, 319, 322, 386. Years later, Jefferson Randolph offered his grandfather similar assurances. See From Thomas Jefferson Randolph, 3 February [1826], in *FLTJ*, 467.

19   Although Virginia law required freed slaves to leave the state, Sally managed to remain. She worked first in the home of a chemistry professor and later as a self-employed seamstress. She eventually married Reuben Cole, a free black man.

Ann Lucas Birle and Lisa A. Francavilla, eds., *Thomas Jefferson's Granddaughter in Queen Victoria's England: The Travel Diary of Ellen Wayles Coolidge, 1838–1839* (Charlottesville: University of Virginia Press for the Massachusetts Historical Society and the Thomas Jefferson Foundation, 2011), xix, 22.

20 Stanton, "Those Who Labor," 3; Stanton, "Free Some Day," 196; Annette Gordon-Reed, *The Hemingses of Monticello: An American Family* (New York: W. W. Norton, 2008), 661.

21 Stanton, "Those Who Labor," 3, 304n2. Gilette purchased his freedom in 1844 and moved to Ohio with his wife, where he changed his name to Israel Jefferson. When interviewed for the *Pike County Republican*, he professed knowledge that his former master and Sally Hemings had been sexually intimate. See Joshua D. Rothman, "James Callender and Knowledge of Interracial Sex in Antebellum Virginia," in Lewis and Onuf, *Sally Hemings and Thomas Jefferson*, 99. The 1827 auction did not end slave sales at Monticello. More slaves were auctioned off in 1829. Jeff Randolph purchased thirty of them. See Stanton, "Free Some Day," 208.

22 Stanton, "Free Some Day," 201.

23 Gaines, *Thomas Mann Randolph*, 184–86.

24 Ibid., 178; Kierner, *Martha Jefferson Randolph*, 214.

25 Kierner, *Martha Jefferson Randolph*, 243, 258 (quote).

26 Stanton, "Free Some Day," 197, 207; Stanton, "Other End of the Telescope," 102; Kierner, *Martha Jefferson Randolph*, 262, 266. Hughes spent the remainder of his life working in the homes of Patsy's children and grandchildren.

27 Kierner, *Martha Jefferson Randolph*, 272.

Chapter 18

1 Ethel Stephens Arnett, *Mrs. James Madison: The Incomparable Dolley* (Greensboro, NC: Piedmont Press, 1972), 20–21, 28; Cutts Memoir I, in *The Queen of America: Mary Cutts's Life of Dolley Madison*, ed. Catherine Allgor (Charlottesville: University of Virginia Press, 2012), 89–90.

2 Catherine Allgor, *A Perfect Union: Dolley Madison and the Creation of the American Nation* (New York: Henry Holt, 2006), 16–17; "The Payne Family of Goochland, &c," *Virginia Magazine of History and Biography* 6 (January 1899): 315.

3 "Payne Family of Goochland," 80–81; Catherine Allgor, "The Lady Vanishes," in Allgor, *Queen of America*, 23.

4 Arnett, *Mrs. James Madison*, 25.

5 Ibid.

6 Holly Cowan Shulman, "History, Memory, and Dolley Madison: Notes from a Documentary Editor," in Allgor, *Queen of America*, 46.

7 Eva Sheppard Wolf, *Race and Liberty in the New Nation: Emancipation in Virginia from the Revolution to Nat Turner's Rebellion* (Baton Rouge: Louisiana State University Press, 2006), chap. 1. The eight counties were Chesterfield, Charles City, Lancaster, Accomack, Mecklenburg, Fauquier, Botetourt, and Wythe.

8 Cutts Memoir I, 90.

9 James Pinckney Pleasant Bell, *Our Quaker Friends of Ye Olden Times, Being in Part a Transcript of the Minute Books of Cedar Creek Meeting, Hanover County, and the South River Meeting, Campbell County, Va.* (Lynchburg, VA: J. P. Bell, 1905); Arnett, *Mrs. James Madison*, 26.

10 Alan Gilbert, *Black Patriots and Loyalists: Fighting for Emancipation in the War for Independence* (Chicago: University of Chicago Press, 2012), 61.

11 Sarah Fatherly, *Gentlewomen and Learned Ladies: Women and Elite Formation in Eighteenth-Century Philadelphia* (Bethlehem, PA: Lehigh University Press, 2008), 53.

12 Fatherly discusses the importance of Quaker support for Quaker businesses. Ibid.

13 Shulman, "History, Memory, and Dolley Madison," 46–59.

14 Allgor, *Perfect Union*, 389; Allgor, "Lady Vanishes," 26–27. Dolley's father had appeared near death, but he lingered until 24 October 1792.

15 Arnett, *Mrs. James Madison*, 41, 44.

16 Ibid., 48.

17 Thomas Jefferson to Mary Jefferson, 17 November 1793, in *FLTJ*, 126; Andrew Burstein and Nancy Isenberg, *Madison and Jefferson* (New York: Random House, 2010), 274. Quoted in Arnett, *Mrs. James Madison*, 49.

18 Later on, she lived some of the time with her daughter Mary Payne Jackson. Arnett, *Mrs. James Madison*, 54; To Margaret Bayard Smith, 31 August 1834, in *SLDPM*, 306.

19 Margaret Bayard Smith, *The First Forty Years of Washington Society*, ed. Gaillard Hunt (New York: Charles Scribner's Sons, 1906), 351–52.

Chapter 19

1 Ethel Stephens Arnett, *Mrs. James Madison: The Incomparable Dolley* (Greensboro, NC: Piedmont Press, 1972), 47; Catherine Allgor, *A Perfect Union: Dolley Madison and the Creation of the American Nation* (New York: Henry Holt, 2006), 27–28. On Burr's guardianship, see Nancy Isenberg, *Fallen Founder: The Life of Aaron Burr* (New York: Viking, 2007), 124.

2 See Cutts Memoir I, in *The Queen of America: Mary Cutts's Life of Dolley Madison*, ed. Catherine Allgor (Charlottesville: University of Virginia Press, 2012), 96.

3   Henry Wiencek, *An Imperfect God: George Washington, His Slaves, and the Creation of America* (New York: Farrar, Straus, and Giroux, 2003), 275, 276.

4   Merrill D. Peterson, ed., *Visitors to Monticello* (Charlottesville: University Press of Virginia, 1989), 42.

5   Glenn A. Crothers, "Quaker Merchants and Slavery in Early National Alexandria, Virginia." *Journal of the Early Republic* 25 (Spring 2005), 52.

6   Allgor, *Perfect Union*, 21; Allgor, "The Lady Vanishes," 24, and Cutts Memoir II, 150, both in Allgor, *Queen of America*, 150.

7   Cutts Memoir I, in Allgor, *Queen of America*, 94.

8   Ibid., 91.

9   Elizabeth Collins Lee to Zaccheus Collins Lee, [1849], in *SLDPM*, 390–91; To Elizabeth Brooke Ellicot, [December 1788], in *DMDE*, http://rotunda.upress .virginia.edu/dmde/DPMO566 (accessed 02/24/2014).

10   To Elizabeth Brooke Ellicott, [December 1788], in *DMDE*.

11   Arnett, *Mrs. James Madison*, 61.

12   Ibid., 65.

13   Ibid., 63; *In Memoriam: Benjamin Ogle Tayloe* (Philadelphia: Sherman and Co., 1872), 118.

14   Cutts Memoir I, 90, 95, 99.

15   Alan Gilbert, *Black Patriots and Loyalists: Fighting for Emancipation in the War for Independence* (Chicago: University of Chicago Press, 2012), 250.

16   John Swanwick to James Madison, 14 June 1795, *Papers of James Madison Digital Edition*, J. C. A. Stagg, ed. (Charlottesville: University of Virginia Press, Rotunda, 2010, http://rotunda.upress.virginia.edu/founders/JSMN-01[16-02 -0019 (accessed 04/24/2016); Cutts Memoir I, 99–103, 105–6. The Philadelphia Quakers also read Anna Payne out of the Meeting in a further rebuke of Dolley, who for years had assumed responsibility for her younger sister.

17   "Ambrose and Frances Madison," https://www.montpelier.org/research-and -collections/people/grandparents (accessed 04/25/2016).

18   Ralph Ketcham, *James Madison: A Biography* (Charlottesville: University Press of Virginia, 1990), 12.

19   "History of Montpelier," Digital Montpelier Project, http://www.digitalmont pelier.org/history.html (accessed 04/24/2016); Cutts Memoir II, 157; Elizabeth Dowling Taylor, *A Slave in the White House: Paul Jennings and the Madisons* (New York: Palgrave Macmillan, 2012), 82.

20   Taylor, *Slave in the White House*, 68.

21   Ibid., 69–70; "South Yard," https://www.montpelier.org/mansion-and-grounds /landscape/south-yard (accessed 05/23/2016). I am grateful to Christian Cotz, director of education and visitor engagement at the Montpelier Foundation, for pointing out the shortcomings of the wood-frame buildings.

22   Taylor, *Slave in the White House*, 20–21, 67–68, 84–85.

23   Cutts Memoir II, 159; Maud Wilder Goodwin, *Dolley Madison* (New York: Charles Scribner's Sons, 1896), 205.

24   Taylor, *Slave in the White House*, 23.

25   Myron Magnet, *The Founders at Home: The Building of America, 1735–1817* (New York: W. W. Norton, 2014), 384; To Elizabeth Parke Custis Law, 17 October 1804, in *SLDPM*, 60.

26   Margaret Bayard Smith, *The First Forty Years of Washington Society*, ed. Gaillard Hunt (New York: Charles Scribner's Sons, 1906), 36, 38.

27   Quoted in Ron Chernow, *Alexander Hamilton* (New York: Penguin, 2004), 362.

28   Arnett, *Mrs. James Madison*, 95. Anna Payne married U.S. representative Richard Cutts of Maine in April 1804.

29   Ibid., 95, 97, 114. Dolley once assured James that she had "resolved not to admit a gentleman, into my room, unless entitled by age and long acquaintance," suggesting she had been seeing men in her private rooms from time to time and James was concerned. To James Madison, [3 November 1805], in *DMDE*, http://rotunda.upress.virginia.edu/dmde/DPM0114 (accessed 02/24/2014).

30   Allgor, *Perfect Union*, 105.

Chapter 20

1   See for example, Catherine Allgor, *A Perfect Union: Dolley Madison and the Creation of the American Nation* (New York: Henry Holt, 2006), esp. chap. 10.

2   Elizabeth Dowling Taylor, *A Slave in the White House: Paul Jennings and the Madisons* (New York: Palgrave Macmillan, 2012), xvi, 28.

3   Ibid., xvi, 1, 3, 7, 79.

4   Ibid., 3, 7.

5   "A Washington Education, 1801–1809," in *SLDPM*, 40.

6   Margaret Bayard Smith, *The First Forty Years of Washington Society*, ed. Gaillard Hunt (New York: Charles Scribner's Sons, 1906), 58–59.

7   Ibid., 58, 61–62; http://www.inaugural.senate.gov/days-events/days-event /inaugural-ball (accessed 02/03/2016).

8   Allgor, *Perfect Union*, 291; Ethel Stephens Arnett, *Mrs. James Madison: The Incomparable Dolley* (Greensboro, NC: Piedmont Press, 1972), 197.

9   Quoted in Kurt E. Leichtle and Bruce G. Carveth, *Crusade against Slavery: Edward Coles, Pioneer of Freedom* (Carbondale: Southern Illinois University Press, 2011), 37.

10   *Montpelier Hospitality Cookbook: Recipes and Traditions from the Home of James and Dolley Madison* (n.p.: Montpelier Foundation, 2010), 22–24; Arnett, *Mrs. James Madison*, 170–71, 177 (quote).

11   Allgor, *Perfect Union*, 245.

12   Ibid., 182; Arnett, *Mrs. James Madison*, 166.

13   Smith, *First Forty Years*, 97; Cutts Memoir I, in *The Queen of America: Mary Cutts's Life of Dolley Madison*, ed. Catherine Allgor (Charlottesville: University of Virginia Press, 2012), 111.

14   Arnett, *Mrs. James Madison*, 167, 177; Allgor, *Perfect Union*, 182, 188–89.

15   Arnett, *Mrs. James Madison*, 180–81.

16   Ibid., 197; Dolley Payne Todd Madison's Memorandum to Mr. Zantzinger for Purchases, [1801–1807], in *DMDE*, http://rotunda.upress.virginia.edu/dmde /DPM3372 (accessed 04/25/2016).

17   Arnett, *Mrs. James Madison*, 177, 200; Andrew Burstein and Nancy Isenberg, *Madison and Jefferson* (New York: Random House, 2010), 471.

18   Allgor, *Perfect Union*, 233–40; Arnett, *Mrs. James Madison*, 184.

19   *Montpelier Hospitality Cookbook*, 8.

20   Allgor, *Perfect Union*, 161.

21   From Benjamin Henry Latrobe, 8 September 1809; To Benjamin Henry Latrobe, 12 September 1809, both in *SLDPM*, 125, 127.

22   From Benjamin Henry Latrobe, 17 March 1809, 20 March 1809, and 22 March 1809, all in *DMDE*, http://rotunda.upress.virginia.edu/dmde/DPM0195, DPM0196, and DPM0197 (accessed 04/25/2016).

23   Arnett, *Mrs. James Madison*, 214, 279; Catherine Allgor, *Parlor Politics, In Which the Ladies of Washington Help Build a City and a Government* (Charlottesville: University Press of Virginia, 2000), 84.

24   To Mary E. E. Cutts, October [1835], in *SLDPM*, 316; Kate Roberts Edenborg, "The First Lady and the Media: Newspaper Coverage of Dolley Madison," in *Seeking a Voice: Images of Race and Gender in the 19th Century Press*, ed. David B. Sachsman, S. Kittrell Rushing, and Ray Morris Jr. (West Lafayette, IN: Purdue University Press, 2009), 169.

25   To Lucy Payne Washington Todd, 23 August 1814, *SLDPM*, 193; Allgor, *Perfect Union*, 313.

26   Paul Jennings, "A Colored Man's Reminiscences of James Madison," reproduced in Taylor, *Slave in the White House*, 231–32; Arnett, *Mrs. James Madison*, 225–26.

27   Burstein and Isenberg, *Madison and Jefferson*, 525–26.

28   Allgor, *Perfect Union*, 3–5. 314, 392, 394.

29   To Lucy Payne Washington Todd, 23 August 1814, in *SLDPM*, 193–94.

30   To Robert G. L. De Peyster, 11 February 1848, in *SLDPM*, 387; Allgor, *Perfect Union*, 313, 394.

31   Allgor, *Perfect Union*, 313.

32   Jennings, "Colored Man's Reminiscences," 230–34.

33   Allgor, *Perfect Union*, 3–5. 392, 394; Taylor, *Slave in the White House*, 51, 219.

34   Arnett, *Mrs. James Madison*, 240; Allgor, *Perfect Union*, 314.

35   Jennings, "Colored Man's Reminiscences," 232.

36 To Mary Elizabeth Hazlehurst Latrobe, 3 December 1814, in *DMDE*, http://rotunda.upress.virginia.edu/dmde/DPM5064 (accessed 09/12/2016); Jennings, "Colored Man's Reminiscences," 232.

37 Smith, *First Forty Years*, 110.

38 Richard S. Dunn, *A Tale of Two Plantations: Slave Life and Labor in Jamaica and Virginia* (Cambridge, MA: Harvard University Press, 2014), 210.

39 Jennings, "Colored Man's Reminiscences," 234.

40 Burstein and Isenberg, *Madison and Jefferson*, 520–21, 531–32; Carl Sferrazza Anthony, *First Ladies: The Saga of the Presidents' Wives and Their Power 1789–1961* (New York: William Morrow & Co., 1990), 80.

41 Arnett, *Mrs. James Madison*, 199; Allgor, *Perfect Union*, 328–29; Anthony, *First Ladies*, 96; Holly Cowan Shulman, "History, Memory, and Dolley Madison: Notes from a Documentary Editor," in Allgor, *Queen of America*, 63.

Chapter 21

1 From Nelly Conway Madison Willis, 24 June 1812, and 14 July 1812, in *DMDE*, http://rotunda.upress.virginia.edu/dmde/DPM0347 (accessed 09/12/2016); Ralph Ketcham, *The Madisons at Montpelier: Reflections on the Founding Couple* (Charlottesville: University of Virginia Press, 2009), 96; Ethel Stephens Arnett, *Mrs. James Madison: The Incomparable Dolley* (Greensboro, NC: Piedmont Press, 1972), 276.

2 From Sarah (Sally) Coles Stevenson, 24 December 1834, in *DMDE*, http://rotunda.upress.virginia.edu/dmde/DPM0802 (accessed 09/12/2016).

3 Cutts Memoir I, in *The Queen of America: Mary Cutts's Life of Dolley Madison*, ed. Catherine Allgor (Charlottesville: University of Virginia Press, 2012), 116.

4 On rituals involving owners and young children, see Marie Jenkins Schwartz, *Born in Bondage: Growing Up Enslaved in the Antebellum South* (Cambridge, MA: Harvard University Press, 2000), esp. chaps. 3 and 4.

5 Ketcham, *Madisons at Montpelier*, 110; Cutts Memoir II, in Allgor, *Queen of America*, 156–57.

6 Margaret Bayard Smith, *The First Forty Years of Washington Society*, ed. Gaillard Hunt (New York: Charles Scribner's Sons, 1906), 380.

7 Ibid., 380; Catherine Allgor, *A Perfect Union: Dolley Madison and the Creation of the American Nation* (New York: Henry Holt, 2006), 349–50.

8 Smith, *First Forty Years*, 81–83, 234; Arnett, *Mrs. James Madison*, 310, 316–18.

9 Ketchum, *The Madisons at Montpelier*, 24; Elizabeth Dowling Taylor, *A Slave in the White House: Paul Jennings and the Madisons* (New York: Palgrave Macmillan, 2012), 84, 86–87.

10 Patricia Brady, ed., *George Washington's Beautiful Nelly: The Letters of Eleanor*

Parke Custis Lewis to Elizabeth Bordley Gibson, 1794–1851 (Columbia: University of South Carolina Press, 2009), 96; To Anna Cutts, [ca. 23 July 1818], in *SLDPM*, 231.

11 To Richard Cutts, 11 August 1833, in *SLDPM*, 300.

12 To Mary Estelle Elizabeth Cutts, October [1834], in *DMDE*, http://rotunda .upress.virginia.edu/dmde/DPM0817 (accessed 09/12/2016).

13 Cutts Memoir II, 159.

14 To Anna Cutts, [ca. 23 July 1818], in *SLDPM*, 231.

15 To Anna Cutts, [June 1820?], To John C. Payne, [4 December 1829], and To Richard D. Cutts, [ca. 1827–29], all in *SLDPM*, 244, 281, 273; Arnett, *Mrs. James Madison*, 273; From Nelly Conway Madison Willis, 24 June 1812, in *DMDE*, http://rotunda.upress.virginia.edu/dmde/DPM0347 (accessed 04/25/2016).

16 Cynthia A. Kierner, *Martha Jefferson Randolph: Daughter of Monticello* (Chapel Hill: University of North Carolina Press, 2012), 247; Ketcham, *Madisons at Montpelier*, 75, 100.

17 Cutts Memoir II, 182.

18 Taylor, *Slave in the White House*, 99. Kathleen M. Hillaird discusses the slaves' internal economy in Virginia and the other seaboard states in *Masters, Slaves, and Exchange: Power's Purchase in the Old South* (New York: Cambridge University Press, 2014); for a list of items purchased in stores, see pp. 84–85.

19 Hillaird, *Masters, Slaves, and Exchange*, 84–85.

20 Schwartz, *Born in Bondage*, 181–82. On such acts as "everyday resistance," see Stephanie M. H. Camp, *Closer to Freedom: Enslaved Women and Everyday Resistance in the Plantation South* (Chapel Hill: University of North Carolina Press, 2004).

21 Taylor, *Slave in the White House*, 84, 86–87.

22 Smith, *First Forty Years*, 234; Taylor, *Slave in the White House*, 105.

23 Taylor, *Slave in the White House*, 72.

24 Ibid., 87, 89, 122.

25 Ibid., 90.

26 Ibid., 90–92.

27 Ibid., 89.

28 Ibid., 91–92. Taylor uses the phrase "garden variety slaveholder" to describe James Madison (21). Fanny had a sixth child (Elizabeth) by a previous marriage.

29 Quoted in Suzanne Cooper Guasco, *Confronting Slavery: Edward Coles and the Rise of Antislavery Politics in Nineteenth-Century America* (DeKalb: Northern Illinois University Press, 2013), 184.

30 Ketcham, *Madisons at Montpelier*, 151.

31 Martineau quoted in Taylor, *Slave in the White House*, 128; quoted in Ketcham, *Madisons at Montpelier*, 152–53.

32   Taylor, *Slave in the White House*, 115.

33   Quoted in Arnett, *Mrs. James Madison*, 296.

34   Allgor, *Perfect Union*, 394.

Chapter 22

1   Cutts Memoir II, in *The Queen of America: Mary Cutts's Life of Dolley Madison*, ed. Catherine Allgor (Charlottesville: University of Virginia Press, 2012), 188–89.

2   James Madison to John Payne Todd, 13 November 1825, and 15 February 1826, in *DMDE*, http://rotunda.upress.virginia.edu/dmde/DPM3203 and DPM3204 (both accessed 09/12/2016).

3   Holly Cowan Shulman, "History, Memory, and Dolley Madison: Notes from a Documentary Editor," in Allgor, *Queen of America*, 56.

4   Ethel Stephens Arnett, *Mrs. James Madison: The Incomparable Dolley* (Greensboro, NC: Piedmont Press, 1972), 283–84.

5   Accounts of Payne Todd are overwhelmingly negative. See for example "Payne Todd: 'The Serpent in the Garden of Eden,'" in Bruce Chadwick, *James and Dolley Madison: America's First Power Couple* (Amherst, NY: Prometheus Books, 2014), chap. 24.

6   Catherine Allgor, *A Perfect Union: Dolley Madison and the Creation of the American Nation* (New York: Henry Holt, 2006), 208–11.

7   Cutts Memoir II, 193–94.

8   Nancy Isenberg, *Fallen Founder: The Life of Aaron Burr* (New York: Viking, 2007), 124; Arnett, *Mrs. James Madison*, 278.

9   See "John Payne Todd," https://www.montpelier.org/research-and-collections /people/john-payne-todd (accessed 04/26/2016).

10   Holly C. Shulman, "Madison vs. Madison: Dolley Payne Madison and Her Inheritance of the Montpelier Estate, 1836–38," *Virginia Magazine of History and Biography* 119, no. 4 (2011): 363; Allgor, *Perfect Union*, 374, 384. Ingersoll's account of his visit is reproduced in Ralph Ketcham, *The Madisons at Montpelier: Reflections on the Founding Couple* (Charlottesville: University of Virginia Press, 2009), 165–71, see also 45.

11   Elizabeth Dowling Taylor, *A Slave in the White House: Paul Jennings and the Madisons* (New York: Palgrave Macmillan, 2012), 123–24.

12   To James Taylor, 25 December 1834, in *DMDE*, http://rotunda.upress.virginia .edu/dmde/DPM0804 (accessed 09/12/2016). James Madison assured Edward Coles that all of those sold had gone with his kinsman "with their own consent." See Edward Coles to Sarah (Sally) Coles Stevenson, 12 November 1836, in *DMDE*, http://rotunda.upress.virginia.edu/dmde/DPM2827 (accessed 09/ 12/2016).

13   To Mary Estelle Elizabeth Cutts, October (1834), in *DMDE*, http://rotunda
     .upress.virginia.edu/dmde/DPM0817 (accessed 09/12/2016).

14   Taylor, *Slave in the White House*, 123–25, 127.

15   Relevant parts of Martinueau's *Retrospect of Western Travel* are reproduced in
     Ketcham, *Madisons at Montpelier*, 150–56. See also Taylor, *Slave in the White
     House*, 126–27.

16   "Property," http://www.monticello.org/site/plantation-and-slavery/property
     (accessed 12/09/2015); Marie Jenkins Schwartz, *Born in Bondage: Growing Up
     Enslaved in the Antebellum South* (Cambridge, MA: Harvard University Press,
     2000); Schwartz, *Birthing a Slave: Motherhood and Medicine in the Antebellum
     South* (Cambridge, MA: Harvard University Press, 2006).

17   Allgor, *Perfect Union*, 365.

18   Taylor, *Slave in the White House*, 14, 105–6. Coles's ties to the Madisons were
     both political and personal. Dolley's mother, Mary Coles Payne, was the double
     first cousin of Edward's father, John Coles II. Dolley's and Edward's grand-
     fathers were brothers who married two sisters from the Winston family.

19   John Coles II invested heavily in slaves after the American Revolution. By 1793
     he claimed eighty-four persons as property; he continued to purchase slaves into
     the nineteenth century. Suzanne Cooper Guasco, *Confronting Slavery: Edward
     Coles and the Rise of Antislavery Politics in Nineteenth-Century America* (DeKalb:
     Northern Illinois University Press, 2013), 15, 27–28. On Edward Coles's efforts
     to free his slaves, see Kurt E. Leichtle and Bruce G. Carveth, *Crusade against
     Slavery: Edward Coles, Pioneer of Freedom* (Carbondale: Southern Illinois Uni-
     versity Press, 2011).

20   Leichtle and Carveth, *Crusade against Slavery*, 4.

21   Ibid., 20, 39, 60.

22   To Edward Coles, 3 September 1819, *The Papers of James Madison*, Retirement
     Series, vol. 1, 4 March 1817–31 January 1820, ed. David B. Matterns, J. C. A. Stagg,
     Mary Parke Johnson, and Anne Manderville Colony (Charlottesville: Univer-
     sity of Virginia Press, 2009), 504–5.

23   When contacted by Coles in July 1814, Jefferson responded that emancipation
     would have to await the efforts of younger men with the fortitude to endure its
     consequences. Twenty-seven years later, Coles pleaded with Jefferson's grand-
     son, who was then serving in the Virginia House of Delegates: "For God's sake
     step forward & put a stop to . . . the evil of slavery." That same year, Coles inten-
     sified his campaign to convince James Madison to free his slaves through his
     will. Leichtle and Carveth, *Crusade against Slavery*, 45–46, 152.

24   Inventory of Effects at Montpelier, 1 July 1836; From Edward Coles, 12 July 1837,
     24 July 1837, and 9 July 1836, all in *DMDE*, http://rotunda.upress.virginia.edu
     /dmde/DPM3019, -1049, and -0885 (accessed 09/12/2016). See also Leichtle
     and Carveth, *Crusade against Slavery*, 158–59.

25 Leichtle and Carveth, *Crusade against Slavery*, 59.

26 Ibid., 153.

27 Gausco, *Confronting Slavery*, 140–41; Taylor, *Slave in the White House*, 133.

28 Leichtle and Carveth, *Crusade against Slavery*, 159.

29 To Anna Cutts, [ca. 15 May 1832], in *SLDPM*, 295; emphasis in original.

30 Ketcham, *Madisons at Montpelier*, 172.

31 Taylor, *Slave in the White House*, 131–32.

32 Cutts Memoir II, 178.

Chapter 23

1 John Coles Payne to Edward Coles, 18 July 1836; Edward Coles to Sarah (Sally) Coles Stevenson, 28 July 1836, in *DMDE*, http://rotunda.upress.virginia.edu/dmde/DPM2842 and -3059 (accessed 09/12/2016); Elizabeth Dowling Taylor, *A Slave in the White House: Paul Jennings and the Madisons* (New York: Palgrave Macmillan, 2012), 132. At first, Coles accused his brother-in-law, Congressman Andrew Stevenson of Virginia, of influencing the President, but Stevenson denied involvement. Coles then turned to the idea of a second will.

2 To Anna Payne Cutts, [June 1804], in *DMDE*, http://rotunda.upress.edu/dmde/DPM0081 (accessed 09/12/2016).

3 Catherine Allgor, *A Perfect Union: Dolley Madison and the Creation of the American Nation* (New York: Henry Holt, 2006), 381–82; Edward Coles to Sarah (Sally) Coles Stevenson, 12 November 1836, in *DMDE*, http://rotunda.upress.virginia.edu/dmde/DPM2827 (accessed 09/12/2016).

4 Ibid.; Ethel Stephens Arnett, *Mrs. James Madison: The Incomparable Dolley* (Greensboro, NC: Piedmont Press, 1972), 276; Ralph Ketcham, *The Madisons at Montpelier: Reflections on the Founding Couple* (Charlottesville: University of Virginia Press, 2009), 160, 162.

5 Edward Coles to Sarah (Sally) Coles Stevenson, 12 November 1836, in *DMDE*. William Lloyd Garrison called James Madison a "man-stealer." His abolitionist newspaper, the *Liberator*, accused the fourth President of having insufficient "principle or generosity" to bring him to emancipate even one of his more than one hundred slaves. Quoted in Taylor, *Slave in the White House*, 139.

6 Allgor, *Perfect Union*, 382.

7 Cutts Memoir II, in *The Queen of America: Mary Cutts's Life of Dolley Madison*, ed. Catherine Allgor (Charlottesville: University of Virginia Press, 2012), 182.

8 To Edward Coles, 26 September 1842, in *SLDPM*, 361; Allgor, *Perfect Union*, 382–83.

9 Holly C. Shulman, "Madison vs. Madison: Dolley Payne Madison and Her Inheritance of the Montpelier Estate, 1836–38," *Virginia Magazine of History and Biography* 119, no. 4 (2011): 350–93. On Dolley's relationship with James's ex-

tended family, see Shulman, "History, Memory, and Dolley Madison: Notes from a Documentary Editor," in Allgor, *Queen of America*, 57–58.

10 Shulman, "Madison vs. Madison," 357–58.
11 Dolley Payne Todd Madison, Bank statement, 14 September 1836, in *DMDE*, http://rotunda.upress.virginia.edu/dmde/DPM2813 (accessed 09/12/2016).
12 Taylor, *Slave in the White House*, 142–43.
13 The house had once belonged to her sister and brother-in-law, Anna and Richard Cutts.
14 Taylor, *Slave in the White House*, 139–40, 148–50. On Dolley's reputed love of children, see Arnett, *Mrs. James Madison*, 254, 257–60.
15 Taylor, *Slave in the White House*, 140–41.

Chapter 24

1 To John Payne Todd, [ca. 1 September 1842], in *SLDPM*, 359–60.
2 To John Payne Todd, 1 September 1842, in *SLDPM*, 360. A few years later, Billy Hubbard stabbed another overseer and was brought to trial, punished with a whipping, and branded on his hand. Alex Rohr, "Popular Forest Symposium Focuses on Slavery at Site," *News and Advance* (Lynchburg, VA), 4 April 2014.
3 Catherine Allgor, *A Perfect Union: Dolley Madison and the Creation of the American Nation* (New York: Henry Holt, 2006), 383; Henry Wood Moncure to Anna Coles Payne Causten, 7 March 1843 and 14 March 1843, in *DMDE*, http://rotunda.upress.virginia.edu/dmde/DPM2998 and -4999 (accessed 09/12/2016).
4 Ethel Stephens Arnett, *Mrs. James Madison: The Incomparable Dolley* (Greensboro, NC: Piedmont Press, 1972), 362.
5 Ibid.
6 Proposed Indenture for the Sale of Montpelier, [1843], in *SLDPM*, 365–67.
7 The letter from Sarah Steward is discussed further below.
8 Deed to John Payne Todd, [16 June 1844], in *SLDPM*, 372.
9 Editorial Note, ibid., 372.
10 From Sarah Steward, 5 July 1844, in *SLDPM*, 372–73.
11 Articles of Agreement between Dolley Payne Madison, John Payne Todd, and Henry W. Moncure, [8 August 1844], *SLDPM*, 373.
12 To Henry W. Moncure, 12 August 1844 and 3 September 1844; From John Payne Todd, [October 1844], in *SLDPM*, 374, 376, 378.
13 From John Payne Todd, 17 October 1844, in *DMDE*, http://rotunda.upress.virginia.edu/dmde/DPM2028 (accessed 09/12/2016).
14 From John Payne Todd, [27 November 1844], in *DMDE*, http://rotunda,upress.virginia.edu/dmde/DPM6282 (accessed 02/26/2014).
15 Henry Wood Moncure to John Payne Todd, 29 October 1844, in *DMDE*, http://rotunda.upress.virginia.edu/dmde/DPM3369 (accessed 08/12/2016).

16 Elizabeth Dowling Taylor, *A Slave in the White House: Paul Jennings and the Madisons* (New York: Palgrave Macmillan, 2012), 152.

17 From John Payne Todd, August 1844, in *SLDPM*, 375.

18 Ralph Ketcham, *The Madisons at Montpelier: Reflections on the Founding Couple* (Charlottesville: University of Virginia Press, 2009), 179; Arnett, *Mrs. James Madison*, 356–57.

19 Holly Cowan Shulman, "History, Memory, and Dolley Madison: Notes from a Documentary Editor," in *The Queen of America: Mary Cutts's Life of Dolley Madison*, ed. Catherine Allgor (Charlottesville: University of Virginia Press, 2012), 65–66, 68–69. In 1848 Congress would buy the remaining papers in Dolley's possession for twenty-five thousand dollars. Allgor, *Perfect Union*, 379.

20 See Jan Lewis, *The Pursuit of Happiness: Family and Values in Jefferson's Virginia* (New York: Cambridge University Press, 1983), 140–41.

21 The slaves who went with Thomas and Sarah Macon were James, Pamela, her son Solomon and daughter Judy, Sam, and Peter. William Madison took Edmund, Joshua, Milly (with her child under the age of fourteen), Betty, Frank, Daniel, Reuben, and Simon. Ketcham, *Madisons at Montpelier*, 76–78.

22 From Sarah Steward, 24 April 1847, in *SLDPM*, 383. See also Allgor, *Perfect Union*, 383–84.

23 From Sarah Steward, 24 April 1847, in *SLDPM*, 383.

Chapter 25

1 To Henry Austin Brady, 21 October 1844; From Joseph Rupert Paxton, 28 December 1844, in *DMDE*, http://rotunda.upress.virginia.edu/dmde/DPM 2027 and -6291 (accessed 09/12/2016).

2 This was in December 1837, before her permanent move to Washington. "Washington Widow, 1836–1849," in *SLDPM*, 320–21.

3 Cutts Memoir II, in *The Queen of America: Mary Cutts's Life of Dolley Madison*, ed. Catherine Allgor (Charlottesville: University of Virginia Press, 2012), 186–87.

4 Ethel Stephens Arnett, *Mrs. James Madison: The Incomparable Dolley* (Greensboro, NC: Piedmont Press, 1972), 346, 375; Memorandum Book of John Payne Todd, 1844–1848, Peter Force Papers and Collection, series 8D, entry 169, Library of Congress.

5 Catherine Allgor, *A Perfect Union: Dolley Madison and the Creation of the American Nation* (New York: Henry Holt, 2006), 380, 387.

6 For a discussion of how slaves viewed owners' spending on alcohol and gambling, see Kathleen M. Hilliard, *Masters, Slaves, and Exchange: Power's Purchase in the Old South* (New York: Cambridge University Press, 2014), 50–51.

7 From Paul Jennings, 23 April [1844]; From John Payne Todd, 14 June 1845 and 17 July 1845, in *SLDPM*, 370, 380, 381. The Polks held slaves at the Hermitage, their Tennessee home, and on a Mississippi cotton plantation that served as an investment property, but they brought only one slave with them to Washington. They bought or hired other slaves in the city. Elizabeth Dowling Taylor, *A Slave in the White House: Paul Jennings and the Madisons* (New York: Palgrave Macmillan, 2012), 153; John Reed Bumgarner, *Sarah Childress Polk: A Biography of a Remarkable First Lady* (Jefferson, NC: MacFarland, 1997).

8 Taylor, *Slave in the White House*, xvii. On how the promise of freedom could strengthen slavery, see Eva Shappard Wolf, *Race and Liberty in the New Nation: Emancipation in Virginia from the Revolution to Nat Turner's Rebellion* (Baton Rouge: Louisiana State University Press, 2006).

9 Taylor, *Slave in the White House*, 155–59.

10 From John Payne Todd, 18 September 1847 and 24 September 1847, in *SLDPM*, 384, 385; emphasis in original.

11 Taylor, *Slave in the White House*, 165.

12 The story of Ellen Stewart's escape is told in Taylor, *Slave in the White House*, 162, 165–76. For the story of the *Pearl*, see Josephine F. Pacheco, *The Pearl: A Failed Slave Escape on the Potomac* (Chapel Hill: University of North Carolina Press, 2005).

13 President Millard Fillmore pardoned both in 1852. Taylor, *Slave in the White House*, 174.

14 To John Payne Todd, [24] April, 1848, in *SLDPM*, 387; Taylor, *Slave in the White House*, 175.

15 Taylor, *Slave in the White House*, 174, 176.

16 Quoted ibid., 174.

17 Ralph Ketcham, *The Madisons at Montpelier: Reflections on the Founding Couple* (Charlottesville: University of Virginia Press, 2009), 180; Cutts Memoir II, in Allgor, *Queen of America*, 189–90; Allgor, *Perfect Union*, 396; To John Payne Todd, 21 May, 1848, in *SLDPM*, 388–89.

18 Holly C. Shulman, "A Constant Attention: Dolley Madison and the Publication of the Papers of James Madison," *Virginia Magazine of History and Biography* 118 (January 2010): 41–70; Statement re: the Terms of Sale of the Madison Papers, [13 December 1847], in *SLDPM*, 386.

Chapter 26

1 Excerpts from the *National Intelligencer* of July 14, 16, 17, and 19, http://www2 .vcdh.virginia.edu/madison/exhibit/widowhood/img/articles.html (accessed 12/15/2015); see also Elizabeth Dowling Taylor, *A Slave in the White House: Paul*

Jennings and the Madisons (New York: Palgrave Macmillan, 2012), 180. Ten years later the family moved Dolley's remains to Montpelier, to rest alongside those of James.

2   Will of Dolley Payne Madison, [1 February 1841], in *SLDPM*, 356; Elizabeth Dowling Taylor, "Miss Cutts," in *The Queen of America: Mary Cutts's Life of Dolley Madison*, ed. Catherine Allgor (Charlottesville: University of Virginia Press, 2012), 77.

3   Ethel Stephens Arnett, *Mrs. James Madison: The Incomparable Dolley* (Greensboro, NC: Piedmont Press, 1972), 396.

4   Will of Dolley Payne Madison, in *SLDPM*, 356; Catherine Allgor, *A Perfect Union: Dolley Madison and the Creation of the American Nation* (New York: Henry Holt, 2006), 400–401.

5   Allgor, *Perfect Union*, 402.

6   Arnett, *Mrs. James Madison*, 397, 399.

7   Cutts Memoir II, in Allgor, *Queen of America*, 193.

8   Holly Cowan Shulman, "History, Memory, and Dolley Madison: Notes from a Documentary Editor," in Allgor, *Queen of America*, 64n59; Allgor, *Perfect Union*, 405. Criticism of Dolley Madison over the disposition of the slaves was short-lived. Her name and image have been invoked over time to sell cookies, cigars, milk, ice cream, dolls, snack cakes, silver cutlery, and other products. In 1980 the U.S. Postal Service issued a fifteen-cent stamp in her honor.

9   Arnett, *Mrs. James Madison*, 400.

10   Allgor, *Perfect Union*, 405; http://www.montpelier.org/research-and-collec tions/people/john-payne-todd (accessed 12/15/2015); Taylor, *Slave in the White House*, 182.

11   Kurt E. Leichtle and Bruce G. Carveth, *Crusade against Slavery: Edward Coles, Pioneer of Freedom* (Carbondale: Southern Illinois University Press, 2011), 161–63; Allgor, *Perfect Union*, 404; Suzanne Cooper Guasco, *Confronting Slavery: Edward Coles and the Rise of Antislavery Politics in Nineteenth-Century America* (DeKalb: Northern Illinois University Press, 2013), 218–19; Taylor, *Slave in the White House*, 132.

12   Holly C. Shulman, "Madison vs. Madison: Dolley Payne Madison and Her Inheritance of the Montpelier Estate, 1836–38," *Virginia Magazine of History and Biography* 119, no. 4 (2011): 361–62.

13   James Madison's Will, 15 April 1835, in *DMDE*, http://rotunda.upress.virginia .edu/dmde/DPM3225 (accessed 09/12/2016). According to Dolley's brother John C. Payne, the American Colonization Society would also get the proceeds from the sale of James's gristmill after Dolley's death. This detail was not included in the former President's will, but perhaps it had been stipulated in the deed or elsewhere. John Coles Payne to Edward Coles, 18 July 1836, in

DMDE, http://rotunda.upress.virginia.edu/dmde/DPM2842 (accessed 09/12/2016). Andrew Burstein and Nancy Isenberg use the term "fantasy" in *Madison and Jefferson* (New York: Random House, 2010), 632.

14   It is difficult to know exactly how much the Madisons spent on Dolley's son over his adult life. Dolley's brother John C. Payne said that James once showed him "vouchers to the amount of about twenty-thousand dollars for the payment of [Payne's] debts." Arnett estimates the amount at forty thousand dollars. See *Mrs. James Madison,* 286.

Index